Ichigo Takano presents

Dreamin' Sun

1

volume
one

SEVEN SEAS ENTERTAINMENT PRESENTS

Dreamin' Sun

story and art by ICHIGO TAKANO   VOLUME 1

TRANSLATION
Amber Tamosaitis

ADAPTATION
Shannon Fay

LETTERING AND RETOUCH
Lys Blakeslee

COVER DESIGN
Nicky Lim

PROOFREADER
Lee Otter

ASSISTANT EDITOR
Jenn Grunigen

PRODUCTION ASSISTANT
CK Russell

PRODUCTION MANAGER
Lissa Pattillo

EDITOR-IN-CHIEF
Adam Arnold

PUBLISHER
Jason DeAngelis

DREAMIN' SUN VOLUME 1
© Ichigo Takano 2007
All rights reserved.
First published in Japan in 2016 by Futabasha Publishers Ltd., Tokyo.
English version published by Seven Seas Entertainment, LLC.
under license from Futabasha Publishers Ltd.

Seven Seas books may be purchased in bulk for educational, business, or
promotional use. For information on bulk purchases, please contact Macmillan
Corporate & Premium Sales Department at 1-800-221-7945 (ext 5442)
or write specialmarkets@macmillan.com.

Seven Seas and the Seven Seas logo are trademarks of
Seven Seas Entertainment, LLC. All rights reserved.

ISBN: 978-1-626925-25-0

Printed in Canada

First Printing: May 2017

10 9 8 7 6 5 4 3 2 1

FOLLOW US ONLINE: **www.gomanga.com**

READING DIRECTIONS

This book reads from **_right to left_**, Japanese style.
If this is your first time reading manga, you start
reading from the top right panel on each page and
take it from there. If you get lost, just follow the
numbered diagram here. It may seem backwards at
first, but you'll get the hang of it! Have fun!!

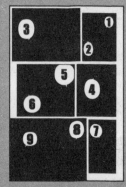

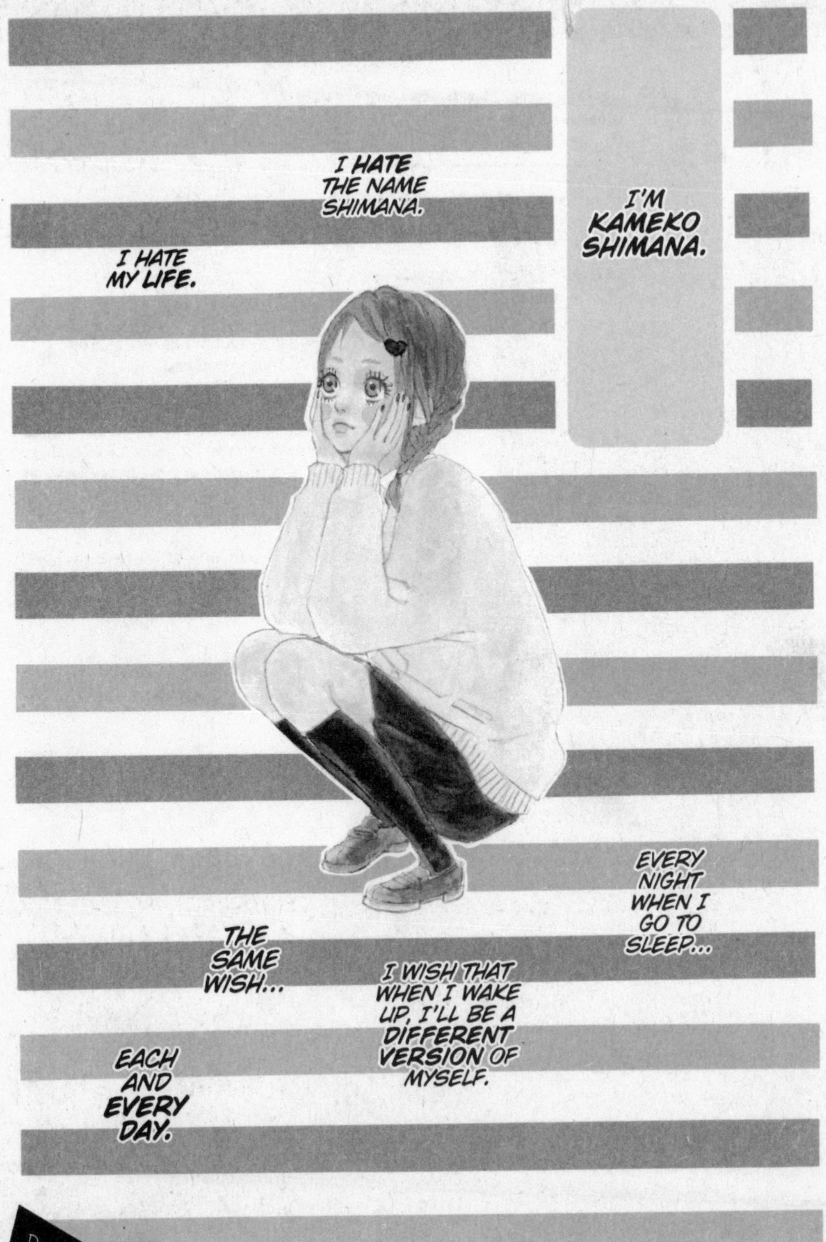
I'M KAMEKO SHIMANA.
I HATE THE NAME SHIMANA.
I HATE MY LIFE.
EVERY NIGHT WHEN I GO TO SLEEP...
I WISH THAT WHEN I WAKE UP, I'LL BE A DIFFERENT VERSION OF MYSELF.
THE SAME WISH...
EACH AND EVERY DAY.
Dreamin' Sun

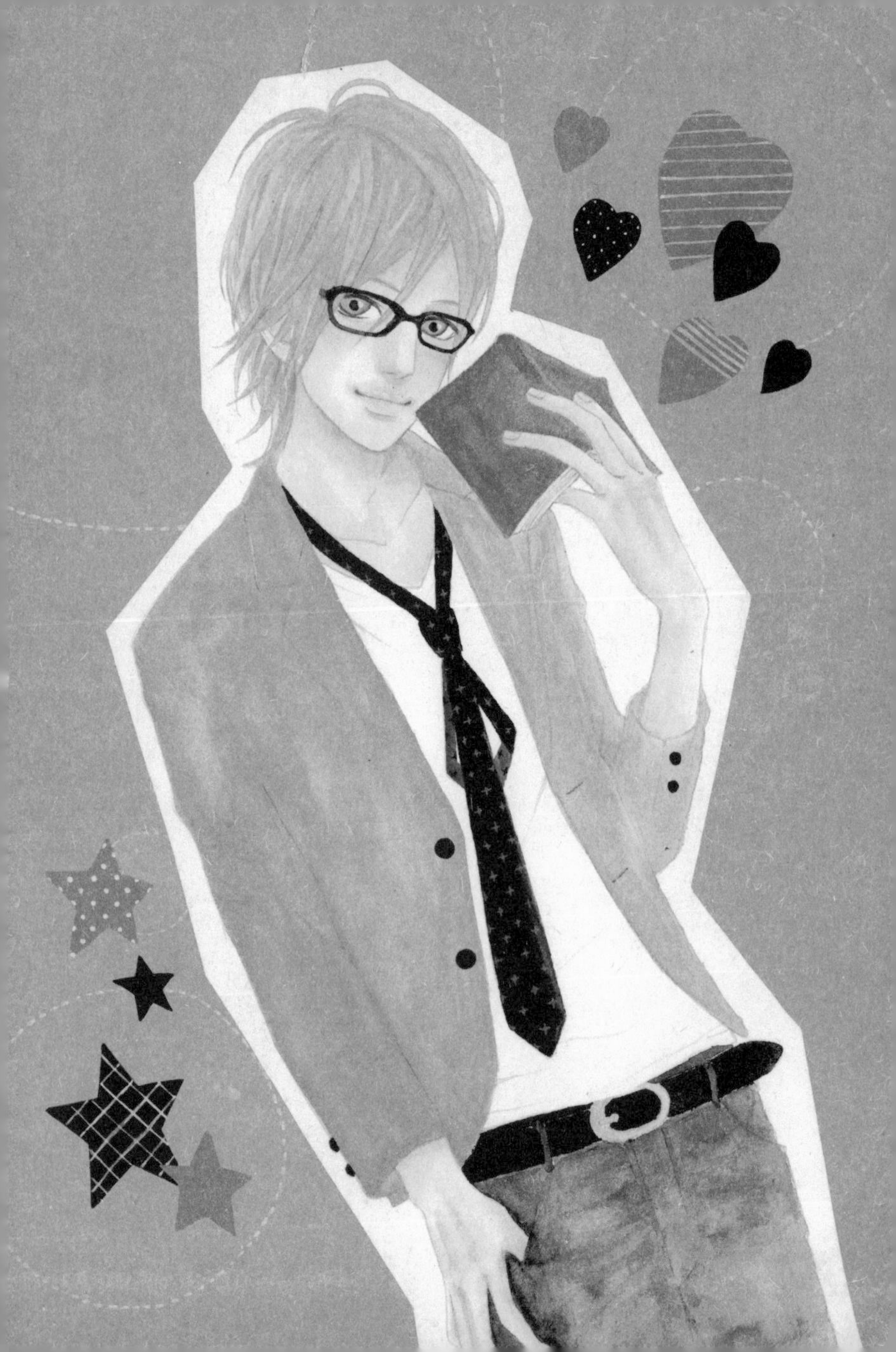

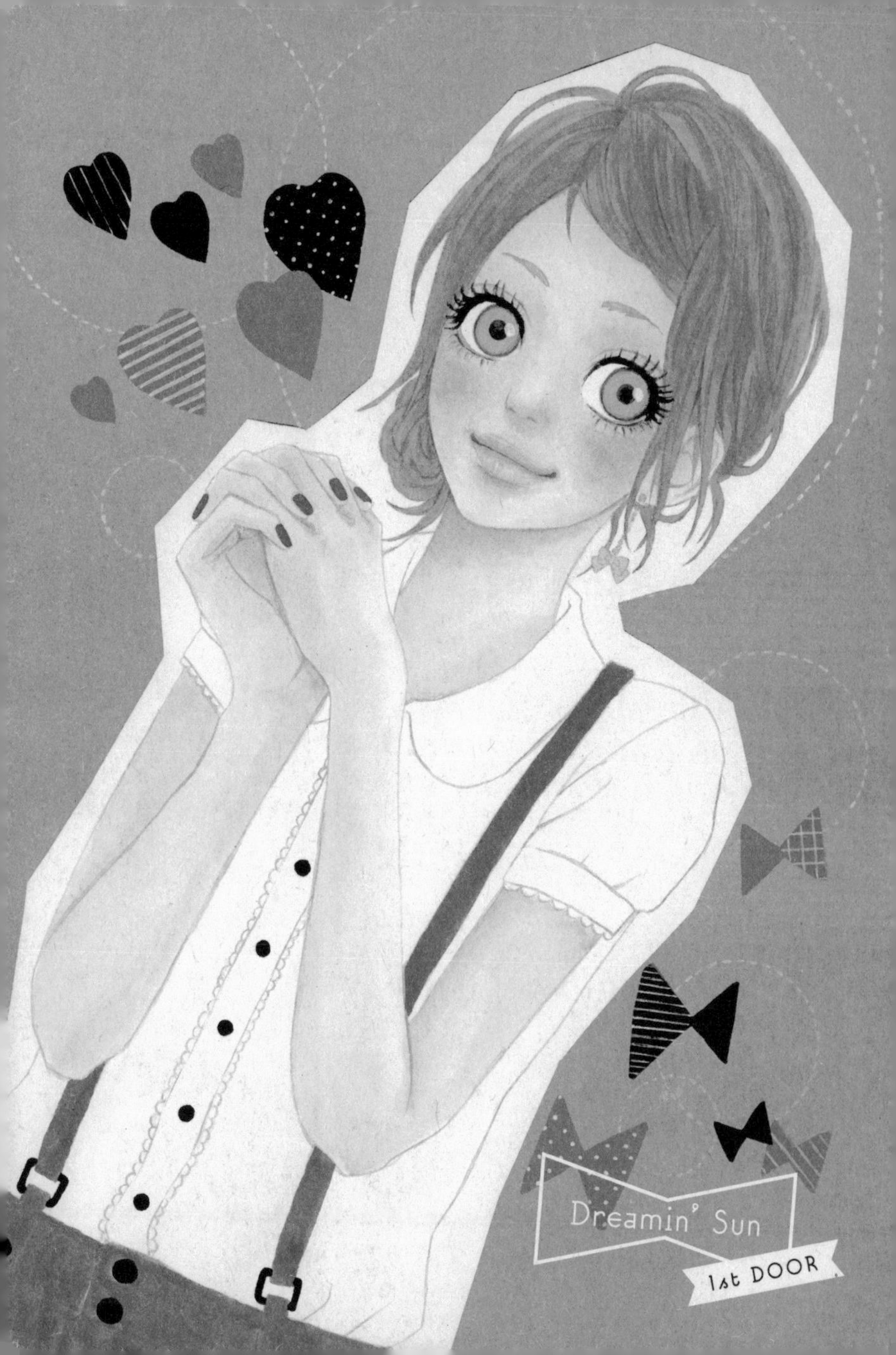
Dreamin' Sun
1st DOOR

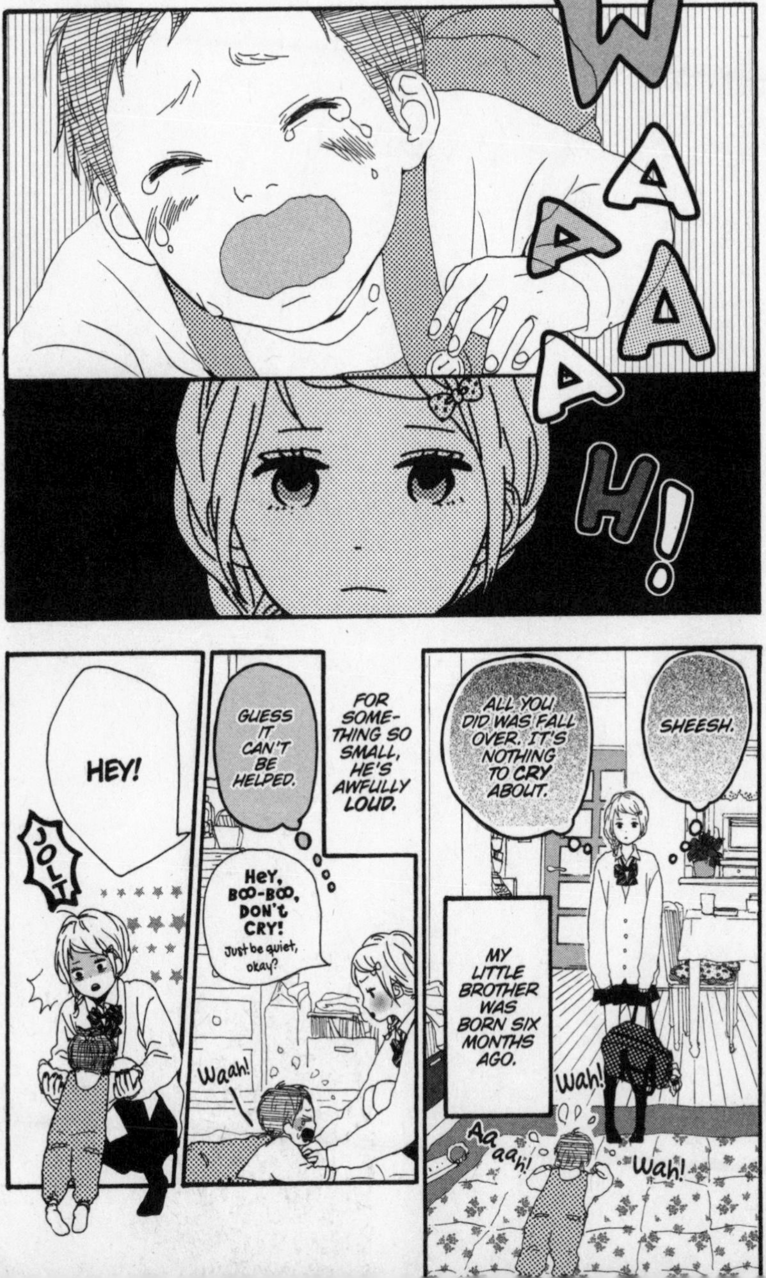
WAAAAAH!
SHEESH.
ALL YOU DID WAS FALL OVER. IT'S NOTHING TO CRY ABOUT.
MY LITTLE BROTHER WAS BORN SIX MONTHS AGO.
Wah!
Aaaah!
Wah!
FOR SOMETHING SO SMALL, HE'S AWFULLY LOUD.
GUESS IT CAN'T BE HELPED.
HEY, BOO-BOO, DON'T CRY!
Just be quiet, okay?
Waah!
HEY!
JOLT

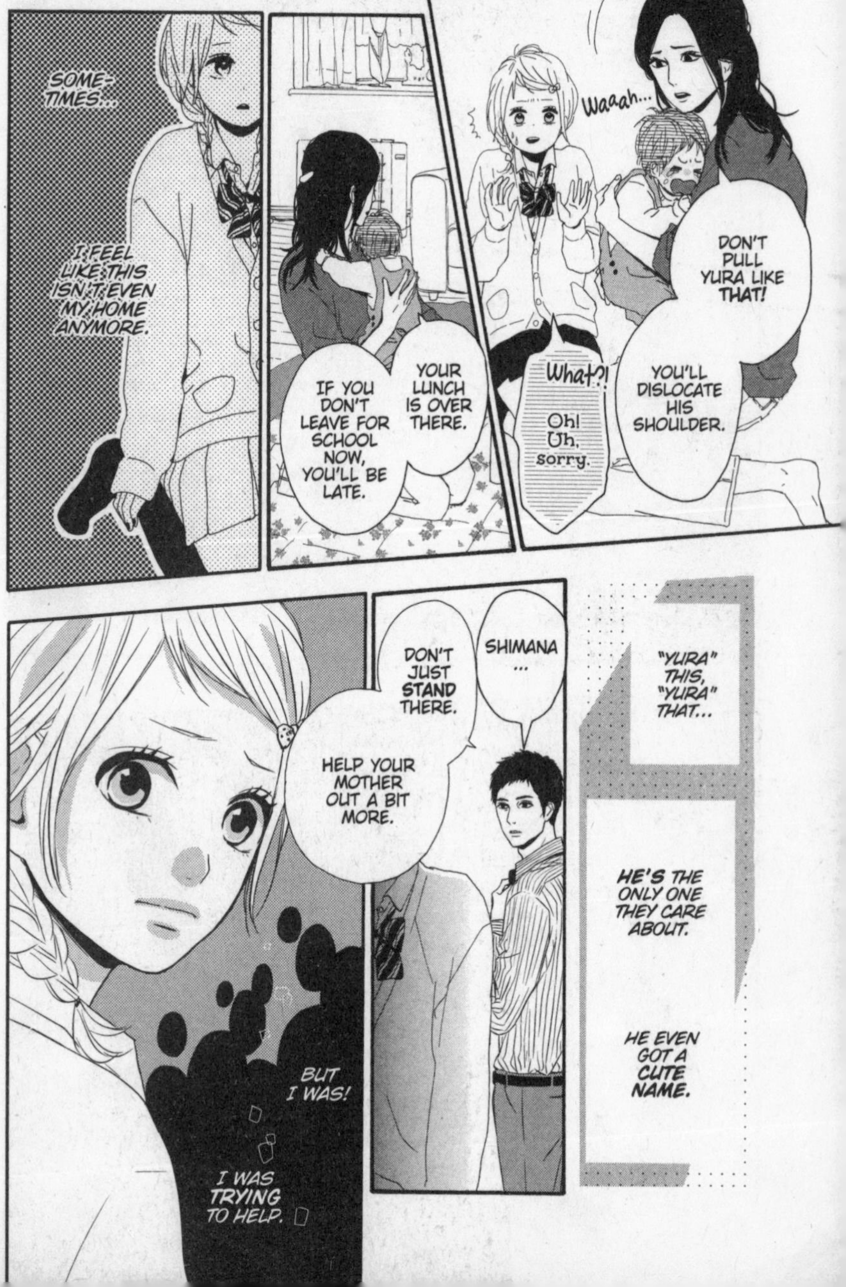
Waaah...
DON'T PULL YURA LIKE THAT!
YOU'LL DISLOCATE HIS SHOULDER.
What?! Oh! Uh, sorry.
YOUR LUNCH IS OVER THERE.
IF YOU DON'T LEAVE FOR SCHOOL NOW, YOU'LL BE LATE.
SOME-TIMES...
I FEEL LIKE THIS ISN'T EVEN MY HOME ANYMORE.
"YURA" THIS, "YURA" THAT...
HE'S THE ONLY ONE THEY CARE ABOUT.
HE EVEN GOT A CUTE NAME.
SHIMANA ...
DON'T JUST STAND THERE.
HELP YOUR MOTHER OUT A BIT MORE.
BUT I WAS!
I WAS TRYING TO HELP.

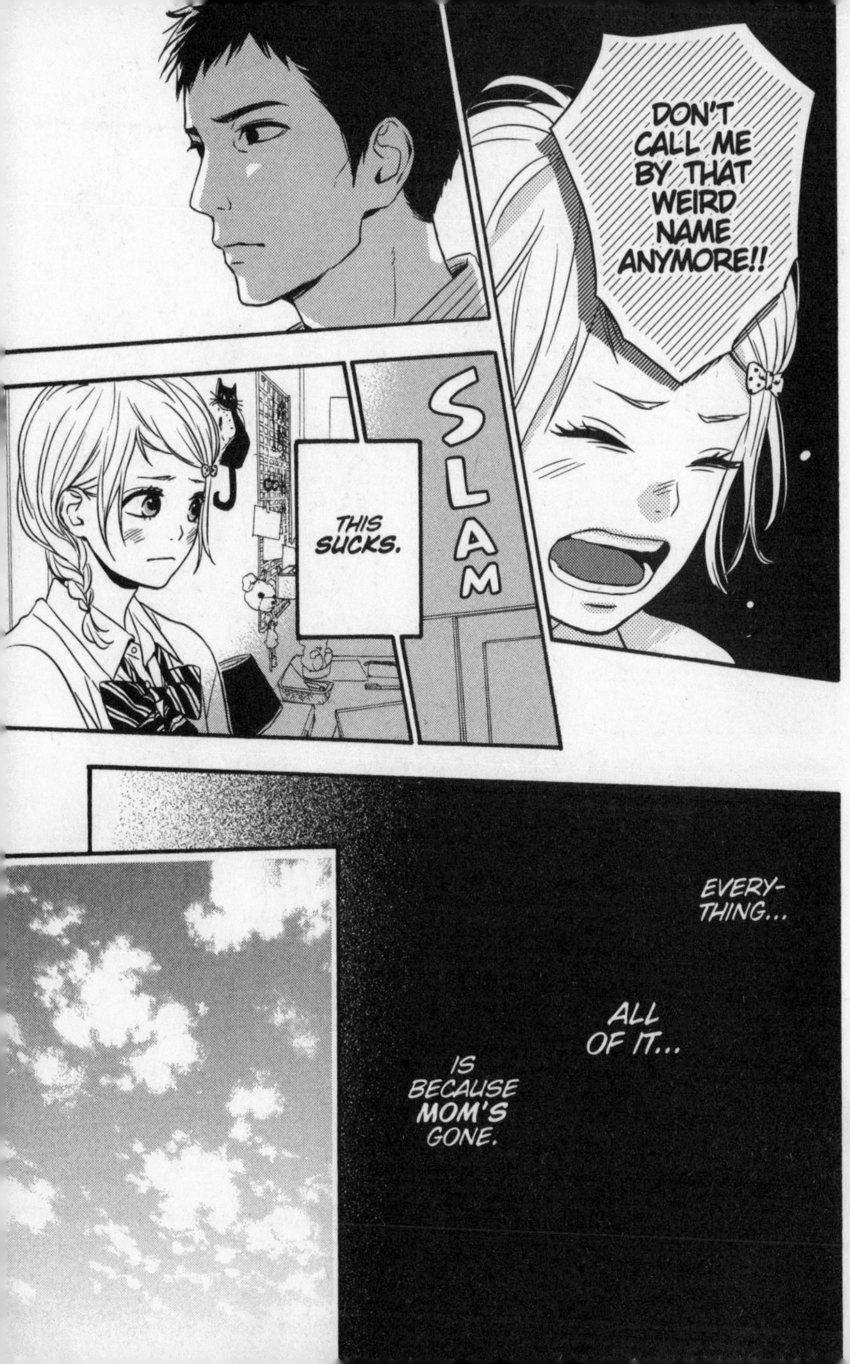
DON'T CALL ME BY THAT WEIRD NAME ANYMORE!!
SLAM
THIS SUCKS.
EVERY-THING...
ALL OF IT...
IS BECAUSE MOM'S GONE.

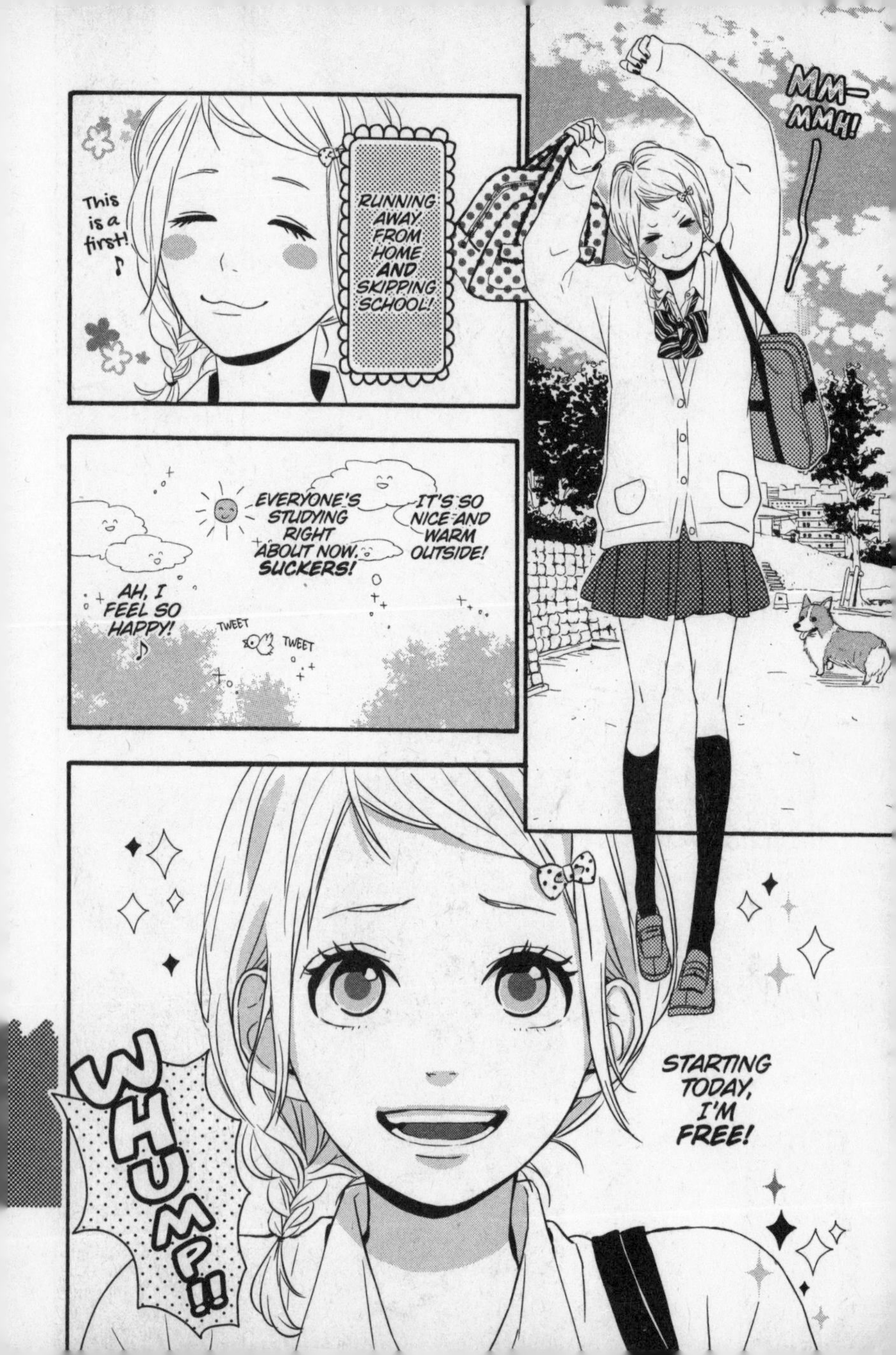
MM-MMH!
RUNNING AWAY FROM HOME AND SKIPPING SCHOOL!
This is a first! ♪
IT'S SO NICE AND WARM OUTSIDE!
EVERYONE'S STUDYING RIGHT ABOUT NOW. SUCKERS!
AH, I FEEL SO HAPPY! ♪
TWEET
TWEET
STARTING TODAY, I'M FREE!
WHUMP!!

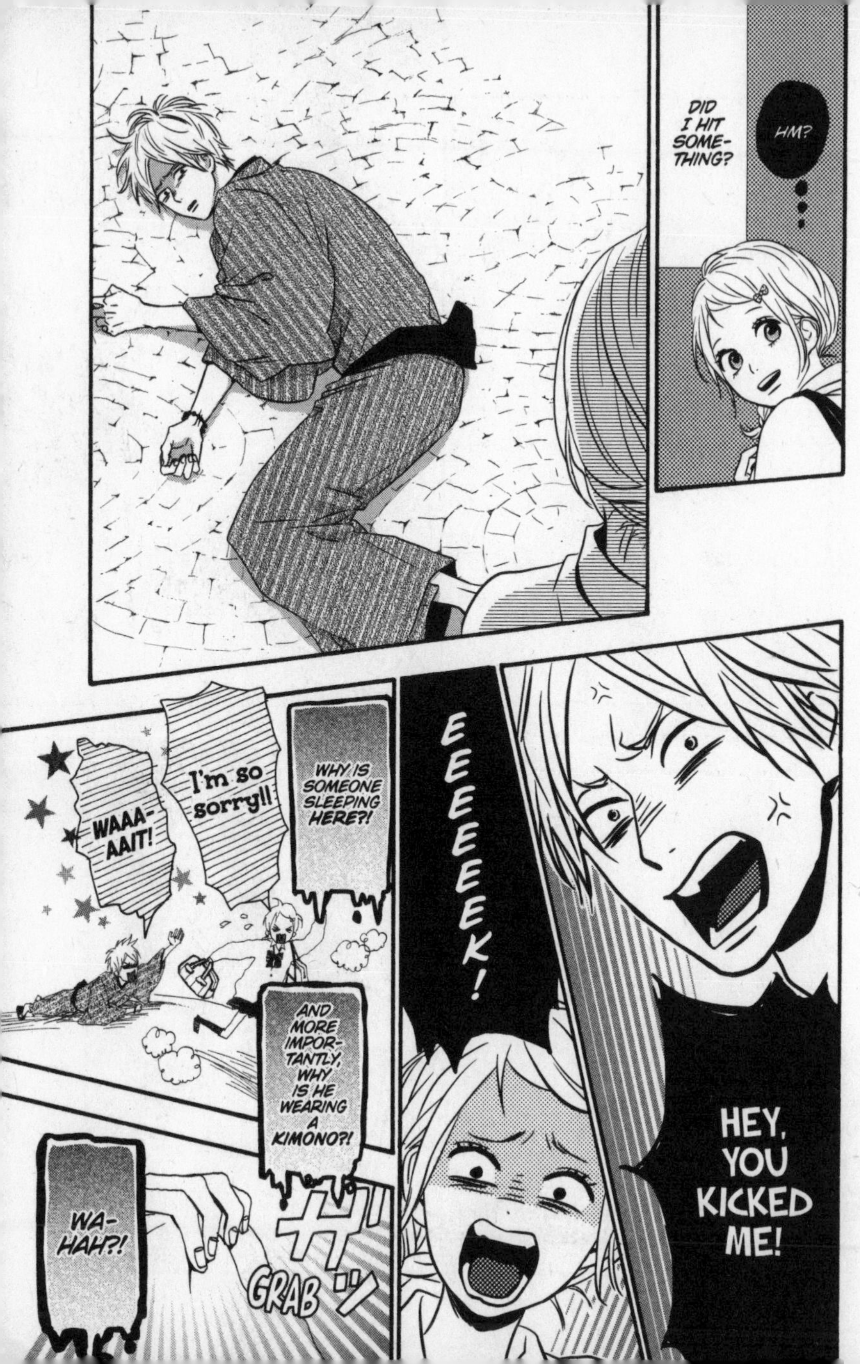
HM?
DID I HIT SOMETHING?
HEY, YOU KICKED ME!
EEEEEEEK!
WHY IS SOMEONE SLEEPING HERE?!
I'm so sorry!!
WAAA-AAIT!
AND MORE IMPORTANTLY, WHY IS HE WEARING A KIMONO?!
GRAB
WA-HAH?!

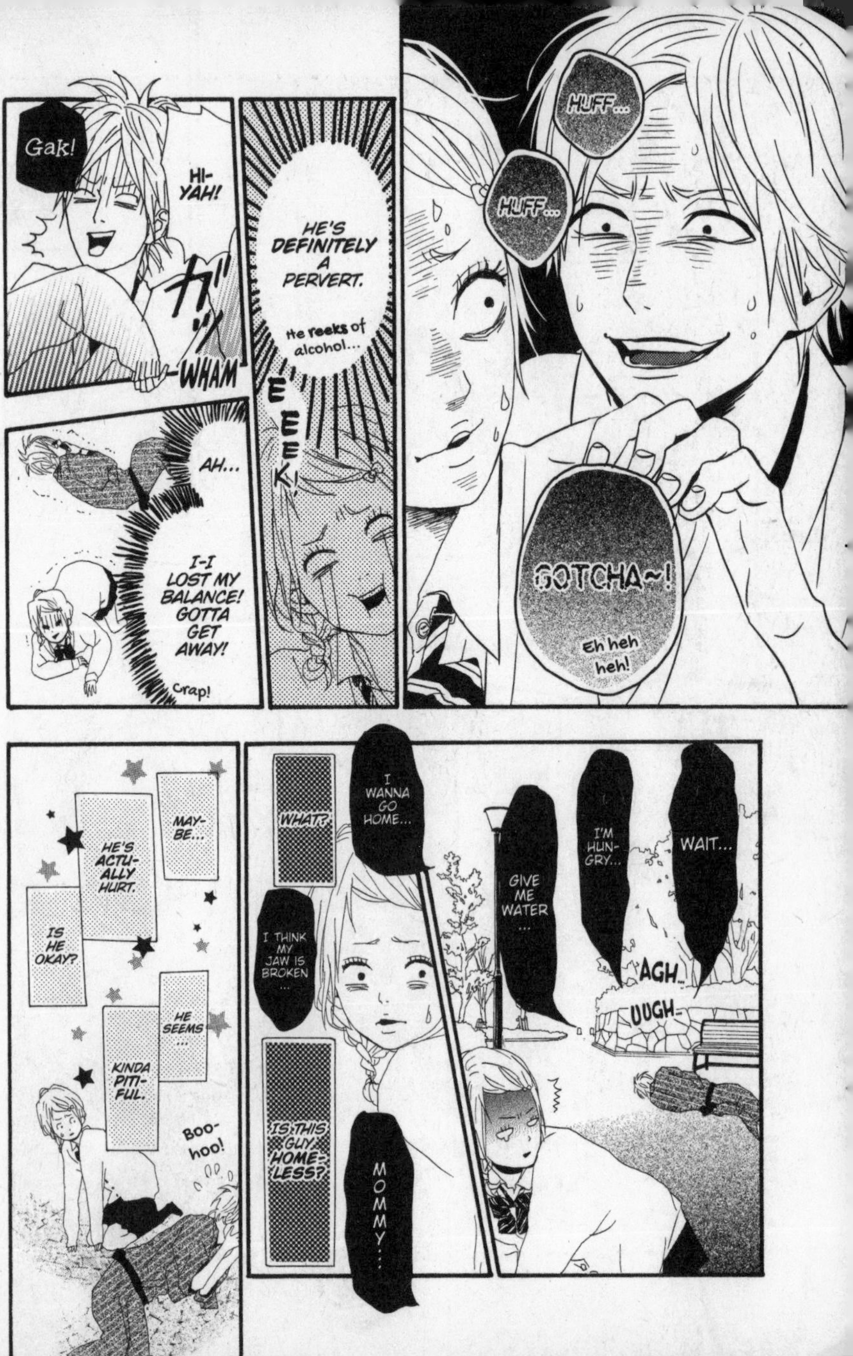
HUFF...
HUFF...
GOTCHA~!
Eh heh heh!
HE'S DEFINITELY A PERVERT.
He reeks of alcohol...
EEEK!
Gak!
HI-YAH!
WHAM
AH...
I-I LOST MY BALANCE! GOTTA GET AWAY!
Crap!
WAIT...
I'M HUN-GRY...
GIVE ME WATER...
I WANNA GO HOME...
WHAT?
AGH..
UUGH..
I THINK MY JAW IS BROKEN...
IS THIS GUY HOME-LESS?
MOMMY...
MAY-BE...
HE'S ACTU-ALLY HURT.
IS HE OKAY?
HE SEEMS...
KINDA PITI-FUL.
Boo-hoo!

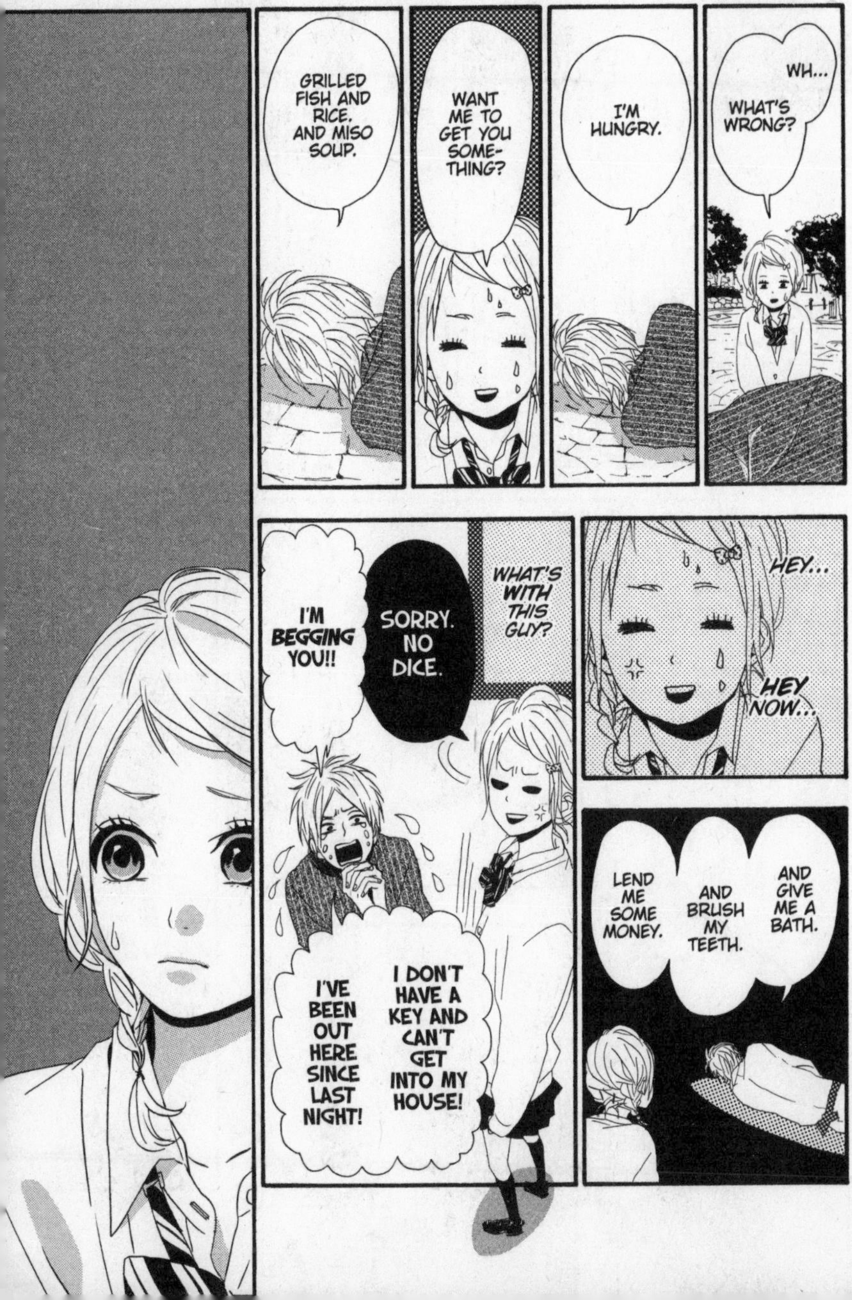
WH...
WHAT'S WRONG?
I'M HUNGRY.
WANT ME TO GET YOU SOME-THING?
GRILLED FISH AND RICE. AND MISO SOUP.
HEY...
HEY NOW...
LEND ME SOME MONEY.
AND BRUSH MY TEETH.
AND GIVE ME A BATH.
WHAT'S WITH THIS GUY?
SORRY. NO DICE.
I'M BEGGING YOU!!
I DON'T HAVE A KEY AND CAN'T GET INTO MY HOUSE!
I'VE BEEN OUT HERE SINCE LAST NIGHT!

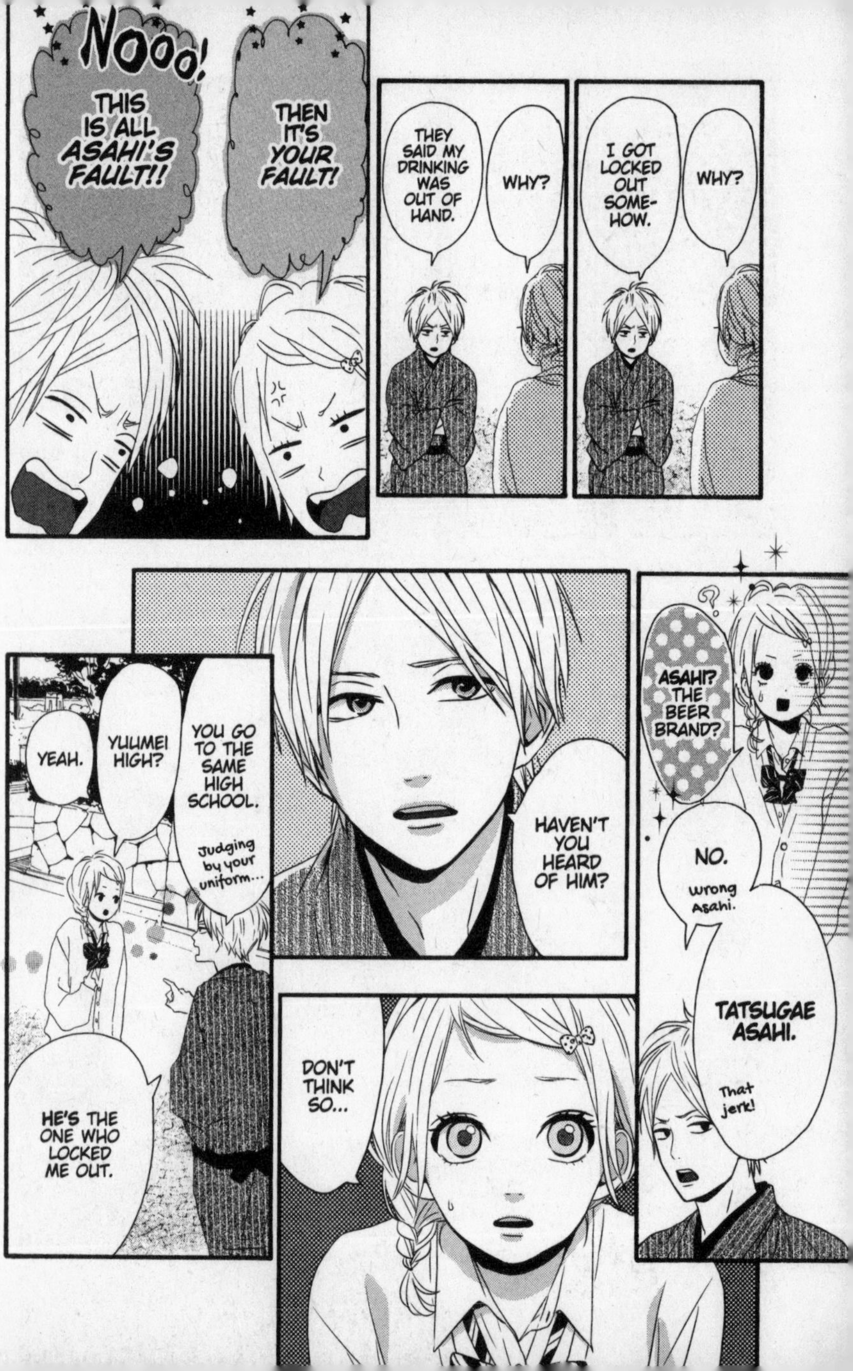
WHY?
I GOT LOCKED OUT SOME-HOW.
WHY?
THEY SAID MY DRINKING WAS OUT OF HAND.
Nooo!
THEN IT'S YOUR FAULT!
THIS IS ALL ASAHI'S FAULT!!
ASAHI? THE BEER BRAND?
NO. wrong Asahi.
TATSUGAE ASAHI. That jerk!
HAVEN'T YOU HEARD OF HIM?
DON'T THINK SO...
YOU GO TO THE SAME HIGH SCHOOL. Judging by your uniform...
YUUMEI HIGH?
YEAH.
HE'S THE ONE WHO LOCKED ME OUT.

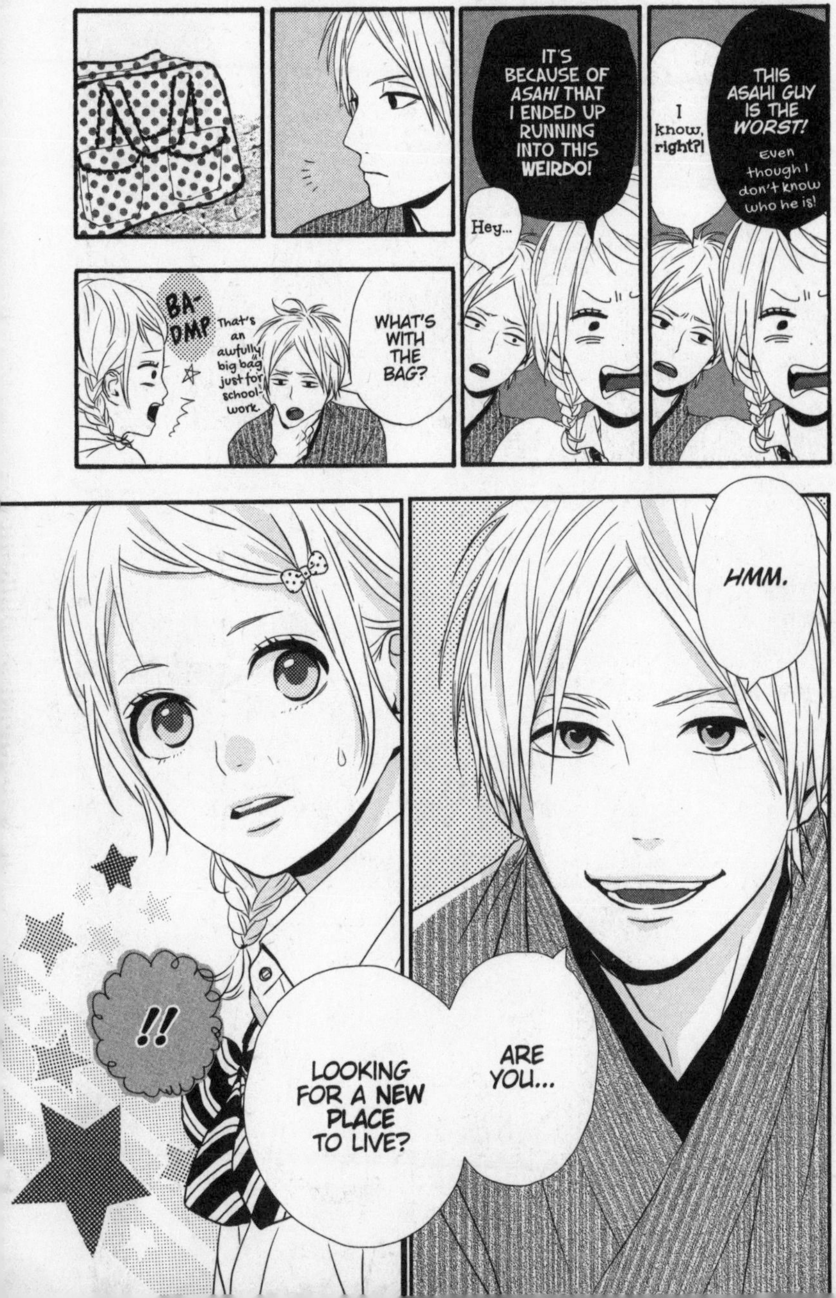
THIS ASAHI GUY IS THE WORST!
Even though I don't know who he is!
I know, right?!
IT'S BECAUSE OF ASAHI THAT I ENDED UP RUNNING INTO THIS WEIRDO!
Hey...
WHAT'S WITH THE BAG?
That's an awfully big bag just for school-work.
BA-DMP
HMM.
ARE YOU...
LOOKING FOR A NEW PLACE TO LIVE?
!!

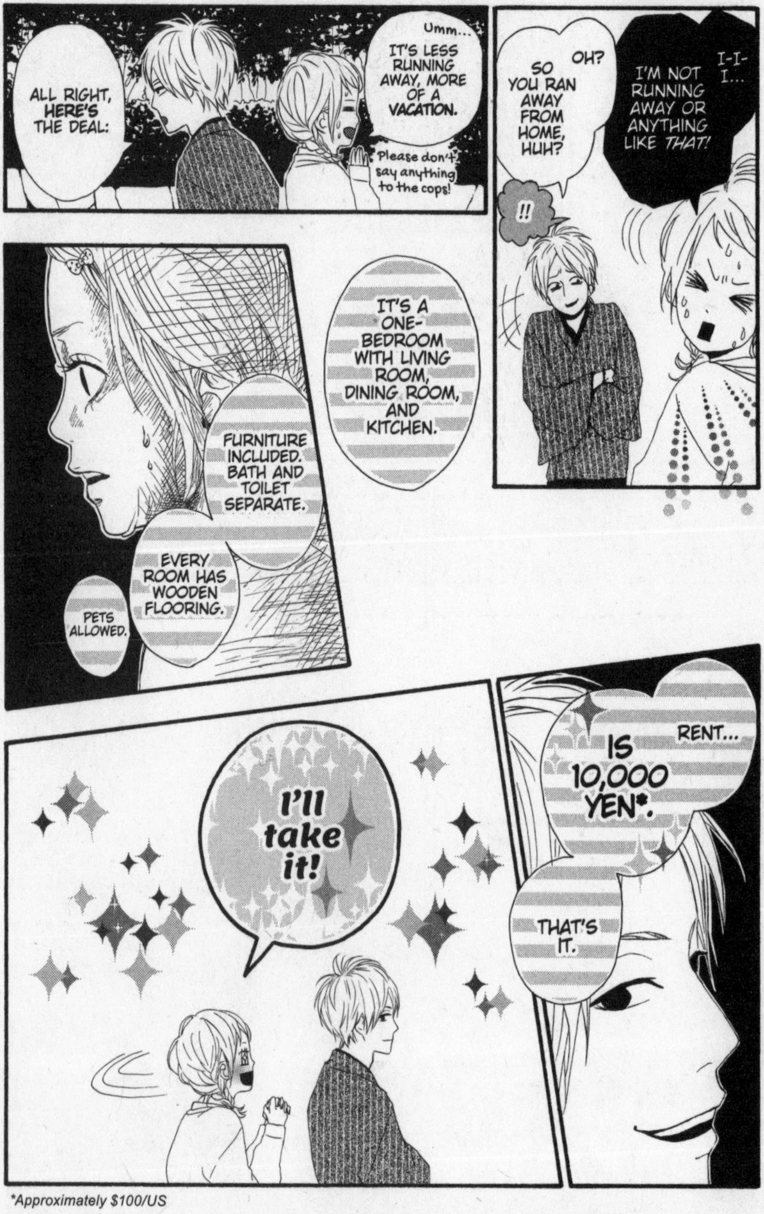
OH? SO YOU RAN AWAY FROM HOME, HUH?
!!
I-I-I...
I'M NOT RUNNING AWAY OR ANYTHING LIKE *THAT!*
Umm...
IT'S LESS RUNNING AWAY, MORE OF A VACATION.
Please don't say anything to the cops!
ALL RIGHT, HERE'S THE DEAL:
IT'S A ONE-BEDROOM WITH LIVING ROOM, DINING ROOM, AND KITCHEN.
FURNITURE INCLUDED. BATH AND TOILET SEPARATE.
EVERY ROOM HAS WOODEN FLOORING.
PETS ALLOWED.
RENT...
IS 10,000 YEN*.
THAT'S IT.
I'll take it!

*Approximately $100/US

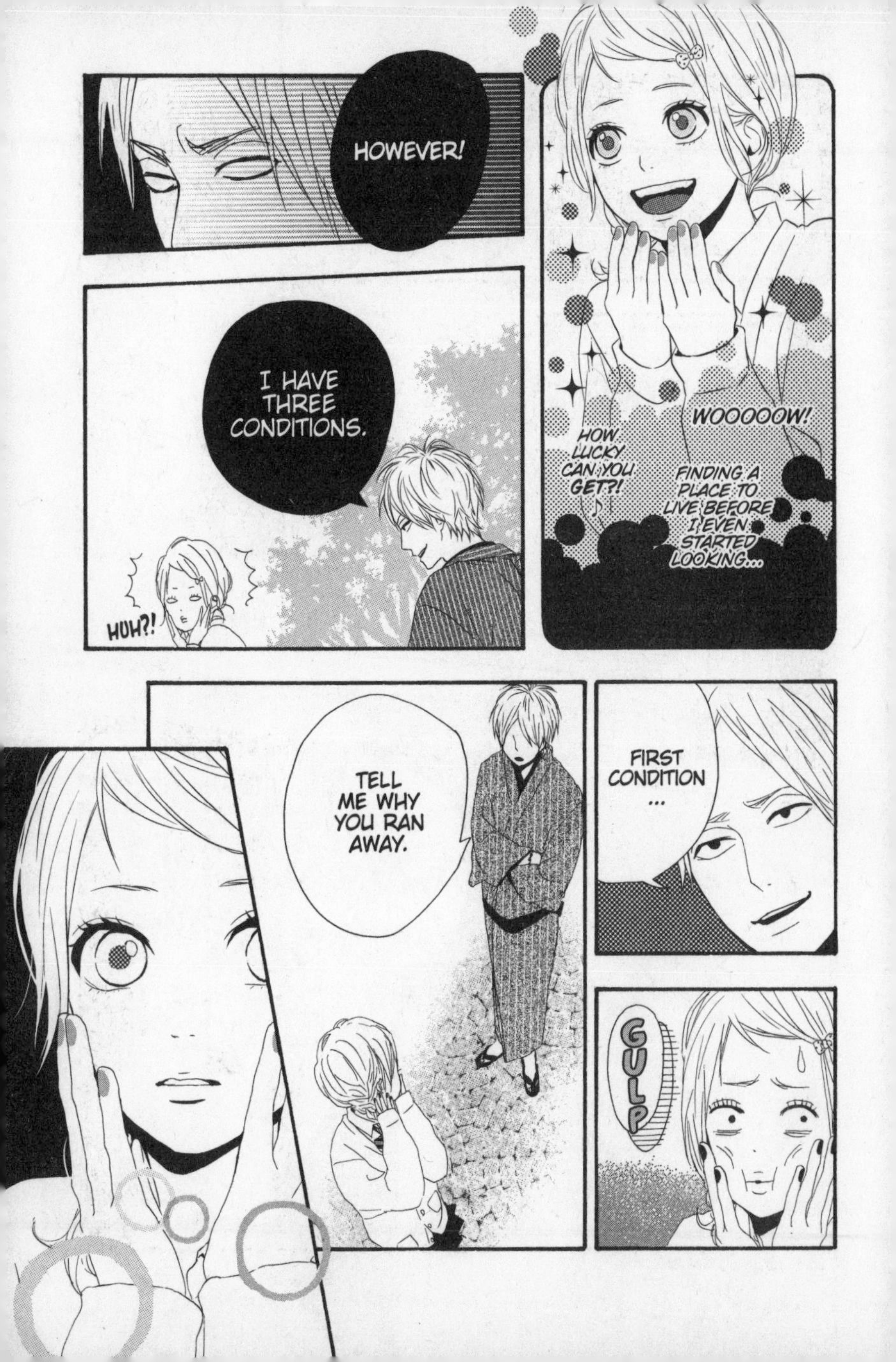
WOOOOOW!
FINDING A PLACE TO LIVE BEFORE I EVEN STARTED LOOKING...
HOW LUCKY CAN YOU GET?! ♪
HOWEVER!
I HAVE THREE CONDITIONS.
HUH?!
FIRST CONDITION ...
GULP
TELL ME WHY YOU RAN AWAY.

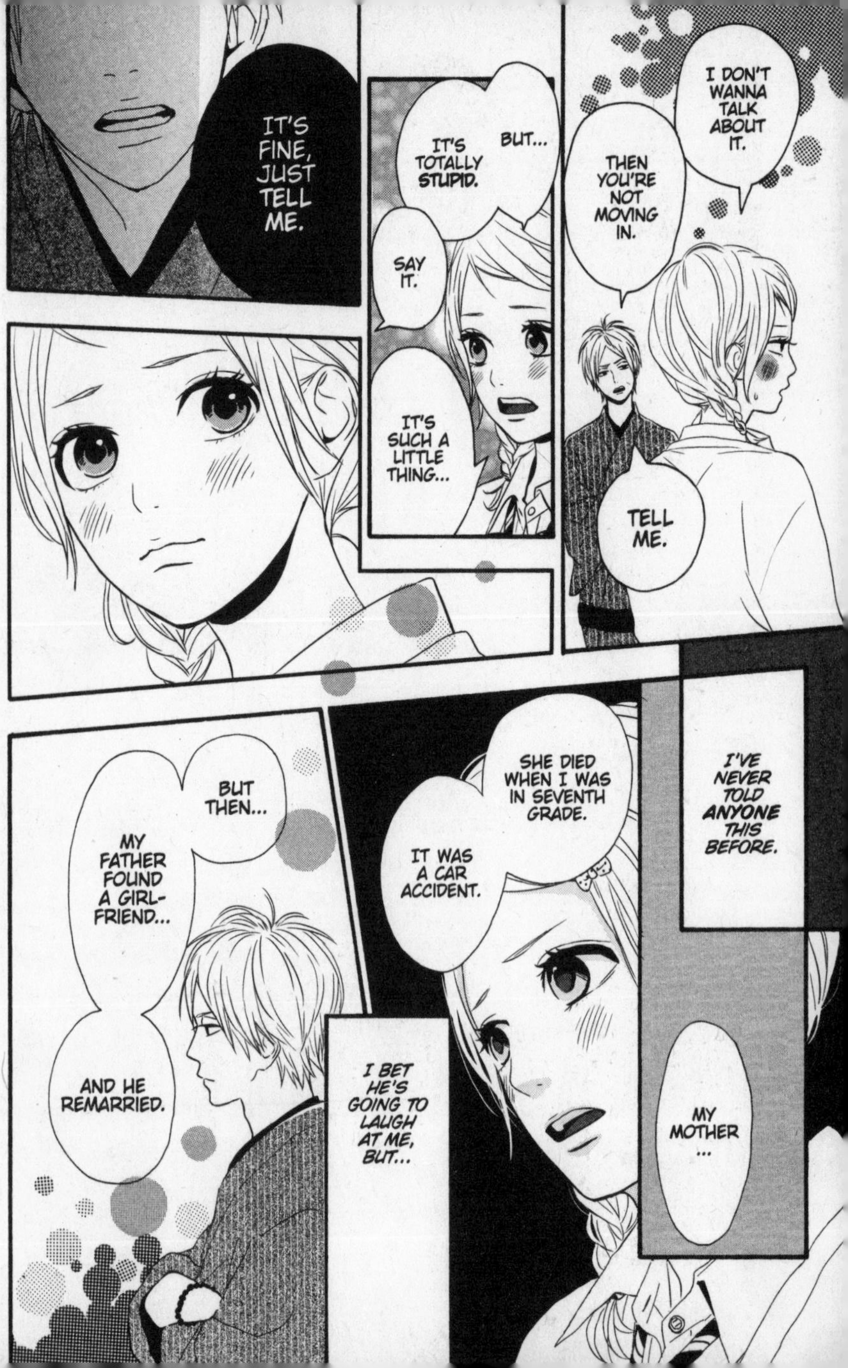
I DON'T WANNA TALK ABOUT IT.
THEN YOU'RE NOT MOVING IN.
TELL ME.
BUT...
IT'S TOTALLY STUPID.
SAY IT.
IT'S SUCH A LITTLE THING...
IT'S FINE, JUST TELL ME.
I'VE NEVER TOLD ANYONE THIS BEFORE.
MY MOTHER...
SHE DIED WHEN I WAS IN SEVENTH GRADE.
IT WAS A CAR ACCIDENT.
I BET HE'S GOING TO LAUGH AT ME, BUT...
BUT THEN...
MY FATHER FOUND A GIRL-FRIEND...
AND HE REMARRIED.

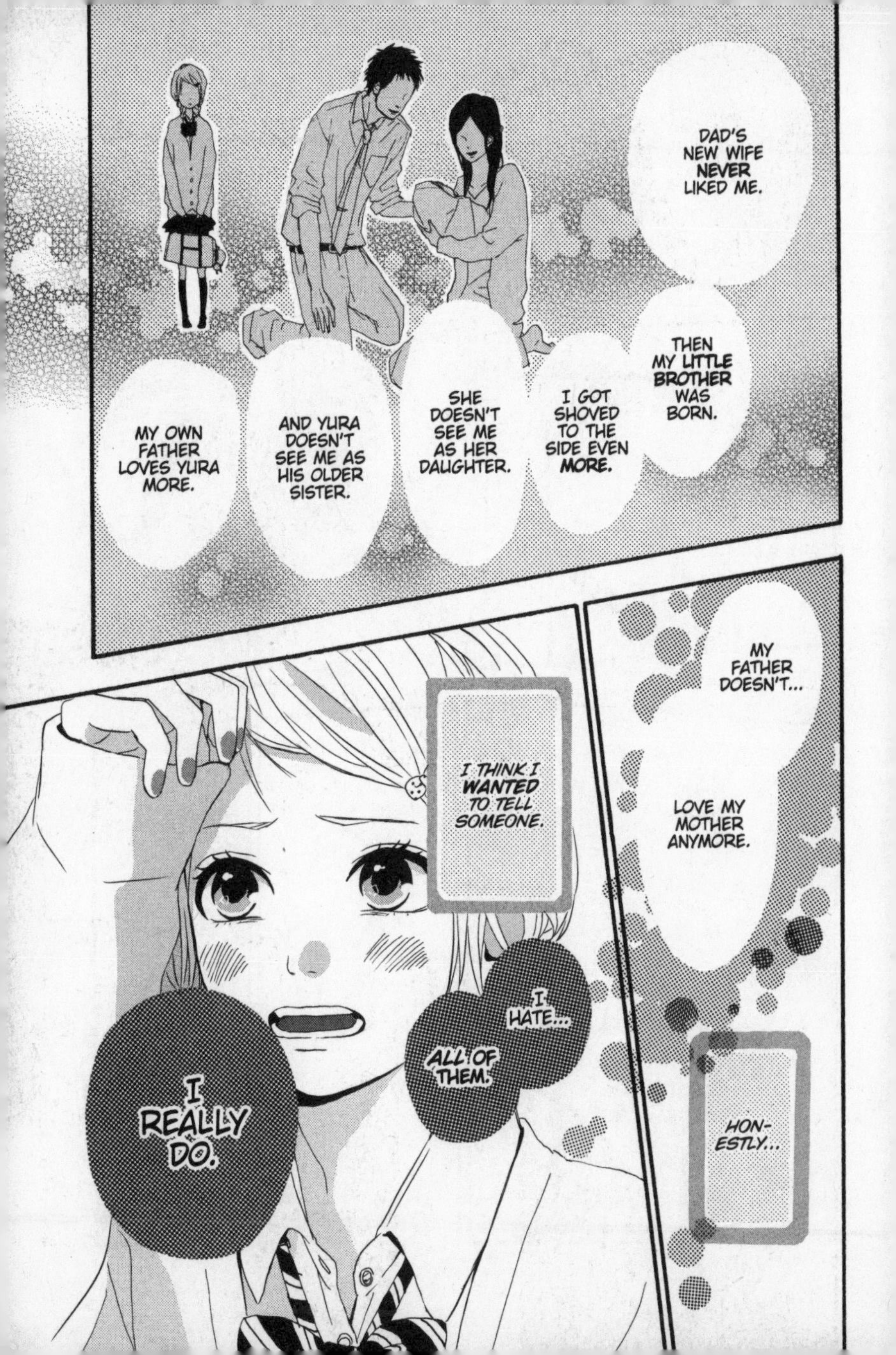
DAD'S NEW WIFE NEVER LIKED ME.
THEN MY LITTLE BROTHER WAS BORN.
I GOT SHOVED TO THE SIDE EVEN MORE.
SHE DOESN'T SEE ME AS HER DAUGHTER.
AND YURA DOESN'T SEE ME AS HIS OLDER SISTER.
MY OWN FATHER LOVES YURA MORE.
MY FATHER DOESN'T...
LOVE MY MOTHER ANYMORE.
HON-ESTLY...
I THINK I WANTED TO TELL SOMEONE.
I HATE...
ALL OF THEM.
I REALLY DO.

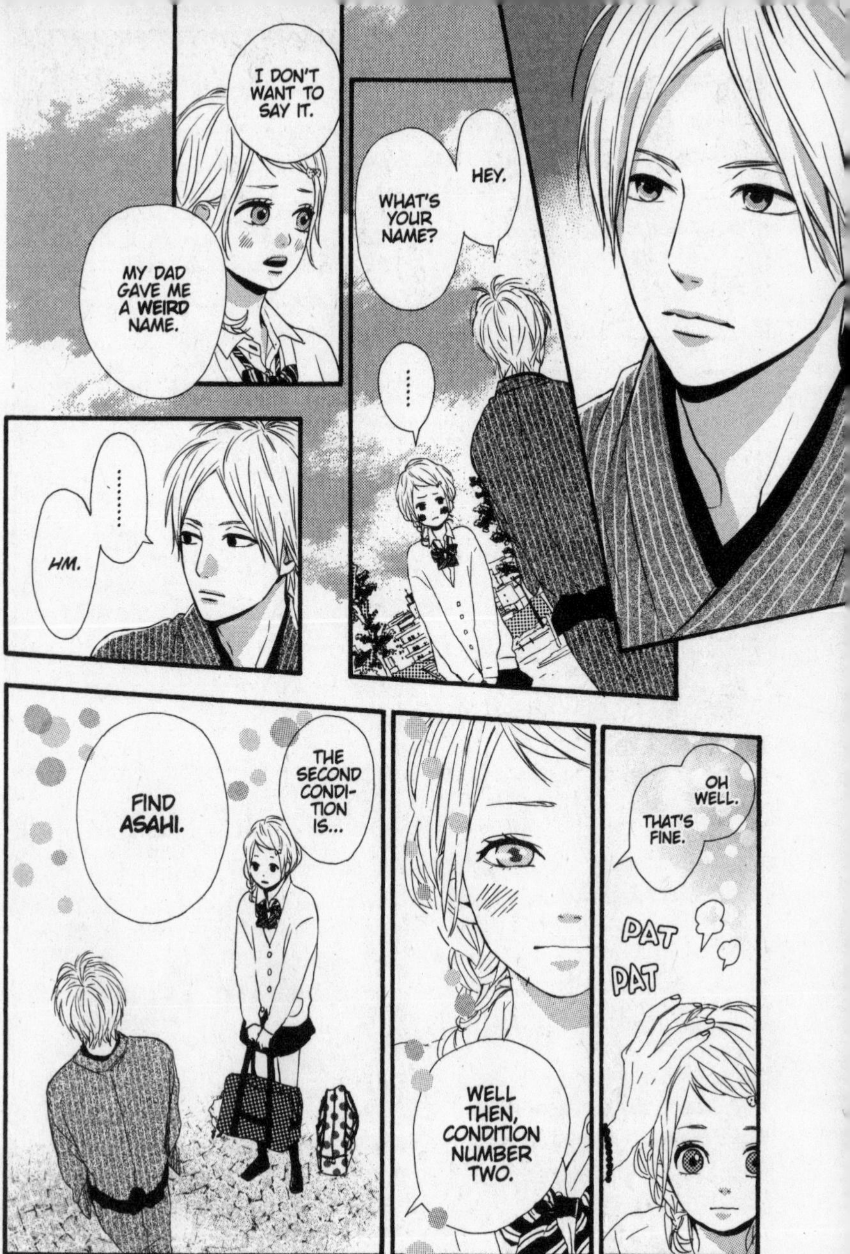
HEY.
WHAT'S YOUR NAME?
......
I DON'T WANT TO SAY IT.
MY DAD GAVE ME A WEIRD NAME.
......
HM.
OH WELL.
THAT'S FINE.
PAT
PAT
WELL THEN, CONDITION NUMBER TWO.
THE SECOND CONDITION IS...
FIND ASAHI.

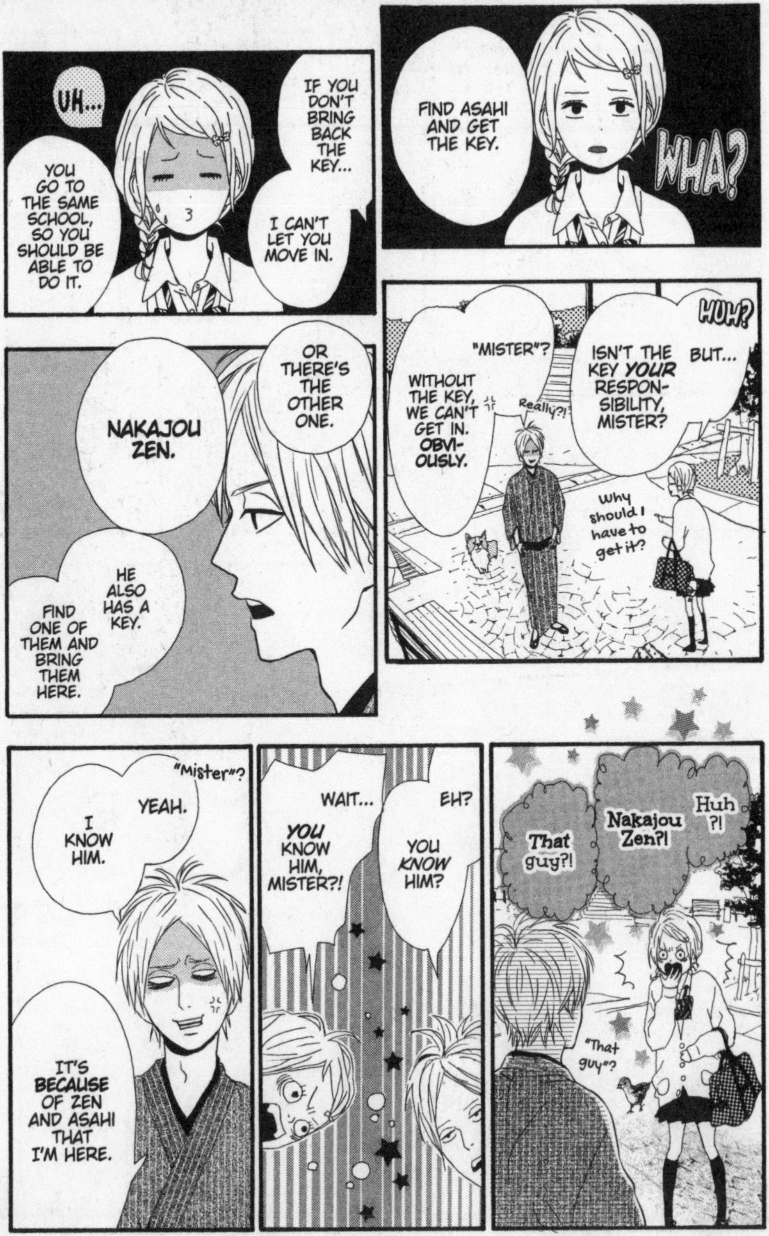
FIND ASAHI AND GET THE KEY.
WHA?
IF YOU DON'T BRING BACK THE KEY...
I CAN'T LET YOU MOVE IN.
UH...
YOU GO TO THE SAME SCHOOL, SO YOU SHOULD BE ABLE TO DO IT.
HUH?
BUT...
ISN'T THE KEY YOUR RESPONSIBILITY, MISTER?
"MISTER"?
Really?!
WITHOUT THE KEY, WE CAN'T GET IN. OBVIOUSLY.
Why should I have to get it?
OR THERE'S THE OTHER ONE.
NAKAJOU ZEN.
HE ALSO HAS A KEY.
FIND ONE OF THEM AND BRING THEM HERE.
Huh?!
Nakajou Zen?!
That guy?!
"That guy"?
EH?
YOU KNOW HIM?
WAIT...
YOU KNOW HIM, MISTER?!
"Mister"?
YEAH.
I KNOW HIM.
IT'S BECAUSE OF ZEN AND ASAHI THAT I'M HERE.

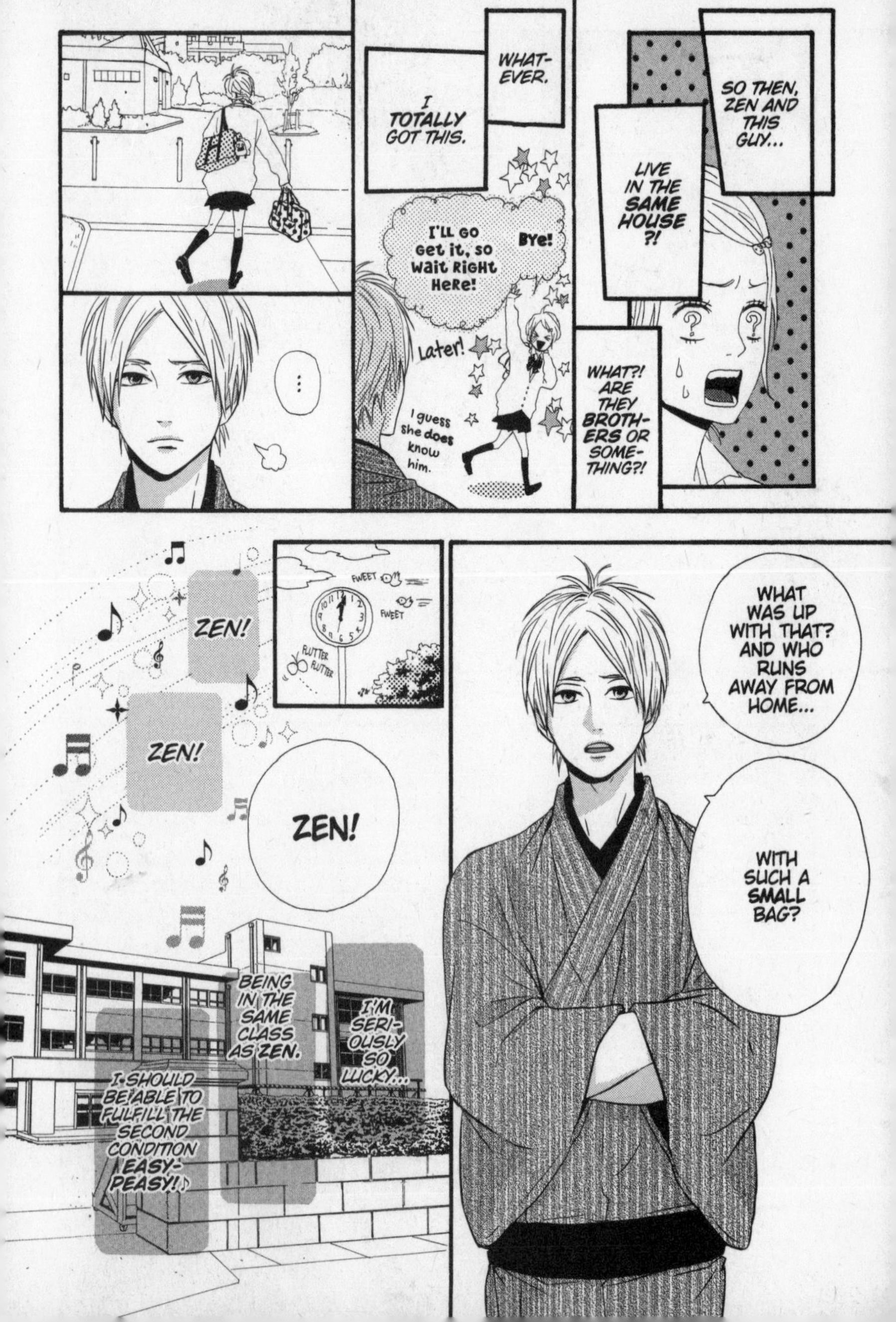
SO THEN, ZEN AND THIS GUY...
LIVE IN THE SAME HOUSE?!
WHAT?! ARE THEY BROTHERS OR SOMETHING?!
WHAT-EVER.
I TOTALLY GOT THIS.
I'LL GO GET IT, SO WAIT RIGHT HERE!
Bye!
Later!
I guess she does know him.
...
WHAT WAS UP WITH THAT? AND WHO RUNS AWAY FROM HOME...
WITH SUCH A SMALL BAG?
FWEET
FWEET
FLUTTER FLUTTER
ZEN!
ZEN!
ZEN!
BEING IN THE SAME CLASS AS ZEN.
I'M SERI-OUSLY SO LUCKY...
I SHOULD BE ABLE TO FULFILL THE SECOND CONDITION EASY-PEASY!♪

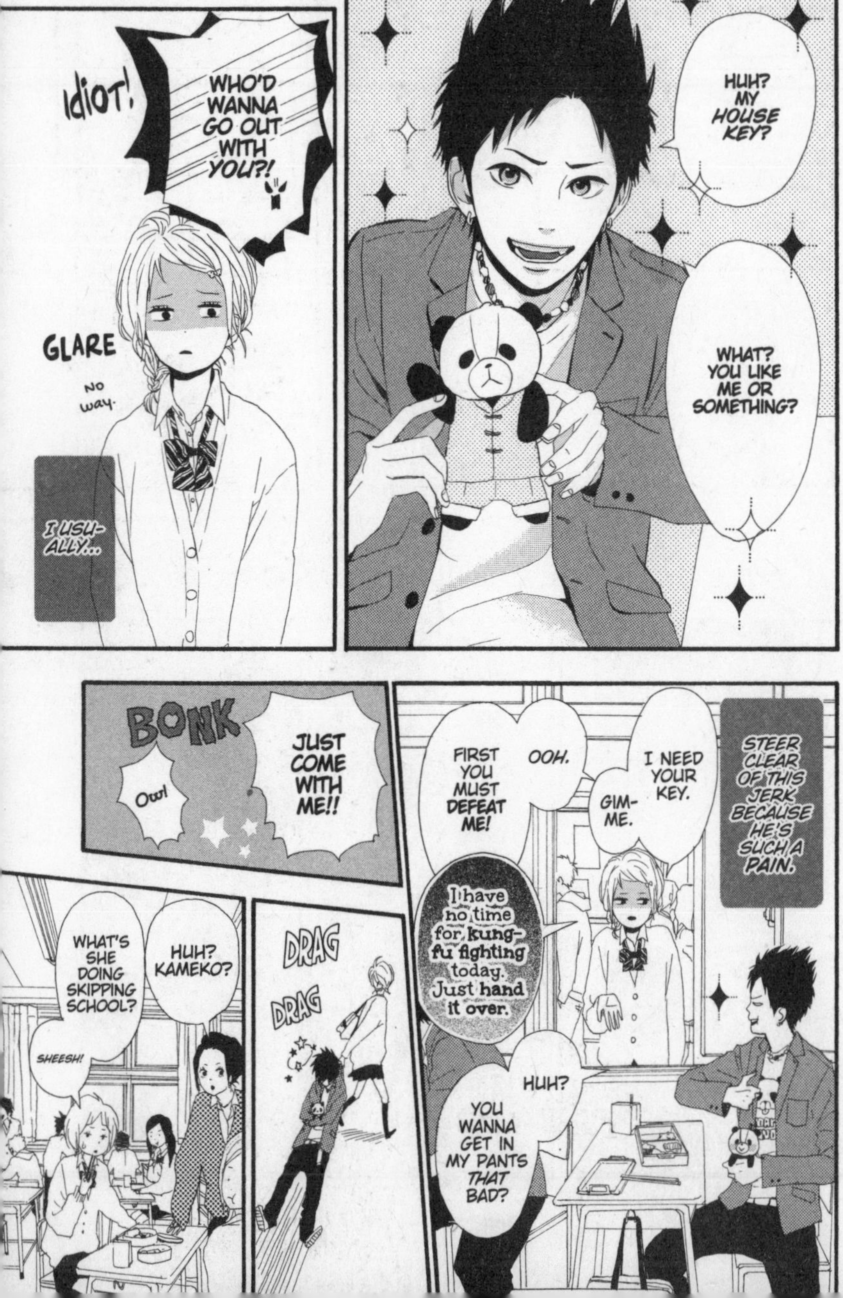

HUH? MY HOUSE KEY?
WHAT? YOU LIKE ME OR SOMETHING?
WHO'D WANNA GO OUT WITH YOU?!
Idiot!
GLARE
No way.
I USU-ALLY...
STEER CLEAR OF THIS JERK BECAUSE HE'S SUCH A PAIN.
I NEED YOUR KEY.
GIM-ME.
OOH.
FIRST YOU MUST DEFEAT ME!
I have no time for kung-fu fighting today. Just hand it over.
HUH?
YOU WANNA GET IN MY PANTS THAT BAD?
JUST COME WITH ME!!
BONK
Ow!
DRAG
DRAG
HUH? KAMEKO?
WHAT'S SHE DOING SKIPPING SCHOOL?
SHEESH!

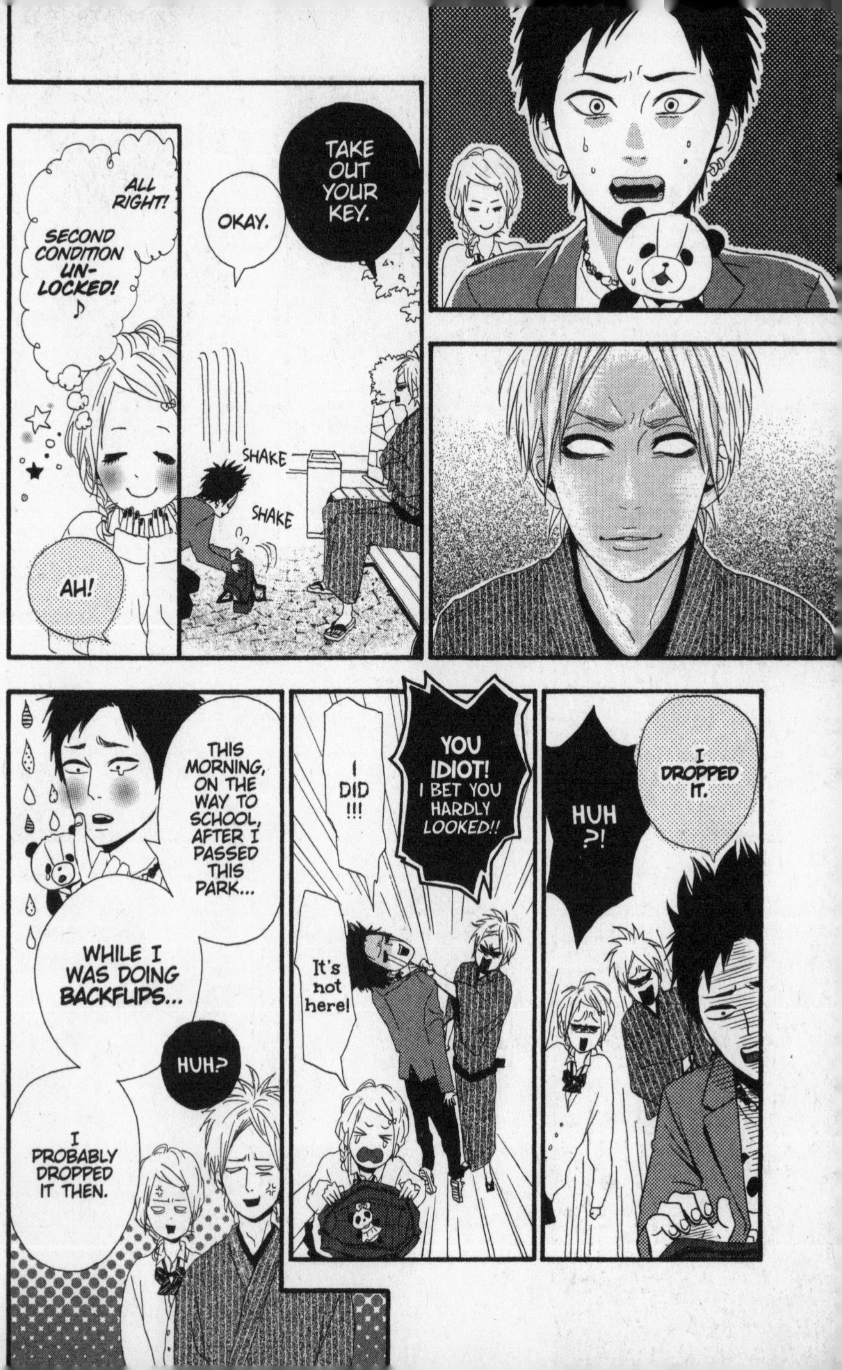
TAKE OUT YOUR KEY.
OKAY.
SHAKE
SHAKE
ALL RIGHT!
SECOND CONDITION UN-LOCKED! ♪
AH!
I DROPPED IT.
HUH ?!
YOU IDIOT! I BET YOU HARDLY LOOKED!!
I DID !!!
It's not here!
THIS MORNING, ON THE WAY TO SCHOOL, AFTER I PASSED THIS PARK...
WHILE I WAS DOING BACKFLIPS...
HUH?
I PROBABLY DROPPED IT THEN.

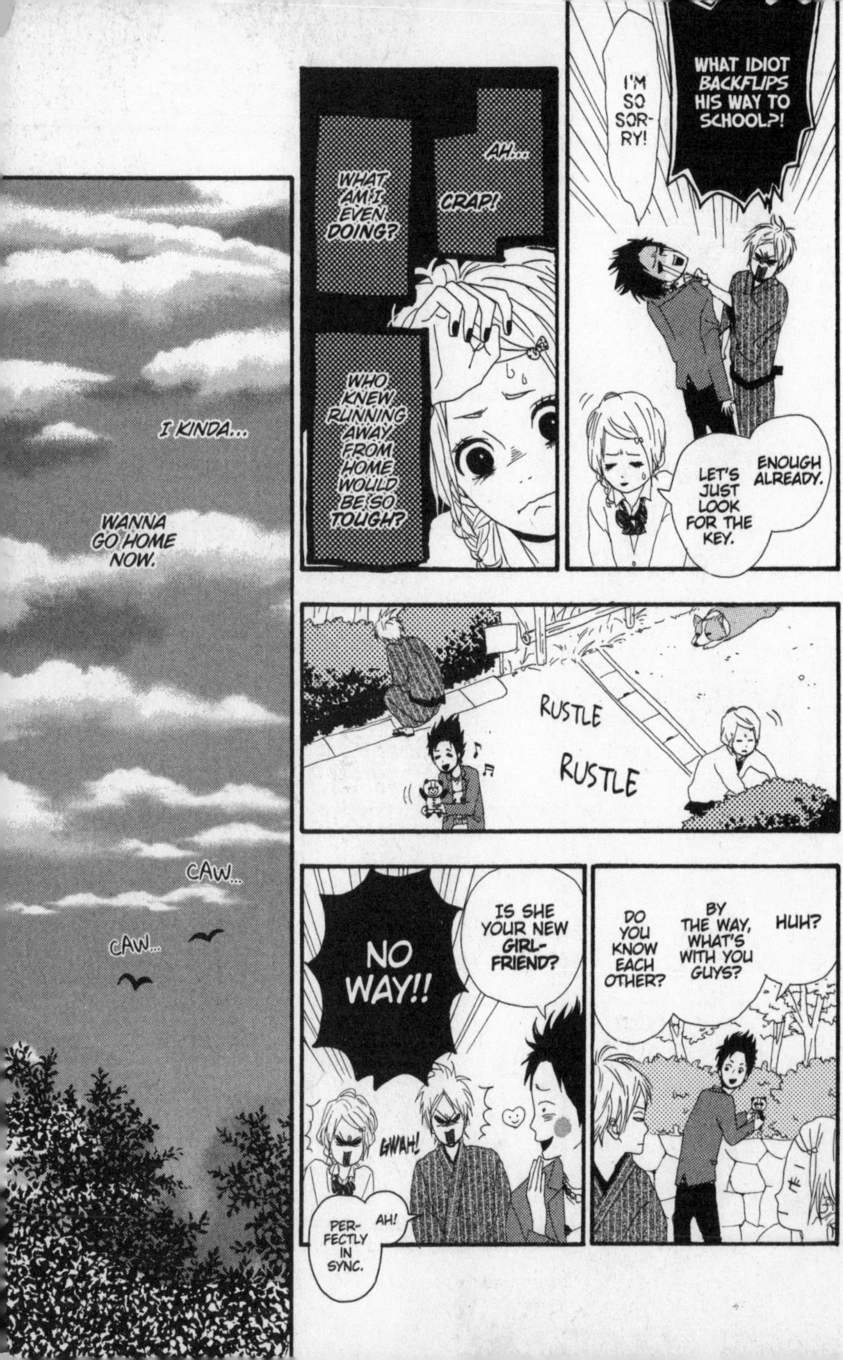
WHAT IDIOT BACKFLIPS HIS WAY TO SCHOOL?!
I'M SO SOR-RY!
ENOUGH ALREADY.
LET'S JUST LOOK FOR THE KEY.
AH...
CRAP!
WHAT AM I EVEN DOING?
WHO KNEW RUNNING AWAY FROM HOME WOULD BE SO TOUGH?
RUSTLE
RUSTLE
HUH?
BY THE WAY, WHAT'S WITH YOU GUYS?
DO YOU KNOW EACH OTHER?
IS SHE YOUR NEW GIRL-FRIEND?
NO WAY!!
GWAH!
AH!
PER-FECTLY IN SYNC.
I KINDA...
WANNA GO HOME NOW.
CAW...
CAW...

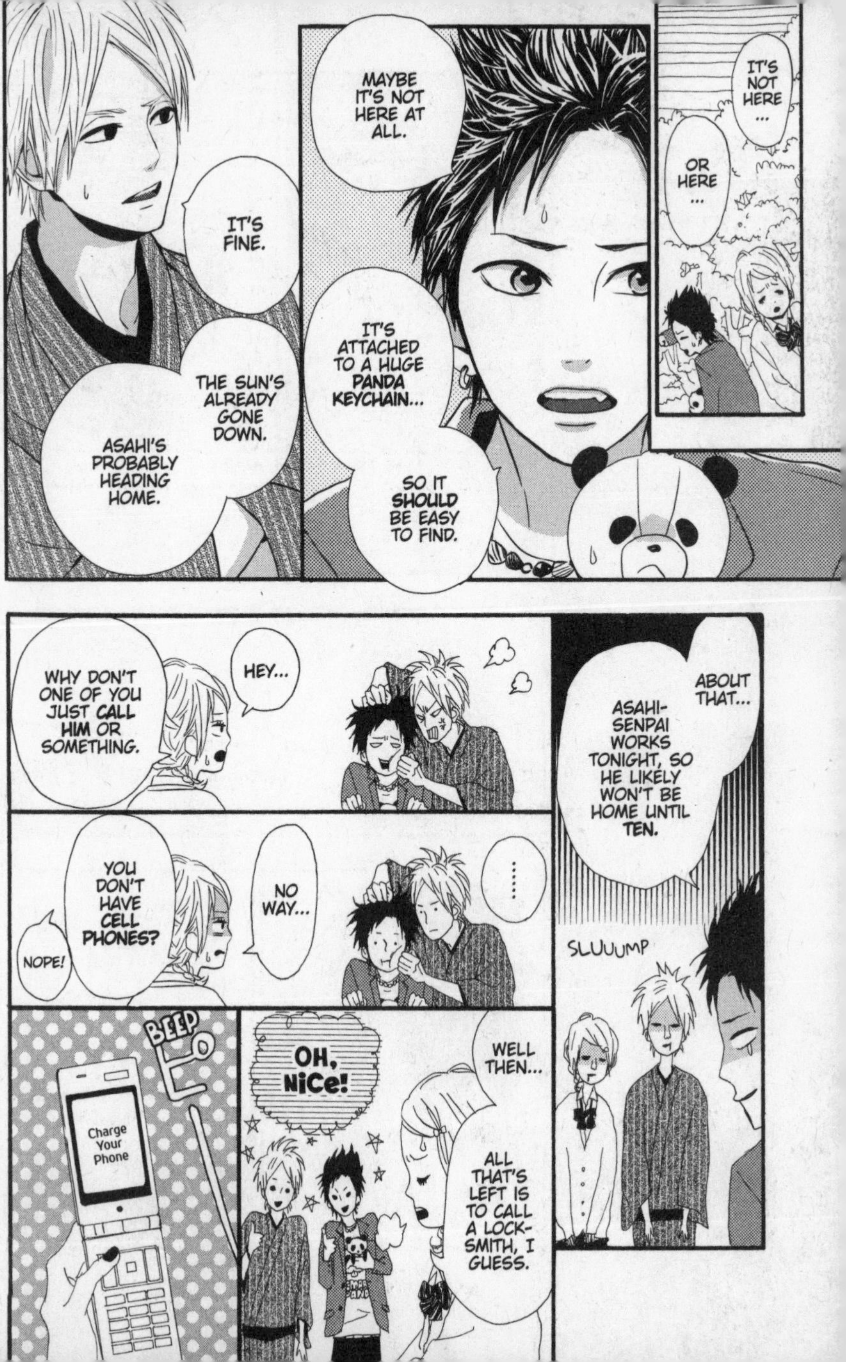
IT'S NOT HERE...
OR HERE...
MAYBE IT'S NOT HERE AT ALL.
IT'S ATTACHED TO A HUGE PANDA KEYCHAIN...
SO IT SHOULD BE EASY TO FIND.
IT'S FINE.
THE SUN'S ALREADY GONE DOWN.
ASAHI'S PROBABLY HEADING HOME.
ABOUT THAT...
ASAHI-SENPAI WORKS TONIGHT, SO HE LIKELY WON'T BE HOME UNTIL TEN.
SLUUUMP
HEY...
WHY DON'T ONE OF YOU JUST CALL HIM OR SOMETHING.
......
NO WAY...
YOU DON'T HAVE CELL PHONES?
NOPE!
WELL THEN...
ALL THAT'S LEFT IS TO CALL A LOCK-SMITH, I GUESS.
OH, NICE!
BEEP
Charge Your Phone

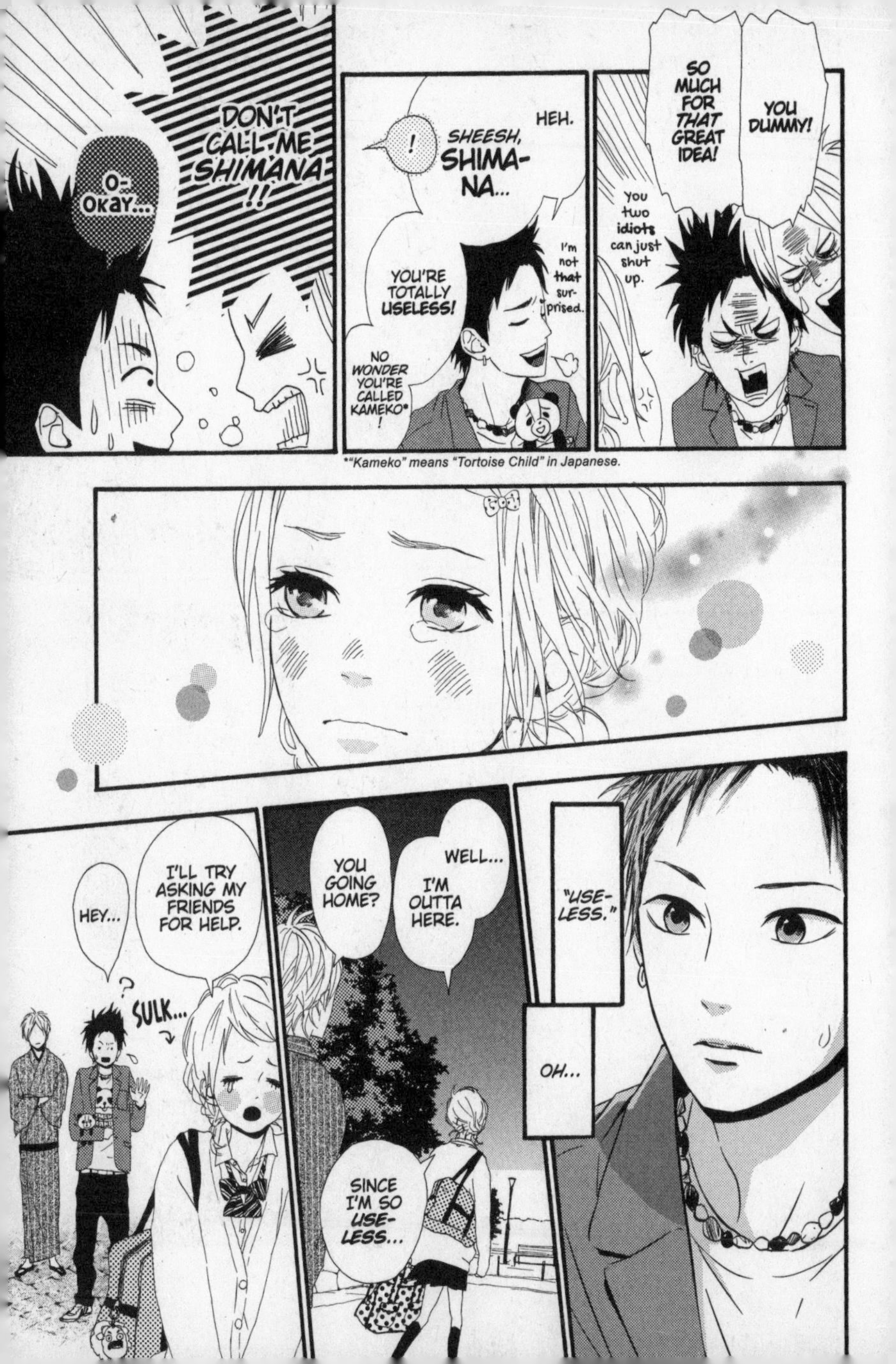
YOU DUMMY!
SO MUCH FOR THAT GREAT IDEA!
You two idiots can just shut up.
HEH.
SHEESH, SHIMANA...
!
I'm not that surprised.
YOU'RE TOTALLY USELESS!
NO WONDER YOU'RE CALLED KAMEKO*!
DON'T CALL ME SHIMANA!!
O-OKAY...
"USELESS."
OH...
WELL... I'M OUTTA HERE.
YOU GOING HOME?
SINCE I'M SO USELESS...
I'LL TRY ASKING MY FRIENDS FOR HELP.
HEY...
?
SULK...

*"Kameko" means "Tortoise Child" in Japanese.

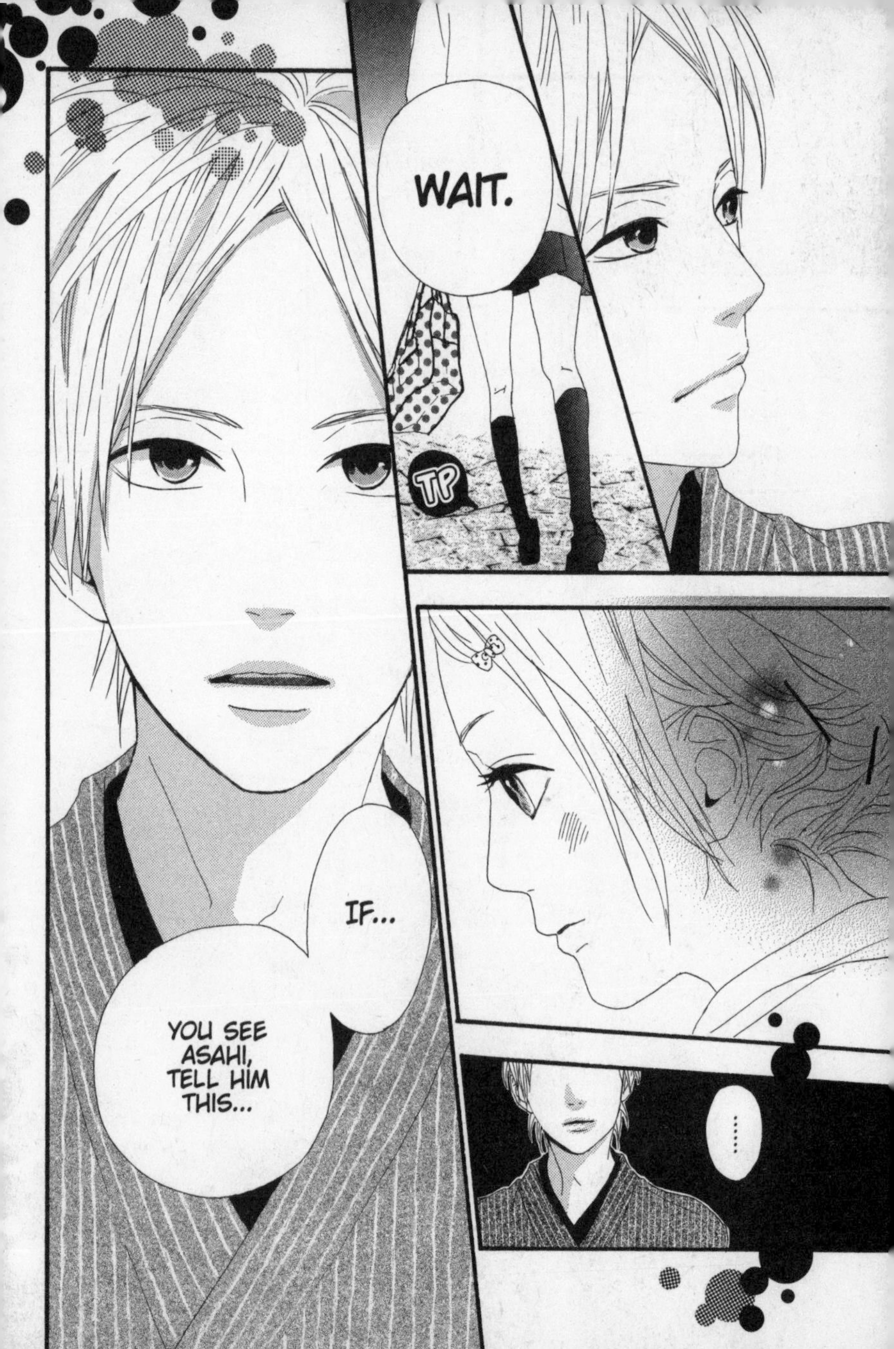
WAIT.
TP
......
IF...
YOU SEE ASAHI, TELL HIM THIS...

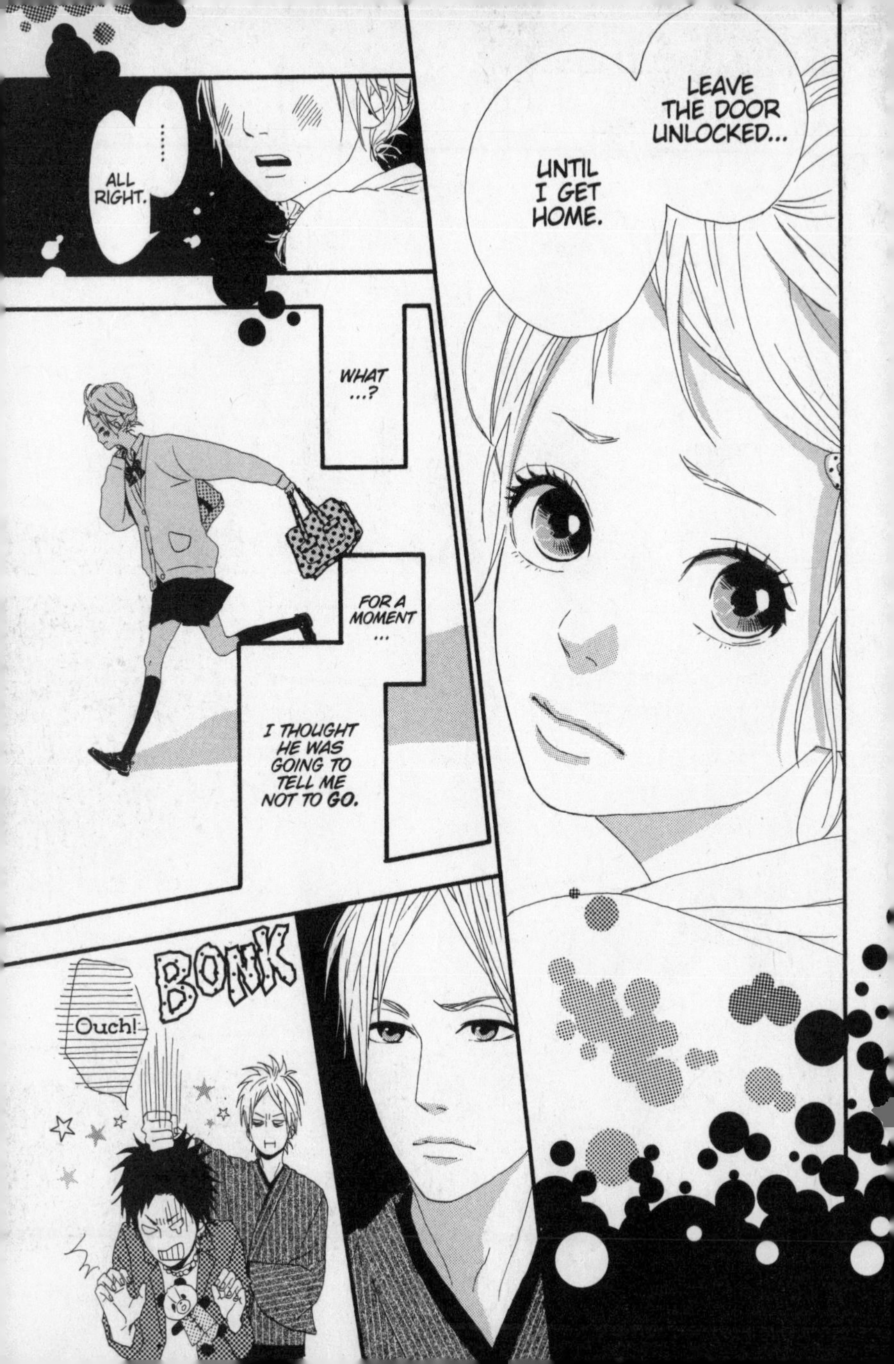
LEAVE THE DOOR UNLOCKED...
UNTIL I GET HOME.
......
ALL RIGHT.
WHAT ...?
FOR A MOMENT ...
I THOUGHT HE WAS GOING TO TELL ME NOT TO GO.
BONK
Ouch!

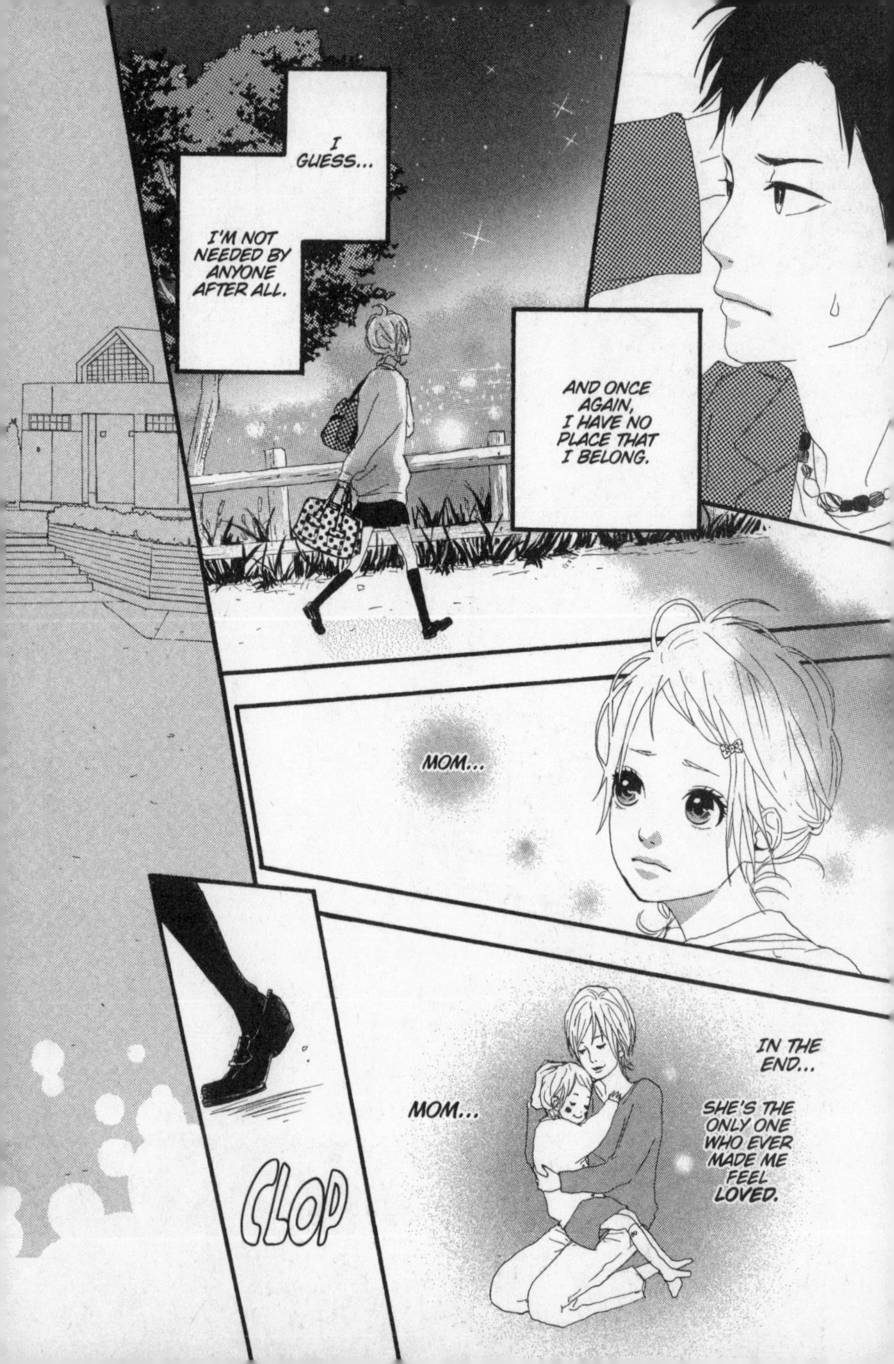
I GUESS...
I'M NOT NEEDED BY ANYONE AFTER ALL.
AND ONCE AGAIN, I HAVE NO PLACE THAT I BELONG.
MOM...
IN THE END...
SHE'S THE ONLY ONE WHO EVER MADE ME FEEL LOVED.
MOM...
CLOP

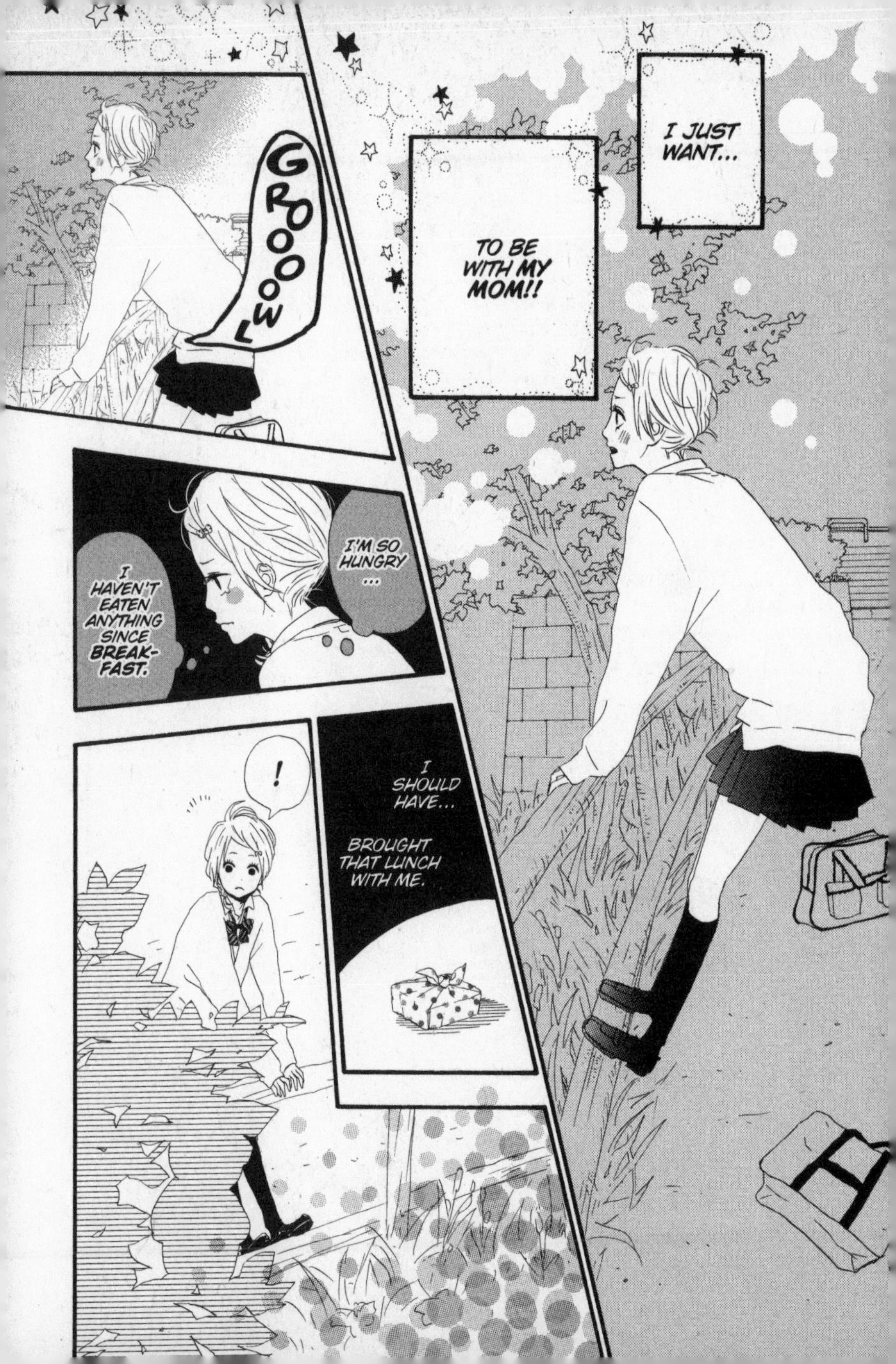

I JUST WANT...
TO BE WITH MY MOM!!
GROOOOWL
I'M SO HUNGRY...
I HAVEN'T EATEN ANYTHING SINCE BREAKFAST.
I SHOULD HAVE...
BROUGHT THAT LUNCH WITH ME.
!

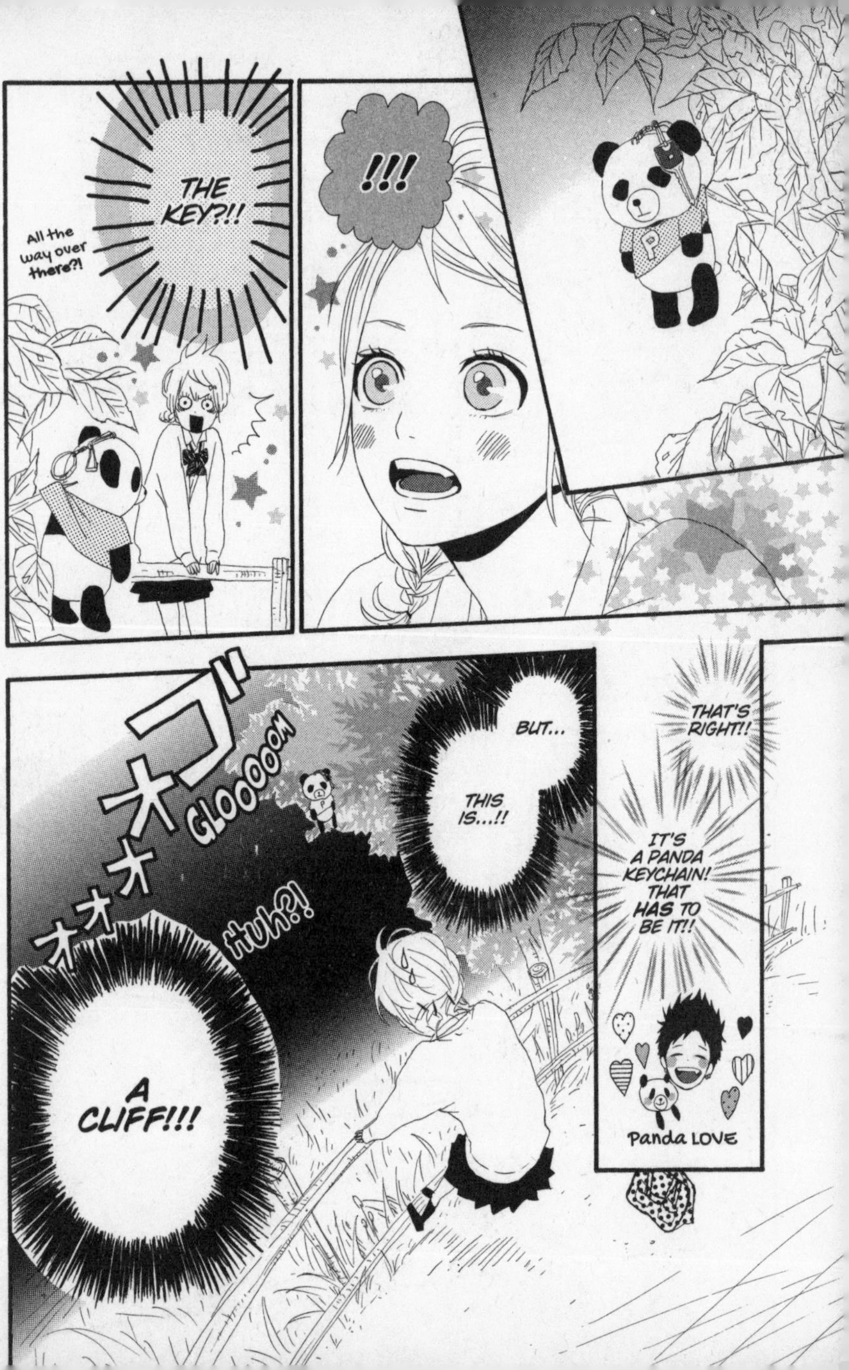
!!!
THE KEY?!!
All the way over there?!
THAT'S RIGHT!!
IT'S A PANDA KEYCHAIN! THAT HAS TO BE IT!!
Panda LOVE
BUT...
THIS IS...!!
ゴオオオ
GLOOOOOM
Huh?!
A CLIFF!!!

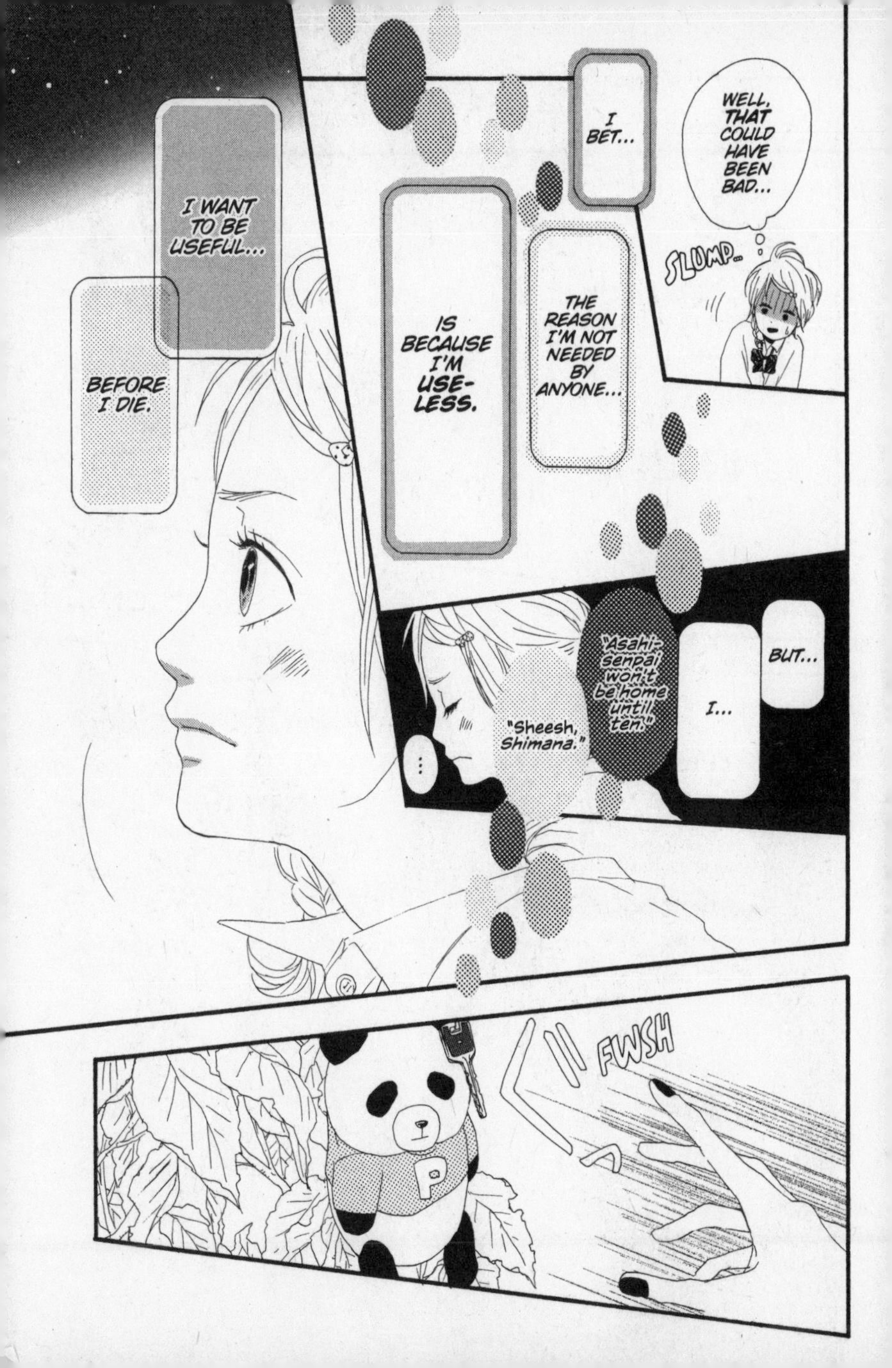

WELL, THAT COULD HAVE BEEN BAD...
SLUMP...
I BET...
THE REASON I'M NOT NEEDED BY ANYONE...
IS BECAUSE I'M USE-LESS.
BUT...
I...
"Asahi-senpai won't be home until ten."
"Sheesh, Shimana."
...
I WANT TO BE USEFUL...
BEFORE I DIE.
FWSH

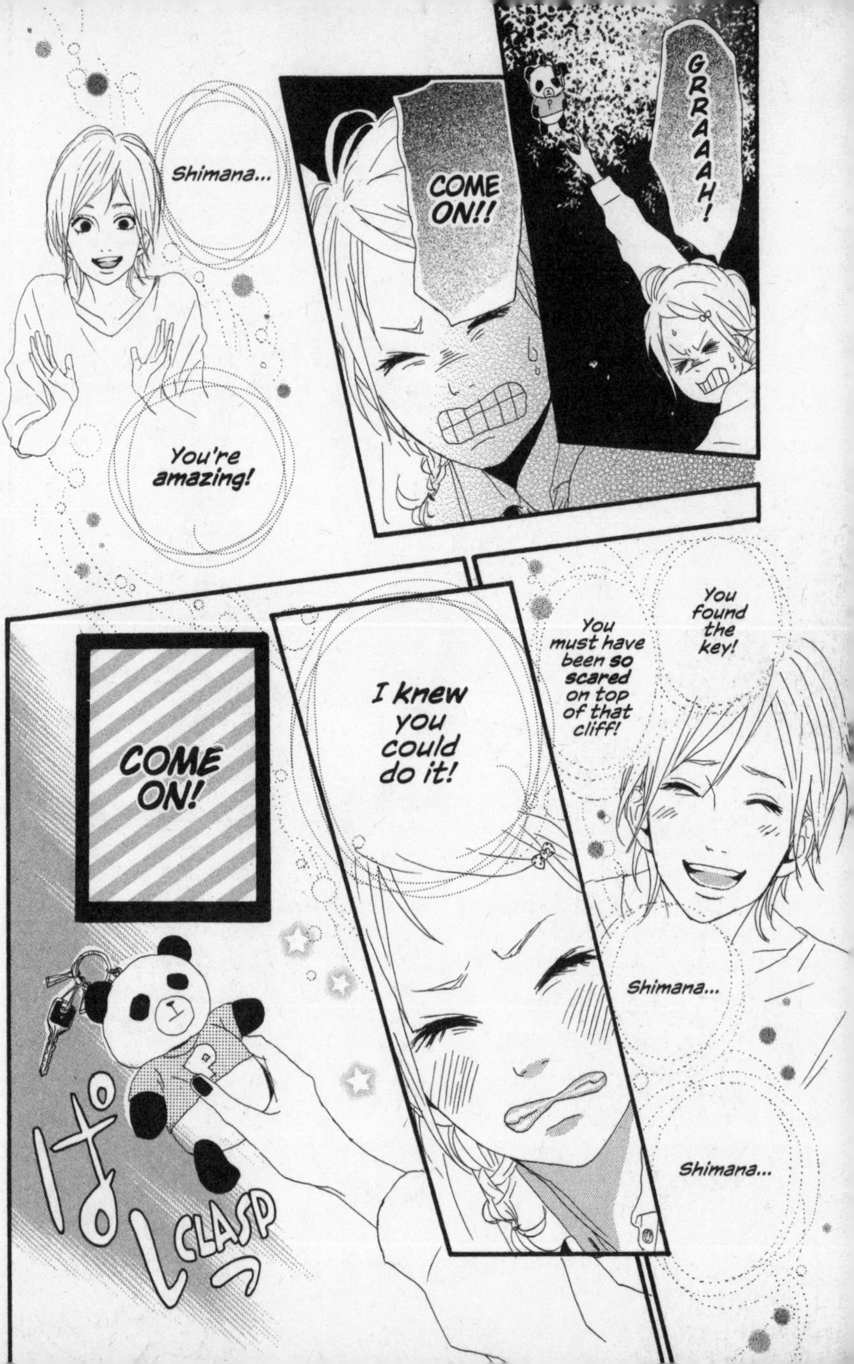
GRRAAAH!
COME ON!!
Shimana...
You're amazing!
You found the key!
You must have been so scared on top of that cliff!
Shimana...
Shimana...
I knew you could do it!
COME ON!
ぱしっ
CLASP

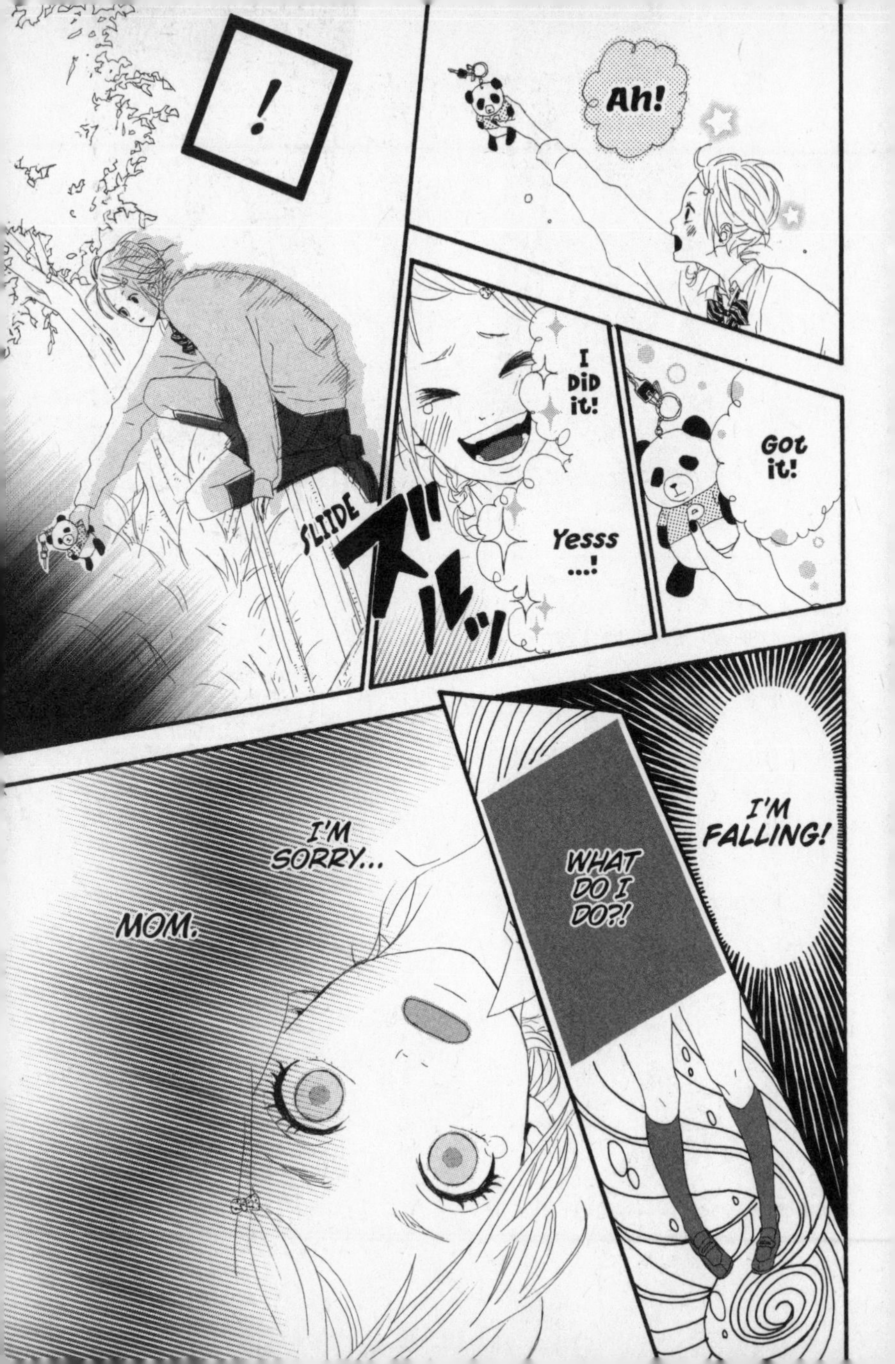
Ah!
Got it!
I DID it!
Yesss ...!
SLIIDE
ズルッ
!
I'M FALLING!
WHAT DO I DO?!
I'M SORRY...
MOM.

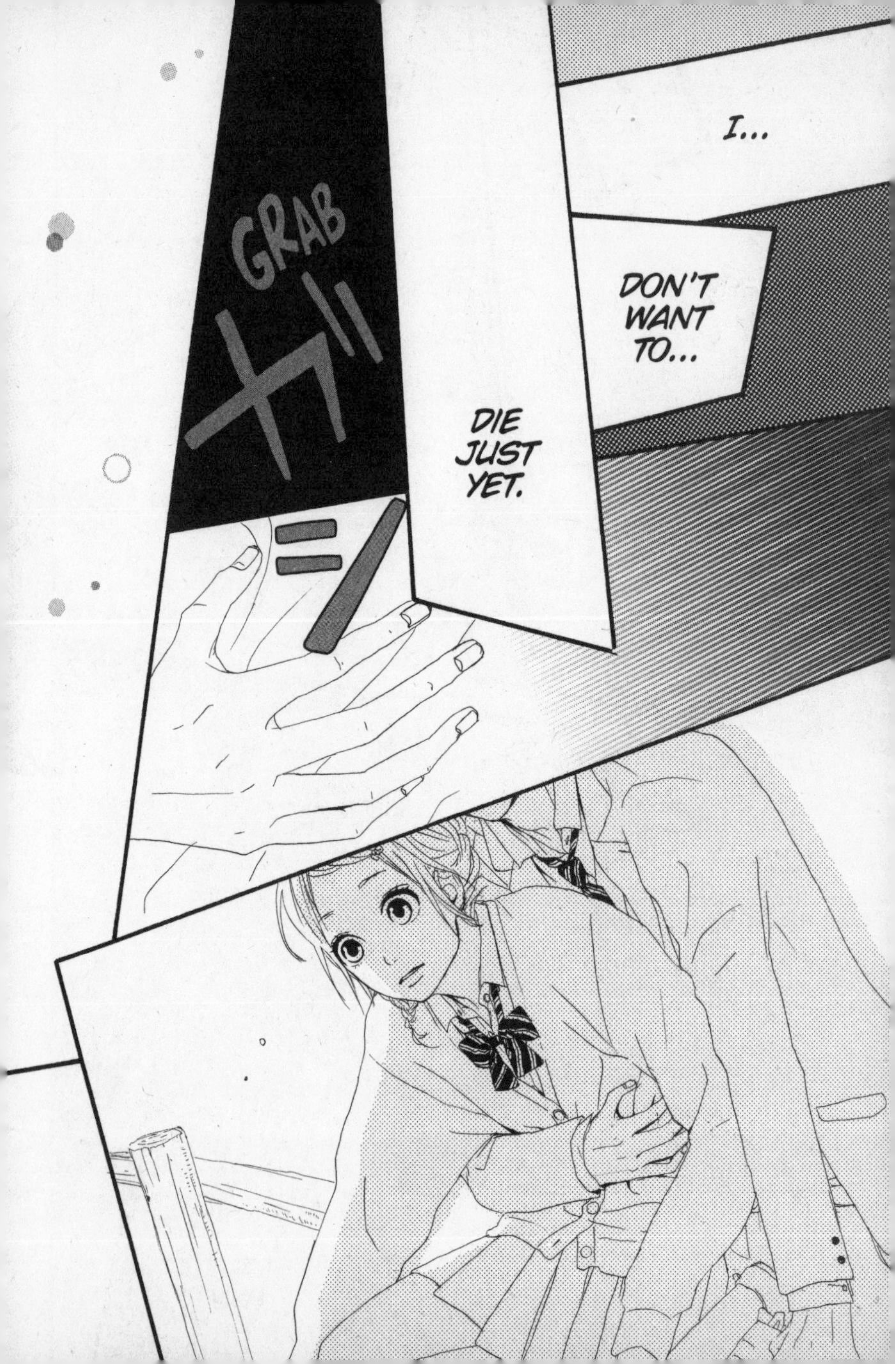
I...
DON'T WANT TO...
GRAB
DIE JUST YET.

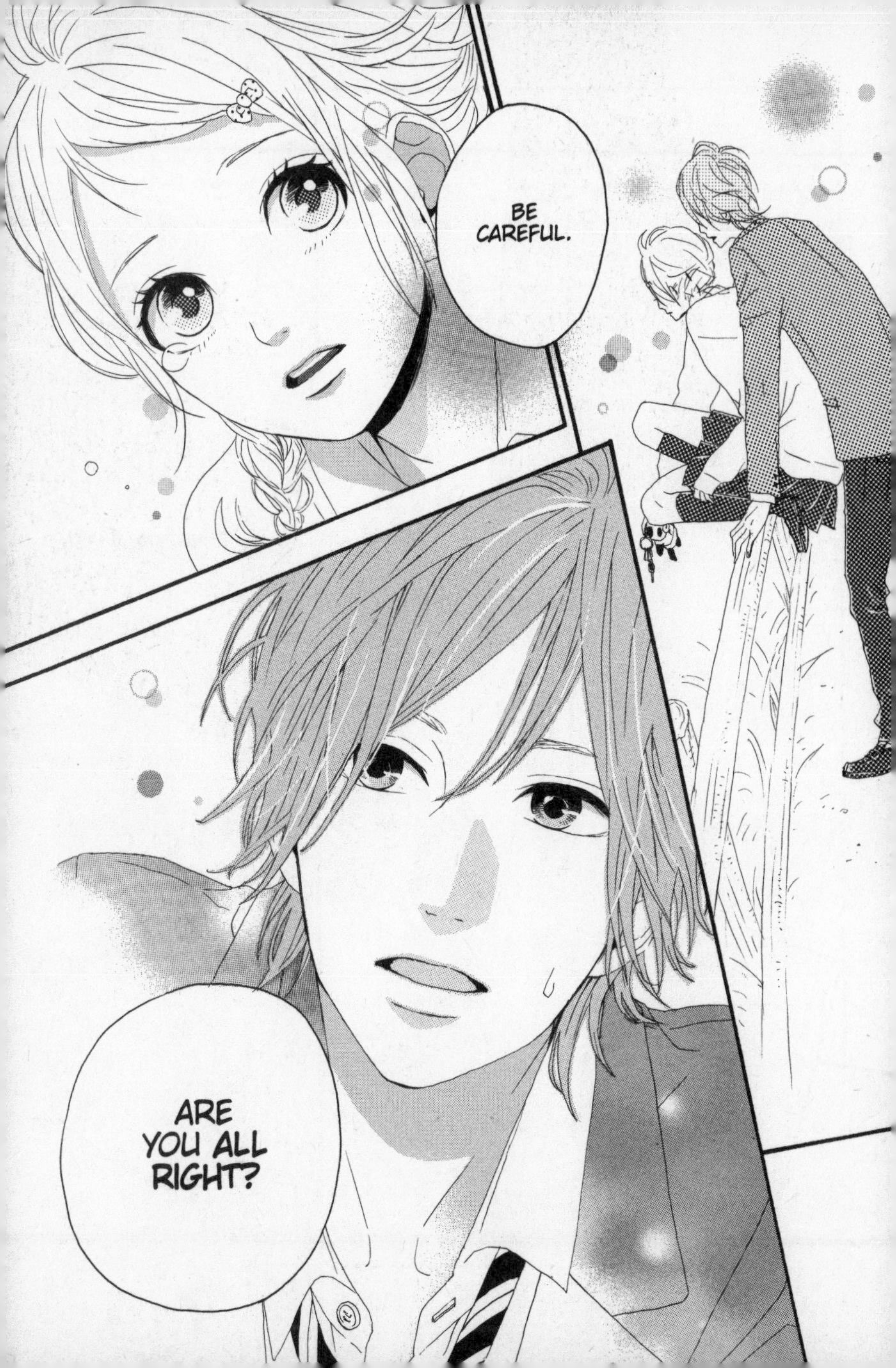
BE CAREFUL.
ARE YOU ALL RIGHT?

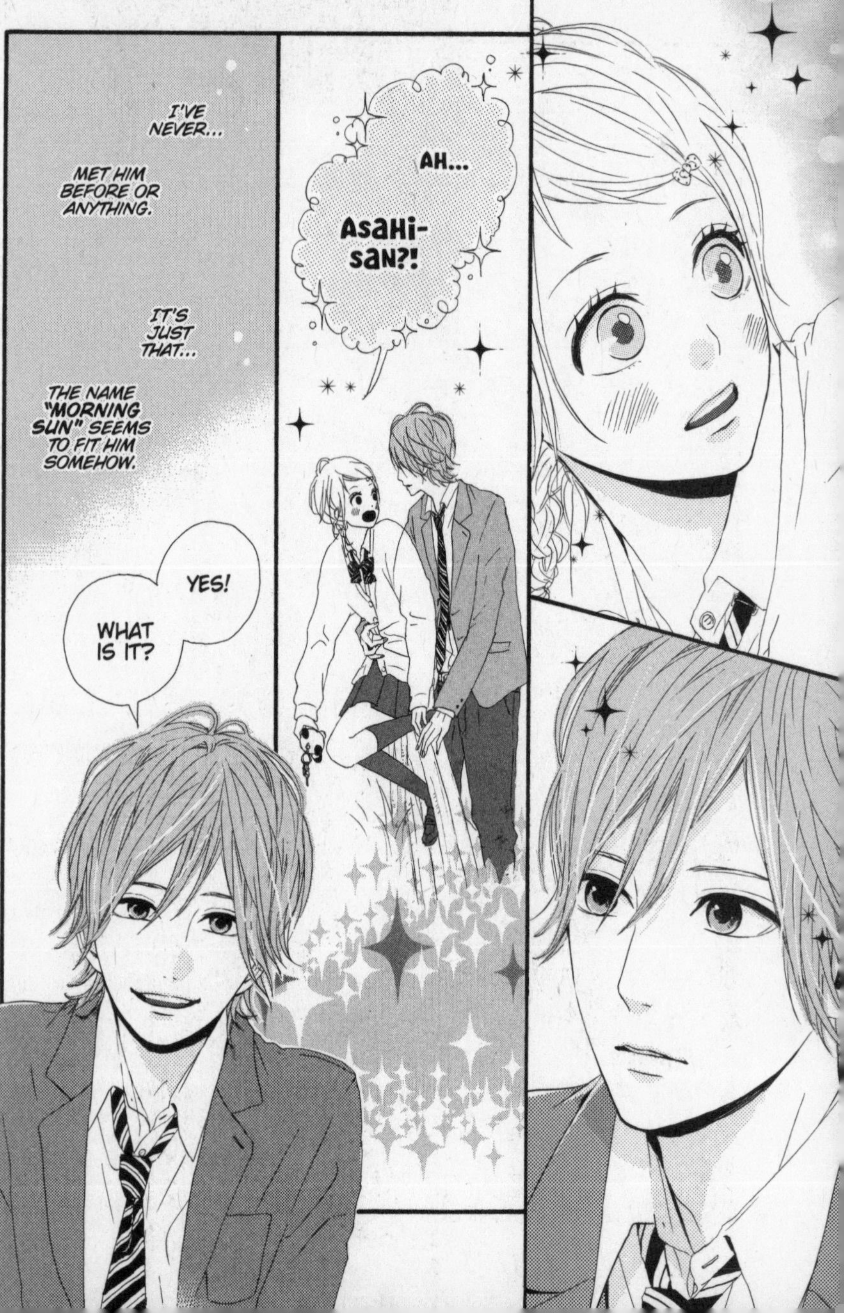
AH... ASAHI-SAN?!
I'VE NEVER...
MET HIM BEFORE OR ANYTHING.
IT'S JUST THAT...
THE NAME "MORNING SUN" SEEMS TO FIT HIM SOMEHOW.
YES! WHAT IS IT?

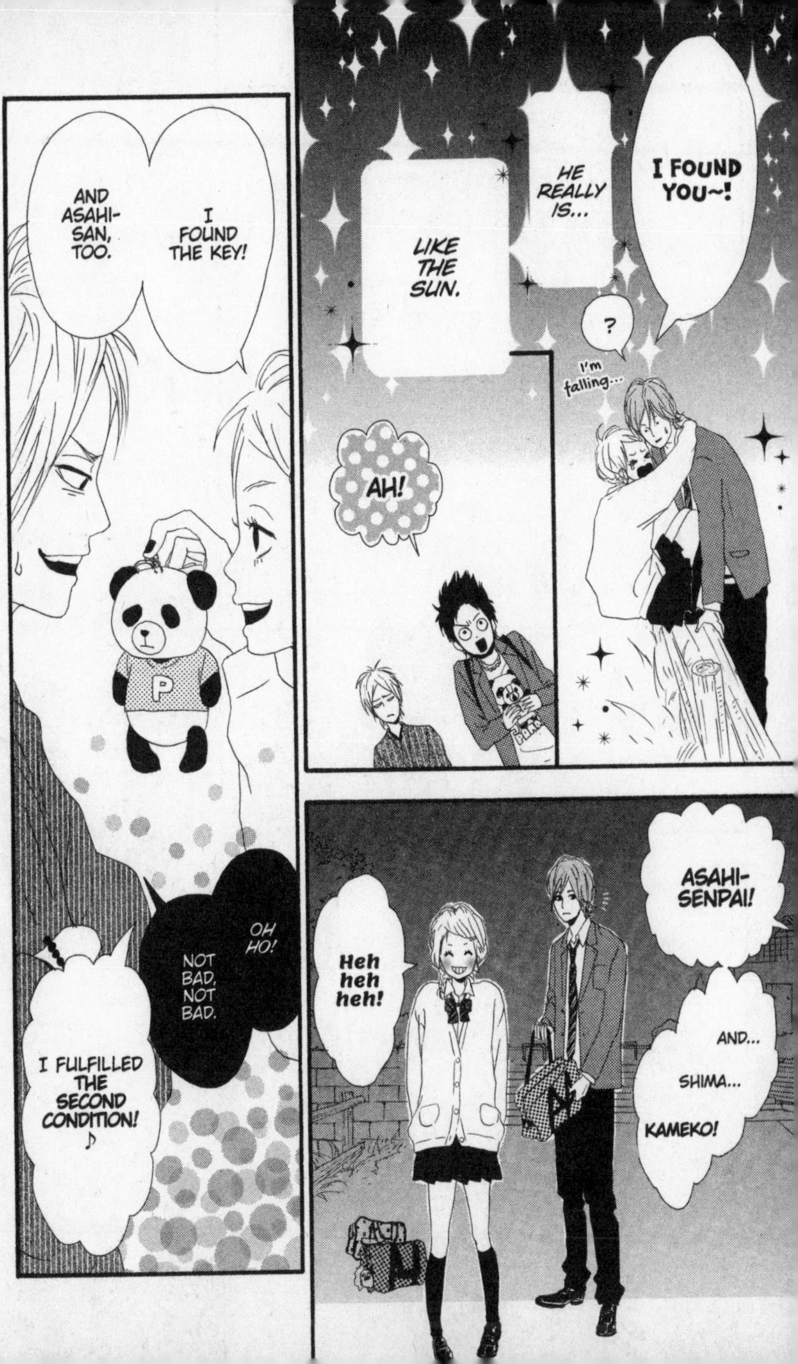
I FOUND YOU~!
HE REALLY IS...
LIKE THE SUN.
?
I'm falling...
AH!
ASAHI-SENPAI!
AND... SHIMA... KAMEKO!
Heh heh heh!
I FOUND THE KEY!
AND ASAHI-SAN, TOO.
OH HO!
NOT BAD, NOT BAD.
I FULFILLED THE SECOND CONDITION! ♪

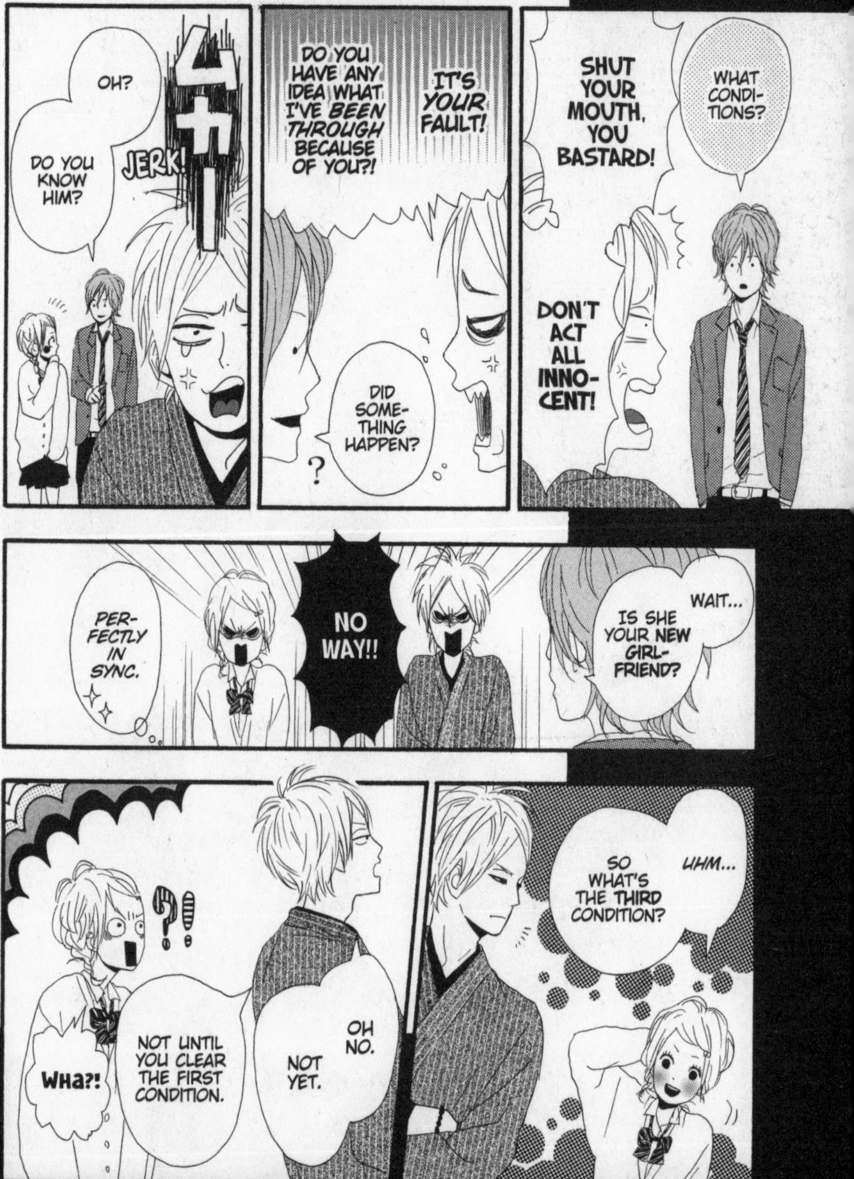
WHAT CONDI-TIONS?
SHUT YOUR MOUTH, YOU BASTARD!
DON'T ACT ALL INNO-CENT!
IT'S YOUR FAULT!
DO YOU HAVE ANY IDEA WHAT I'VE BEEN THROUGH BECAUSE OF YOU?!
DID SOME-THING HAPPEN?
?
JERK!
OH?
DO YOU KNOW HIM?
WAIT...
IS SHE YOUR NEW GIRL-FRIEND?
NO WAY!!
PER-FECTLY IN SYNC.
UHM...
SO WHAT'S THE THIRD CONDITION?
OH NO.
NOT YET.
?!
NOT UNTIL YOU CLEAR THE FIRST CONDITION.
Wha?!

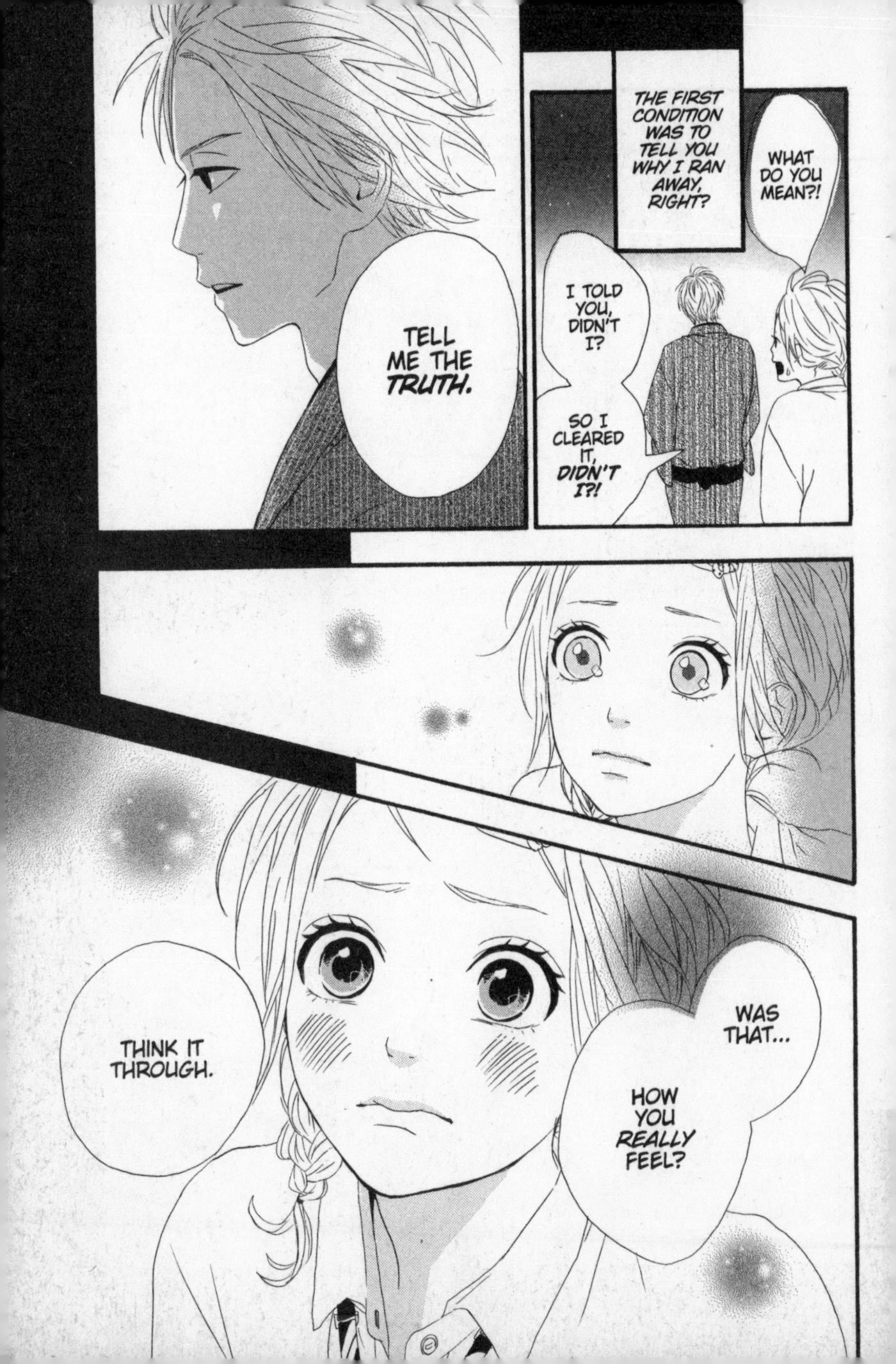

WHAT DO YOU MEAN?!
THE FIRST CONDITION WAS TO TELL YOU WHY I RAN AWAY, RIGHT?
I TOLD YOU, DIDN'T I?
SO I CLEARED IT, *DIDN'T I?!*
TELL ME THE *TRUTH.*
WAS THAT...
HOW YOU *REALLY* FEEL?
THINK IT THROUGH.

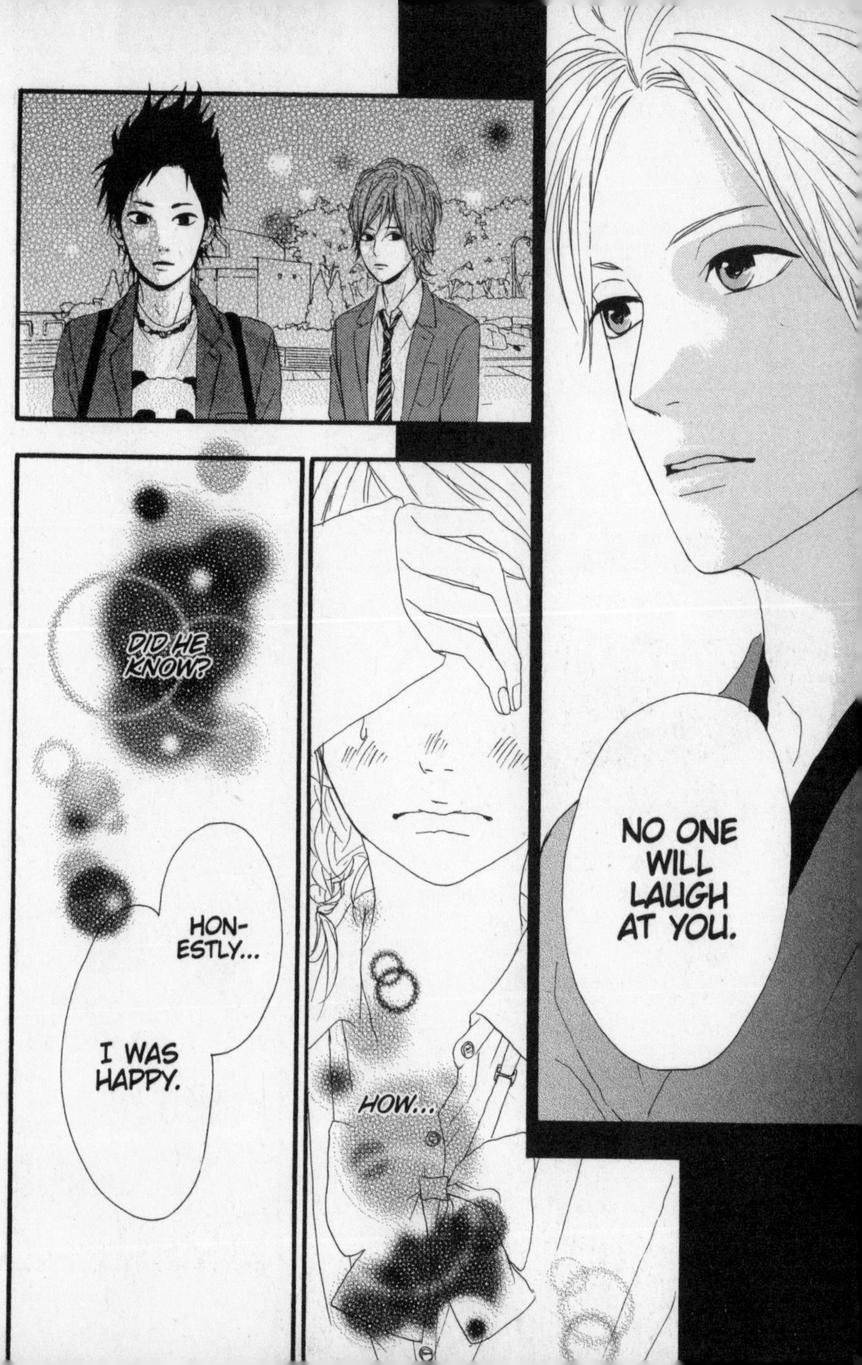
NO ONE WILL LAUGH AT YOU.
HOW...
DID HE KNOW?
HON-ESTLY...
I WAS HAPPY.

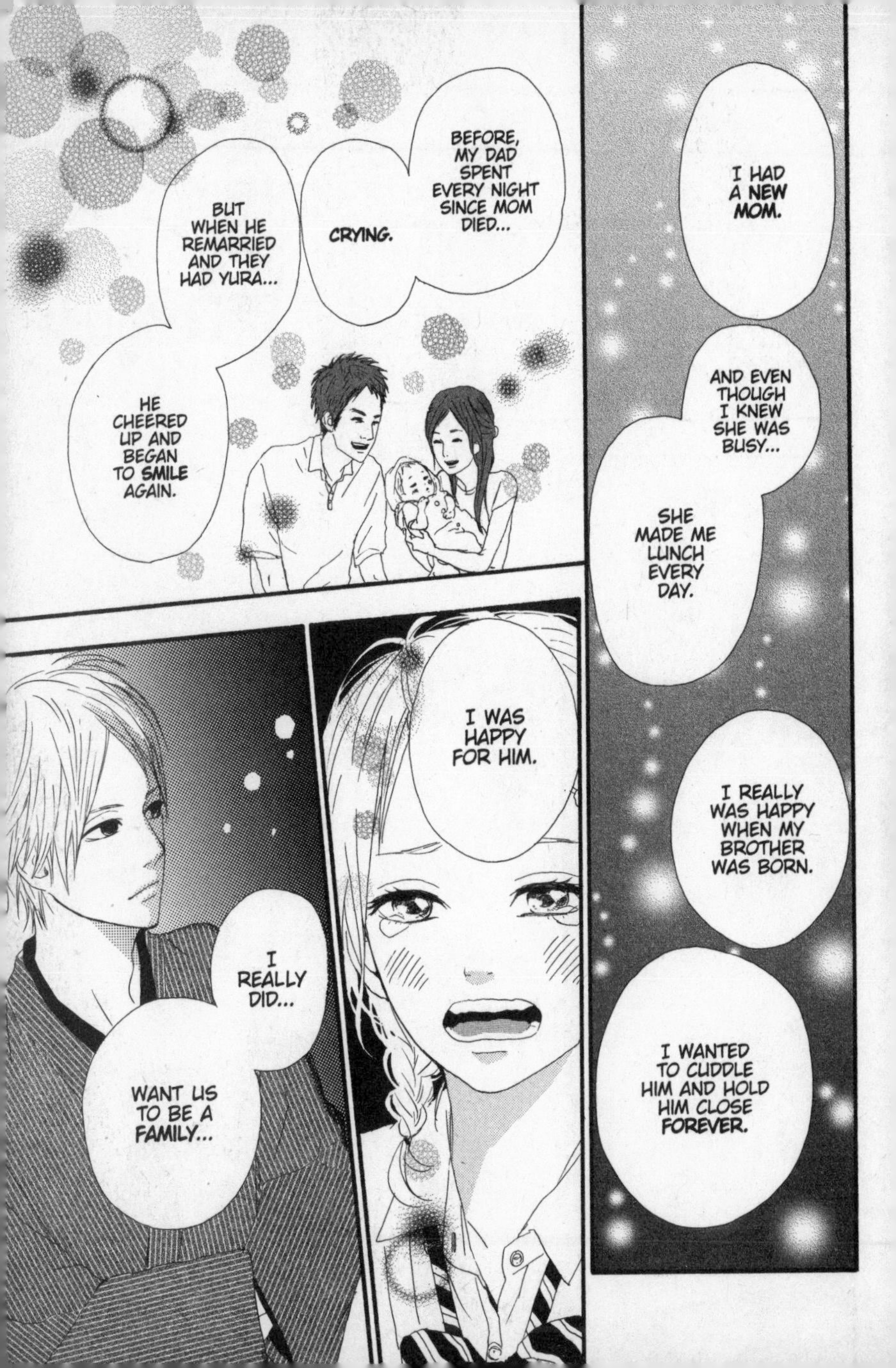
I HAD A NEW MOM.
AND EVEN THOUGH I KNEW SHE WAS BUSY...
SHE MADE ME LUNCH EVERY DAY.
I REALLY WAS HAPPY WHEN MY BROTHER WAS BORN.
I WANTED TO CUDDLE HIM AND HOLD HIM CLOSE FOREVER.
BEFORE, MY DAD SPENT EVERY NIGHT SINCE MOM DIED...
CRYING.
BUT WHEN HE REMARRIED AND THEY HAD YURA...
HE CHEERED UP AND BEGAN TO SMILE AGAIN.
I WAS HAPPY FOR HIM.
I REALLY DID...
WANT US TO BE A FAMILY...

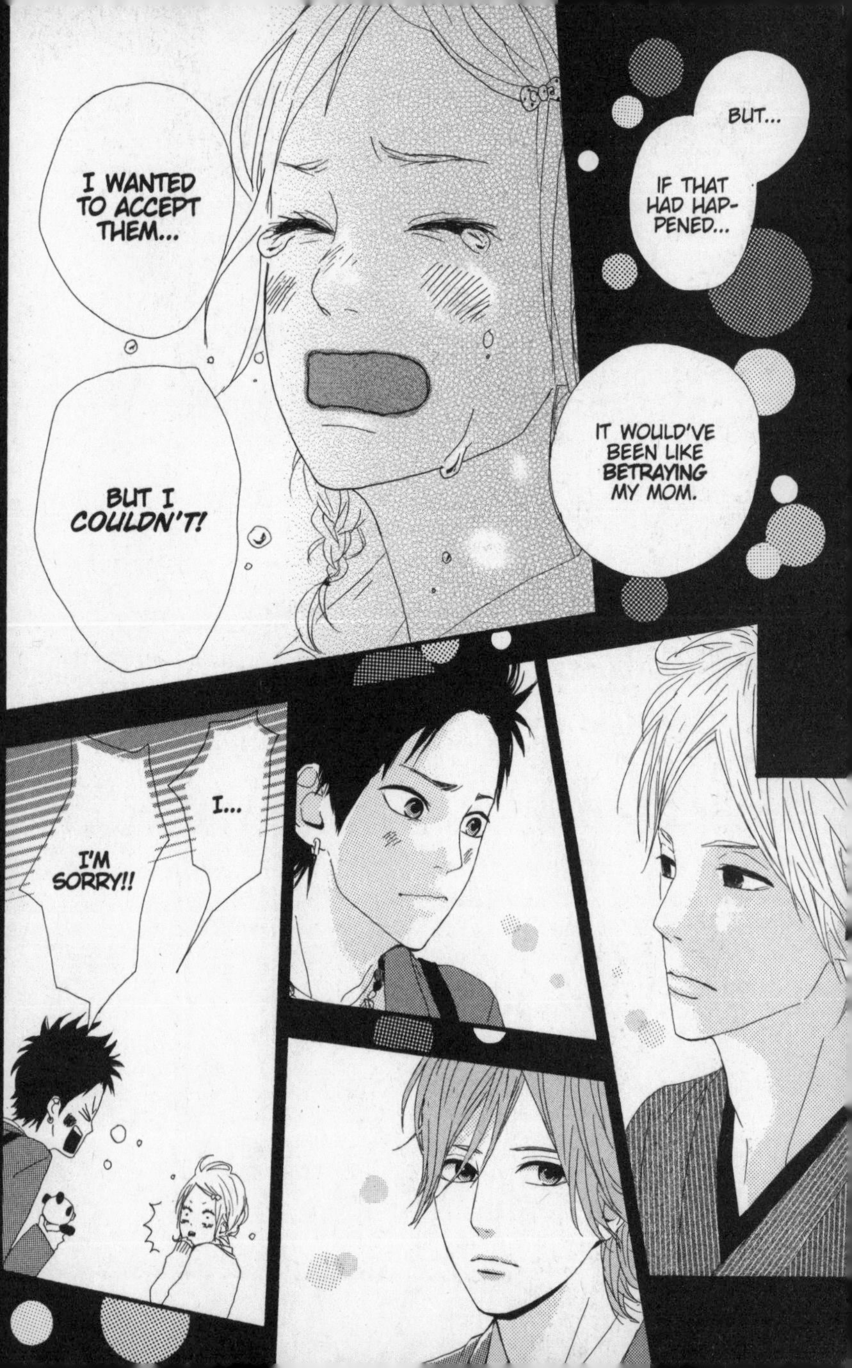
BUT...
IF THAT HAD HAP-PENED...
IT WOULD'VE BEEN LIKE BETRAYING MY MOM.
I WANTED TO ACCEPT THEM...
BUT I COULDN'T!
I...
I'M SORRY!!

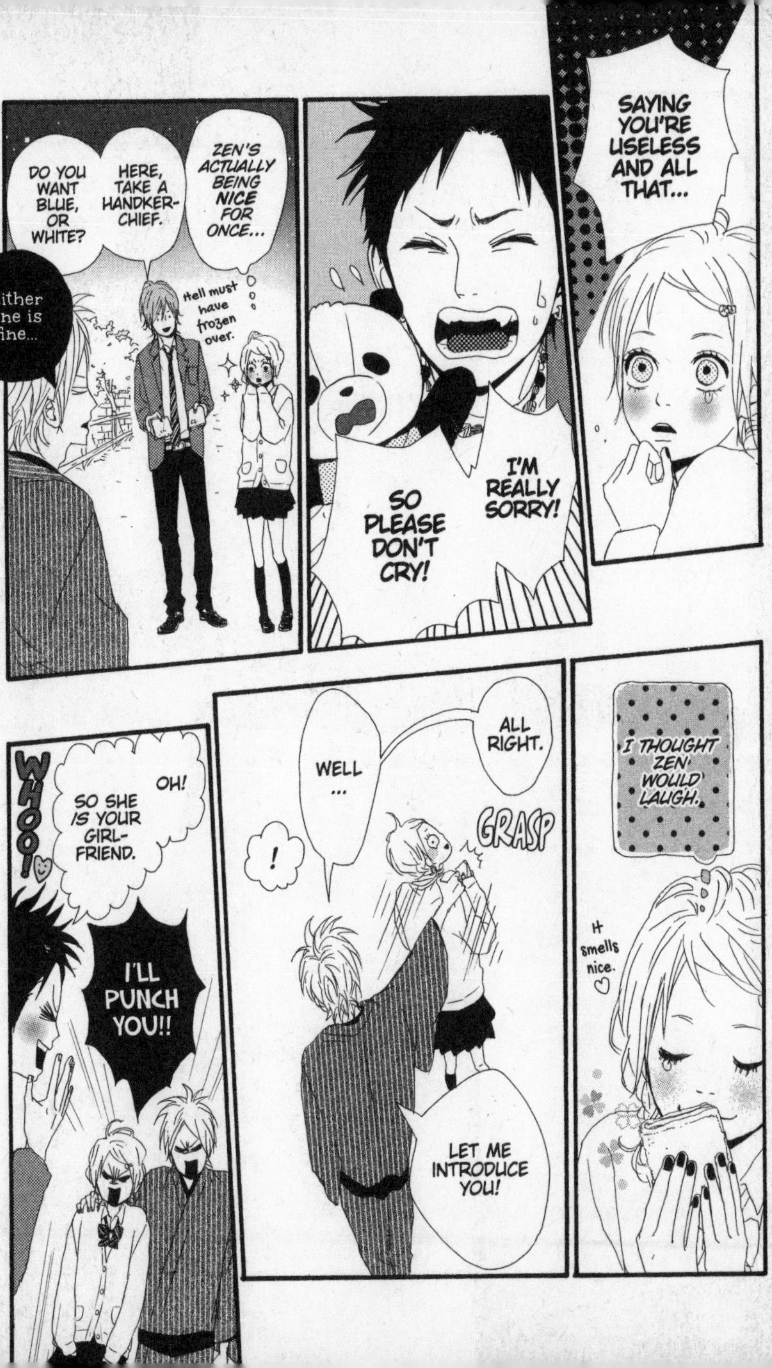
SAYING YOU'RE USELESS AND ALL THAT...
I'M REALLY SORRY!
SO PLEASE DON'T CRY!
ZEN'S ACTUALLY BEING NICE FOR ONCE...
Hell must have frozen over.
HERE, TAKE A HANDKER-CHIEF.
DO YOU WANT BLUE, OR WHITE?
Either one is fine...
I THOUGHT ZEN WOULD LAUGH.
It smells nice.
ALL RIGHT.
WELL ...
!
GRASP
LET ME INTRODUCE YOU!
OH!
SO SHE IS YOUR GIRL-FRIEND.
WHOO!
I'LL PUNCH YOU!!

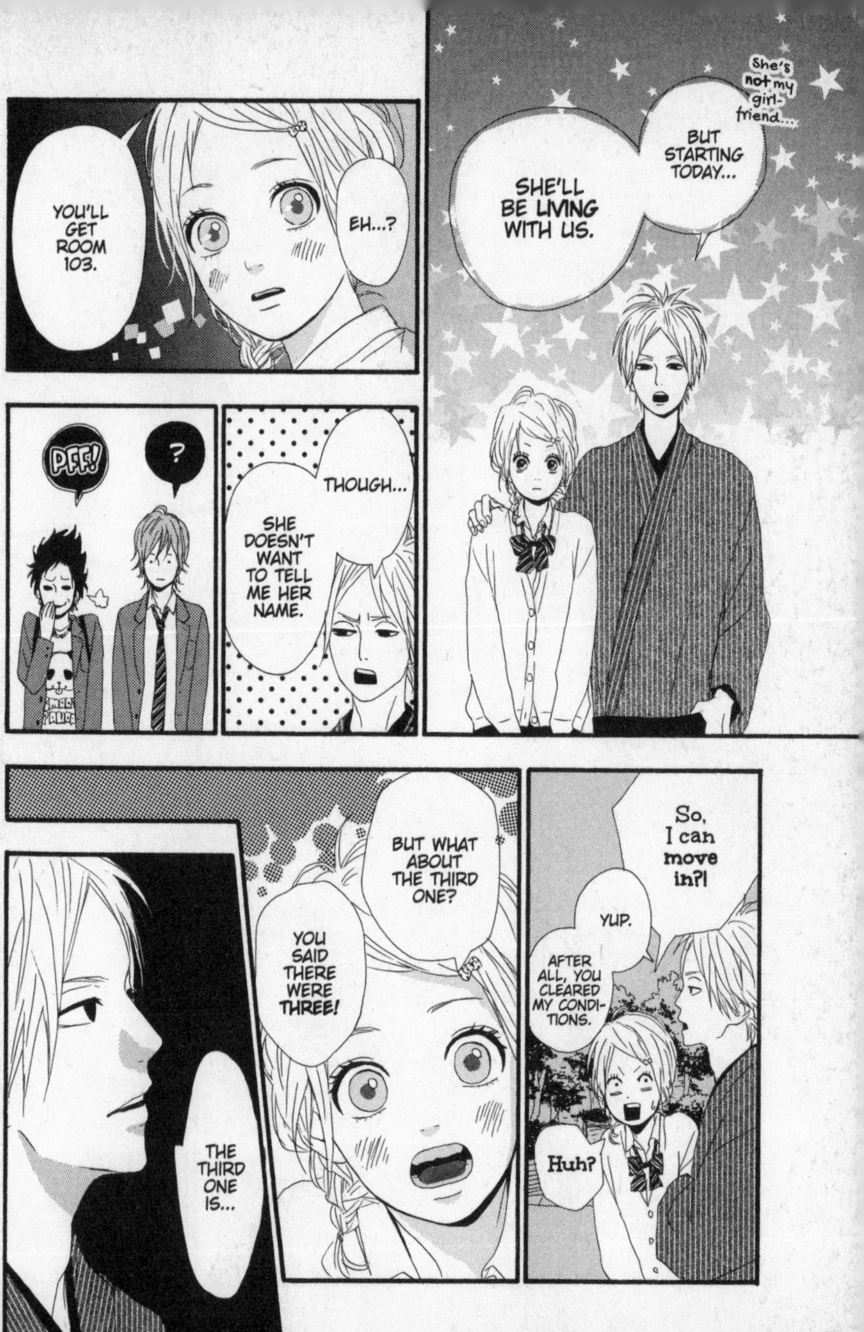
She's not my girl-friend...
BUT STARTING TODAY...
SHE'LL BE LIVING WITH US.
EH...?
YOU'LL GET ROOM 103.
THOUGH...
SHE DOESN'T WANT TO TELL ME HER NAME.
?
PFF!
So, I can move in?!
YUP.
AFTER ALL, YOU CLEARED MY CONDI-TIONS.
Huh?
BUT WHAT ABOUT THE THIRD ONE?
YOU SAID THERE WERE THREE!
THE THIRD ONE IS...

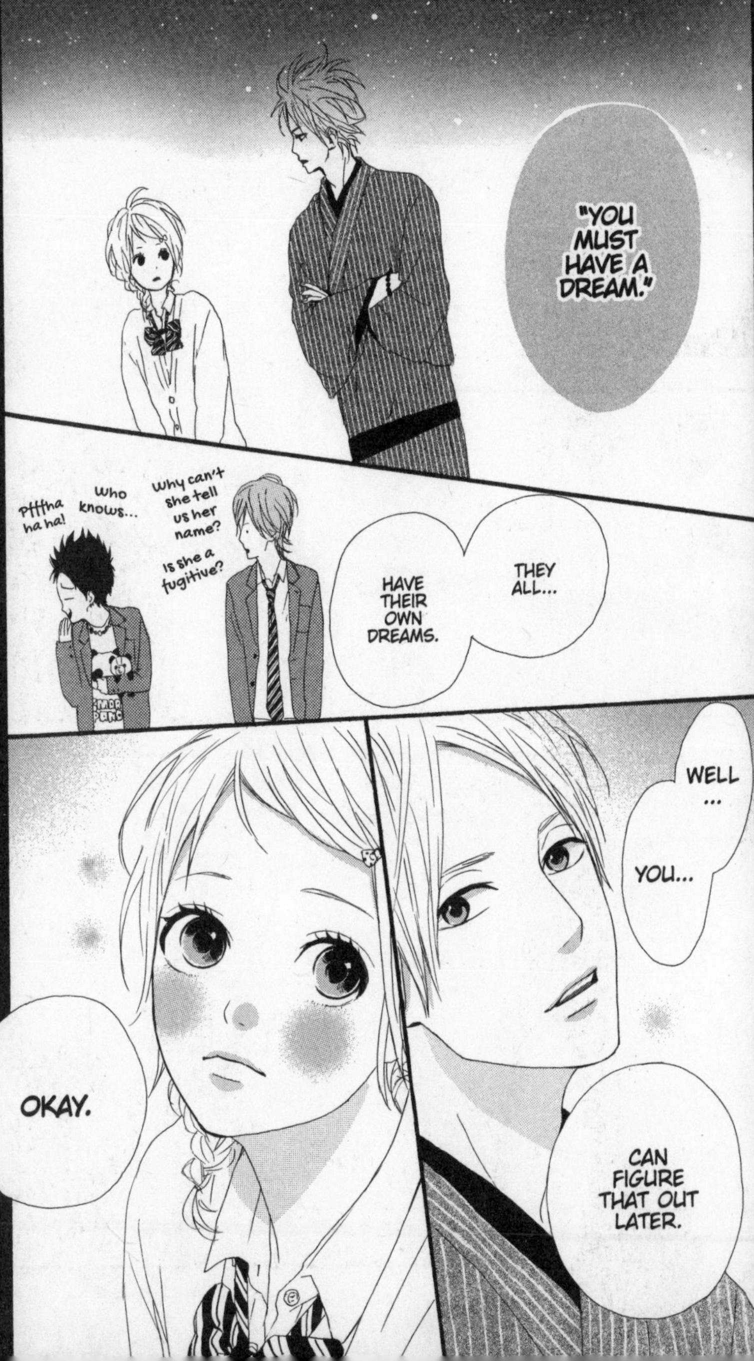
"YOU MUST HAVE A DREAM."
THEY ALL...
HAVE THEIR OWN DREAMS.
Why can't she tell us her name?
Is she a fugitive?
Who knows...
Pfffha ha ha!
WELL...
YOU...
CAN FIGURE THAT OUT LATER.
OKAY.

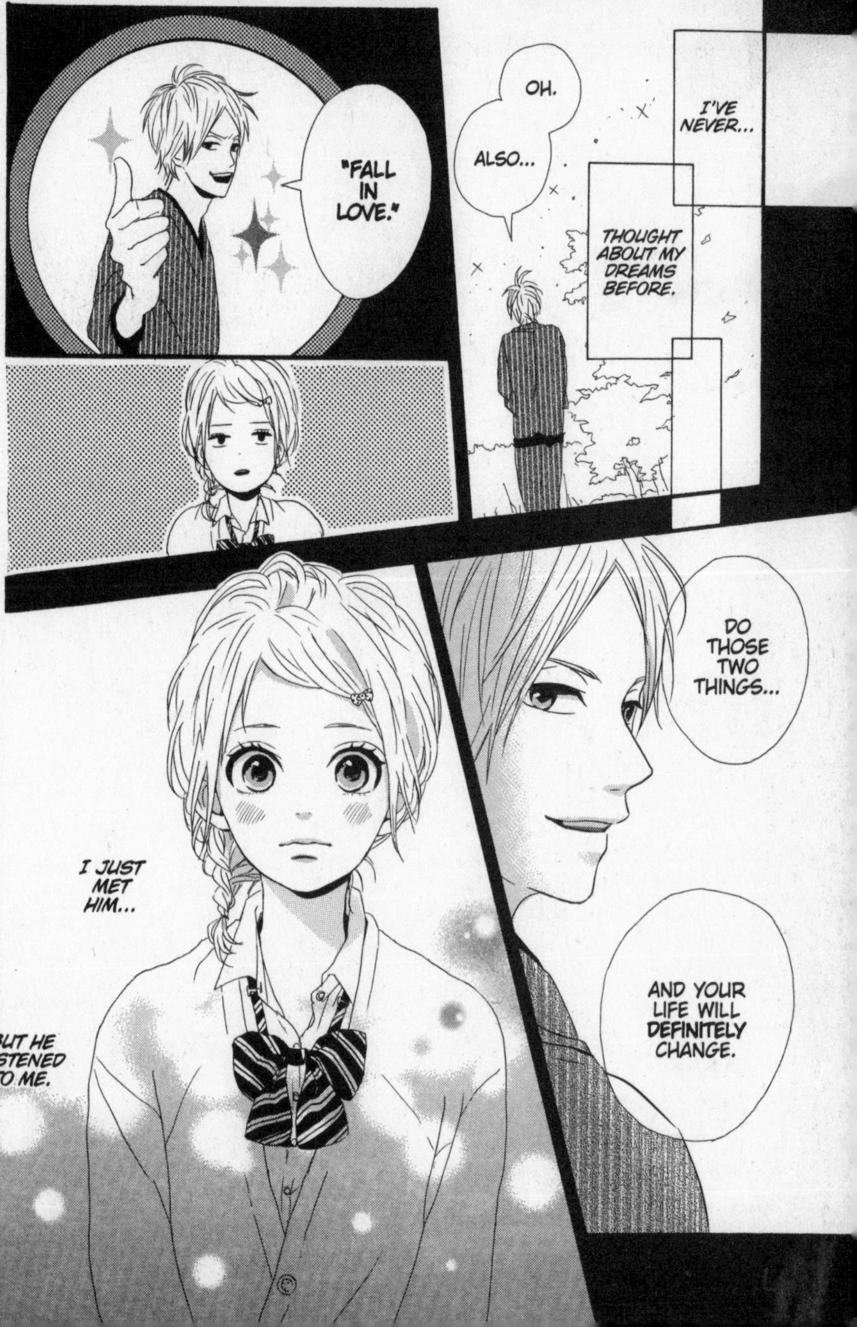
I'VE NEVER...
THOUGHT ABOUT MY DREAMS BEFORE.
OH.
ALSO...
"FALL IN LOVE."
DO THOSE TWO THINGS...
AND YOUR LIFE WILL DEFINITELY CHANGE.
I JUST MET HIM...
BUT HE LISTENED TO ME.

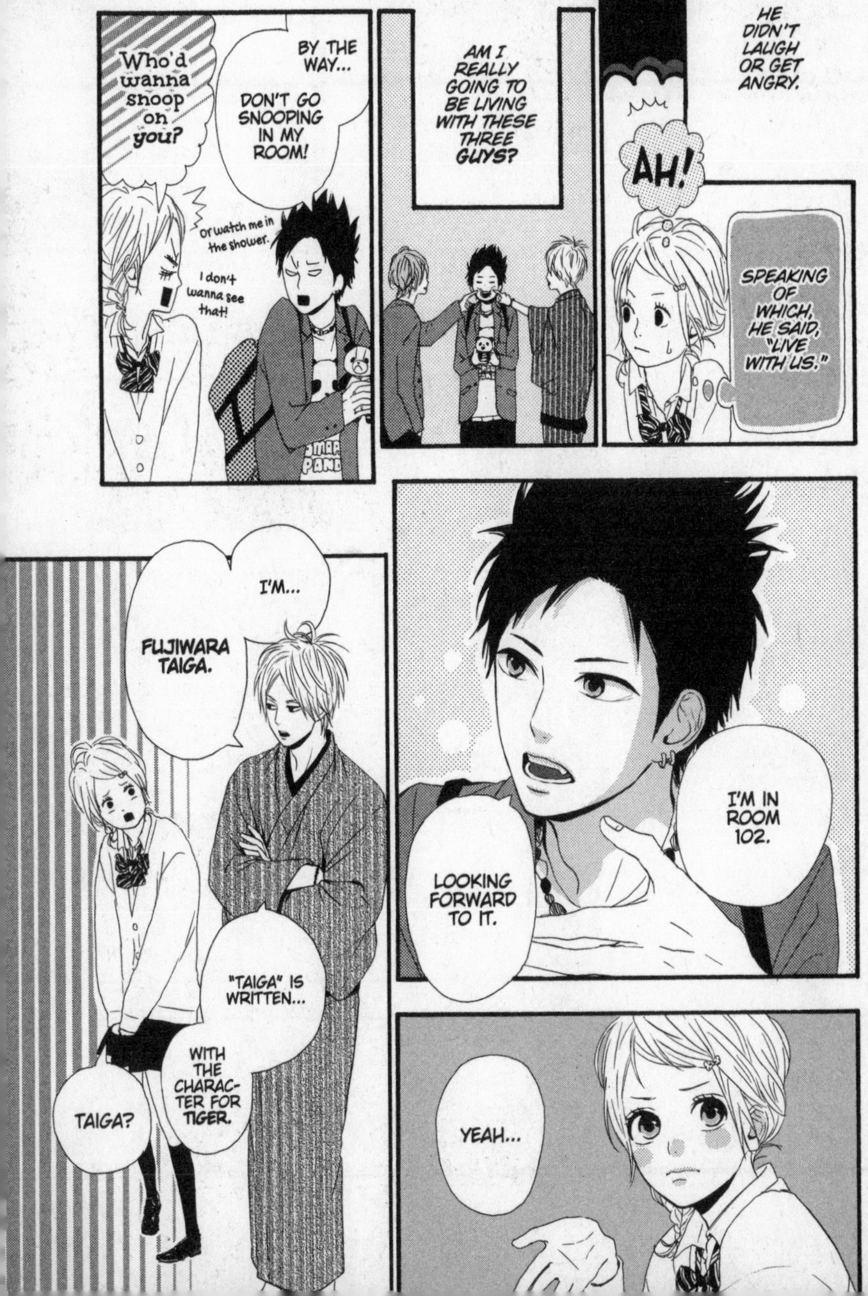
HE DIDN'T LAUGH OR GET ANGRY.
AH!
SPEAKING OF WHICH, HE SAID, "LIVE WITH US."
AM I REALLY GOING TO BE LIVING WITH THESE THREE GUYS?
BY THE WAY...
DON'T GO SNOOPING IN MY ROOM!
Who'd wanna snoop on you?
Or watch me in the shower.
I don't wanna see that!
I'M IN ROOM 102.
LOOKING FORWARD TO IT.
YEAH...
I'M...
FUJIWARA TAIGA.
"TAIGA" IS WRITTEN...
WITH THE CHARACTER FOR TIGER.
TAIGA?

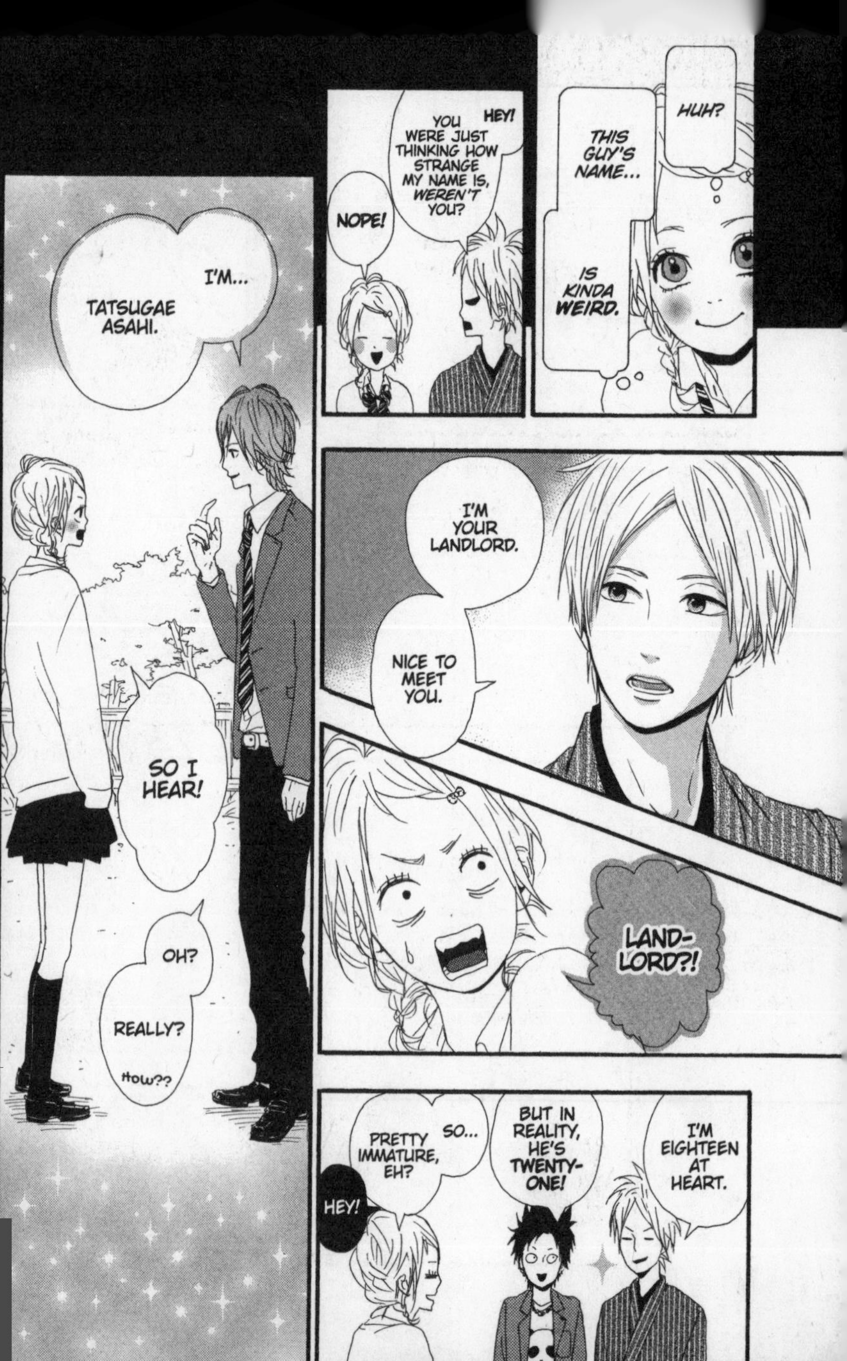
HUH?
THIS GUY'S NAME...
IS KINDA WEIRD.
HEY!
YOU WERE JUST THINKING HOW STRANGE MY NAME IS, WEREN'T YOU?
NOPE!
I'M YOUR LANDLORD.
NICE TO MEET YOU.
LAND-LORD?!
I'M EIGHTEEN AT HEART.
BUT IN REALITY, HE'S TWENTY-ONE!
SO...
PRETTY IMMATURE, EH?
HEY!
I'M...
TATSUGAE ASAHI.
SO I HEAR!
OH?
REALLY?
HOW??

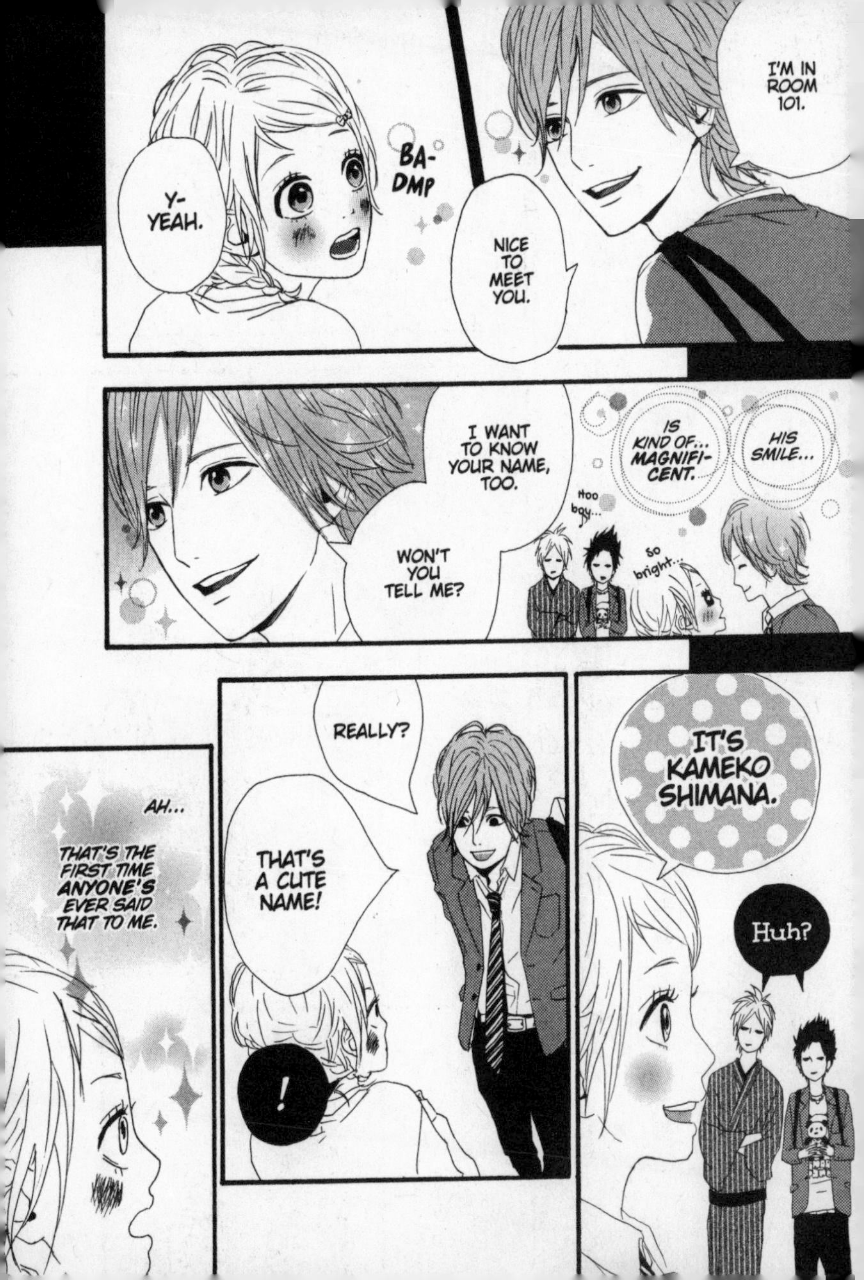
I'M IN ROOM 101.
NICE TO MEET YOU.
BA-DMP
Y-YEAH.
HIS SMILE...
IS KIND OF... MAGNIFI-CENT.
so bright...
Hoo boy...
I WANT TO KNOW YOUR NAME, TOO.
WON'T YOU TELL ME?
IT'S KAMEKO SHIMANA.
Huh?
REALLY?
THAT'S A CUTE NAME!
!
AH...
THAT'S THE FIRST TIME ANYONE'S EVER SAID THAT TO ME.

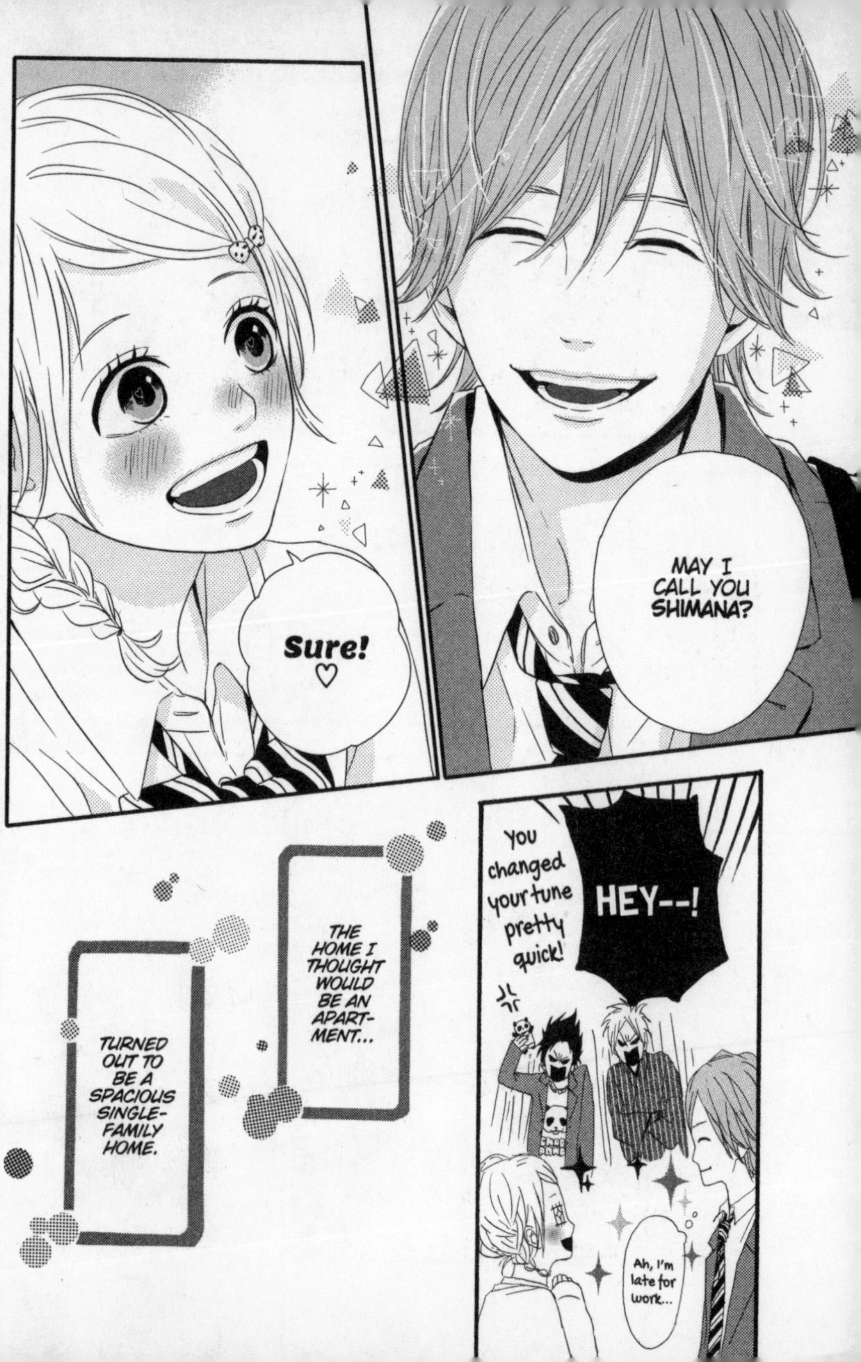
MAY I CALL YOU SHIMANA?
Sure! ♡
HEY--!
You changed your tune pretty quick!
Ah, I'm late for work...
THE HOME I THOUGHT WOULD BE AN APARTMENT...
TURNED OUT TO BE A SPACIOUS SINGLE-FAMILY HOME.

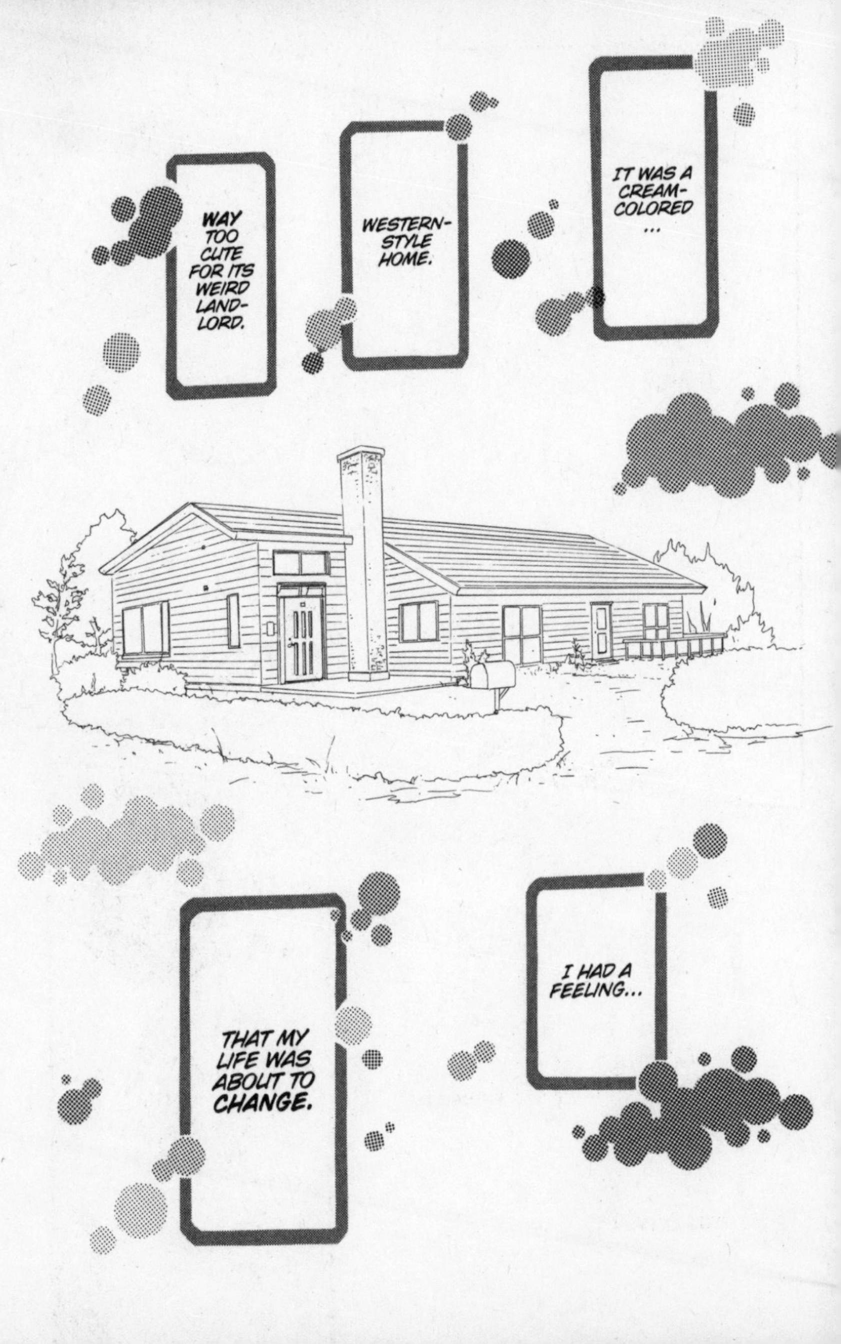
IT WAS A CREAM-COLORED ...
WESTERN-STYLE HOME.
WAY TOO CUTE FOR ITS WEIRD LANDLORD.
I HAD A FEELING...
THAT MY LIFE WAS ABOUT TO CHANGE.

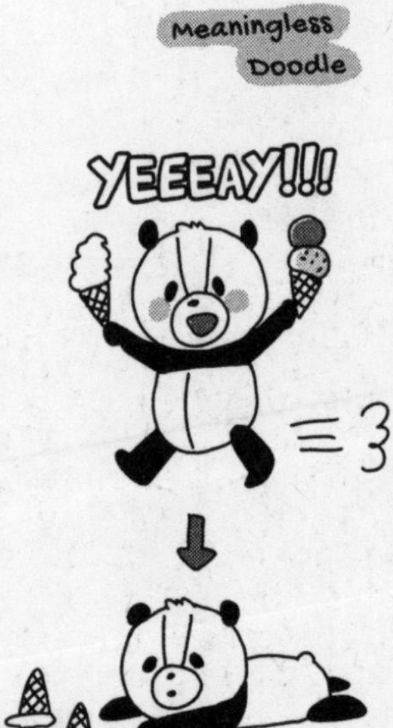
Meaningless Doodle
YEEEAY!!!

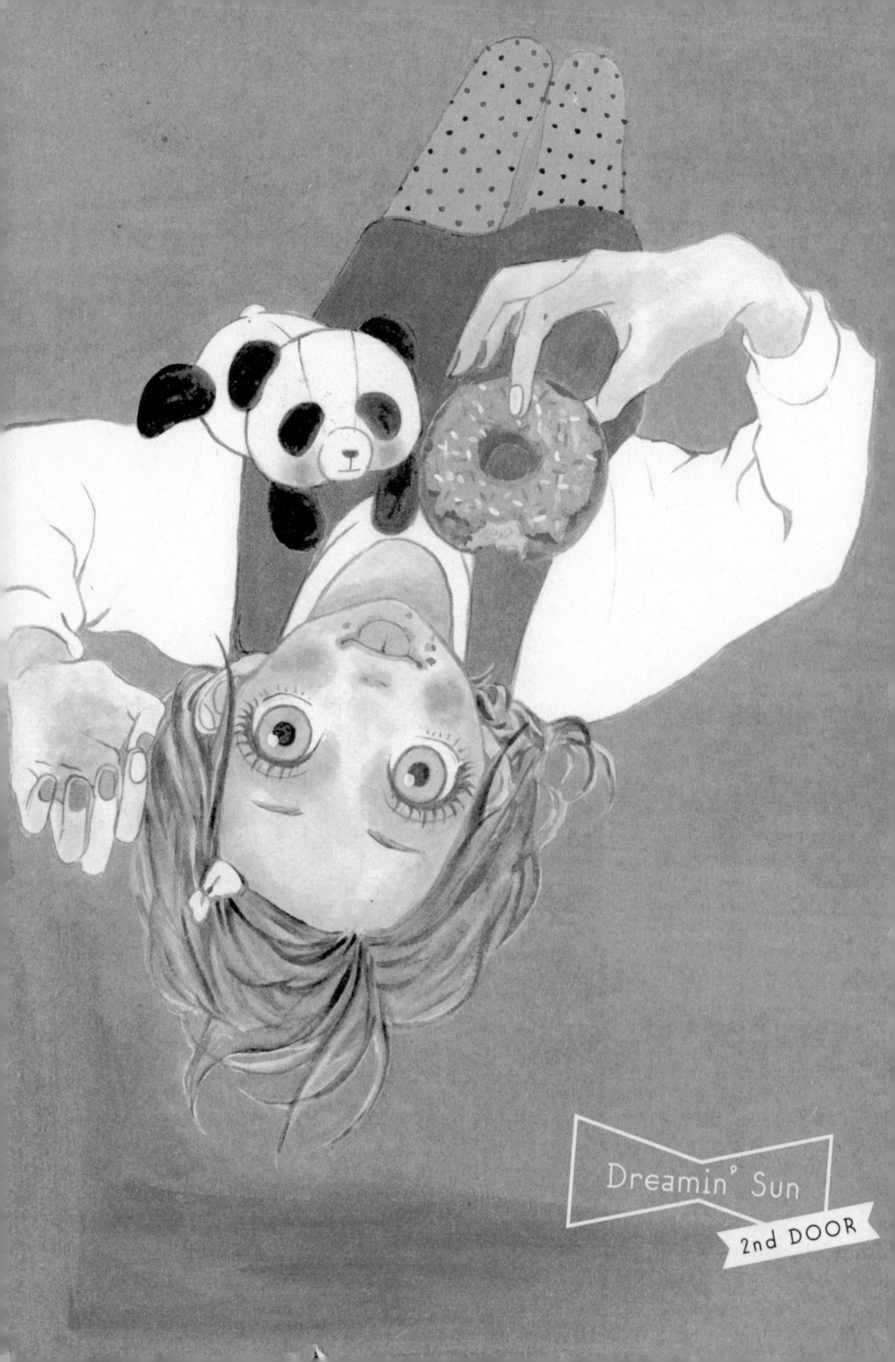
Dreamin' Sun
2nd DOOR

Dreamin'
Sun

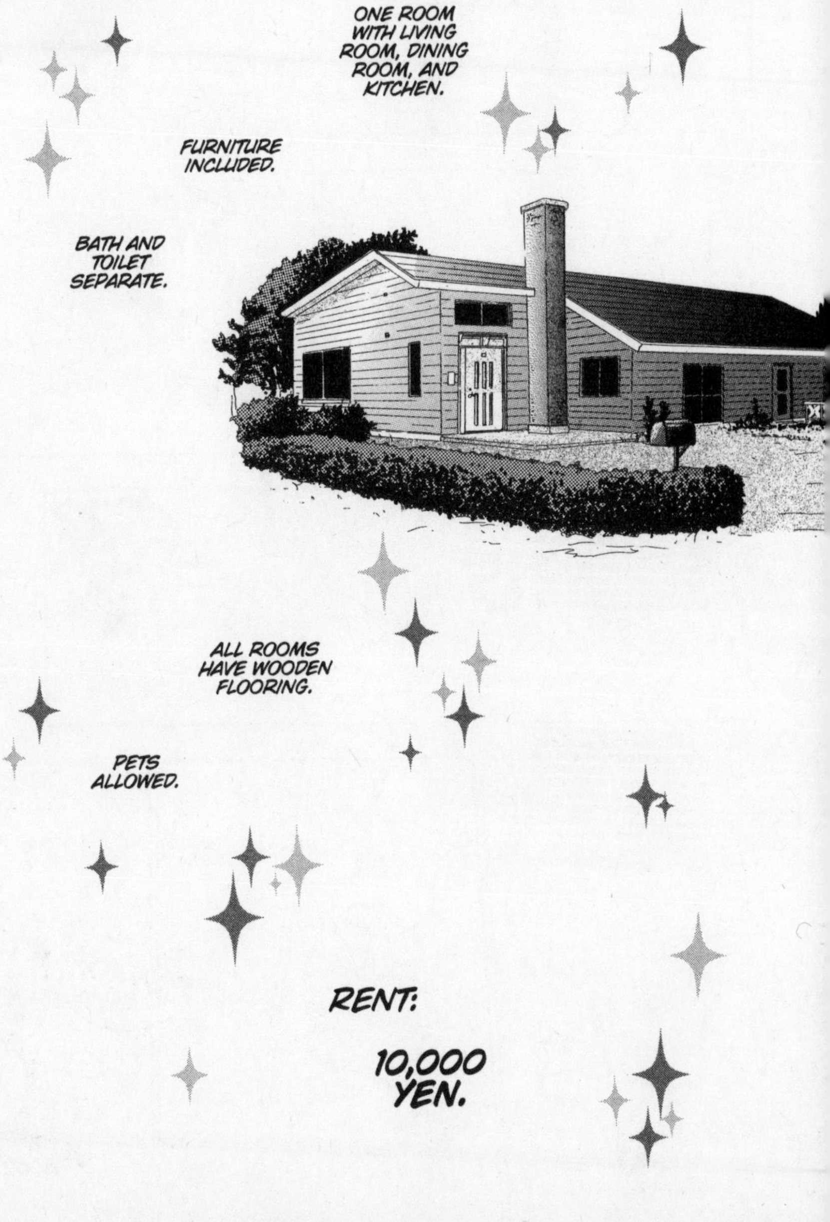
ONE ROOM WITH LIVING ROOM, DINING ROOM, AND KITCHEN.
FURNITURE INCLUDED.
BATH AND TOILET SEPARATE.
ALL ROOMS HAVE WOODEN FLOORING.
PETS ALLOWED.
RENT:
10,000 YEN.

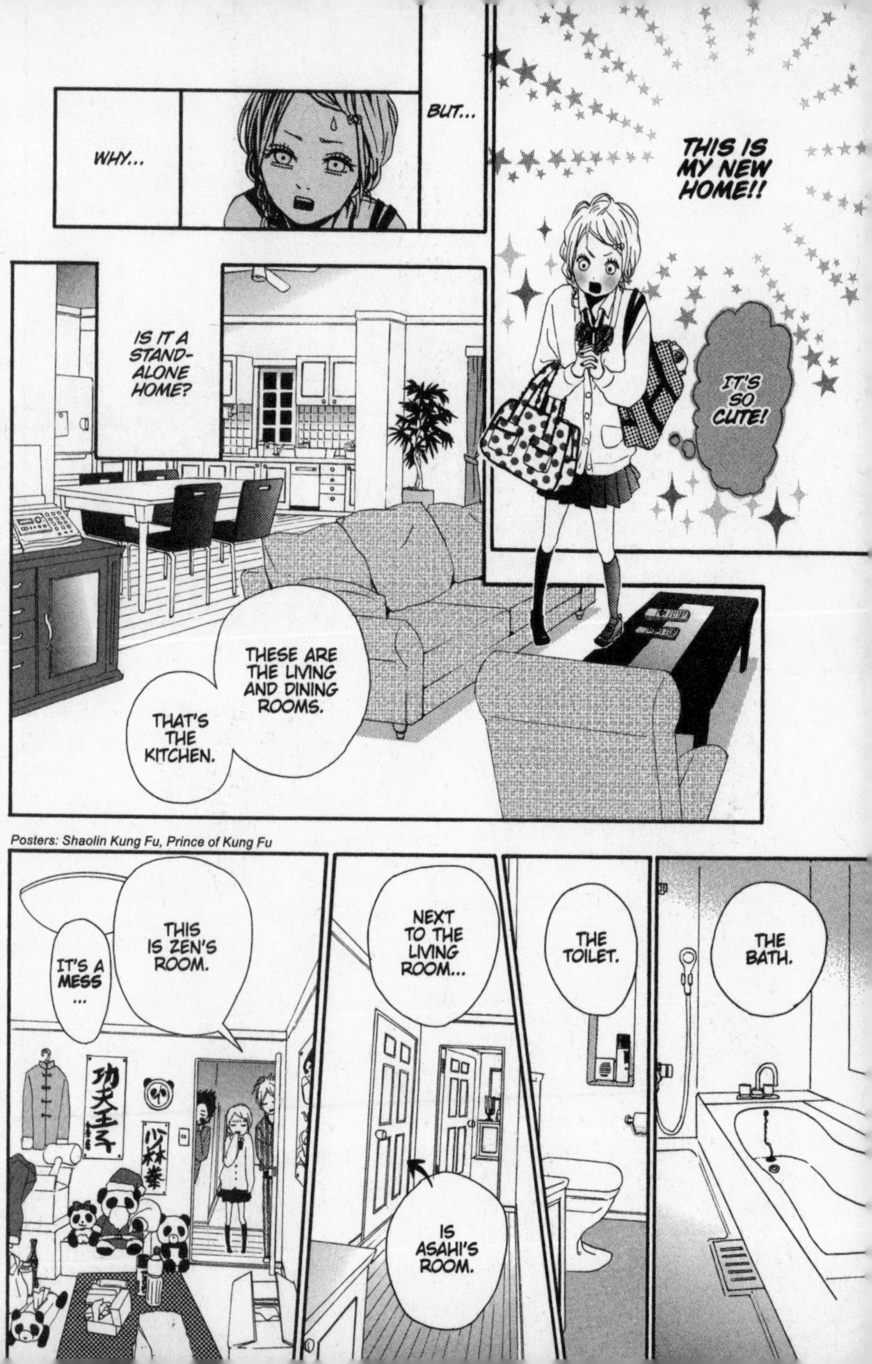
THIS IS MY NEW HOME!!
IT'S SO CUTE!
BUT...
WHY...
IS IT A STAND-ALONE HOME?
THESE ARE THE LIVING AND DINING ROOMS.
THAT'S THE KITCHEN.
Posters: Shaolin Kung Fu, Prince of Kung Fu
THE BATH.
THE TOILET.
NEXT TO THE LIVING ROOM...
IS ASAHI'S ROOM.
THIS IS ZEN'S ROOM.
IT'S A MESS ...
功夫王子
少林拳

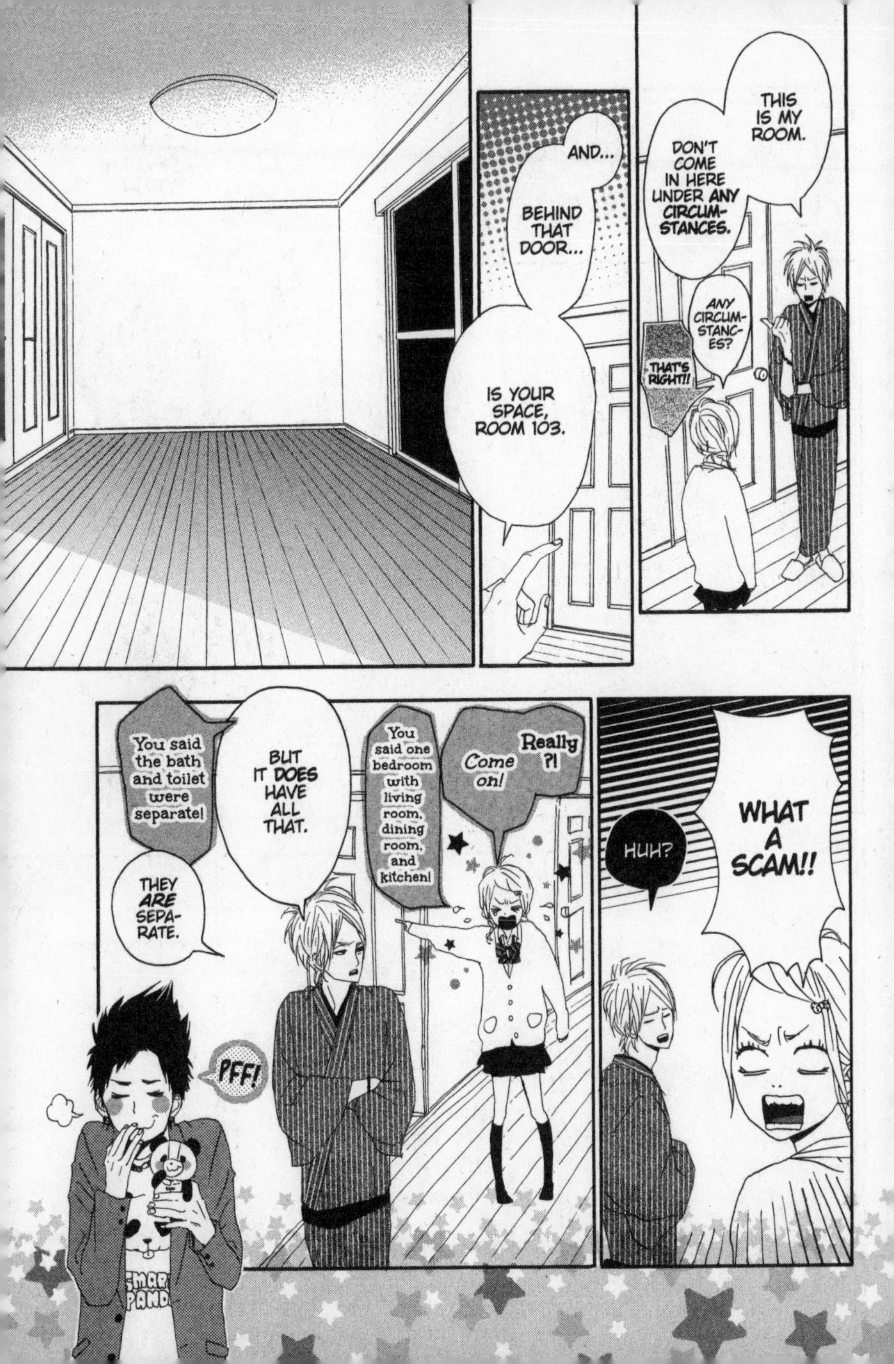
THIS IS MY ROOM.
DON'T COME IN HERE UNDER ANY CIRCUMSTANCES.
ANY CIRCUMSTANCES?
THAT'S RIGHT!!
AND...
BEHIND THAT DOOR...
IS YOUR SPACE, ROOM 103.
WHAT A SCAM!!
HUH?
Really ?!
Come on!
You said one bedroom with living room, dining room, and kitchen!
BUT IT DOES HAVE ALL THAT.
You said the bath and toilet were separate!
THEY ARE SEPARATE.
PFF!

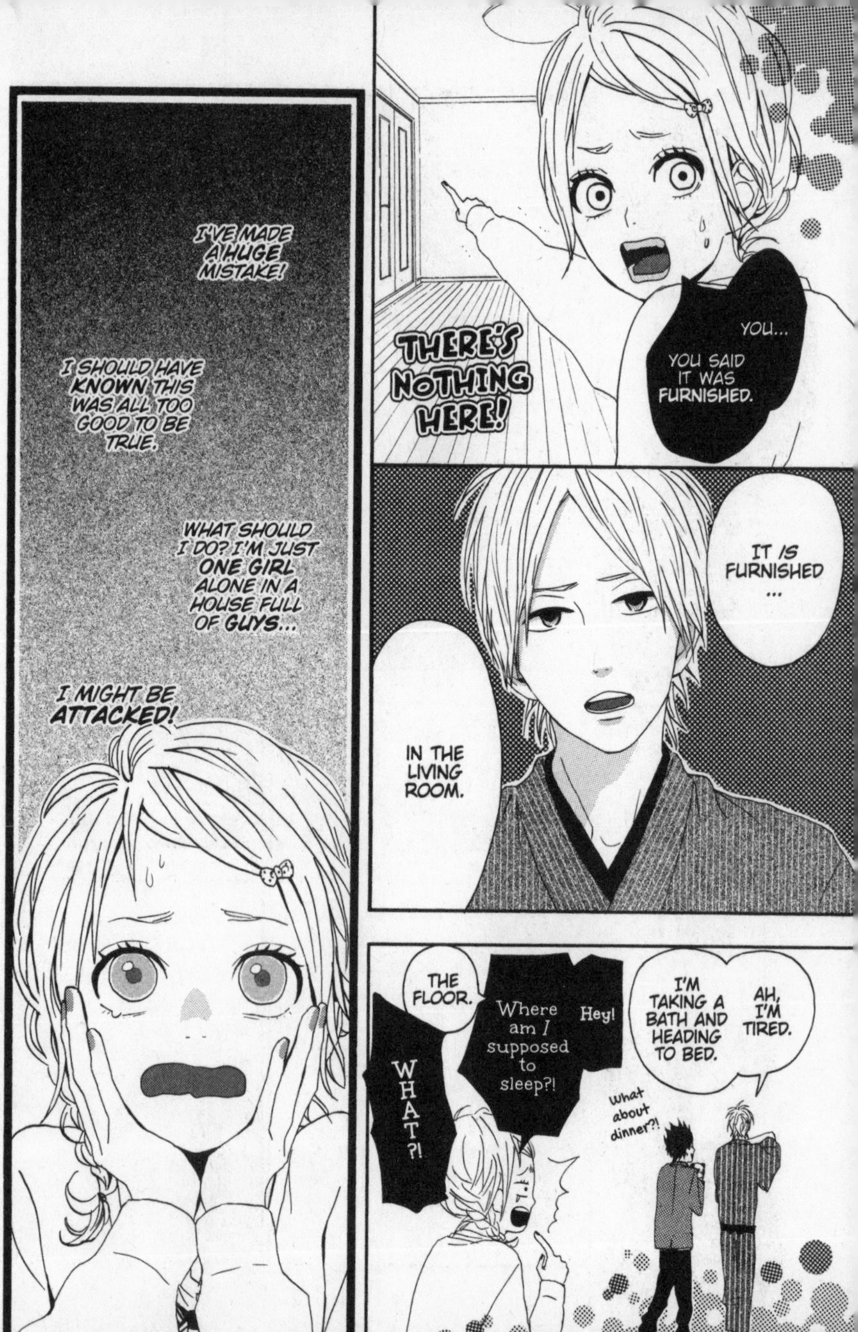
YOU...
YOU SAID IT WAS FURNISHED.
THERE'S NOTHING HERE!
IT IS FURNISHED ...
IN THE LIVING ROOM.
AH, I'M TIRED.
I'M TAKING A BATH AND HEADING TO BED.
Hey!
Where am I supposed to sleep?!
THE FLOOR.
WHAT?!
What about dinner?!
I'VE MADE A HUGE MISTAKE!
I SHOULD HAVE KNOWN THIS WAS ALL TOO GOOD TO BE TRUE.
WHAT SHOULD I DO? I'M JUST ONE GIRL ALONE IN A HOUSE FULL OF GUYS...
I MIGHT BE ATTACKED!

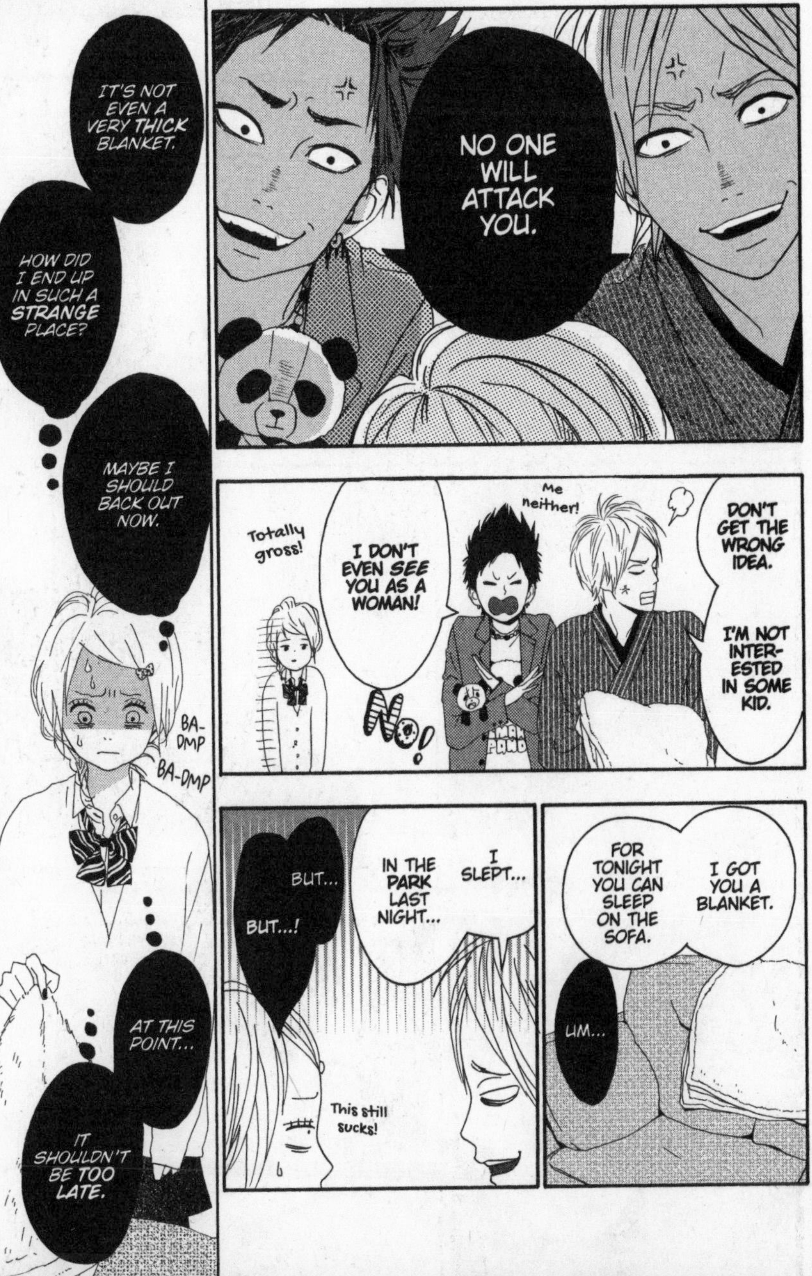
NO ONE WILL ATTACK YOU.
DON'T GET THE WRONG IDEA.
I'M NOT INTERESTED IN SOME KID.
Me neither!
I DON'T EVEN SEE YOU AS A WOMAN!
Totally gross!
NO!
I GOT YOU A BLANKET.
FOR TONIGHT YOU CAN SLEEP ON THE SOFA.
UM...
I SLEPT...
IN THE PARK LAST NIGHT...
BUT...
BUT...!
This still sucks!
IT'S NOT EVEN A VERY THICK BLANKET.
HOW DID I END UP IN SUCH A STRANGE PLACE?
MAYBE I SHOULD BACK OUT NOW.
BA-DMP
BA-DMP
AT THIS POINT...
IT SHOULDN'T BE TOO LATE.

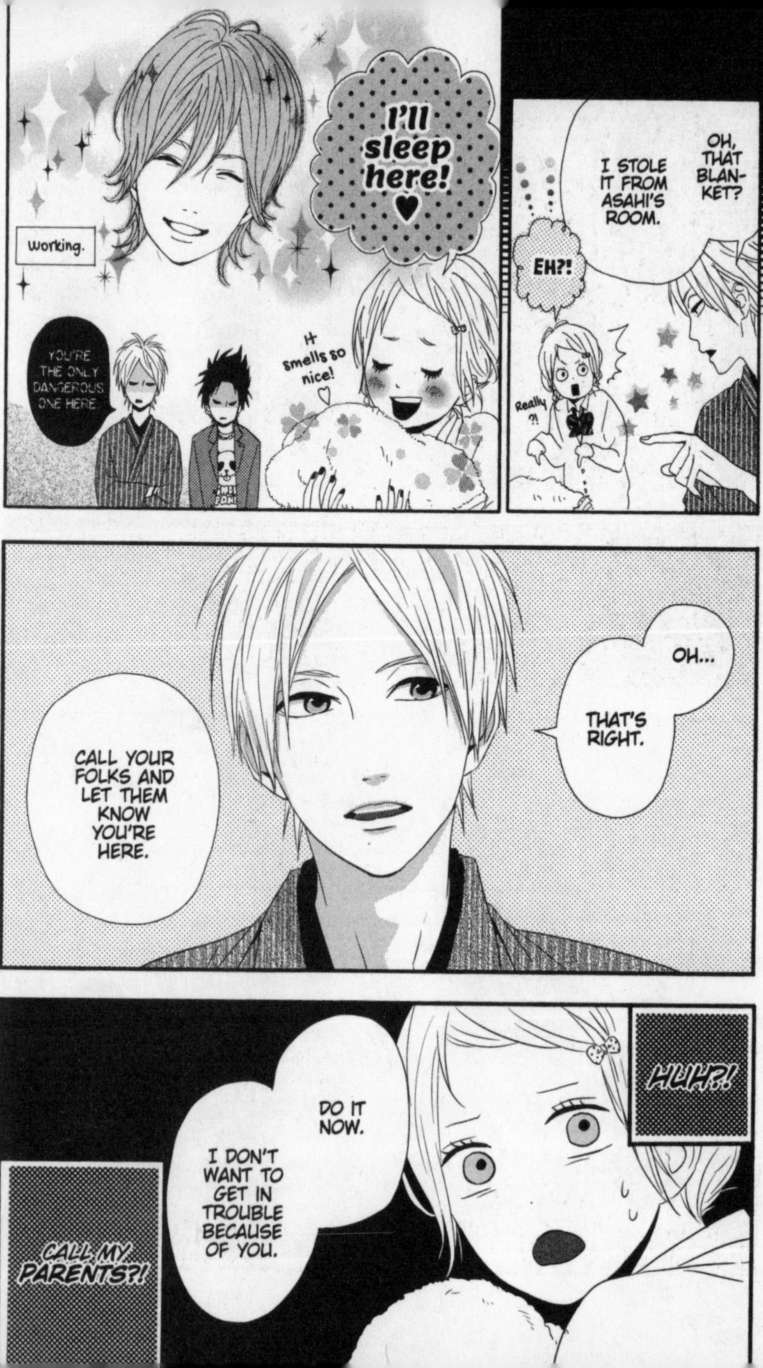
OH, THAT BLANKET?
I STOLE IT FROM ASAHI'S ROOM.
EH?!
Really?!
I'll sleep here!
working.
It smells so nice!
YOU'RE THE ONLY DANGEROUS ONE HERE.
OH... THAT'S RIGHT.
CALL YOUR FOLKS AND LET THEM KNOW YOU'RE HERE.
HUH?!
DO IT NOW.
I DON'T WANT TO GET IN TROUBLE BECAUSE OF YOU.
CALL MY PARENTS?!

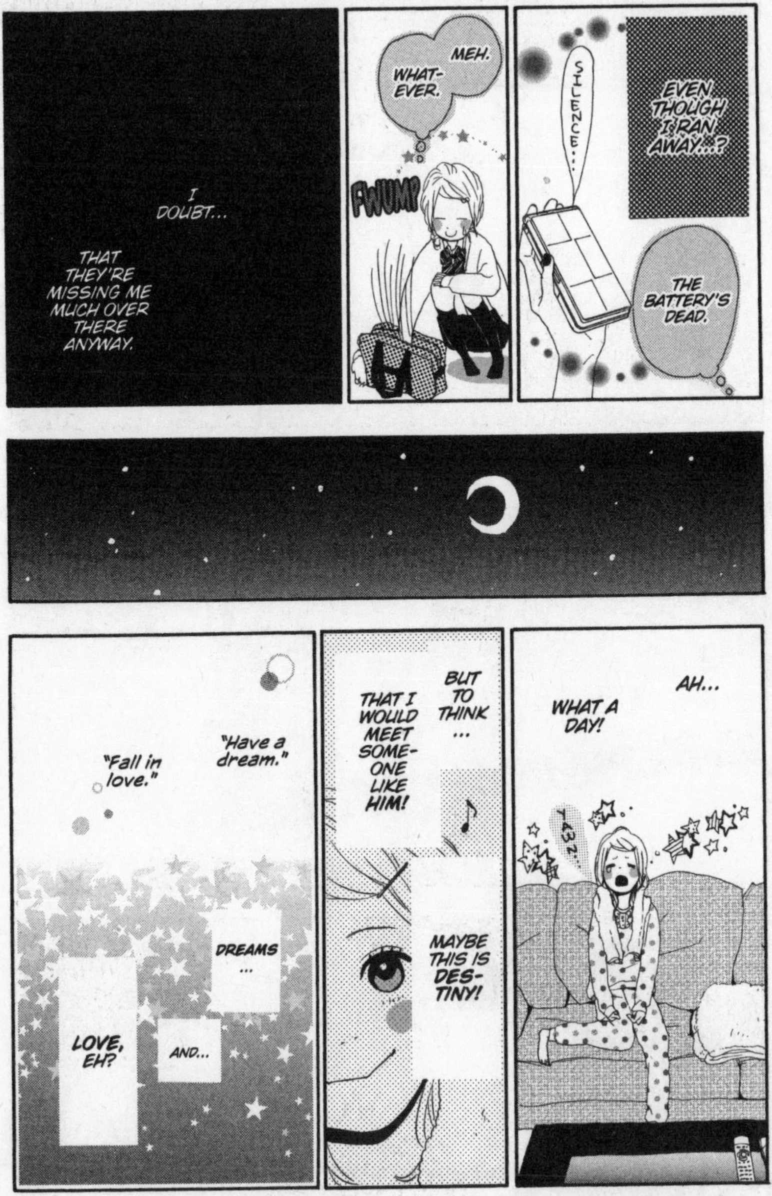
EVEN THOUGH I RAN AWAY...?
SILENCE...
THE BATTERY'S DEAD.
MEH. WHAT-EVER.
FWUMP
I DOUBT...
THAT THEY'RE MISSING ME MUCH OVER THERE ANYWAY.
AH...
WHAT A DAY!
BUT TO THINK...
THAT I WOULD MEET SOME-ONE LIKE HIM!
MAYBE THIS IS DES-TINY!
"Have a dream."
"Fall in love."
DREAMS...
AND...
LOVE, EH?

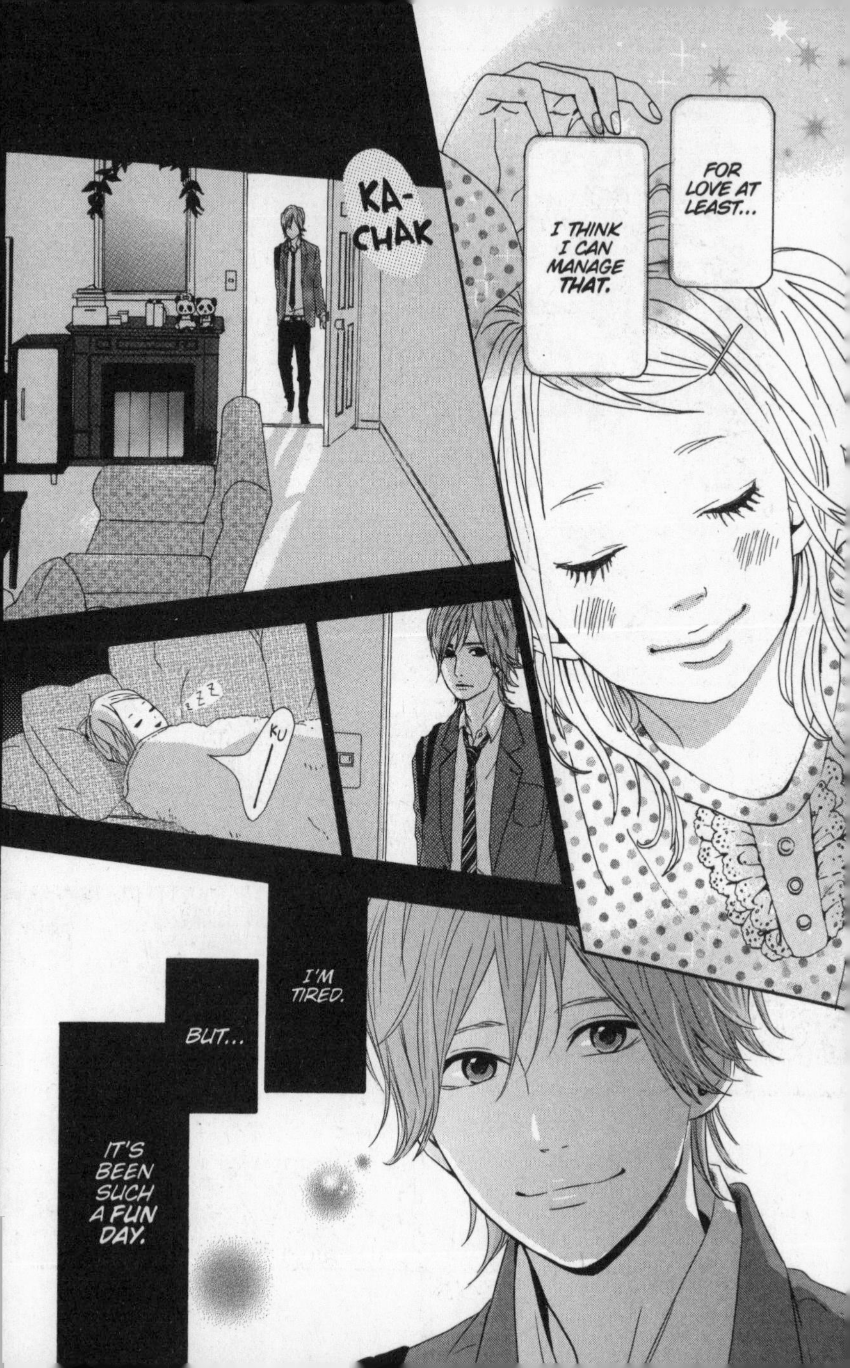
FOR LOVE AT LEAST...
I THINK I CAN MANAGE THAT.
KA-CHAK
Z Z Z
KU—
I'M TIRED.
BUT...
IT'S BEEN SUCH A FUN DAY.

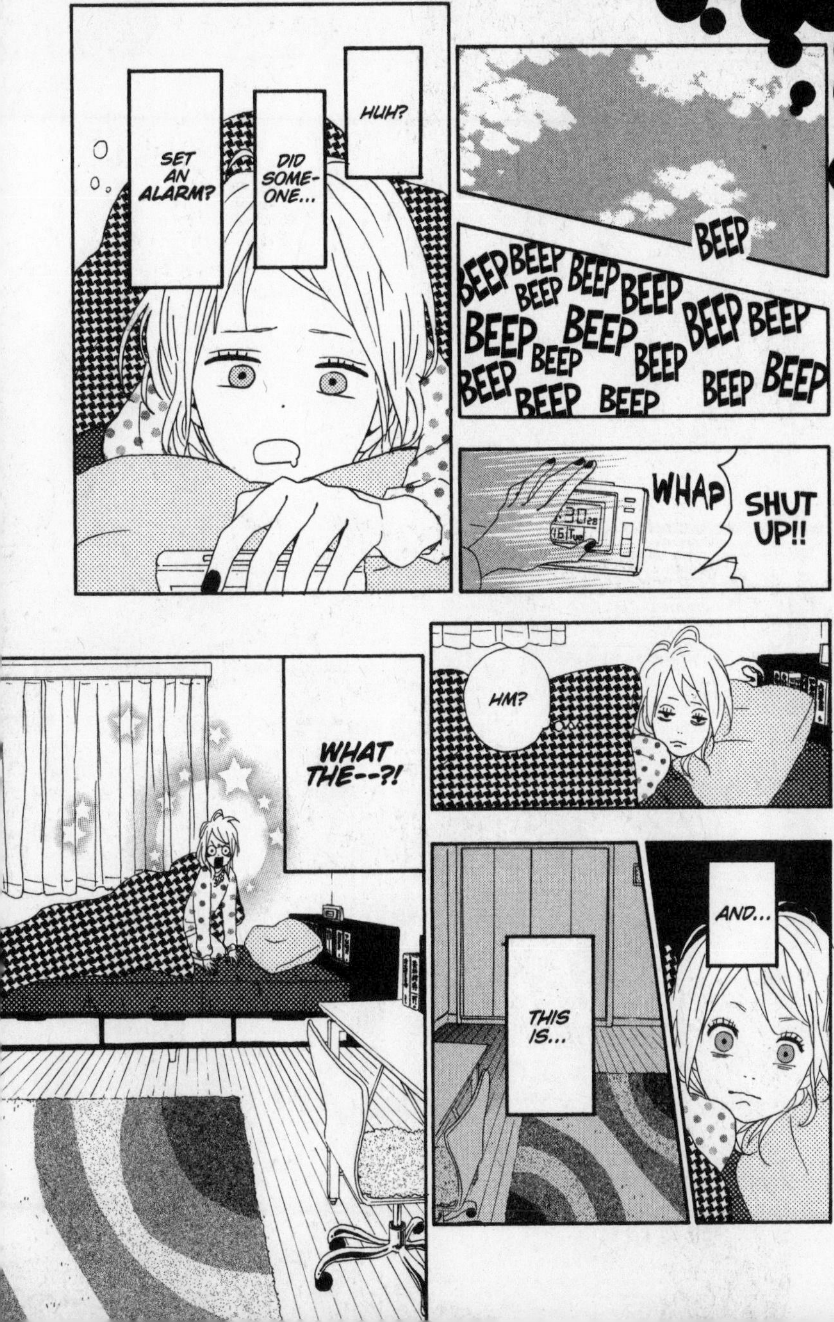
BEEP
BEEP BEEP BEEP BEEP BEEP BEEP BEEP BEEP BEEP BEEP BEEP BEEP BEEP BEEP BEEP BEEP
WHAP
SHUT UP!!
HUH?
DID SOME-ONE...
SET AN ALARM?
HM?
AND...
THIS IS...
WHAT THE--?!

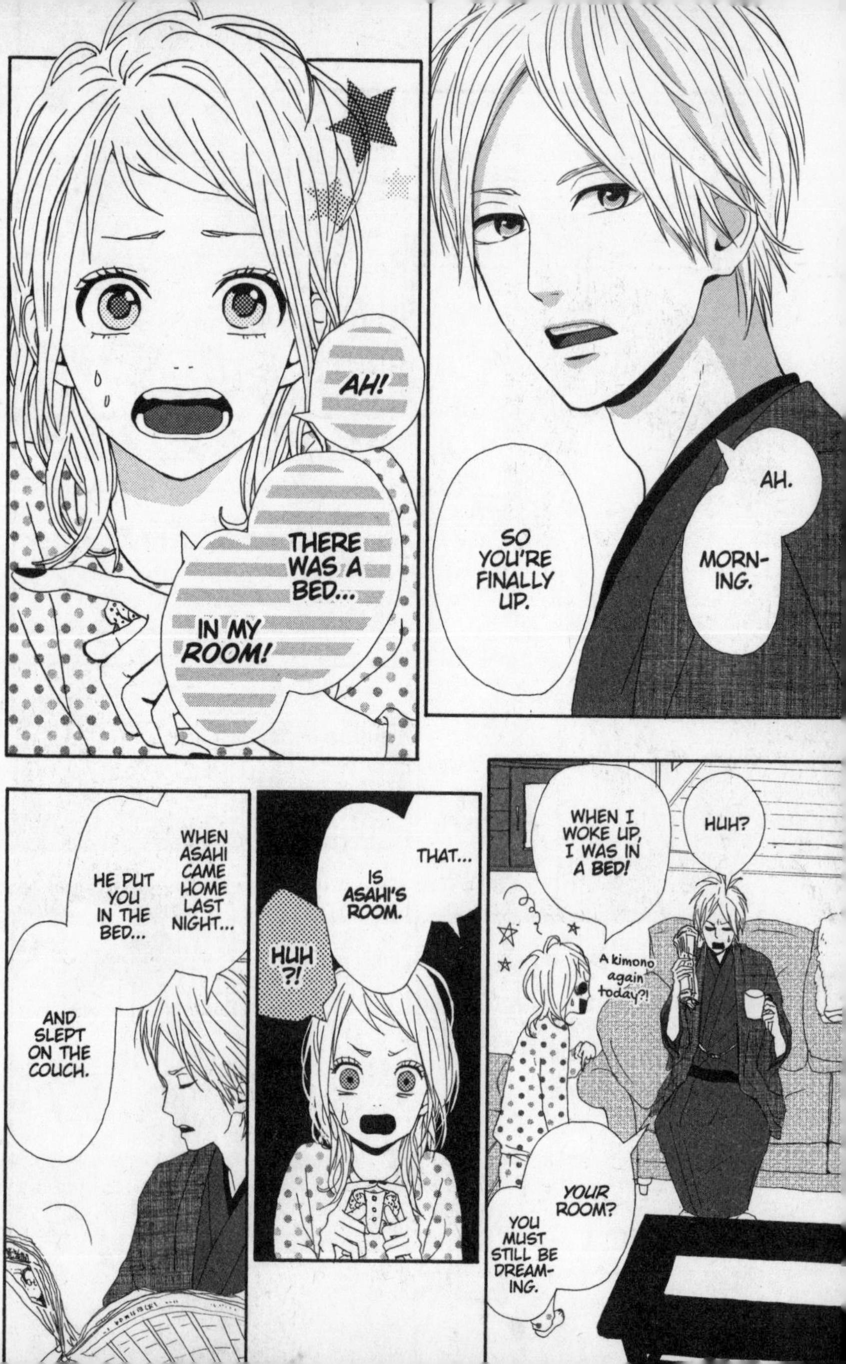
AH.
MORNING.
SO YOU'RE FINALLY UP.
AH!
THERE WAS A BED...
IN MY ROOM!
HUH?
WHEN I WOKE UP, I WAS IN A BED!
A kimono again today?!
YOUR ROOM?
YOU MUST STILL BE DREAMING.
THAT...
IS ASAHI'S ROOM.
HUH?!
WHEN ASAHI CAME HOME LAST NIGHT...
HE PUT YOU IN THE BED...
AND SLEPT ON THE COUCH.

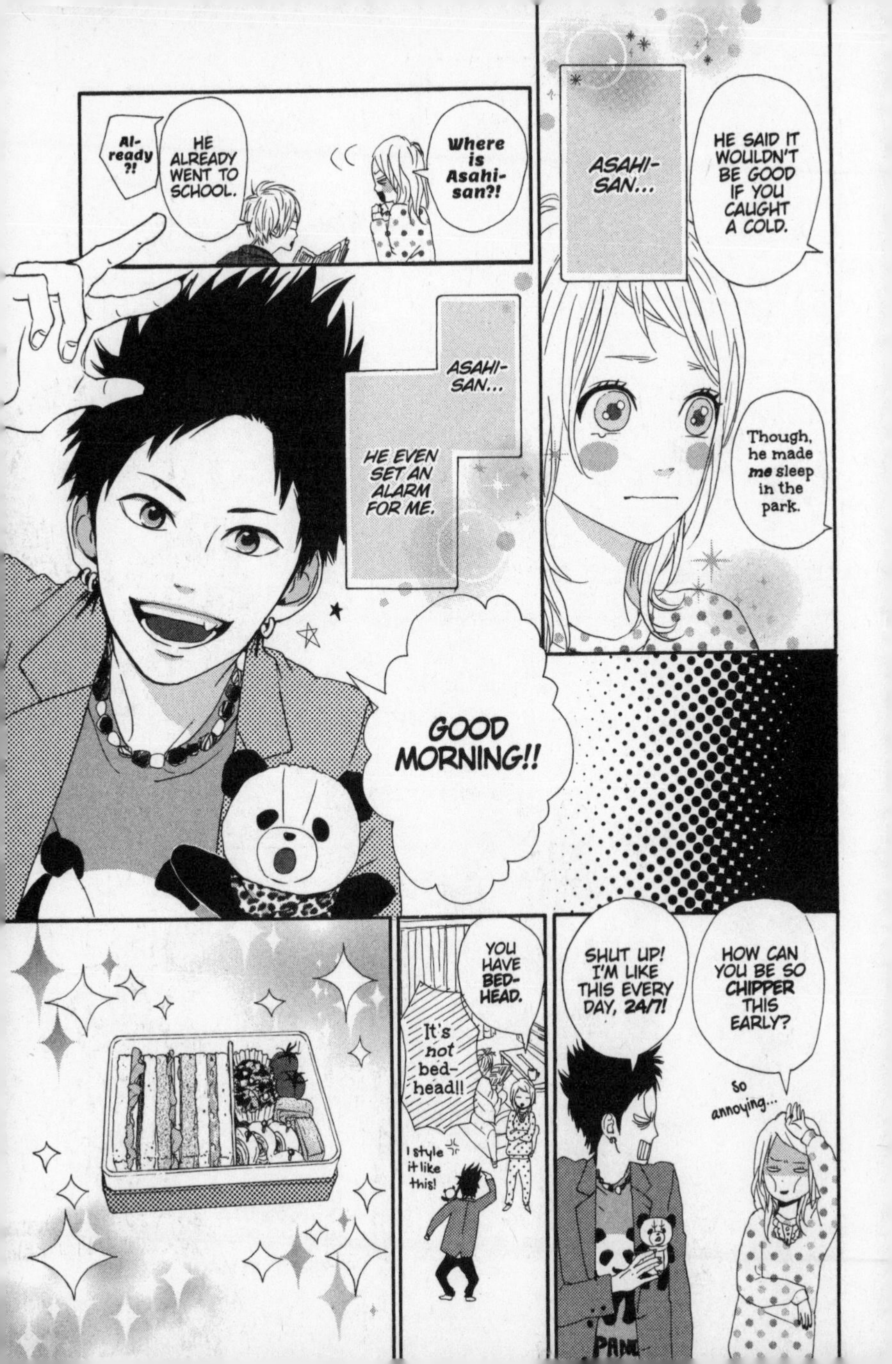

ASAHI-SAN...
HE SAID IT WOULDN'T BE GOOD IF YOU CAUGHT A COLD.
Though, he made me sleep in the park.
Where is Asahi-san?!
HE ALREADY WENT TO SCHOOL.
Al-ready?!
ASAHI-SAN...
HE EVEN SET AN ALARM FOR ME.
GOOD MORNING!!
HOW CAN YOU BE SO CHIPPER THIS EARLY?
SHUT UP! I'M LIKE THIS EVERY DAY, 24/7!
so annoying...
YOU HAVE BED-HEAD.
It's not bed-head!!
I style it like this!

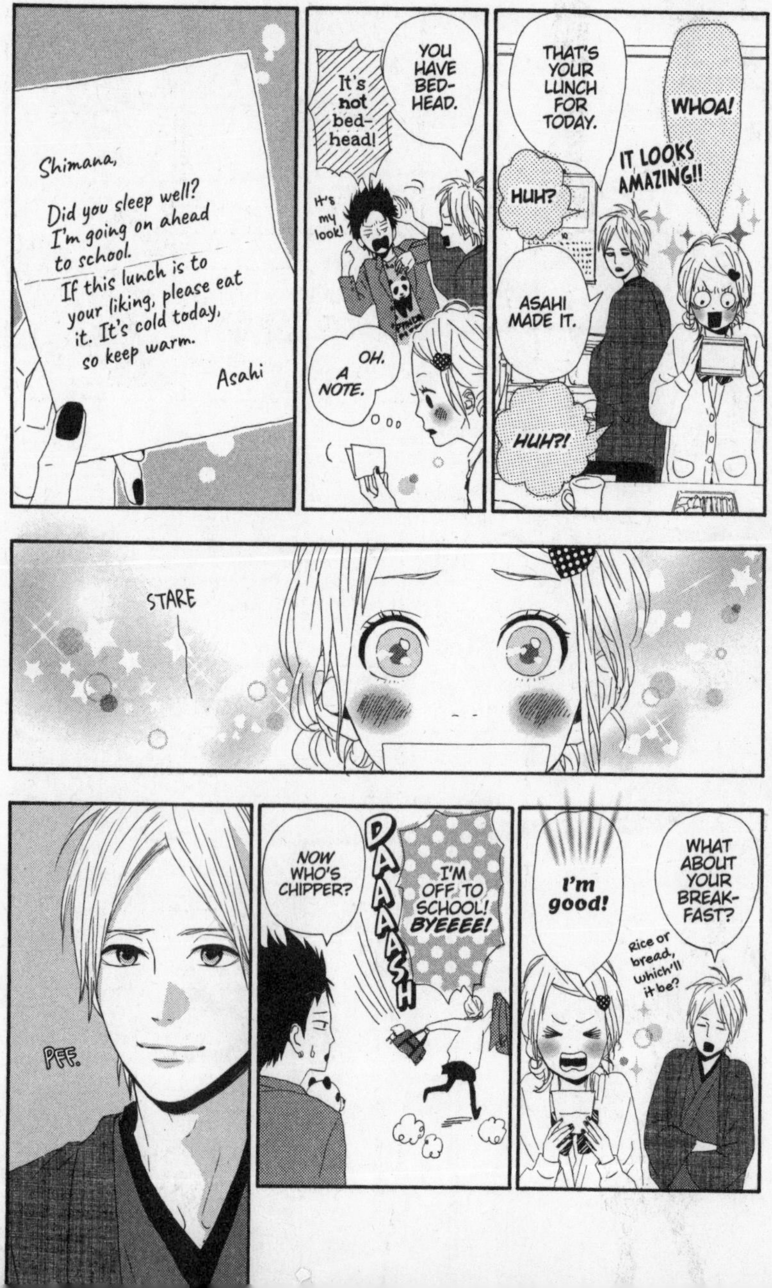
THAT'S YOUR LUNCH FOR TODAY.
WHOA!
IT LOOKS AMAZING!!
HUH?
ASAHI MADE IT.
HUH?!
YOU HAVE BED-HEAD.
It's not bed-head!
It's my look!
OH. A NOTE.
Shimana,
Did you sleep well? I'm going on ahead to school.
If this lunch is to your liking, please eat it. It's cold today, so keep warm.
Asahi
STARE
WHAT ABOUT YOUR BREAK-FAST?
Rice or bread, which'll it be?
I'm good!
I'M OFF TO SCHOOL! BYEEEE!
DAAAASH
NOW WHO'S CHIPPER?
PFF.

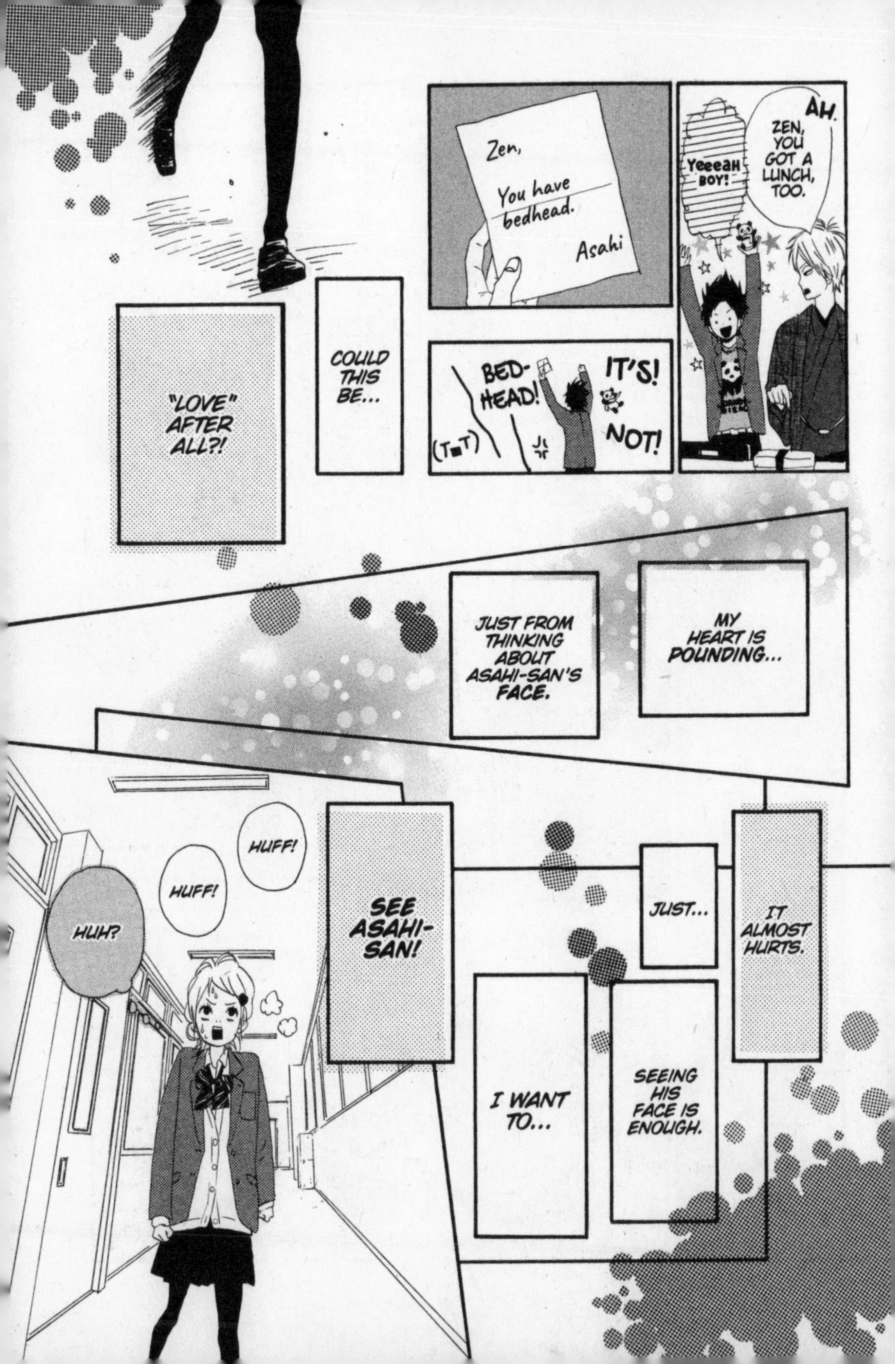
AH. ZEN, YOU GOT A LUNCH, TOO.
YeeeaH BOY!
Zen, You have bedhead. Asahi
IT'S! NOT!
BED-HEAD!
(T■T)
COULD THIS BE...
"LOVE" AFTER ALL?!
MY HEART IS POUNDING...
JUST FROM THINKING ABOUT ASAHI-SAN'S FACE.
IT ALMOST HURTS.
JUST...
SEEING HIS FACE IS ENOUGH.
I WANT TO...
SEE ASAHI-SAN!
HUFF!
HUFF!
HUH?

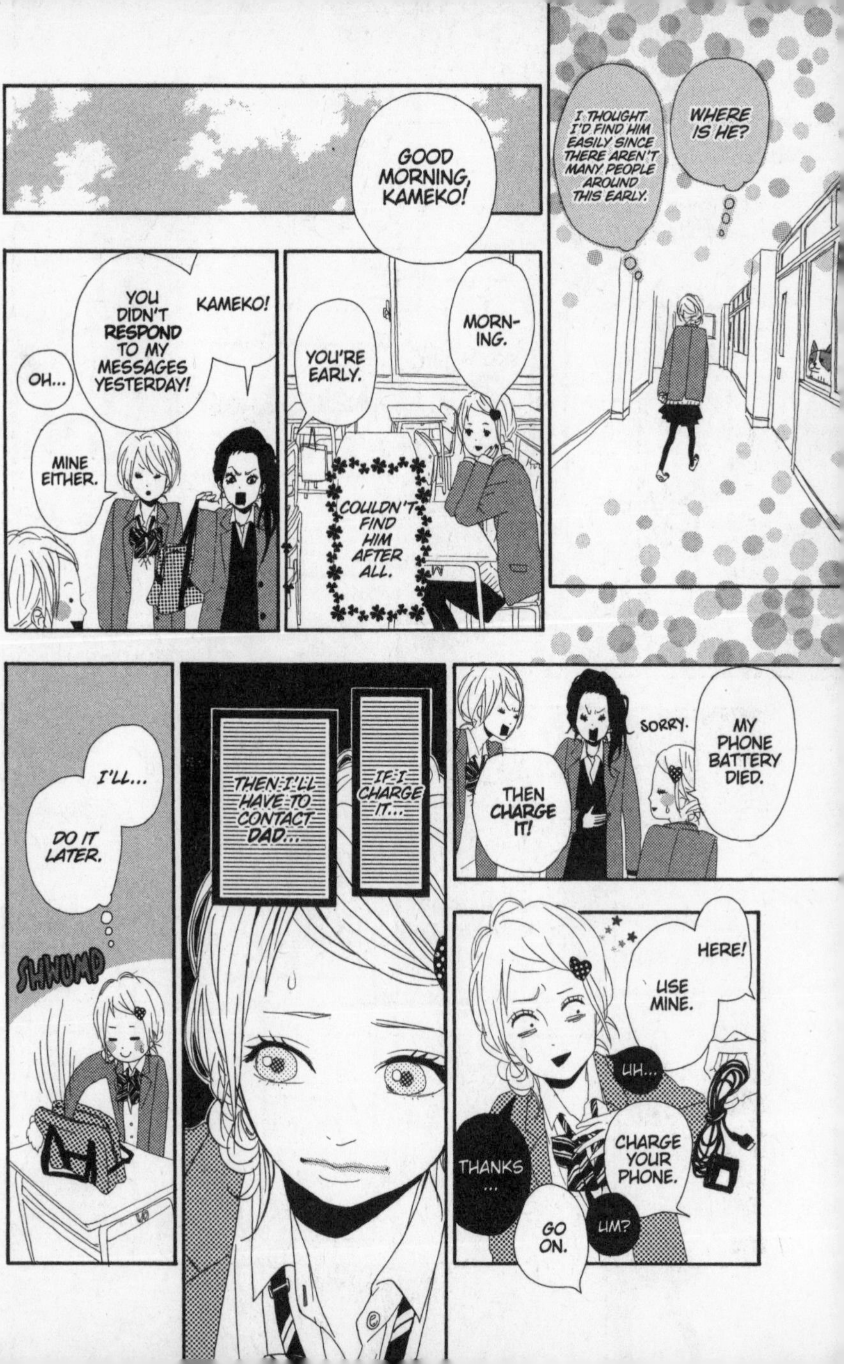
WHERE IS HE?
I THOUGHT I'D FIND HIM EASILY SINCE THERE AREN'T MANY PEOPLE AROUND THIS EARLY.
GOOD MORNING, KAMEKO!
MORN-ING.
YOU'RE EARLY.
COULDN'T FIND HIM AFTER ALL.
KAMEKO!
YOU DIDN'T RESPOND TO MY MESSAGES YESTERDAY!
OH...
MINE EITHER.
MY PHONE BATTERY DIED.
SORRY.
THEN CHARGE IT!
HERE!
USE MINE.
UH...
CHARGE YOUR PHONE.
THANKS ...
UM?
GO ON.
IF I CHARGE IT...
THEN I'LL HAVE TO CONTACT DAD...
I'LL...
DO IT LATER.
SHWOMP

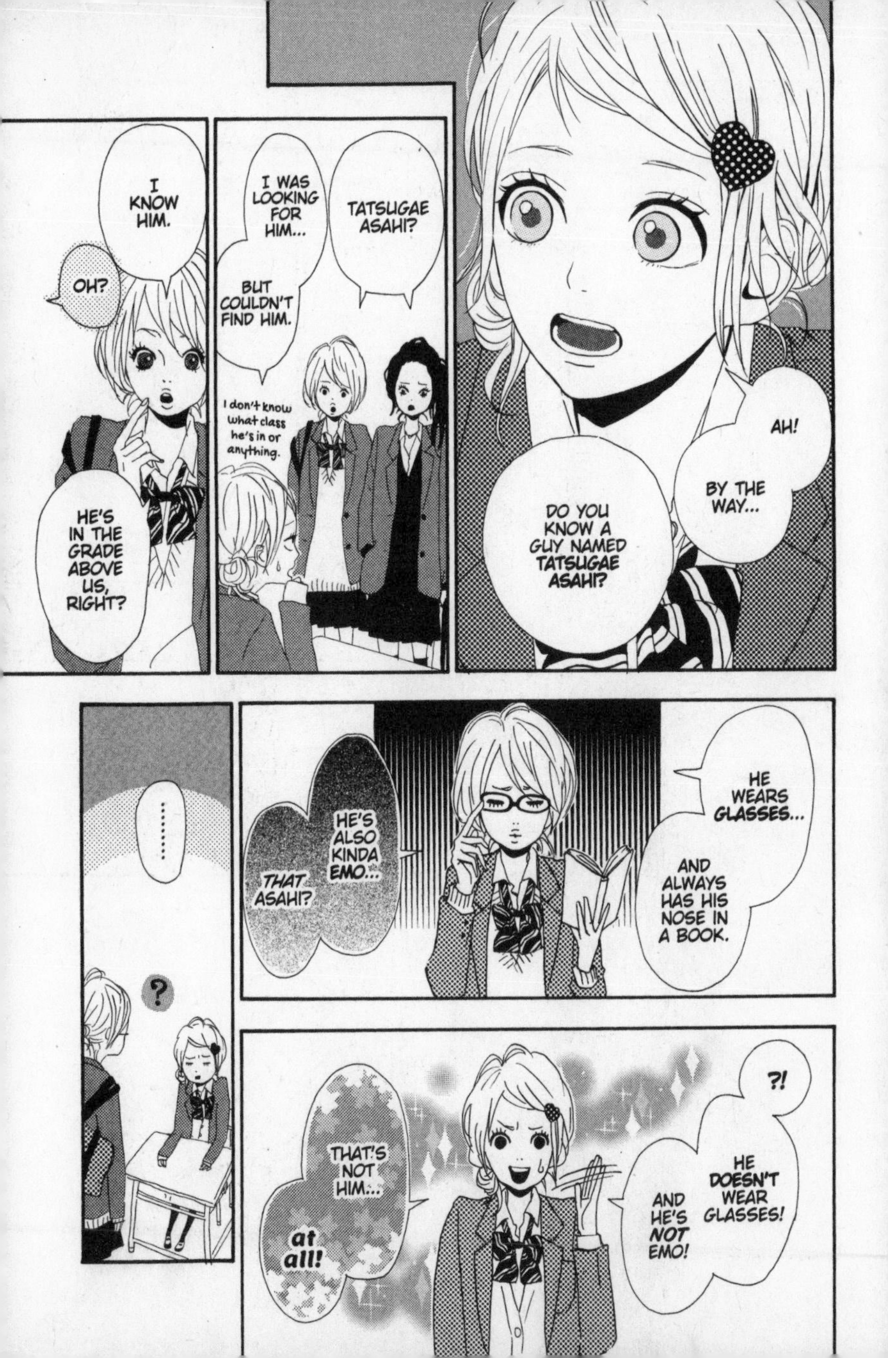
AH!
BY THE WAY...
DO YOU KNOW A GUY NAMED TATSUGAE ASAHI?
TATSUGAE ASAHI?
I WAS LOOKING FOR HIM...
BUT COULDN'T FIND HIM.
I don't know what class he's in or anything.
I KNOW HIM.
OH?
HE'S IN THE GRADE ABOVE US, RIGHT?
HE WEARS GLASSES...
AND ALWAYS HAS HIS NOSE IN A BOOK.
HE'S ALSO KINDA EMO...
THAT ASAHI?
?!
HE DOESN'T WEAR GLASSES!
AND HE'S NOT EMO!
THAT'S NOT HIM...
at all!
......
?

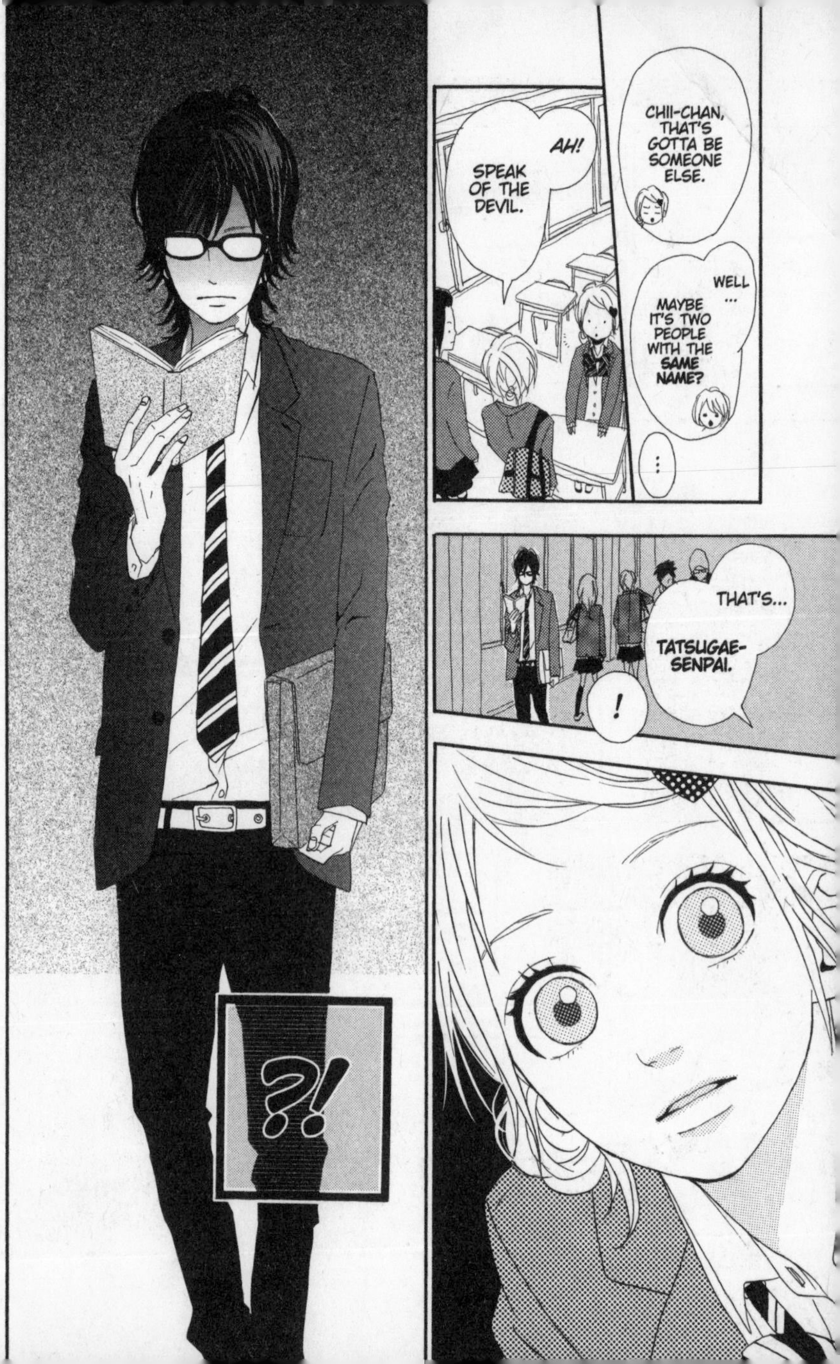
CHII-CHAN, THAT'S GOTTA BE SOMEONE ELSE.
WELL ...
MAYBE IT'S TWO PEOPLE WITH THE SAME NAME?
...
AH!
SPEAK OF THE DEVIL.
THAT'S...
TATSUGAE-SENPAI.
!
?!

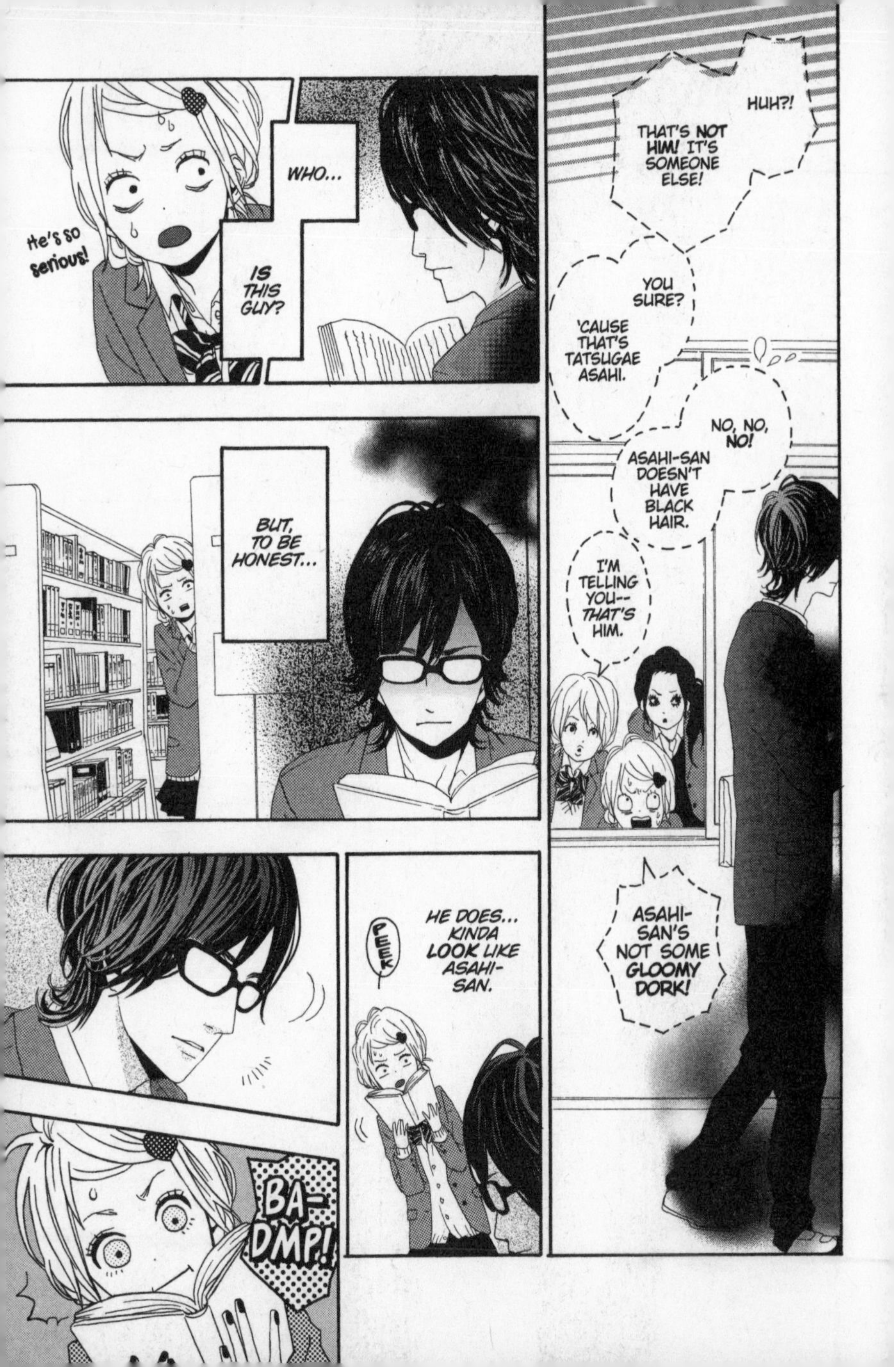
HUH?! THAT'S NOT HIM! IT'S SOMEONE ELSE!
YOU SURE? 'CAUSE THAT'S TATSUGAE ASAHI.
NO, NO, NO! ASAHI-SAN DOESN'T HAVE BLACK HAIR.
I'M TELLING YOU-- THAT'S HIM.
ASAHI-SAN'S NOT SOME GLOOMY DORK!
WHO...
IS THIS GUY?
He's so serious!
BUT, TO BE HONEST...
HE DOES... KINDA LOOK LIKE ASAHI-SAN.
PEEK
BA-DMP!

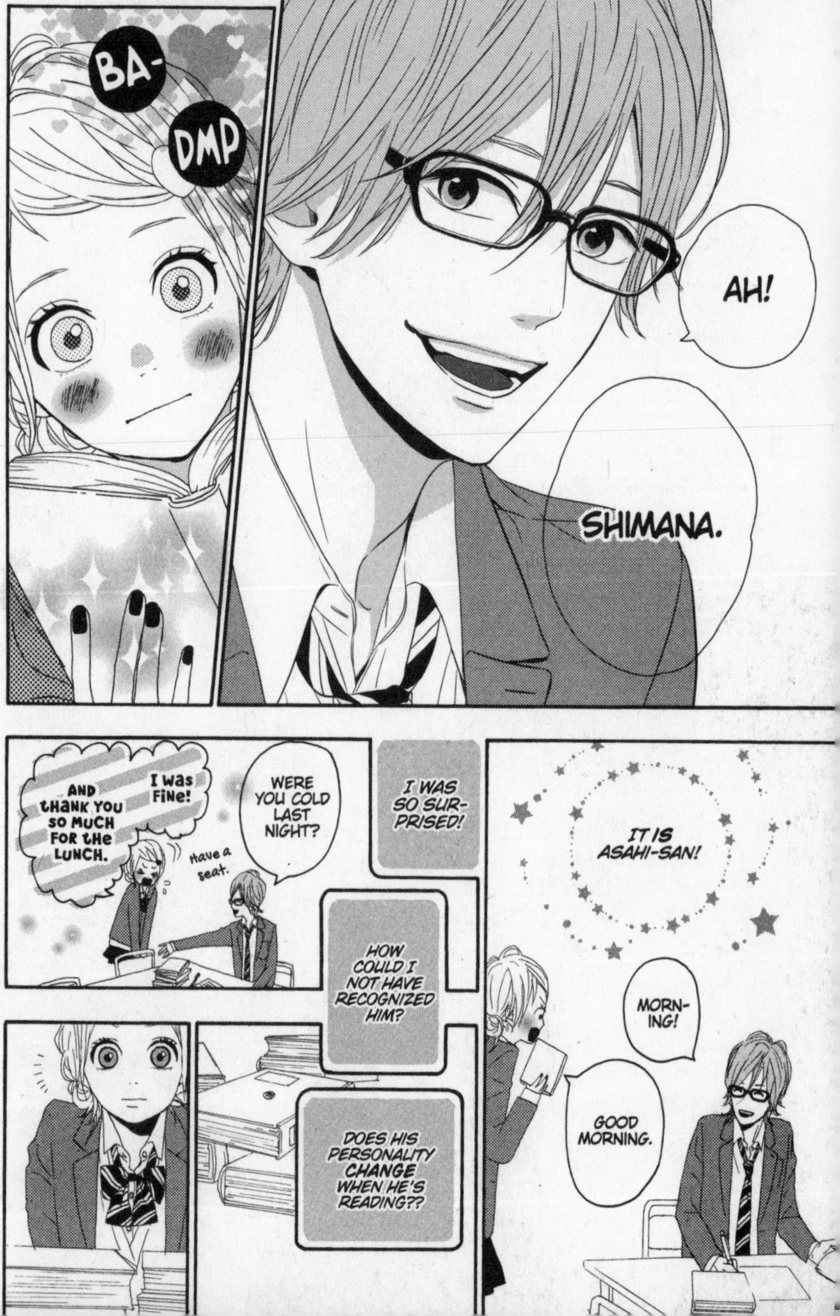
AH!
SHIMANA.
BA-
DMP
IT IS ASAHI-SAN!
MORN-ING!
GOOD MORNING.
I WAS SO SUR-PRISED!
WERE YOU COLD LAST NIGHT?
I was fine!
And thank you so much for the lunch.
Have a seat.
HOW COULD I NOT HAVE RECOGNIZED HIM?
DOES HIS PERSONALITY CHANGE WHEN HE'S READING??

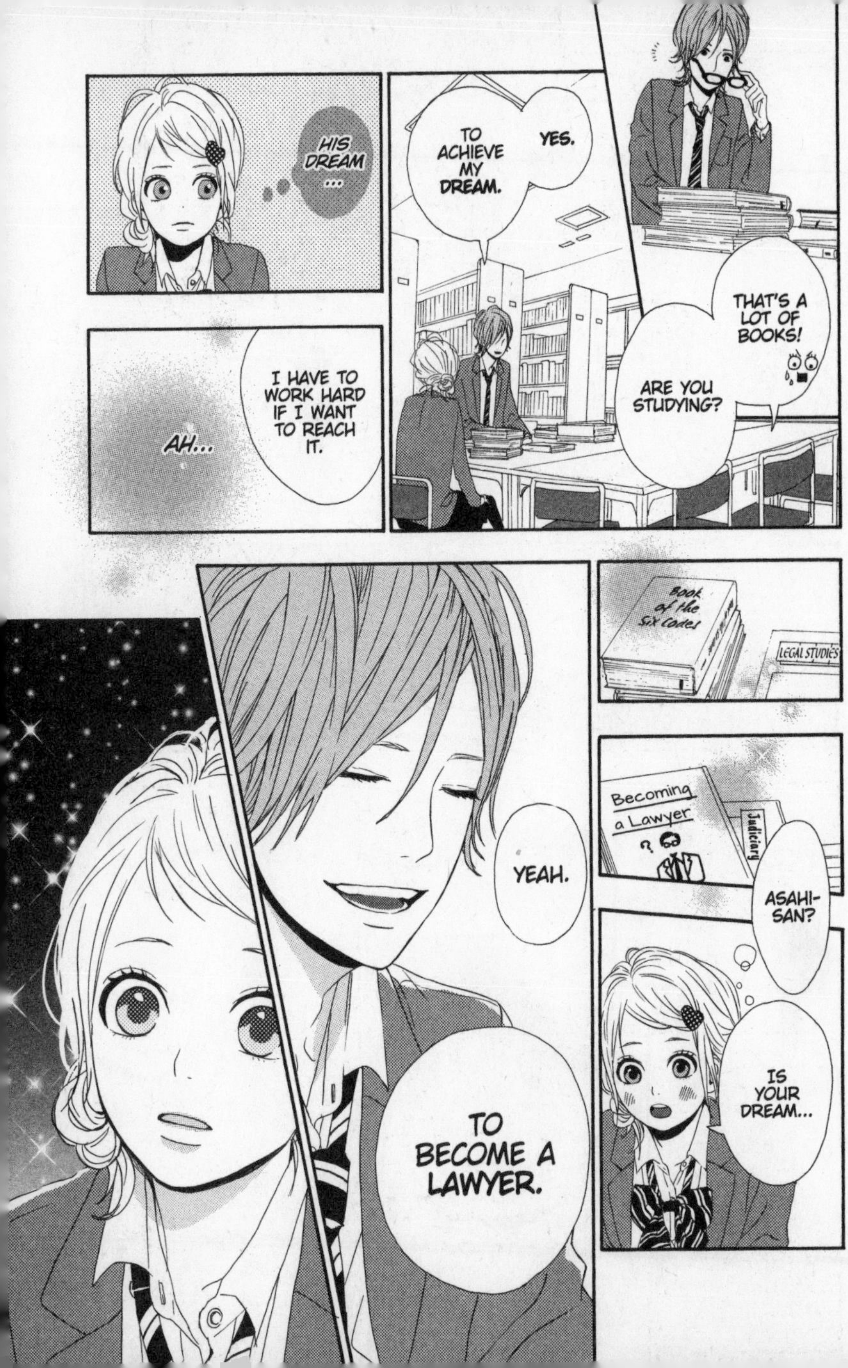
THAT'S A LOT OF BOOKS!
ARE YOU STUDYING?
YES.
TO ACHIEVE MY DREAM.
HIS DREAM...
I HAVE TO WORK HARD IF I WANT TO REACH IT.
AH...
Book of the Six Codes
LEGAL STUDIES
Becoming a Lawyer
Judiciary
ASAHI-SAN?
IS YOUR DREAM...
YEAH.
TO BECOME A LAWYER.

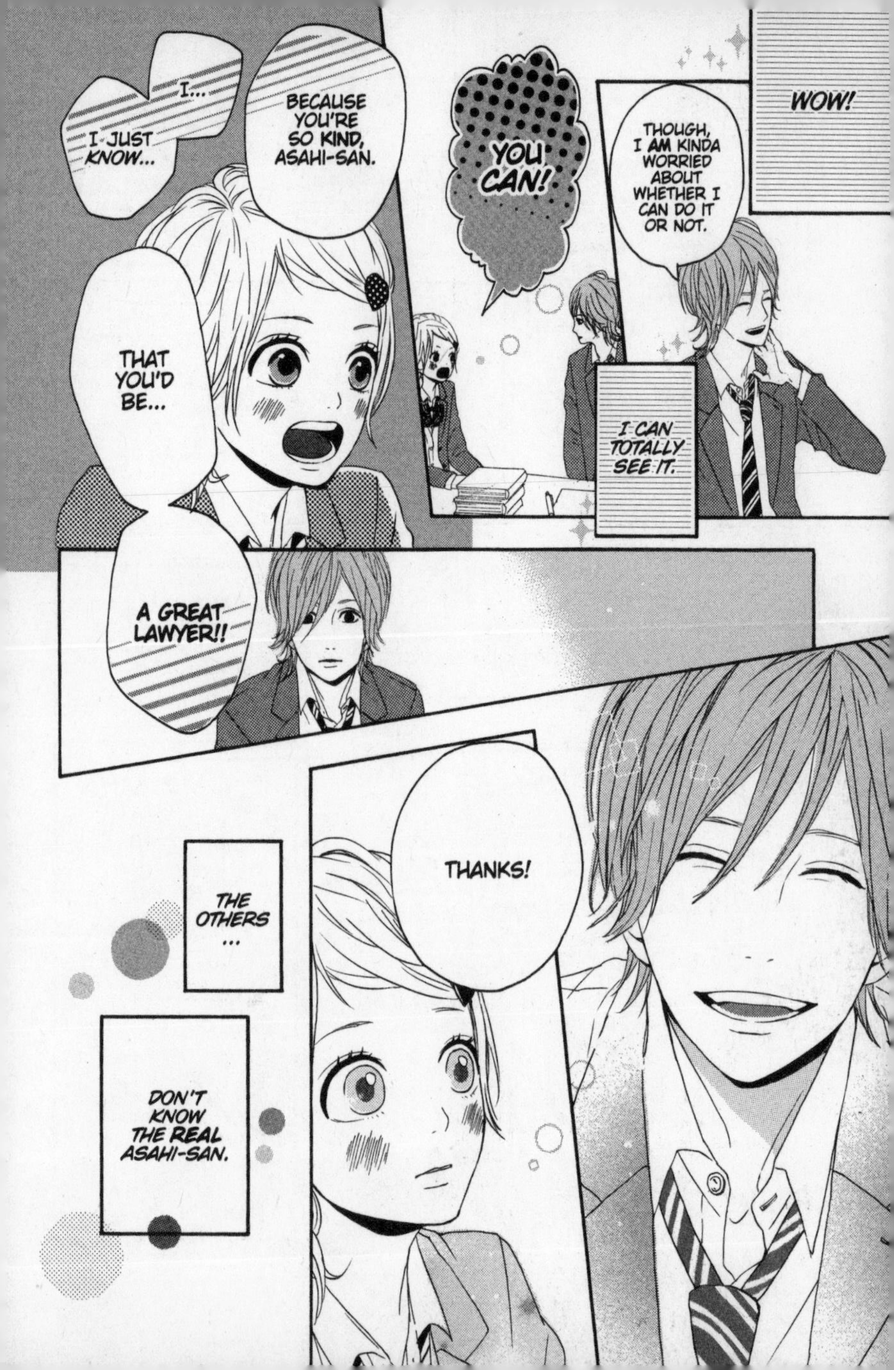
WOW!
THOUGH, I AM KINDA WORRIED ABOUT WHETHER I CAN DO IT OR NOT.
YOU CAN!
I CAN TOTALLY SEE IT.
BECAUSE YOU'RE SO KIND, ASAHI-SAN.
I... I JUST KNOW...
THAT YOU'D BE...
A GREAT LAWYER!!
THANKS!
THE OTHERS...
DON'T KNOW THE REAL ASAHI-SAN.

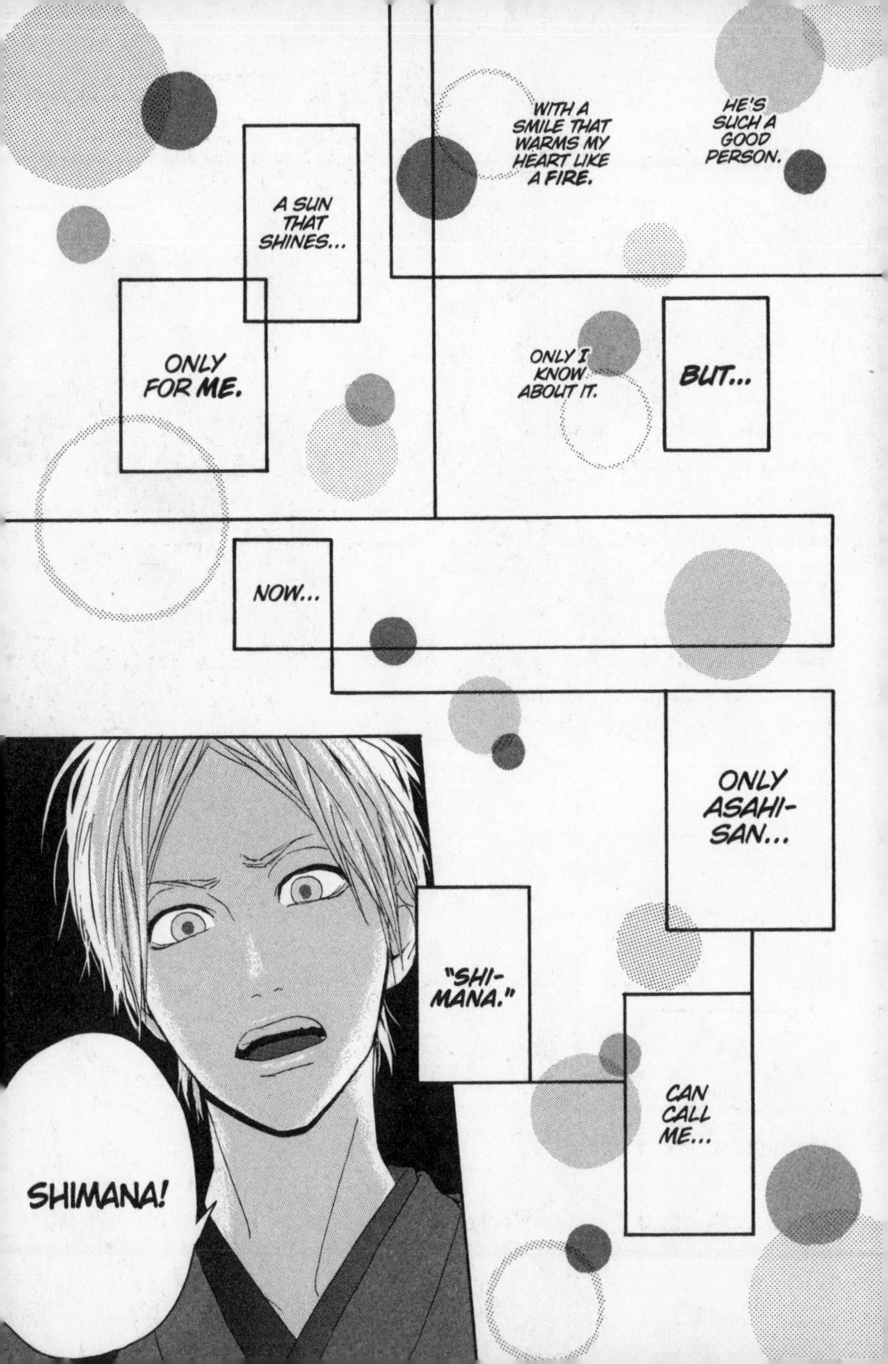
HE'S SUCH A GOOD PERSON.
WITH A SMILE THAT WARMS MY HEART LIKE A FIRE.
BUT...
ONLY I KNOW ABOUT IT.
A SUN THAT SHINES...
ONLY FOR ME.
NOW...
ONLY ASAHI-SAN...
CAN CALL ME...
"SHI-MANA."
SHIMANA!

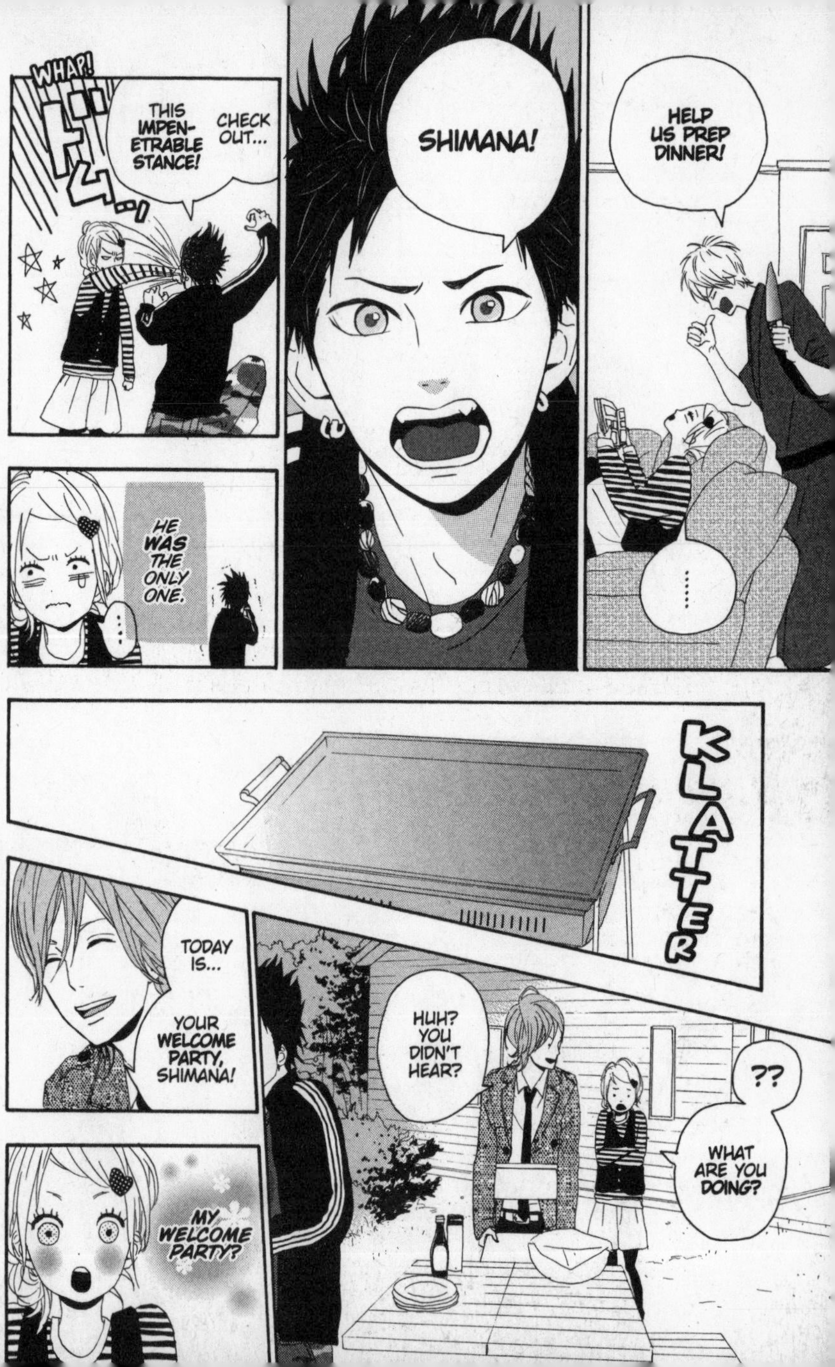
HELP US PREP DINNER!
......
SHIMANA!
WHAP!
CHECK OUT... THIS IMPENETRABLE STANCE!
HE WAS THE ONLY ONE.
...
KLATTER
??
WHAT ARE YOU DOING?
HUH? YOU DIDN'T HEAR?
TODAY IS...
YOUR WELCOME PARTY, SHIMANA!
MY WELCOME PARTY?

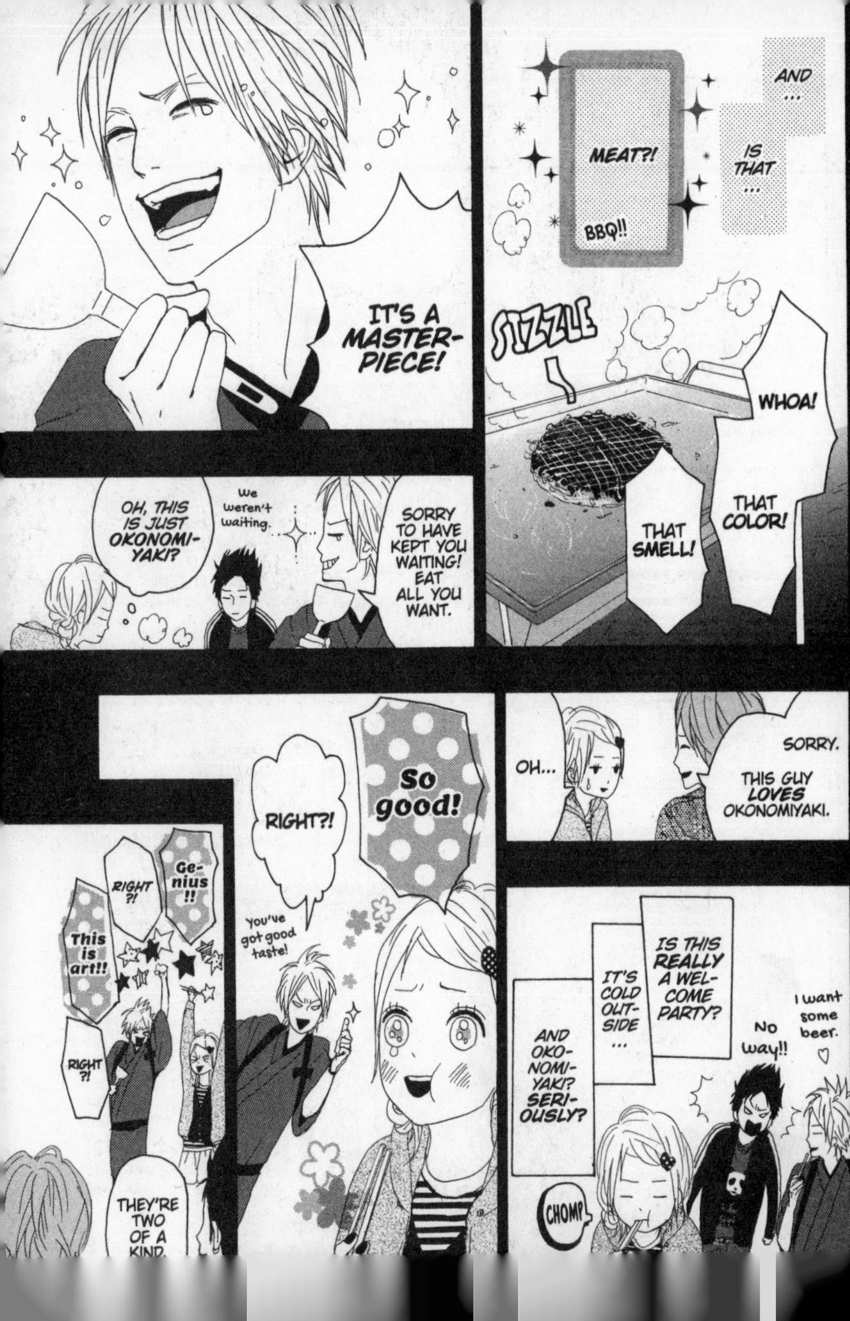
AND ...
IS THAT ...
MEAT?!
BBQ!!
SIZZLE
WHOA!
THAT COLOR!
THAT SMELL!
IT'S A MASTER-PIECE!
SORRY TO HAVE KEPT YOU WAITING! EAT ALL YOU WANT.
We weren't waiting.
OH, THIS IS JUST OKONOMI-YAKI?
SORRY.
THIS GUY LOVES OKONOMIYAKI.
OH...
I want some beer. ♡
No way!!
IS THIS REALLY A WEL-COME PARTY?
IT'S COLD OUT-SIDE ...
AND OKO-NOMI-YAKI? SERI-OUSLY?
CHOMP
So good!
RIGHT?!
You've got good taste!
Ge-nius !!
RIGHT ?!
This is art!!
RIGHT ?!
THEY'RE TWO OF A KIND.

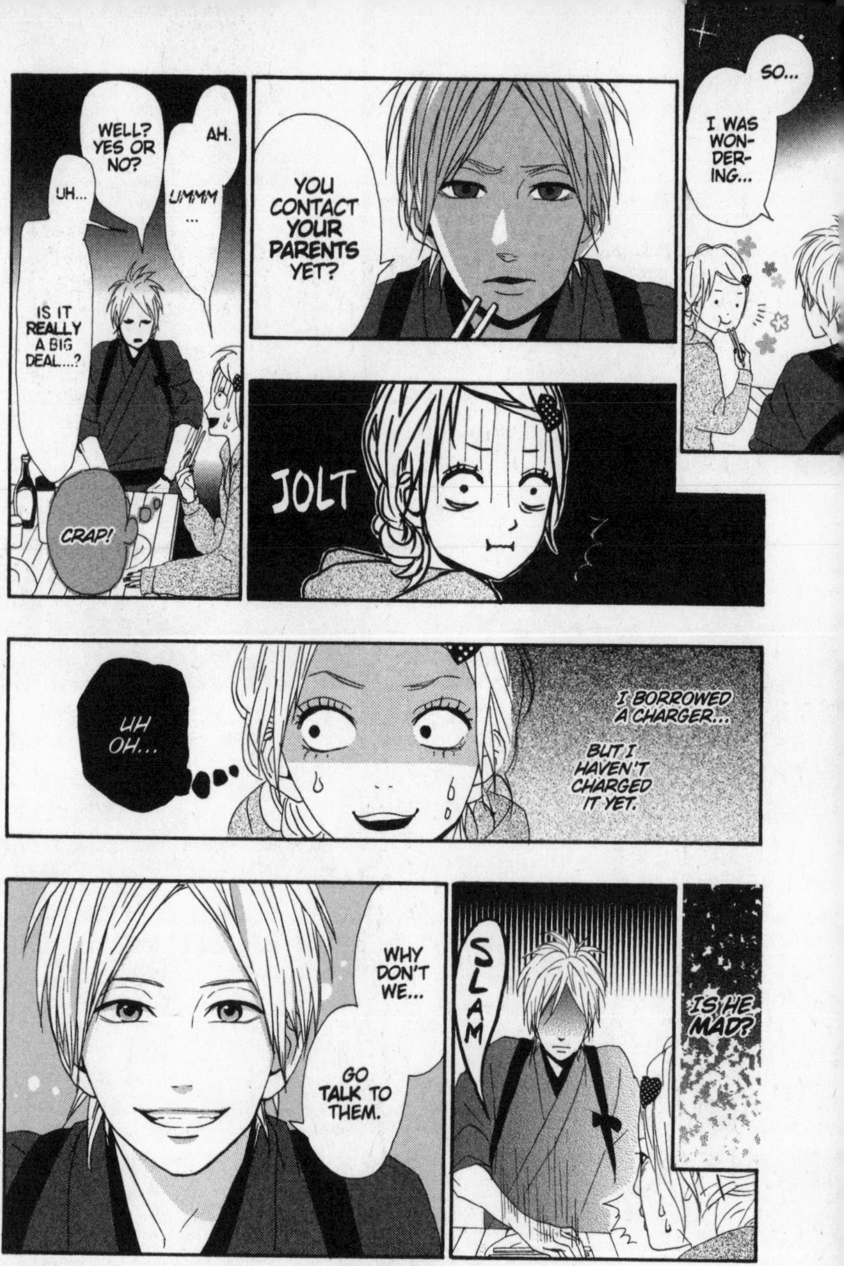
SO...
I WAS WONDERING...
YOU CONTACT YOUR PARENTS YET?
JOLT
AH.
WELL? YES OR NO?
UMMM...
UH...
IS IT REALLY A BIG DEAL...?
CRAP!
I BORROWED A CHARGER...
BUT I HAVEN'T CHARGED IT YET.
UH OH...
IS HE MAD?
SLAM
WHY DON'T WE...
GO TALK TO THEM.

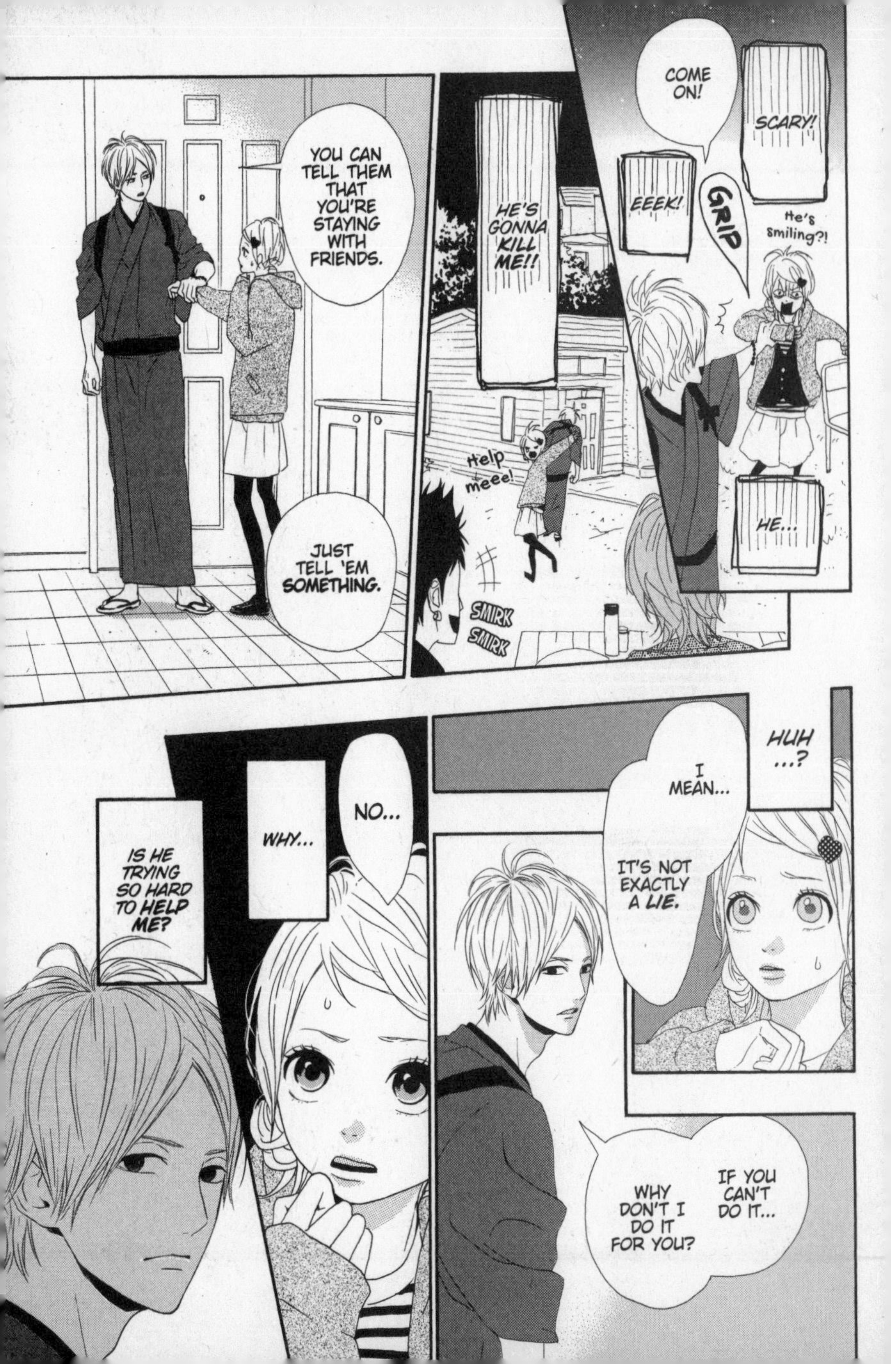
SCARY!
COME ON!
EEEK!
GRIP
He's smiling?!
HE...
HE'S GONNA KILL ME!!
Help meee!
SMIRK
SMIRK
YOU CAN TELL THEM THAT YOU'RE STAYING WITH FRIENDS.
JUST TELL 'EM SOMETHING.
HUH ...?
I MEAN...
IT'S NOT EXACTLY A LIE.
IF YOU CAN'T DO IT...
WHY DON'T I DO IT FOR YOU?
NO...
WHY...
IS HE TRYING SO HARD TO HELP ME?

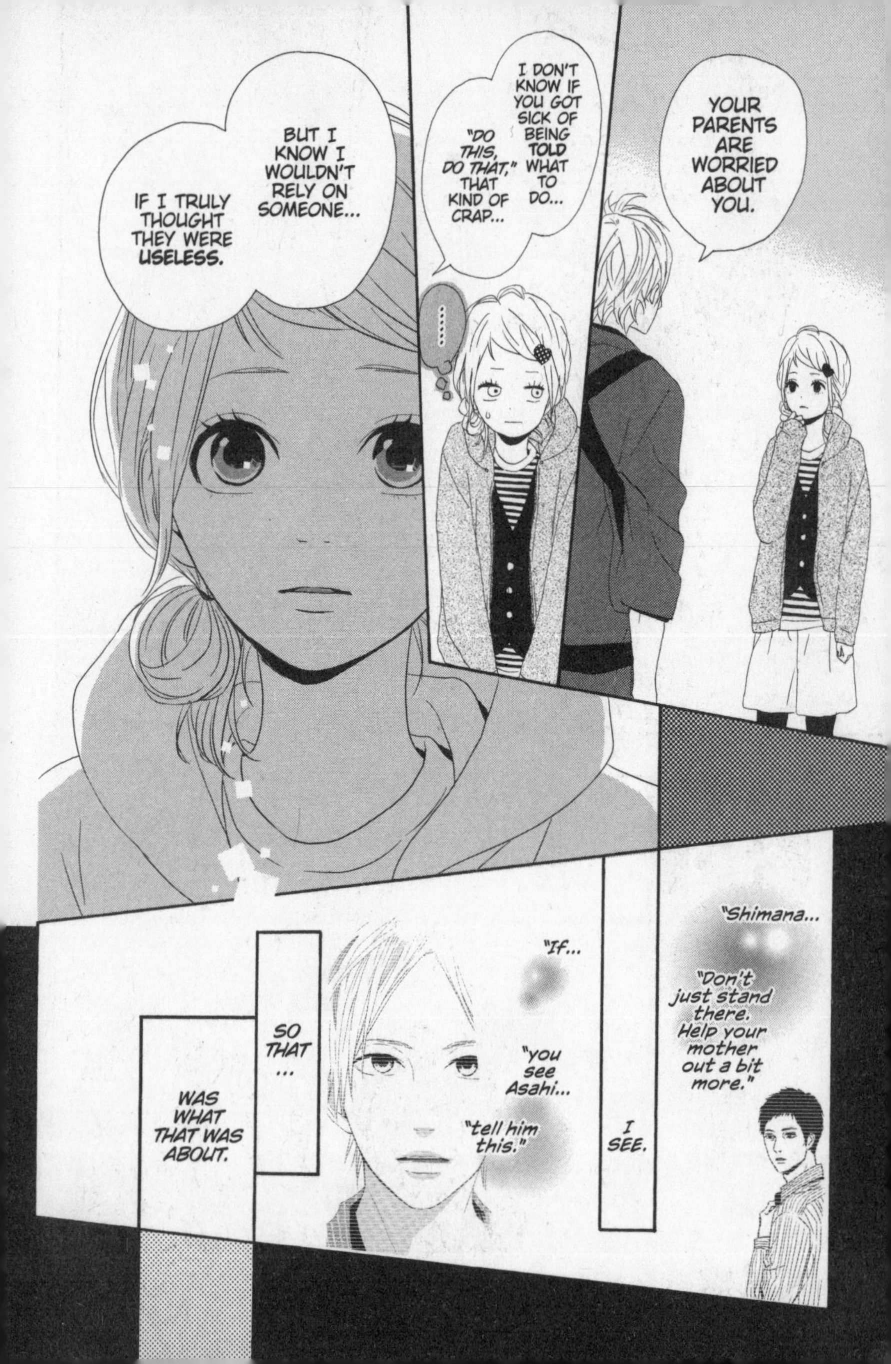
YOUR PARENTS ARE WORRIED ABOUT YOU.
I DON'T KNOW IF YOU GOT SICK OF BEING TOLD WHAT TO DO...
"DO THIS, DO THAT," THAT KIND OF CRAP...
......
BUT I KNOW I WOULDN'T RELY ON SOMEONE...
IF I TRULY THOUGHT THEY WERE USELESS.
"Shimana...
"Don't just stand there. Help your mother out a bit more."
I SEE.
"If...
"you see Asahi...
"tell him this."
SO THAT ...
WAS WHAT THAT WAS ABOUT.

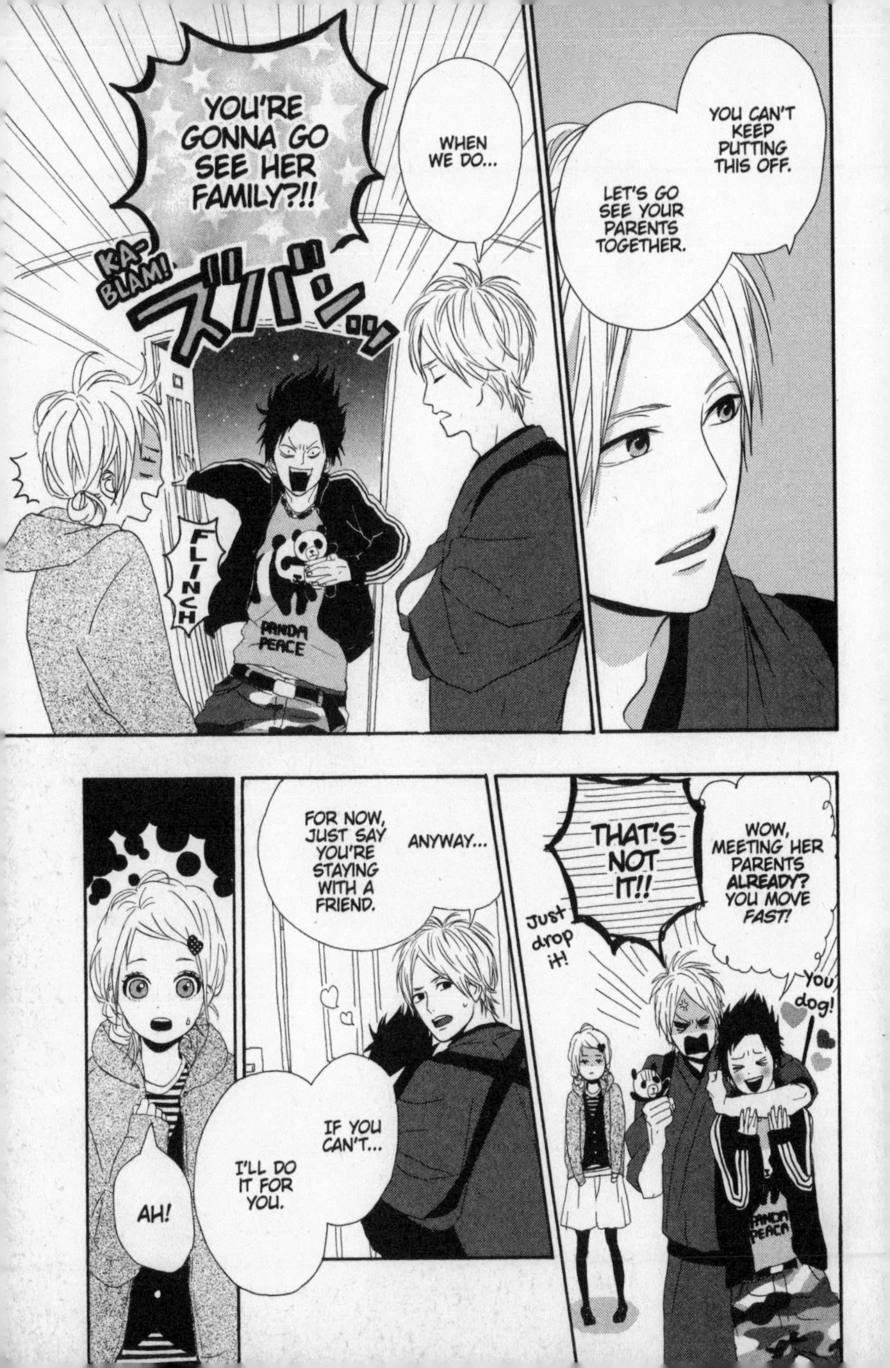
YOU CAN'T KEEP PUTTING THIS OFF.
LET'S GO SEE YOUR PARENTS TOGETHER.
WHEN WE DO...
YOU'RE GONNA GO SEE HER FAMILY?!!
KA-BLAM!
FLINCH
PANDA PEACE
WOW, MEETING HER PARENTS ALREADY? YOU MOVE FAST!
THAT'S NOT IT!!
Just drop it!
You dog!
ANYWAY...
FOR NOW, JUST SAY YOU'RE STAYING WITH A FRIEND.
IF YOU CAN'T...
I'LL DO IT FOR YOU.
AH!

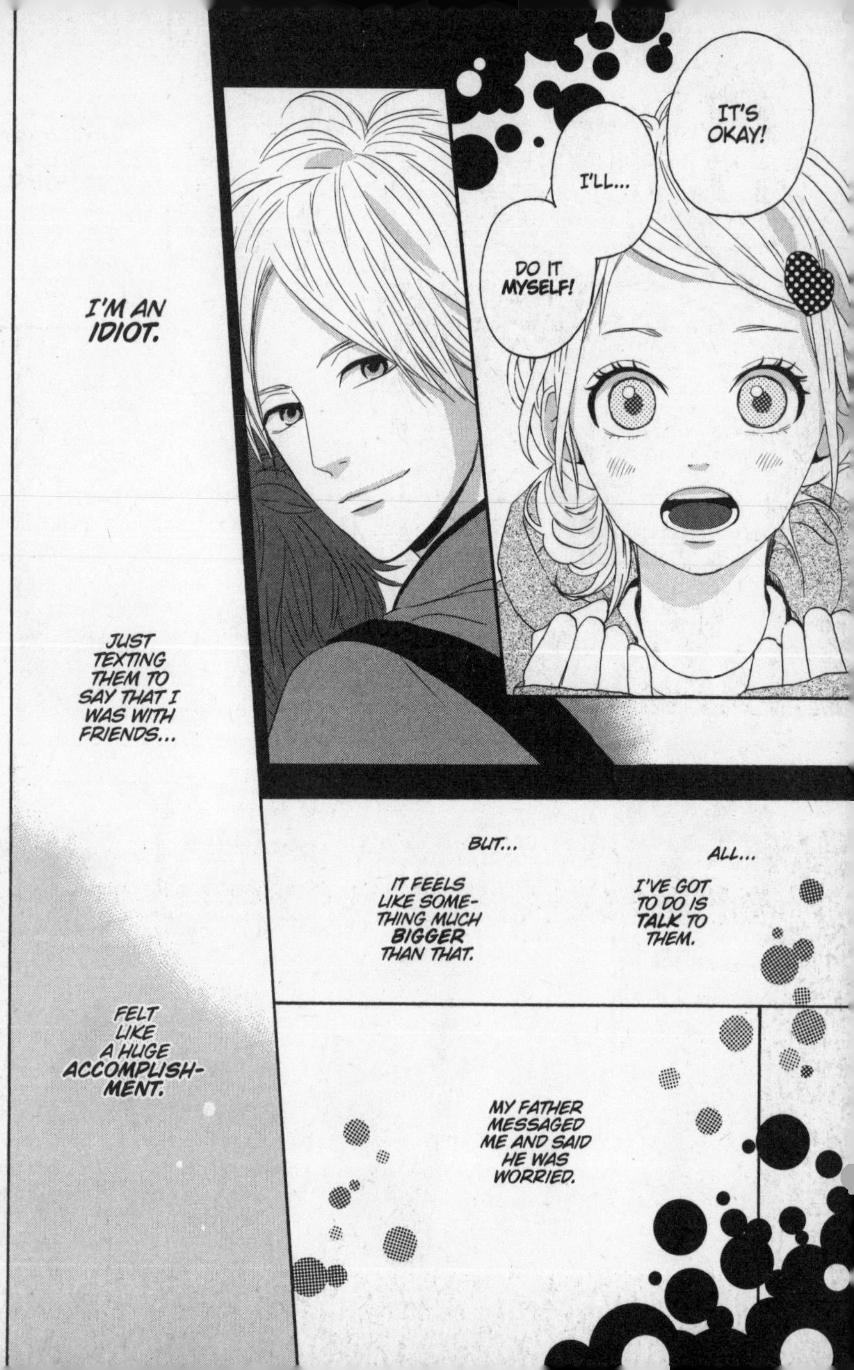
IT'S OKAY!
I'LL...
DO IT MYSELF!
ALL...
I'VE GOT TO DO IS TALK TO THEM.
BUT...
IT FEELS LIKE SOMETHING MUCH BIGGER THAN THAT.
MY FATHER MESSAGED ME AND SAID HE WAS WORRIED.
I'M AN IDIOT.
JUST TEXTING THEM TO SAY THAT I WAS WITH FRIENDS...
FELT LIKE A HUGE ACCOMPLISHMENT.

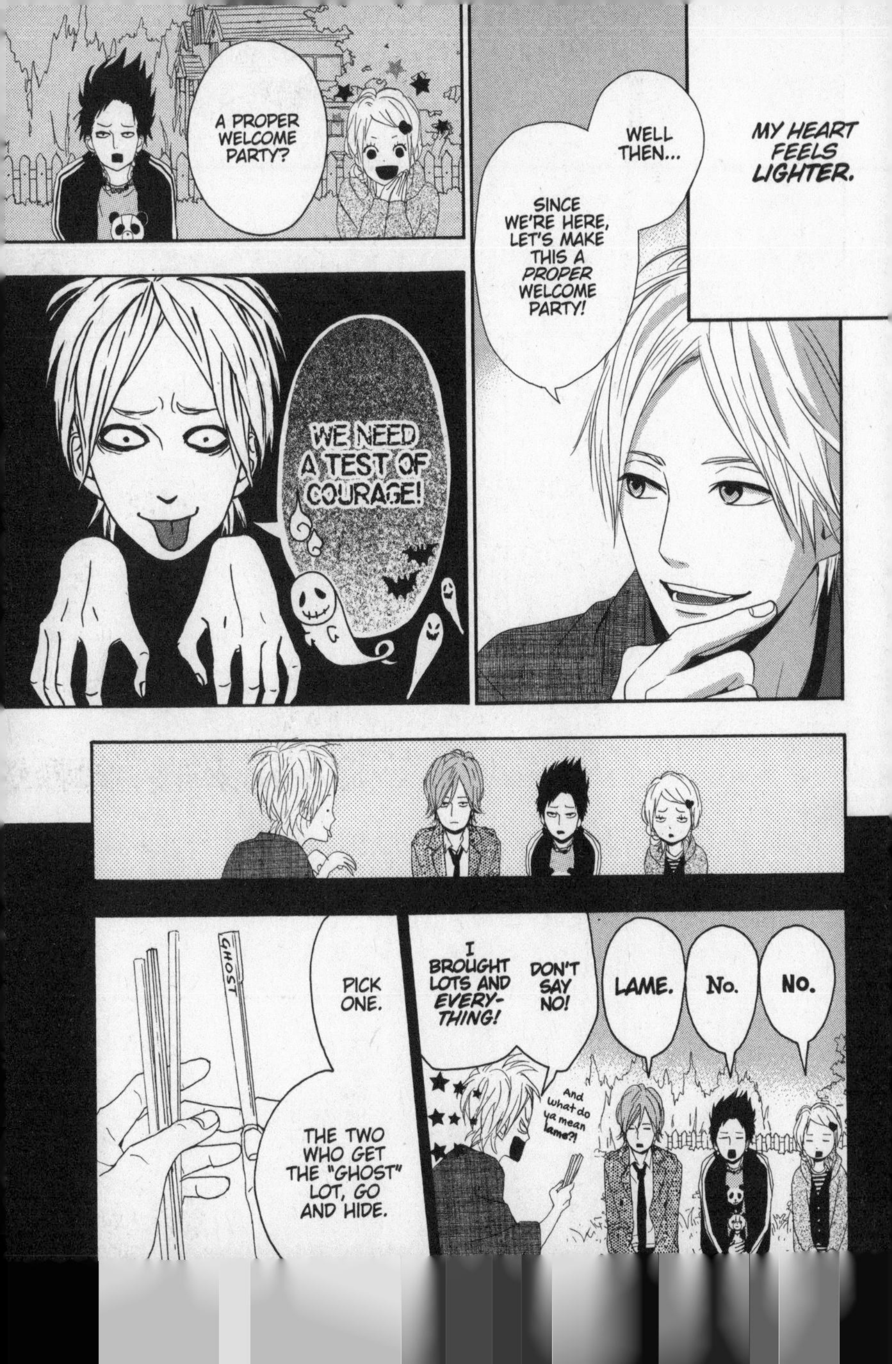
MY HEART FEELS LIGHTER.
WELL THEN...
SINCE WE'RE HERE, LET'S MAKE THIS A *PROPER* WELCOME PARTY!
A PROPER WELCOME PARTY?
WE NEED A TEST OF COURAGE!
No.
No.
LAME.
DON'T SAY NO!
I BROUGHT LOTS AND *EVERYTHING!*
And what do ya mean lame?!
PICK ONE.
GHOST
THE TWO WHO GET THE "GHOST" LOT, GO AND HIDE.

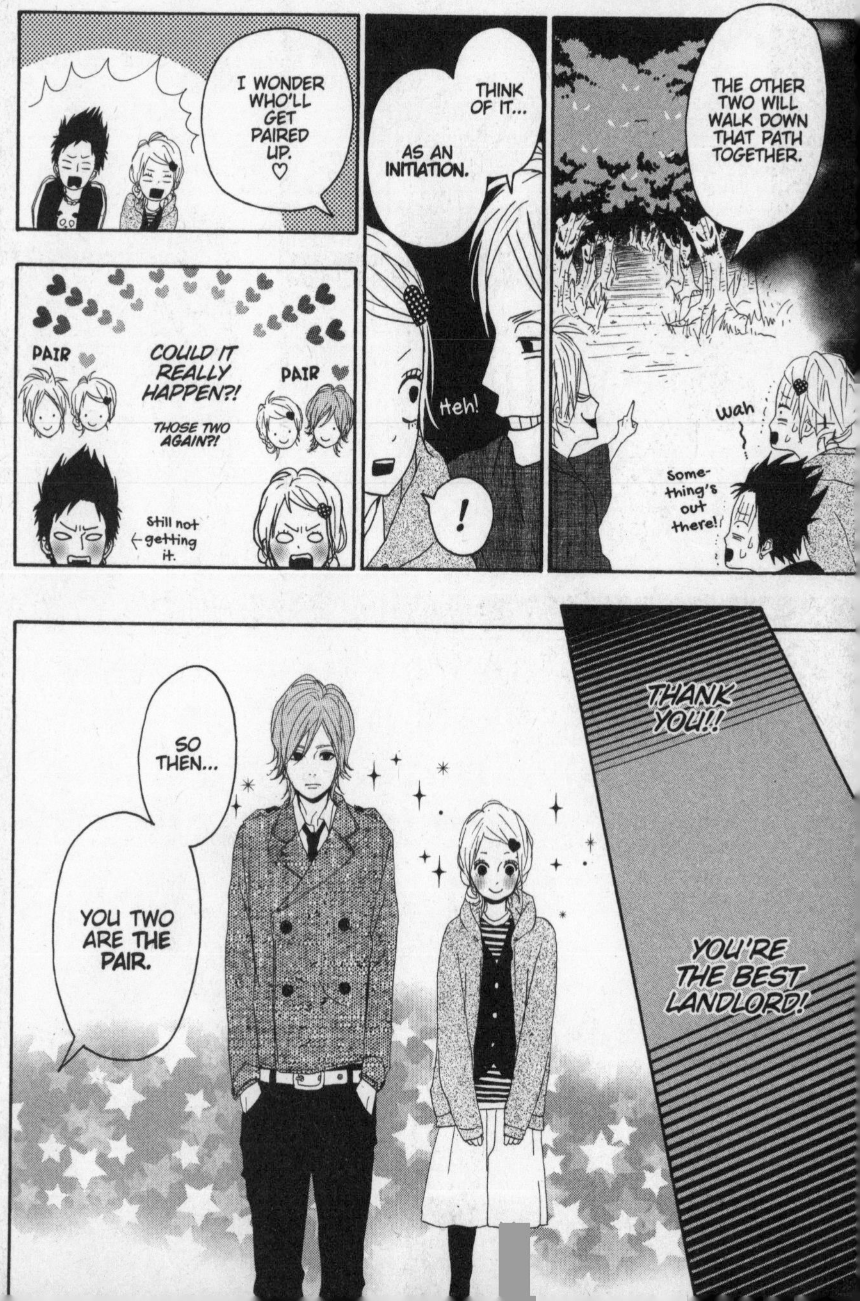
THE OTHER TWO WILL WALK DOWN THAT PATH TOGETHER.
wah
Some-thing's out there!
THINK OF IT...
AS AN INITIATION.
Heh!
!
I WONDER WHO'LL GET PAIRED UP. ♡
PAIR ♥
COULD IT REALLY HAPPEN?!
THOSE TWO AGAIN?!
PAIR ♥
Still not ← getting it.
SO THEN...
YOU TWO ARE THE PAIR.
THANK YOU!!
YOU'RE THE BEST LANDLORD!

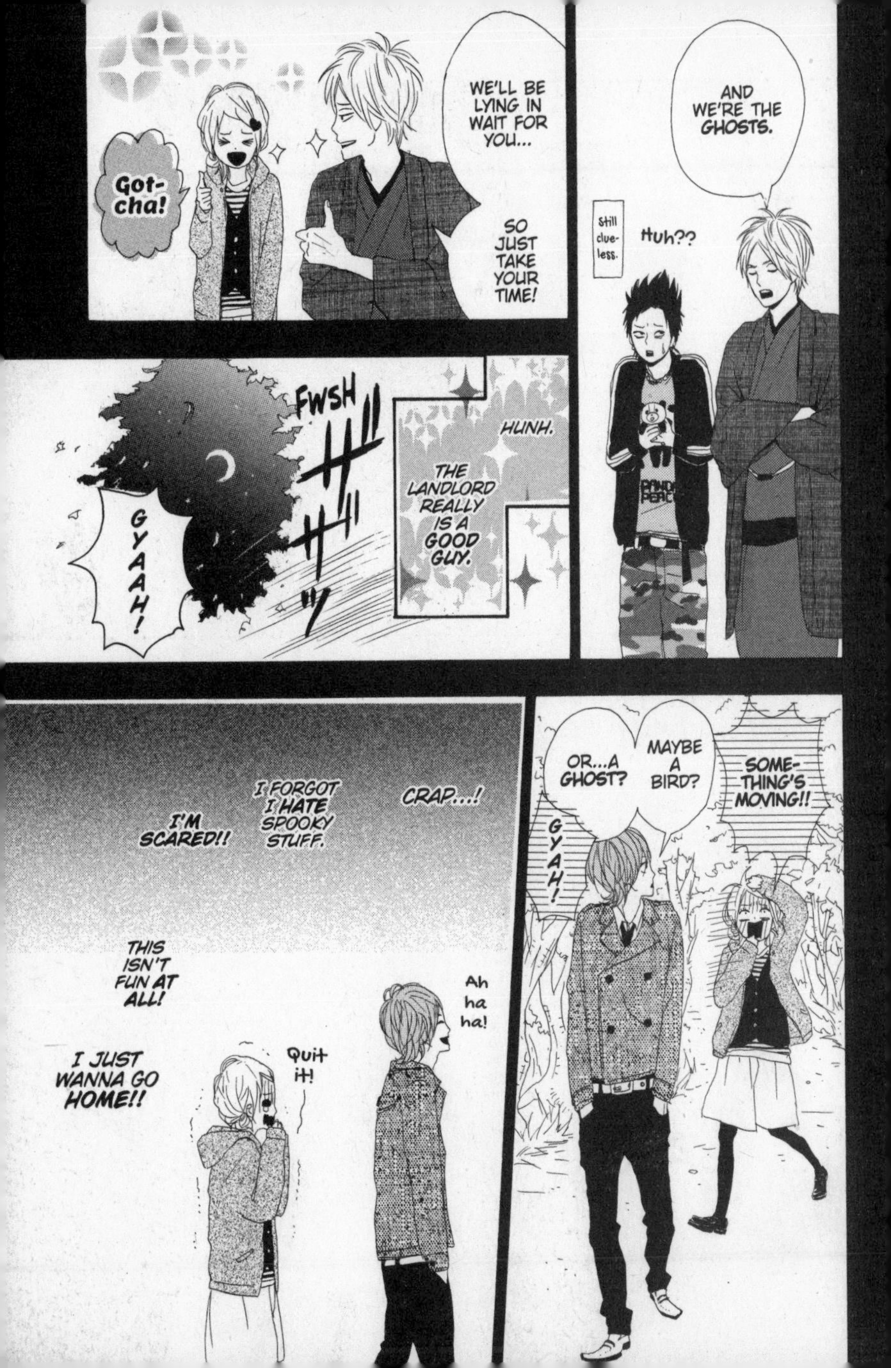
AND WE'RE THE GHOSTS.
Still clueless.
Huh??
WE'LL BE LYING IN WAIT FOR YOU...
SO JUST TAKE YOUR TIME!
Got-cha!
HUNH.
THE LANDLORD REALLY IS A GOOD GUY.
FWSH
GYAAH!
SOME-THING'S MOVING!!
MAYBE A BIRD?
OR...A GHOST?
GYAH!
CRAP...!
I FORGOT I HATE SPOOKY STUFF.
I'M SCARED!!
Ah ha ha!
Quit it!
THIS ISN'T FUN AT ALL!
I JUST WANNA GO HOME!!

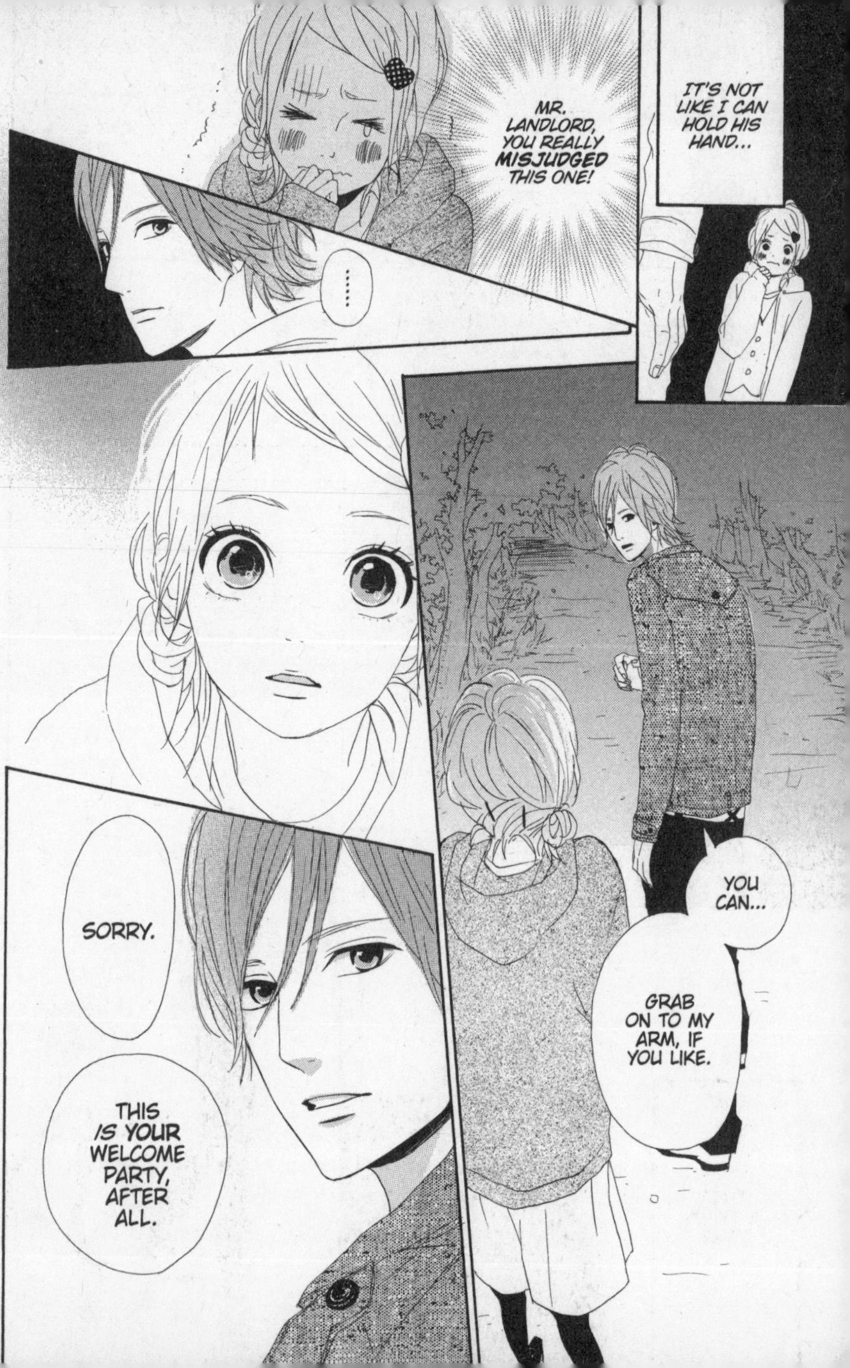
IT'S NOT LIKE I CAN HOLD HIS HAND...
MR. LANDLORD, YOU REALLY MISJUDGED THIS ONE!
......
YOU CAN...
GRAB ON TO MY ARM, IF YOU LIKE.
SORRY.
THIS IS YOUR WELCOME PARTY, AFTER ALL.

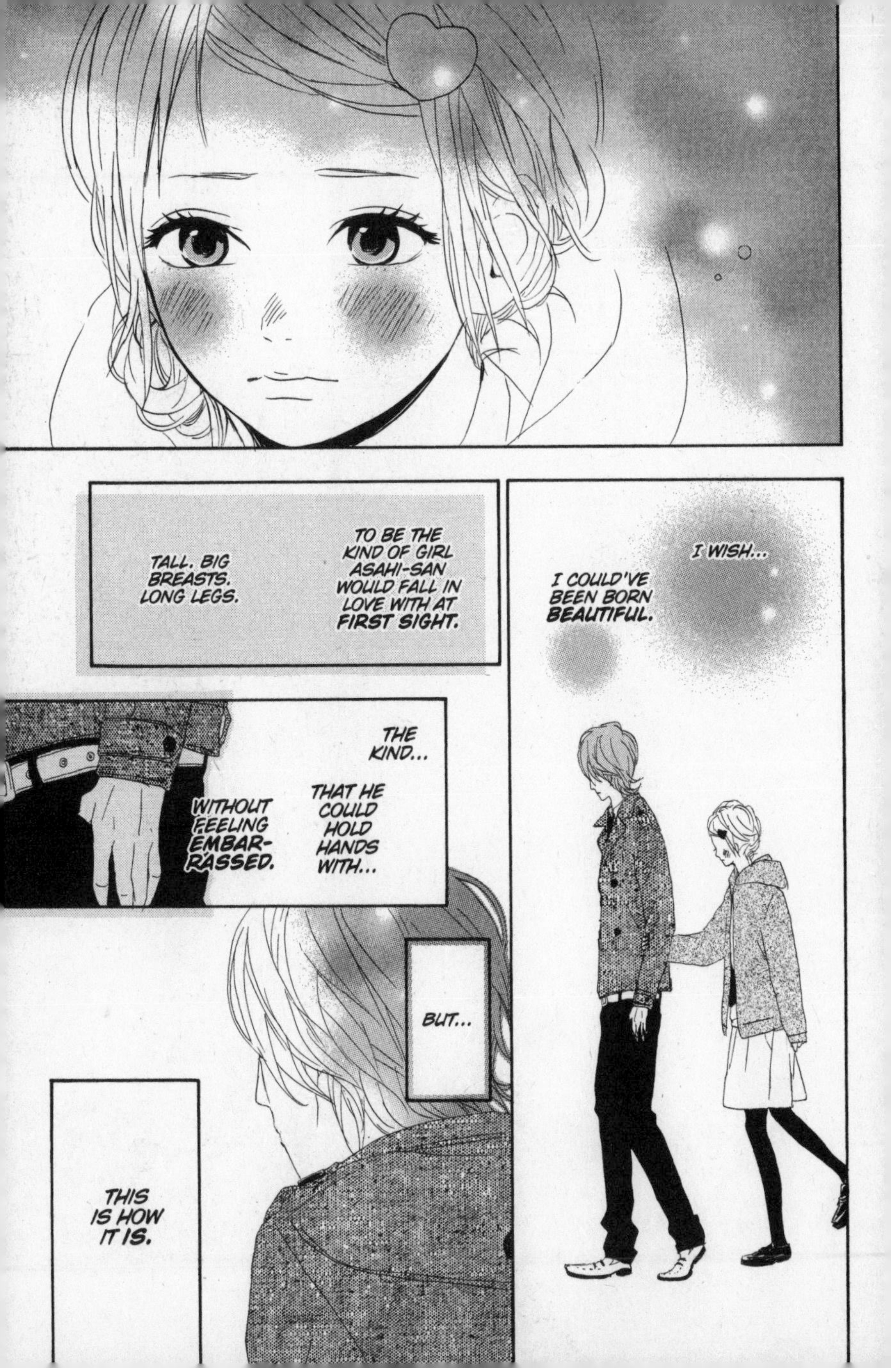
I WISH...
I COULD'VE BEEN BORN BEAUTIFUL.
TO BE THE KIND OF GIRL ASAHI-SAN WOULD FALL IN LOVE WITH AT FIRST SIGHT.
TALL. BIG BREASTS. LONG LEGS.
THE KIND...
THAT HE COULD HOLD HANDS WITH...
WITHOUT FEELING EMBAR-RASSED.
BUT...
THIS IS HOW IT IS.

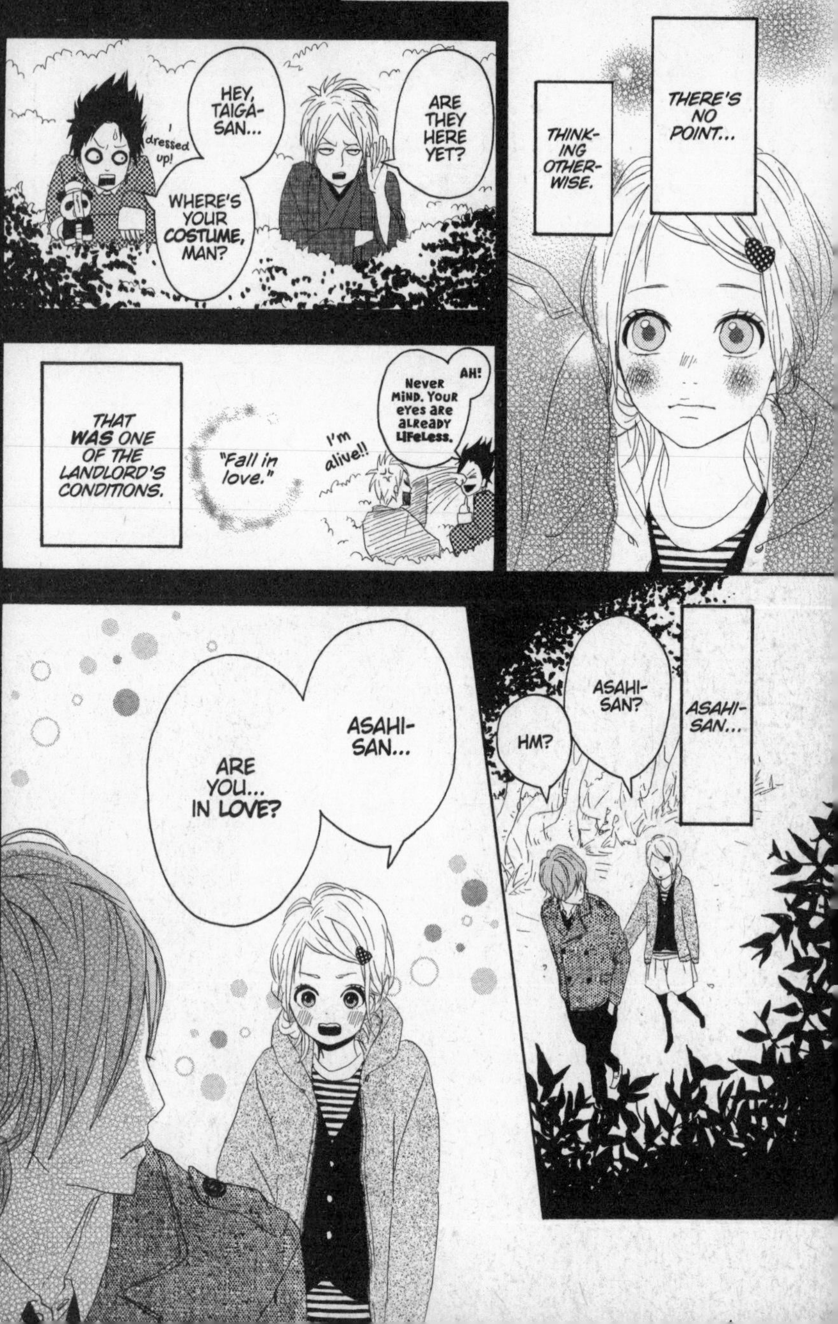
THERE'S NO POINT...
THINKING OTHERWISE.
ARE THEY HERE YET?
HEY, TAIGA-SAN... WHERE'S YOUR COSTUME, MAN?
I dressed up!
AH! Never mind. Your eyes are already lifeless.
I'm alive!!
"Fall in love."
THAT WAS ONE OF THE LANDLORD'S CONDITIONS.
ASAHI-SAN...
ASAHI-SAN?
HM?
ASAHI-SAN... ARE YOU... IN LOVE?

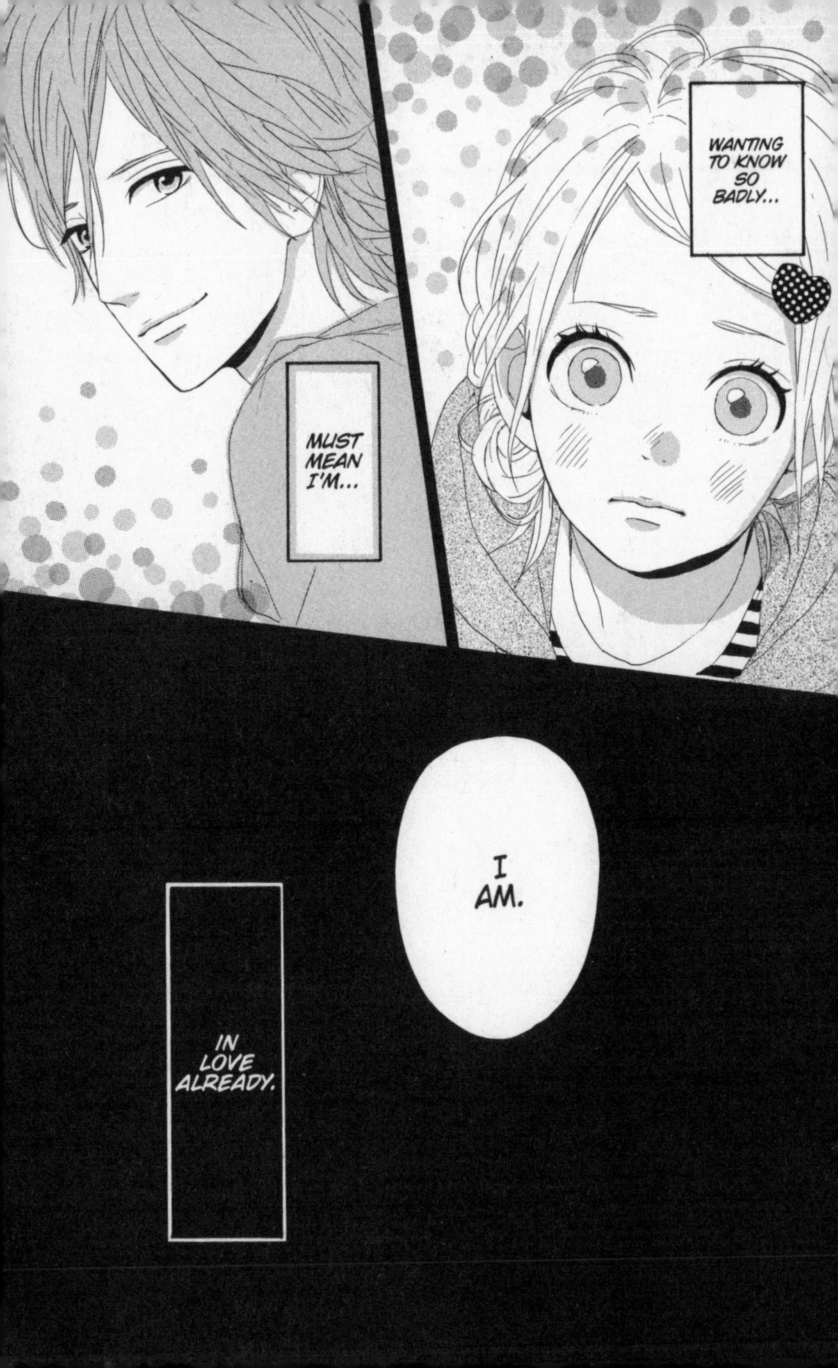
WANTING TO KNOW SO BADLY...
MUST MEAN I'M...
I AM.
IN LOVE ALREADY.

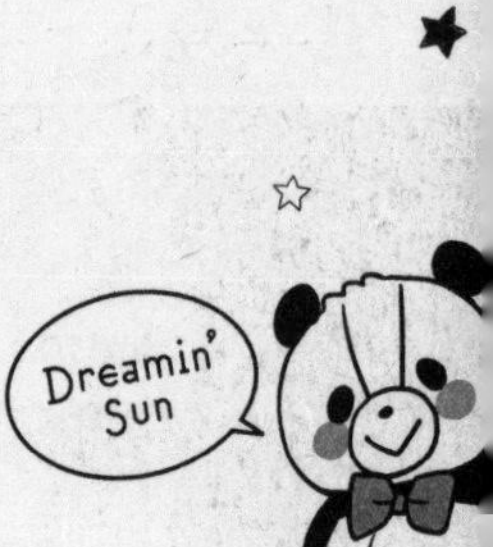
Dreamin' Sun

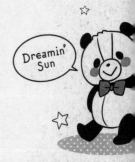

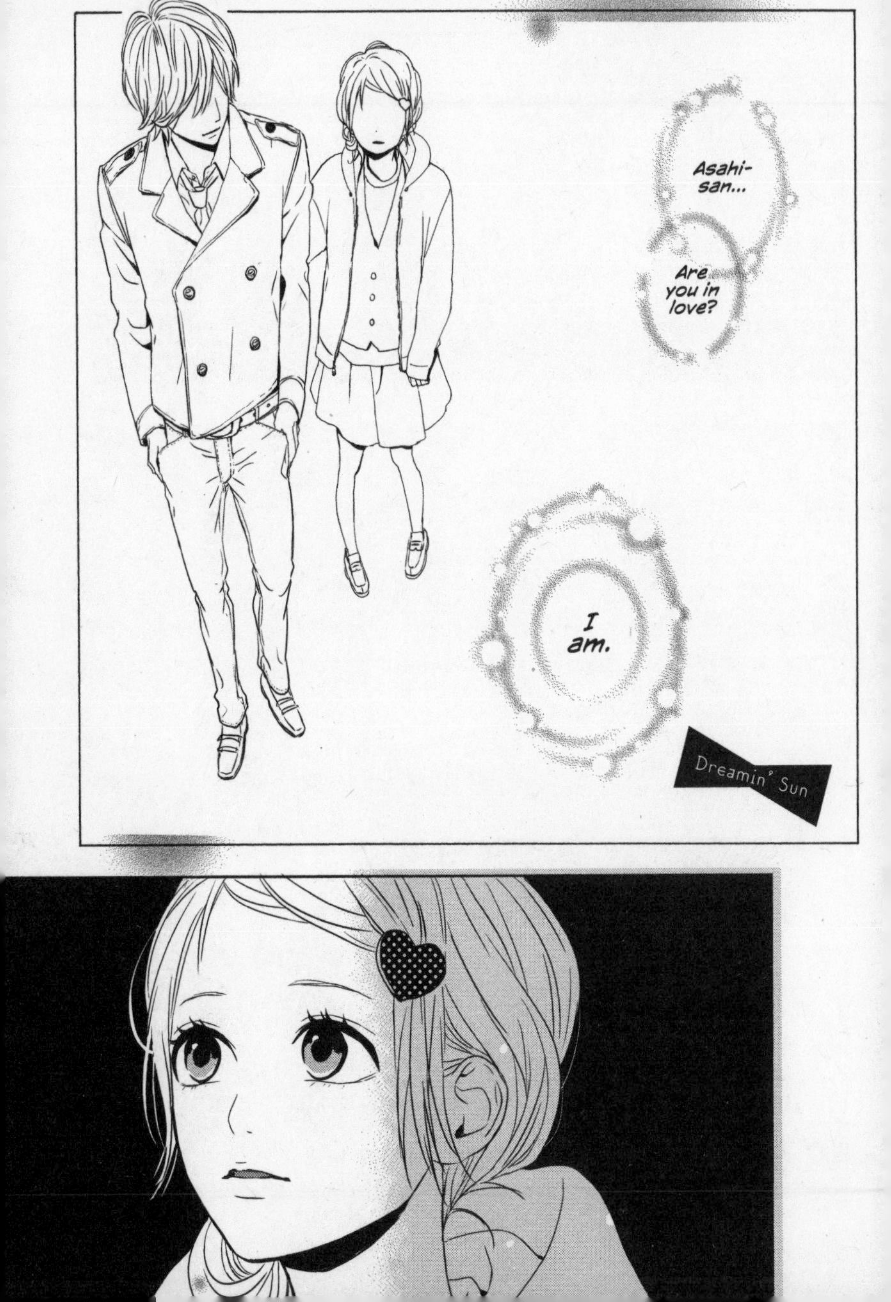
Asahi-san...
Are you in love?
I am.
Dreamin' Sun

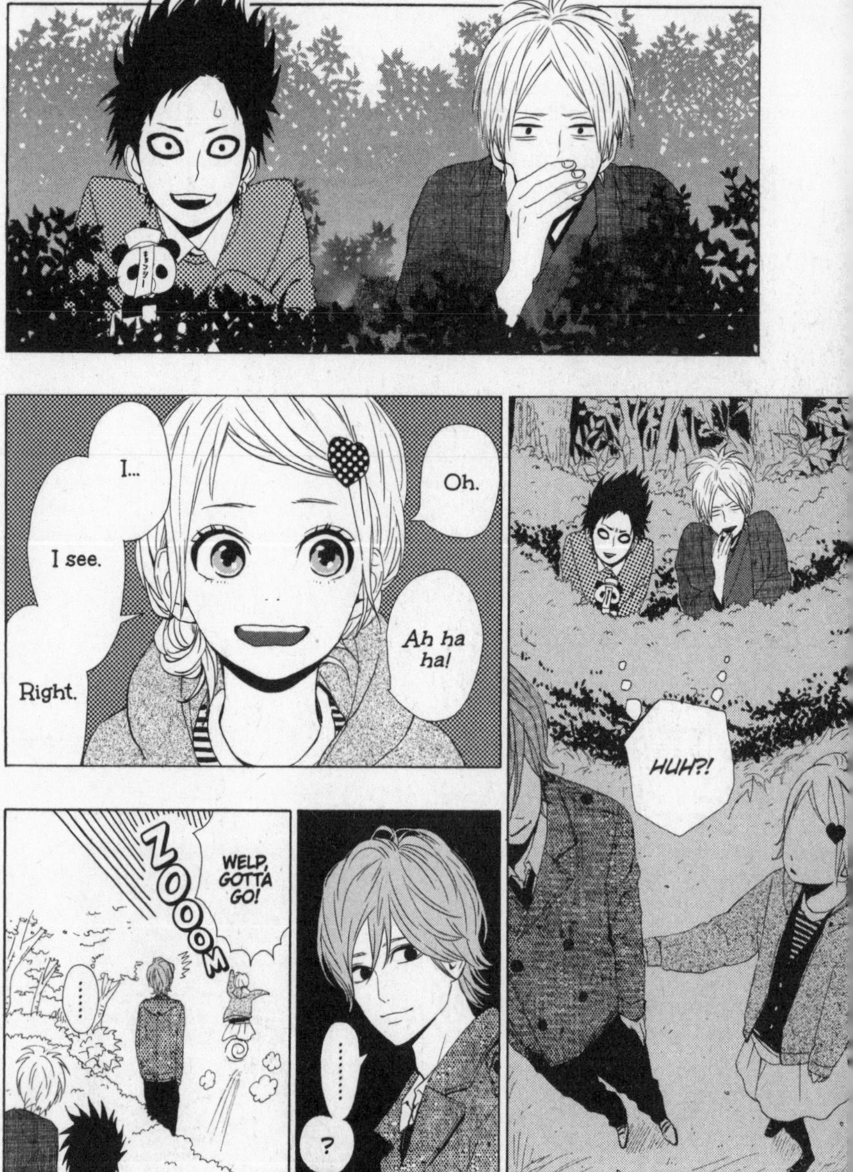
HUH?!
Oh.
Ah ha ha!
I... I see. Right.
....
?
ZOOOM
WELP, GOTTA GO!
......

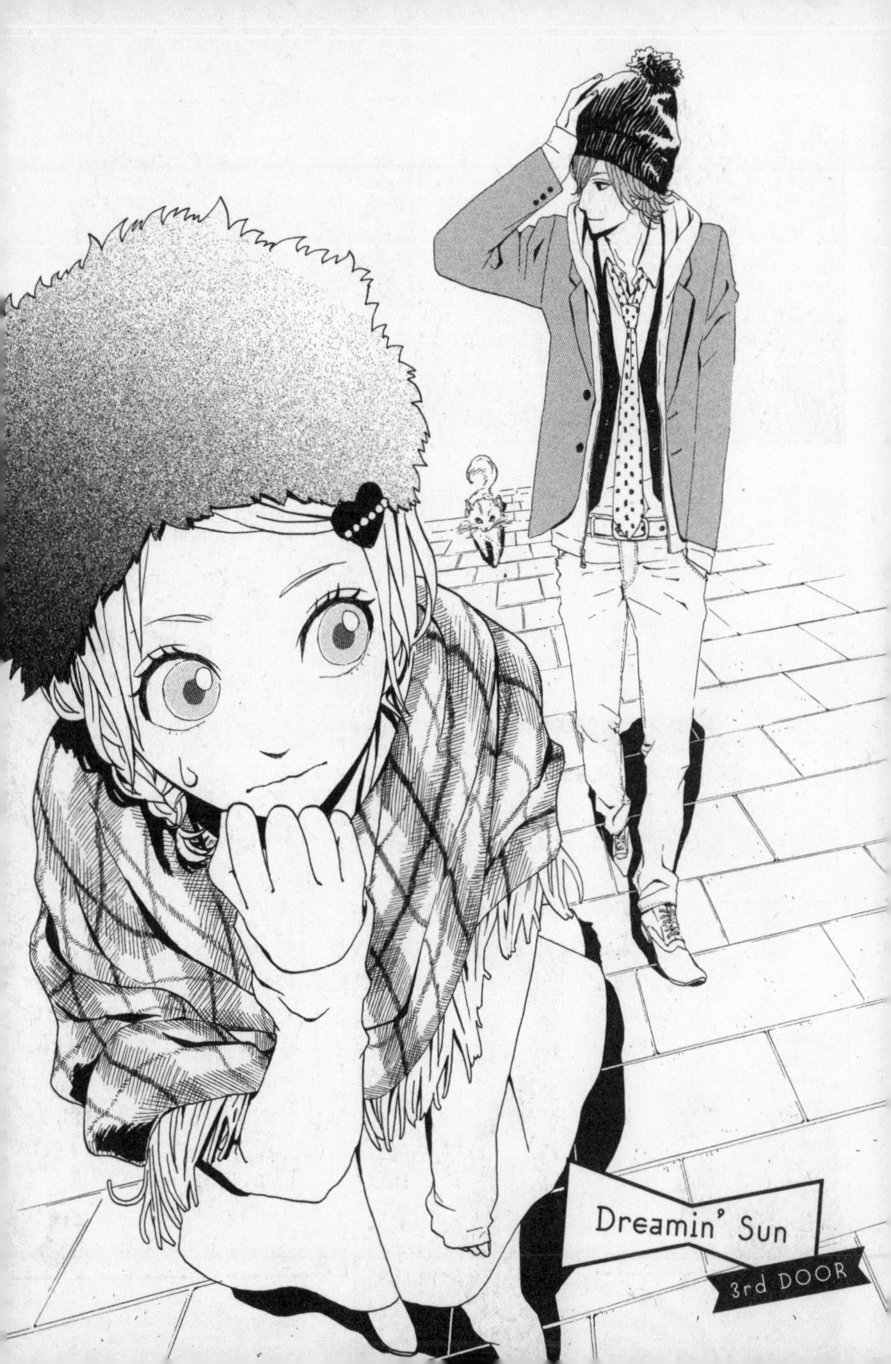
Dreamin' Sun
3rd DOOR

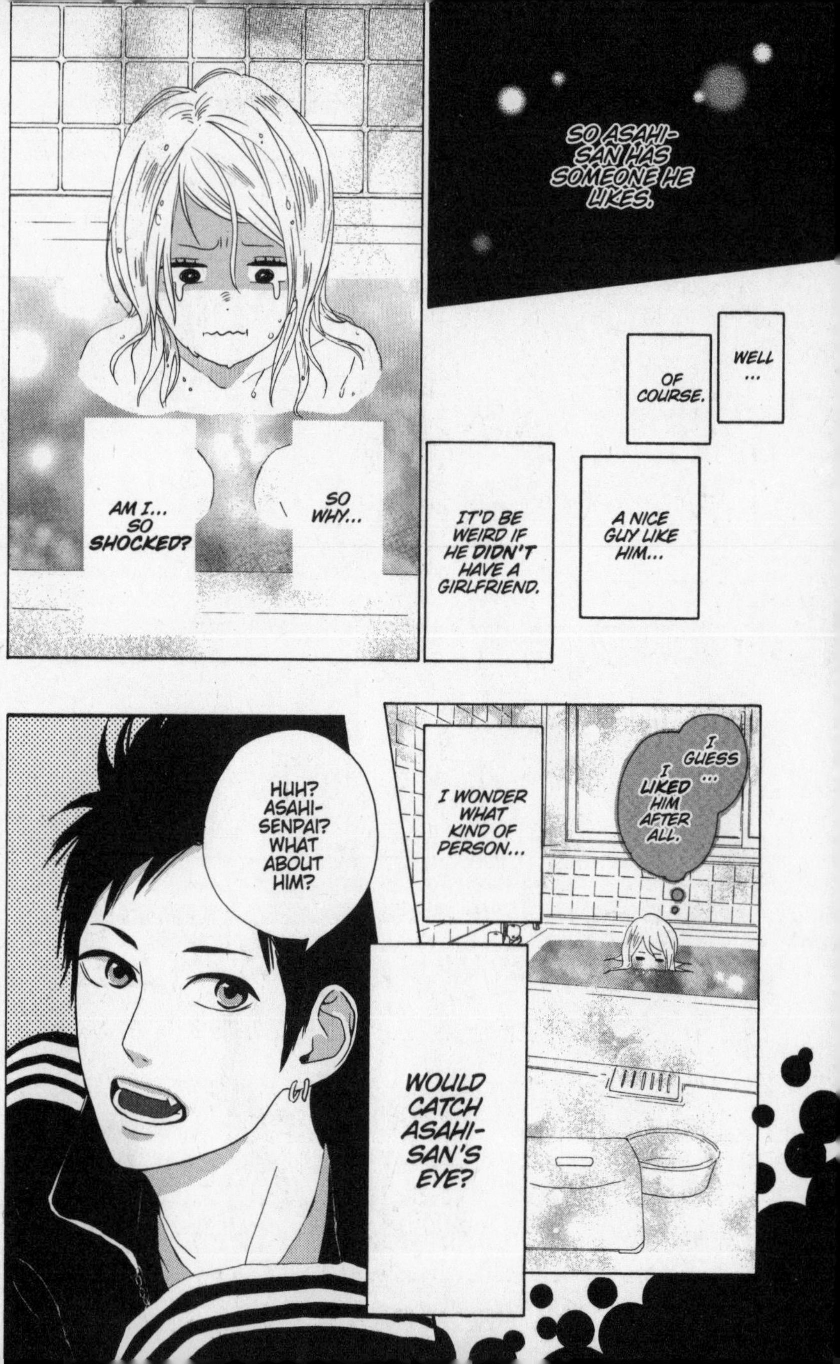
SO ASAHI-SAN HAS SOMEONE HE LIKES.
WELL...
OF COURSE.
A NICE GUY LIKE HIM...
IT'D BE WEIRD IF HE DIDN'T HAVE A GIRLFRIEND.
SO WHY...
AM I... SO SHOCKED?
I GUESS... I LIKED HIM AFTER ALL.
I WONDER WHAT KIND OF PERSON...
WOULD CATCH ASAHI-SAN'S EYE?
HUH? ASAHI-SENPAI? WHAT ABOUT HIM?

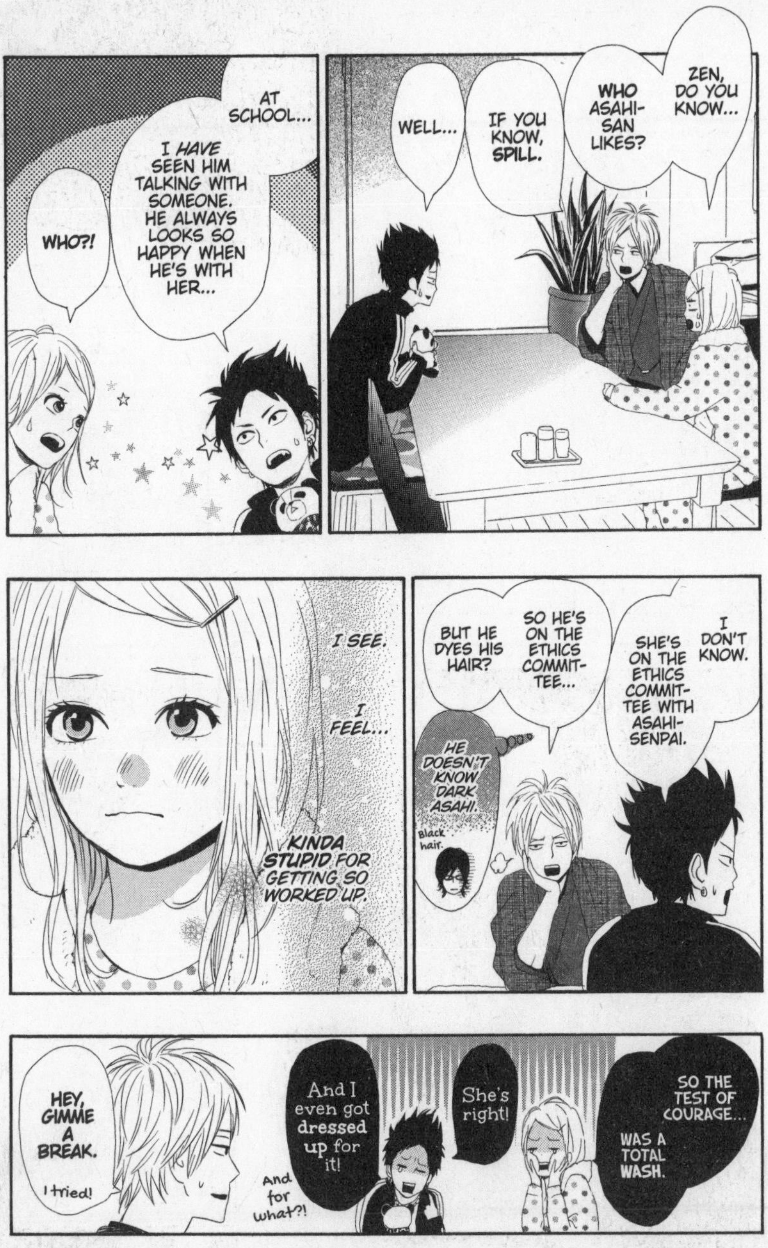
ZEN, DO YOU KNOW...
WHO ASAHI-SAN LIKES?
IF YOU KNOW, SPILL.
WELL...
AT SCHOOL...
I HAVE SEEN HIM TALKING WITH SOMEONE. HE ALWAYS LOOKS SO HAPPY WHEN HE'S WITH HER...
WHO?!
I DON'T KNOW.
SHE'S ON THE ETHICS COMMITTEE WITH ASAHI-SENPAI.
SO HE'S ON THE ETHICS COMMITTEE...
BUT HE DYES HIS HAIR?
HE DOESN'T KNOW DARK ASAHI.
Black hair.
I SEE.
I FEEL...
KINDA STUPID FOR GETTING SO WORKED UP.
SO THE TEST OF COURAGE...
WAS A TOTAL WASH.
She's right!
And I even got dressed up for it!
And for what?!
HEY, GIMME A BREAK.
I tried!

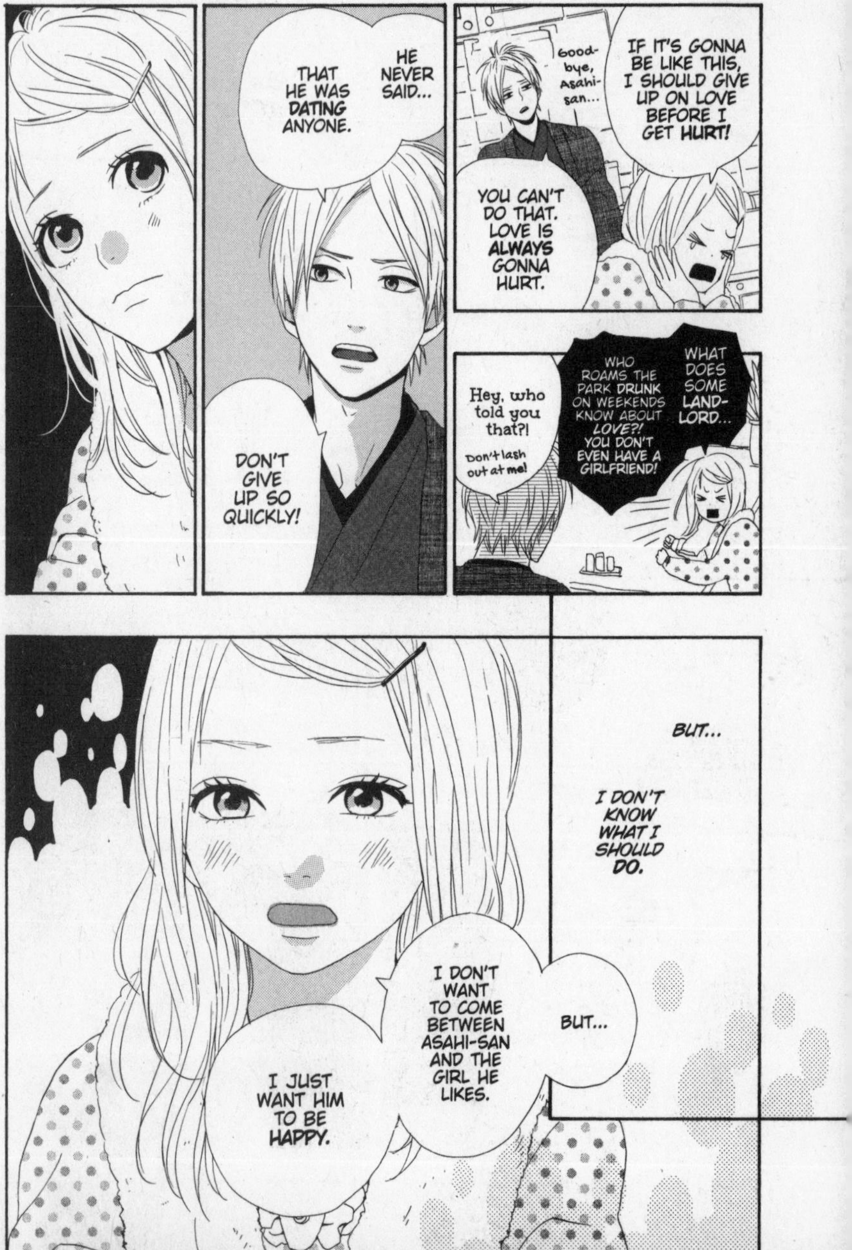
IF IT'S GONNA BE LIKE THIS, I SHOULD GIVE UP ON LOVE BEFORE I GET HURT!
Good-bye, Asahi-san...
YOU CAN'T DO THAT. LOVE IS ALWAYS GONNA HURT.
WHAT DOES SOME LANDLORD...
WHO ROAMS THE PARK DRUNK ON WEEKENDS KNOW ABOUT LOVE?! YOU DON'T EVEN HAVE A GIRLFRIEND!
Hey, who told you that?!
Don't lash out at me!
HE NEVER SAID...
THAT HE WAS DATING ANYONE.
DON'T GIVE UP SO QUICKLY!
BUT...
I DON'T KNOW WHAT I SHOULD DO.
BUT...
I DON'T WANT TO COME BETWEEN ASAHI-SAN AND THE GIRL HE LIKES.
I JUST WANT HIM TO BE HAPPY.

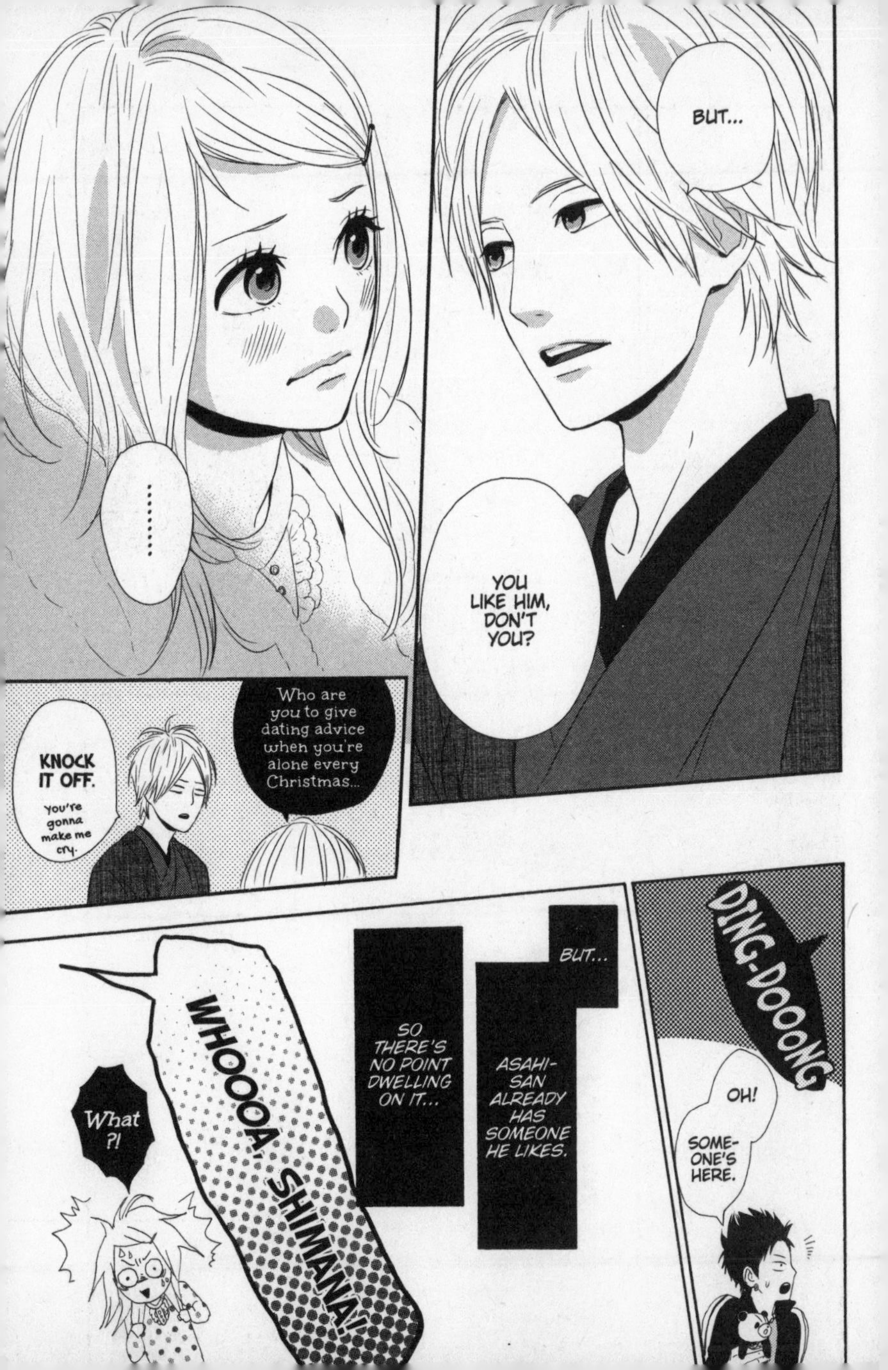
BUT...
YOU LIKE HIM, DON'T YOU?
......
Who are you to give dating advice when you're alone every Christmas...
KNOCK IT OFF.
You're gonna make me cry.
DING-DOOONG
OH!
SOME-ONE'S HERE.
BUT...
ASAHI-SAN ALREADY HAS SOMEONE HE LIKES.
SO THERE'S NO POINT DWELLING ON IT...
WHOOOA, SHIMANA!
What?!

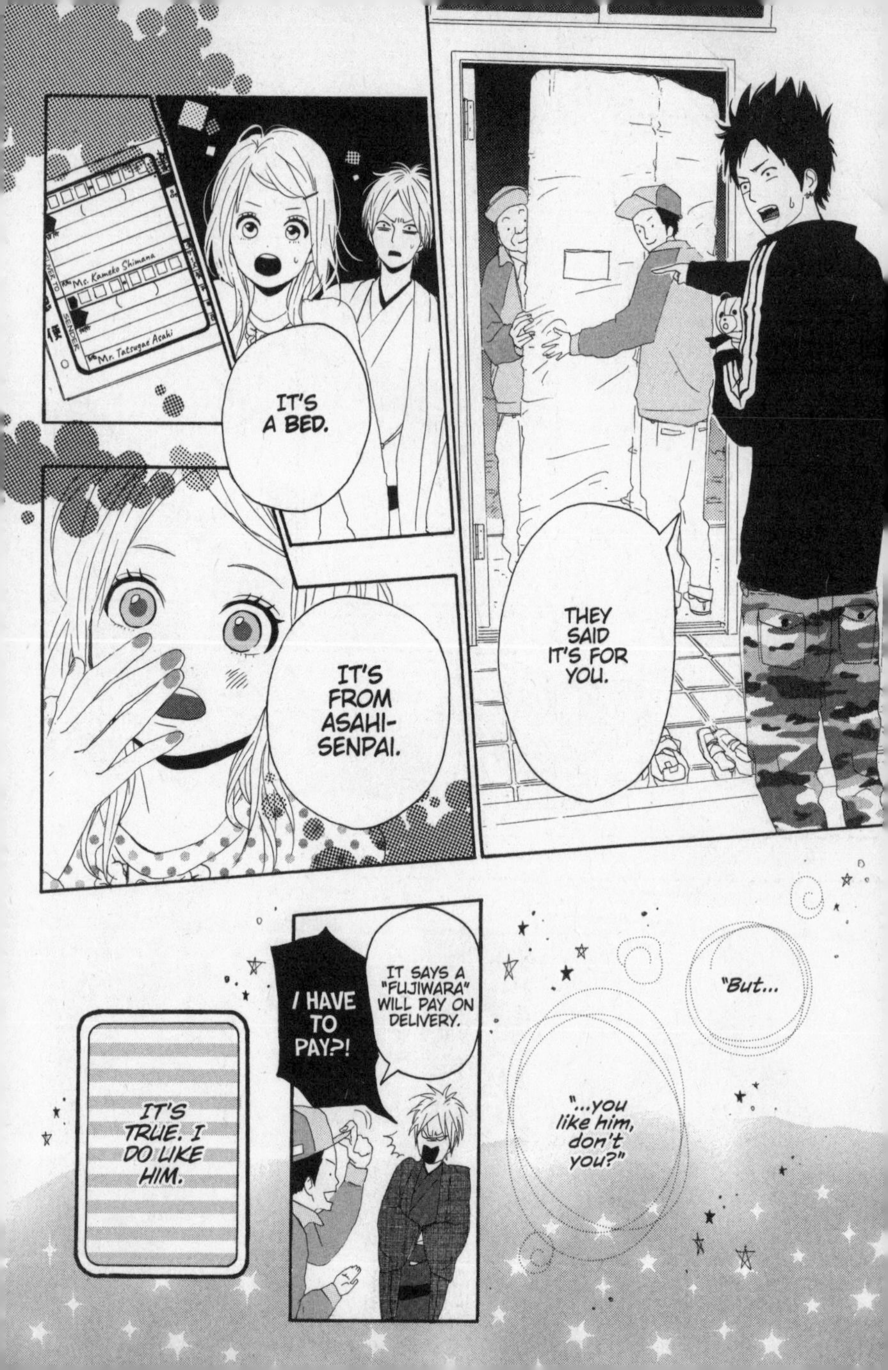
THEY SAID IT'S FOR YOU.
Mr. Kameko Shimana
SENDER
Mr. Tatsugae Asahi
IT'S A BED.
IT'S FROM ASAHI-SENPAI.
"But...
"...you like him, don't you?"
IT SAYS A "FUJIWARA" WILL PAY ON DELIVERY.
I HAVE TO PAY?!
IT'S TRUE. I DO LIKE HIM.

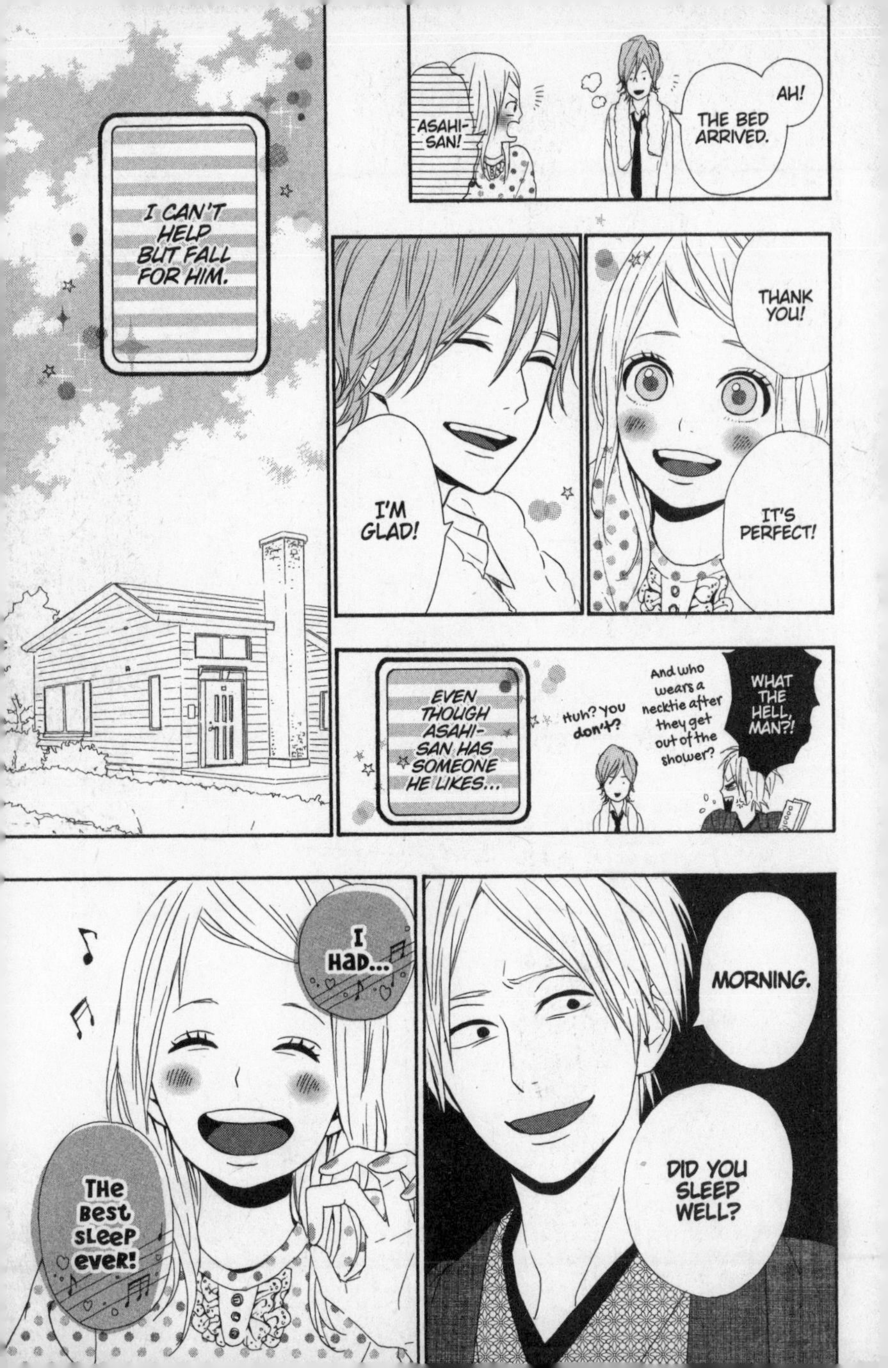

AH! THE BED ARRIVED.
ASAHI-SAN!
THANK YOU!
IT'S PERFECT!
I'M GLAD!
WHAT THE HELL, MAN?!
And who wears a necktie after they get out of the shower?
Huh? You don't?
EVEN THOUGH ASAHI-SAN HAS SOMEONE HE LIKES...
I CAN'T HELP BUT FALL FOR HIM.
MORNING.
DID YOU SLEEP WELL?
I HAD...
The best sleep ever!

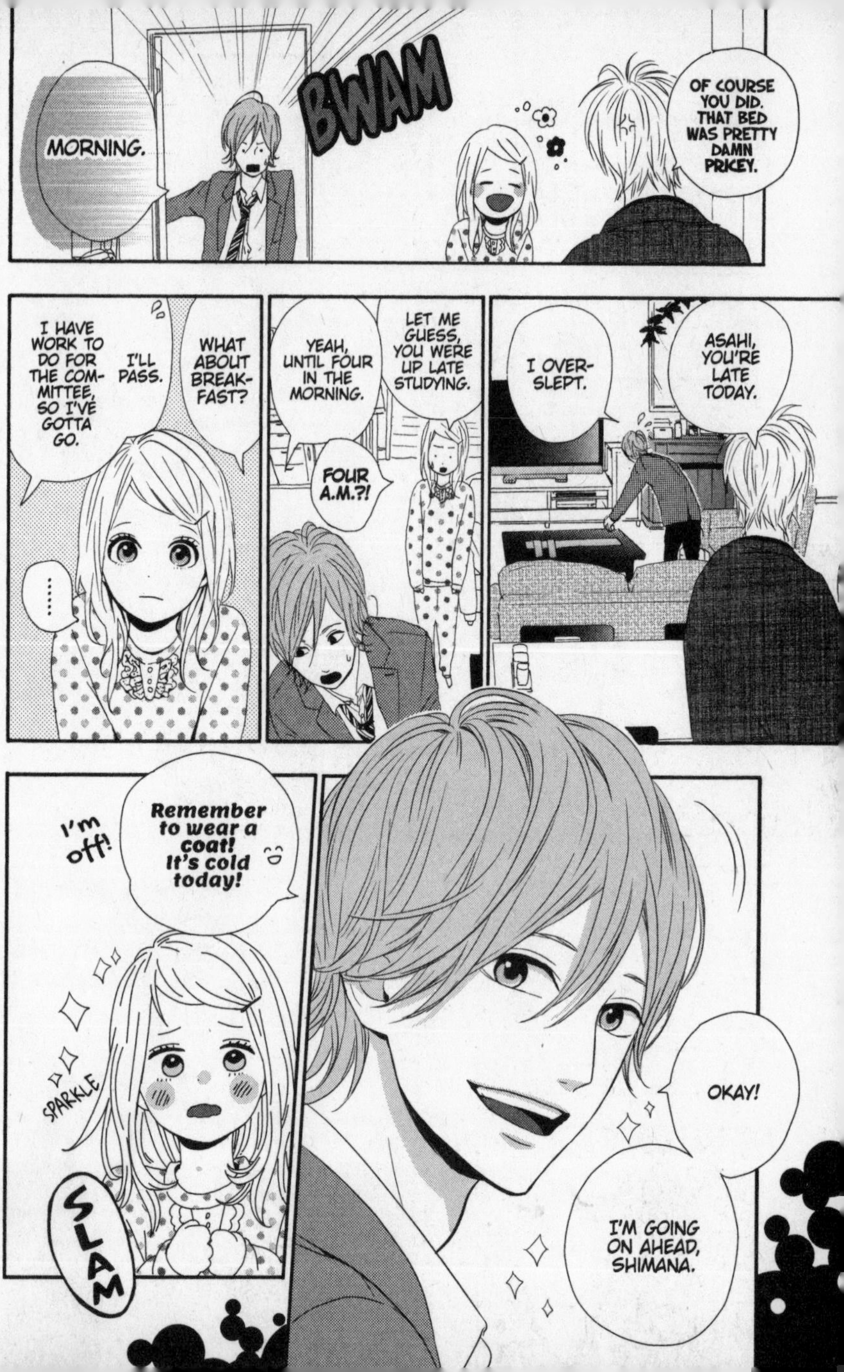
OF COURSE YOU DID. THAT BED WAS PRETTY DAMN PRICEY.
BWAM
MORNING.
ASAHI, YOU'RE LATE TODAY.
I OVER-SLEPT.
LET ME GUESS, YOU WERE UP LATE STUDYING.
YEAH, UNTIL FOUR IN THE MORNING.
FOUR A.M.?!
WHAT ABOUT BREAK-FAST?
I'LL PASS.
I HAVE WORK TO DO FOR THE COM-MITTEE, SO I'VE GOTTA GO.
......
OKAY!
I'M GOING ON AHEAD, SHIMANA.
Remember to wear a coat! It's cold today!
I'm off!
SPARKLE
SLAM

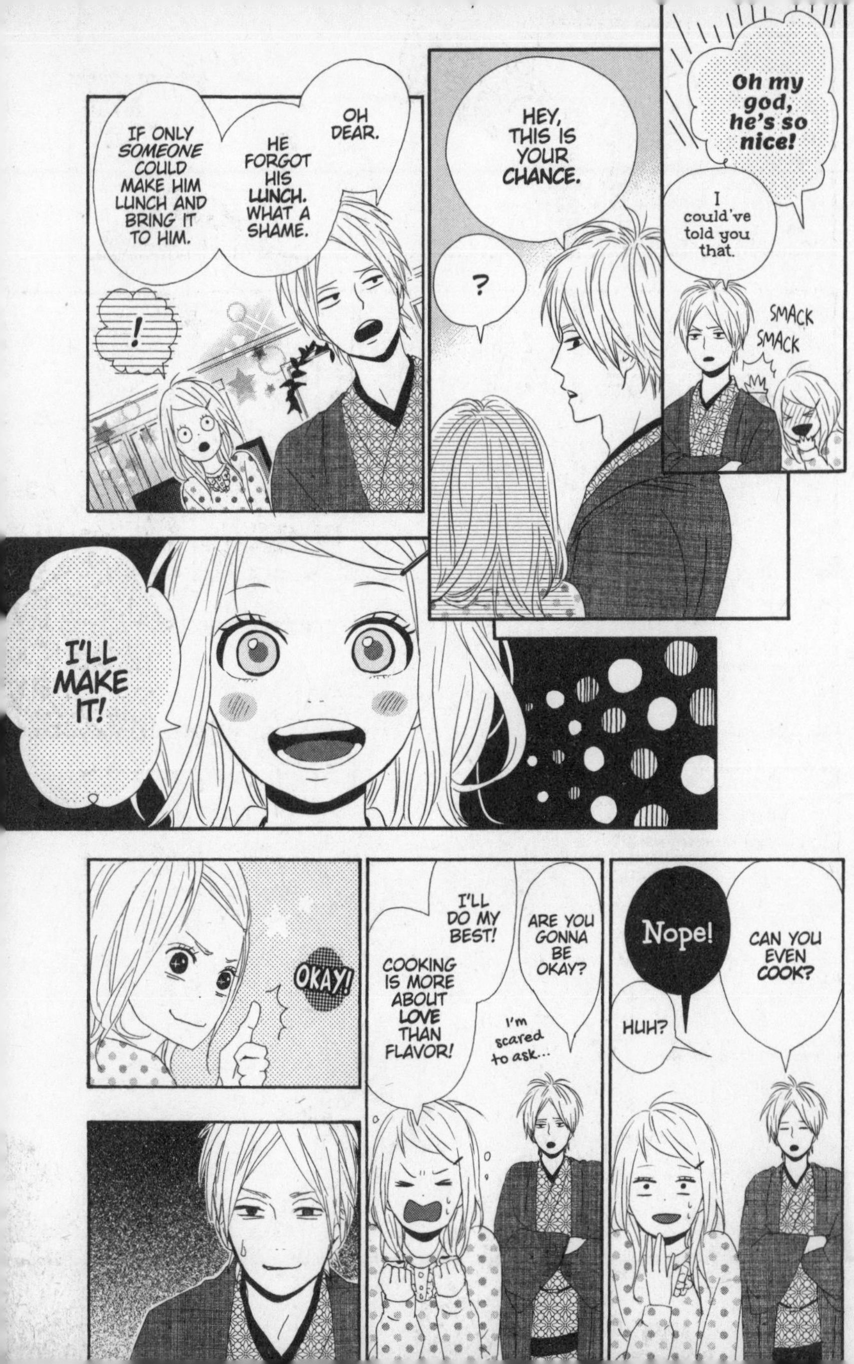
Oh my god, he's so nice!
I could've told you that.
SMACK SMACK
HEY, THIS IS YOUR CHANCE.
?
OH DEAR.
HE FORGOT HIS LUNCH. WHAT A SHAME.
IF ONLY SOMEONE COULD MAKE HIM LUNCH AND BRING IT TO HIM.
!
I'LL MAKE IT!
CAN YOU EVEN COOK?
Nope!
HUH?
ARE YOU GONNA BE OKAY?
I'm scared to ask...
I'LL DO MY BEST!
COOKING IS MORE ABOUT LOVE THAN FLAVOR!
OKAY!

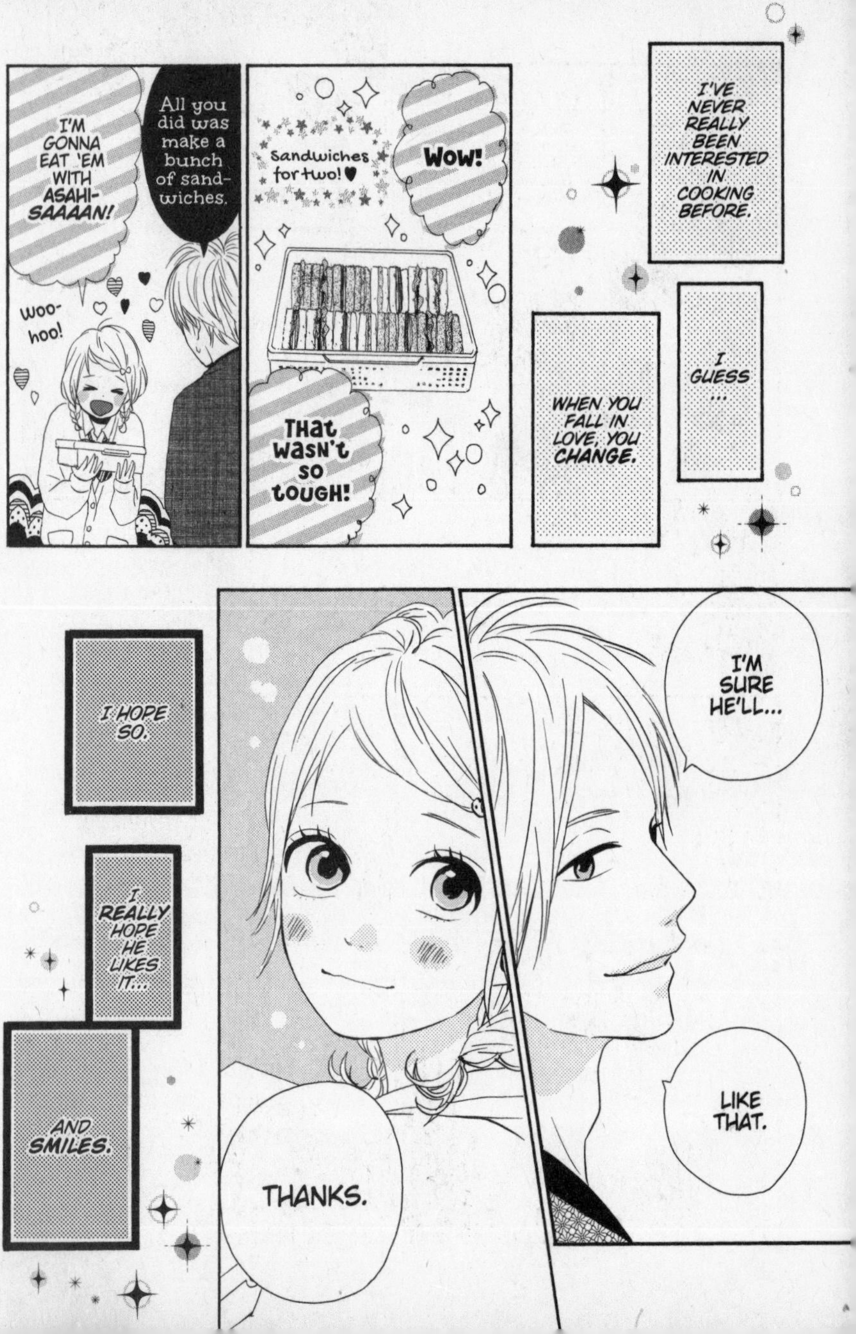
I'VE NEVER REALLY BEEN INTERESTED IN COOKING BEFORE.
I GUESS...
WHEN YOU FALL IN LOVE, YOU CHANGE.
WOW!
Sandwiches for two! ♥
THAT WASN'T SO TOUGH!
All you did was make a bunch of sandwiches.
I'M GONNA EAT 'EM WITH ASAHI-SAAAAN!
Woo-hoo!
I'M SURE HE'LL...
LIKE THAT.
THANKS.
I HOPE SO.
I REALLY HOPE HE LIKES IT...
AND SMILES.

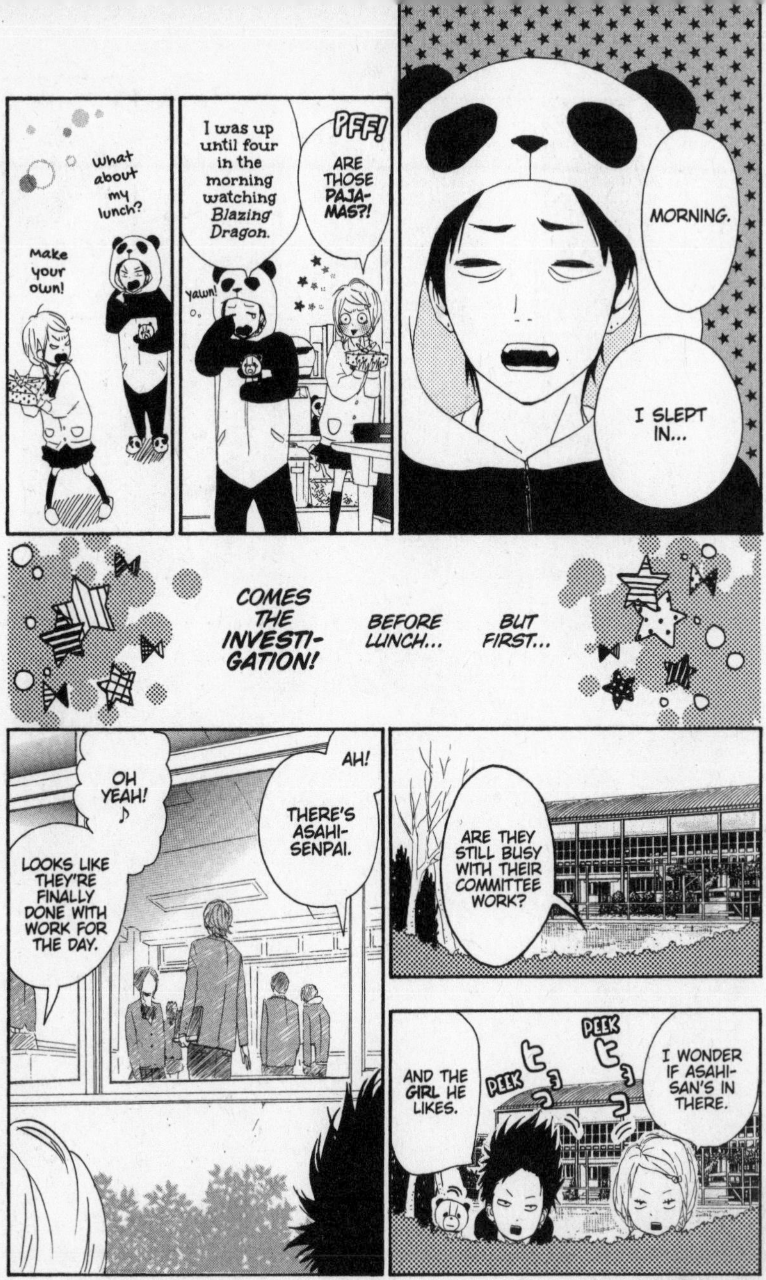
MORNING.
I SLEPT IN...
PFF!
ARE THOSE PAJAMAS?!
I was up until four in the morning watching *Blazing Dragon*.
yawn!
what about my lunch?
Make your own!
BUT FIRST...
BEFORE LUNCH...
COMES THE INVESTIGATION!
ARE THEY STILL BUSY WITH THEIR COMMITTEE WORK?
I WONDER IF ASAHI-SAN'S IN THERE.
PEEK
PEEK
AND THE GIRL HE LIKES.
AH!
THERE'S ASAHI-SENPAI.
OH YEAH! ♪
LOOKS LIKE THEY'RE FINALLY DONE WITH WORK FOR THE DAY.

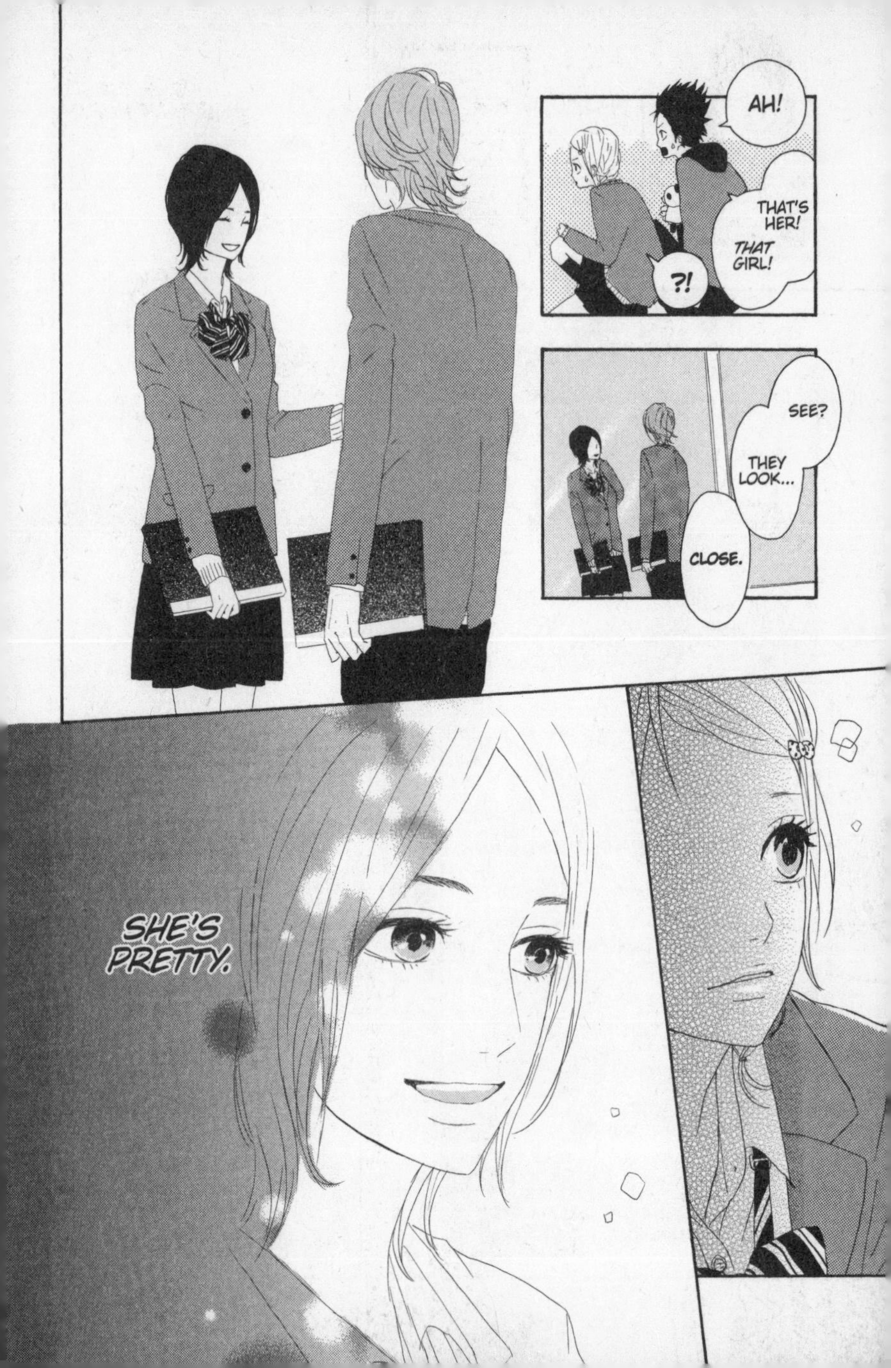
AH!
THAT'S HER! THAT GIRL!
?!
SEE?
THEY LOOK...
CLOSE.
SHE'S PRETTY.

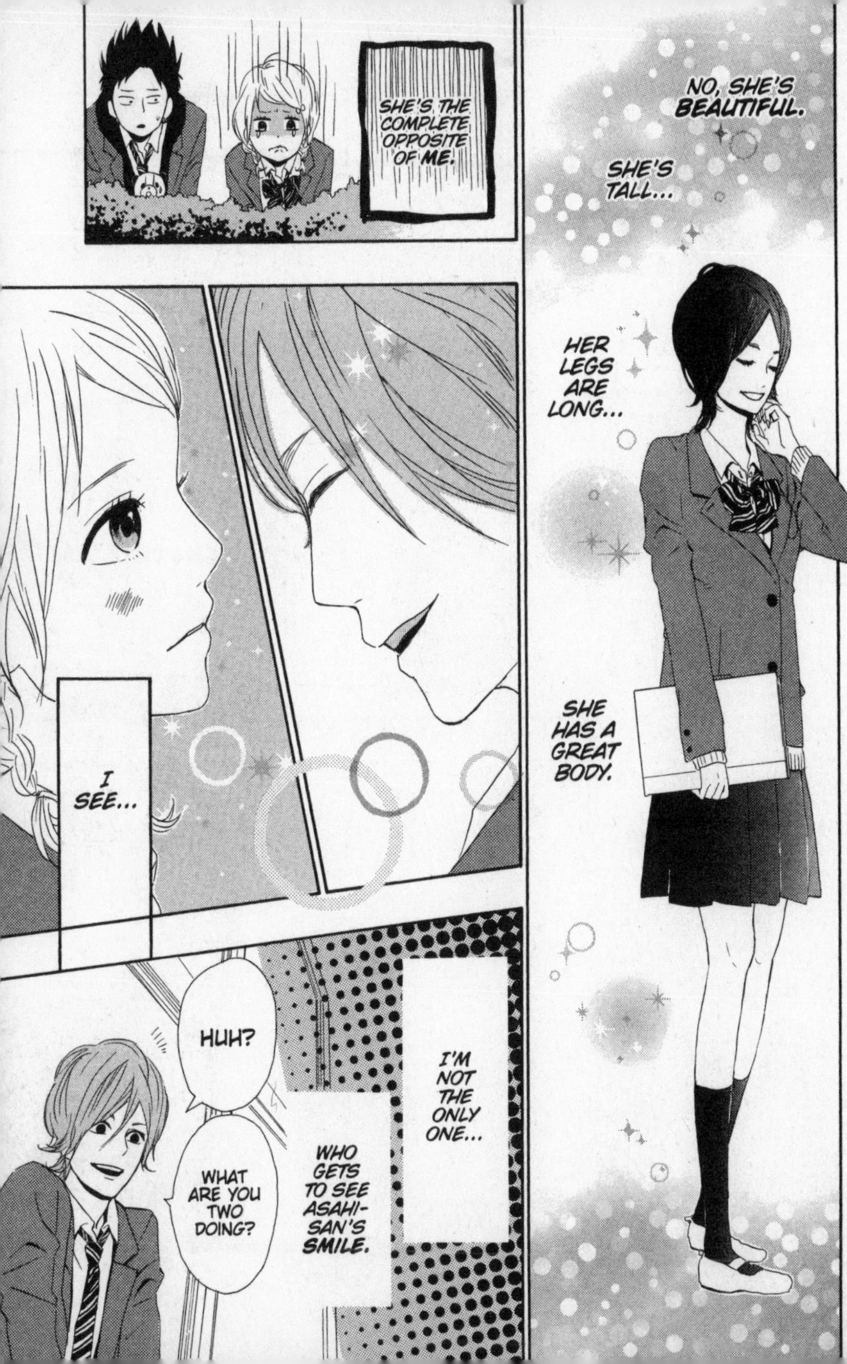

NO, SHE'S BEAUTIFUL.
SHE'S TALL...
HER LEGS ARE LONG...
SHE HAS A GREAT BODY.
SHE'S THE COMPLETE OPPOSITE OF ME.
I SEE...
I'M NOT THE ONLY ONE...
WHO GETS TO SEE ASAHI-SAN'S SMILE.
HUH?
WHAT ARE YOU TWO DOING?

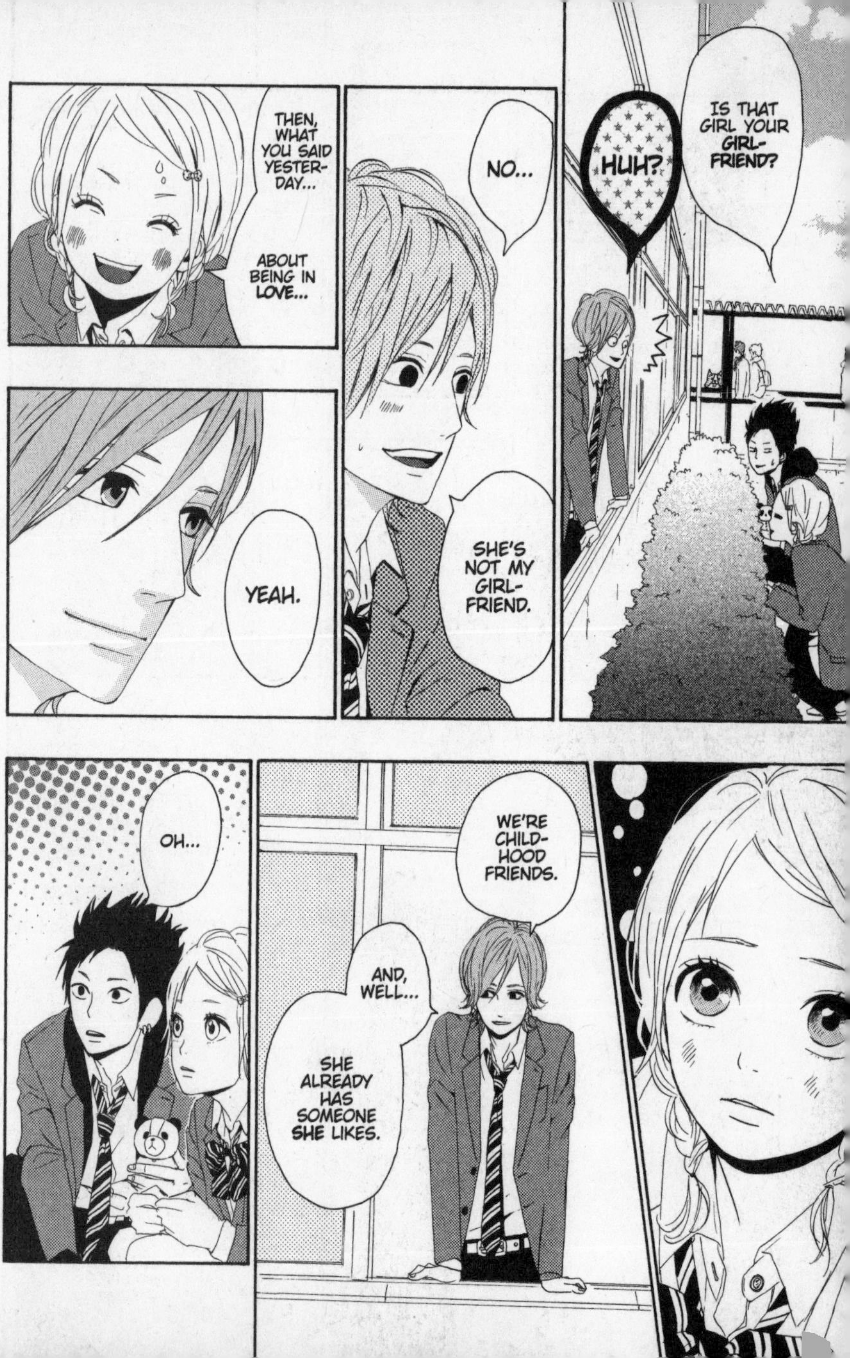
IS THAT GIRL YOUR GIRL-FRIEND?
HUH?
NO...
SHE'S NOT MY GIRL-FRIEND.
THEN, WHAT YOU SAID YESTER-DAY...
ABOUT BEING IN LOVE...
YEAH.
WE'RE CHILD-HOOD FRIENDS.
AND, WELL...
SHE ALREADY HAS SOMEONE SHE LIKES.
OH...

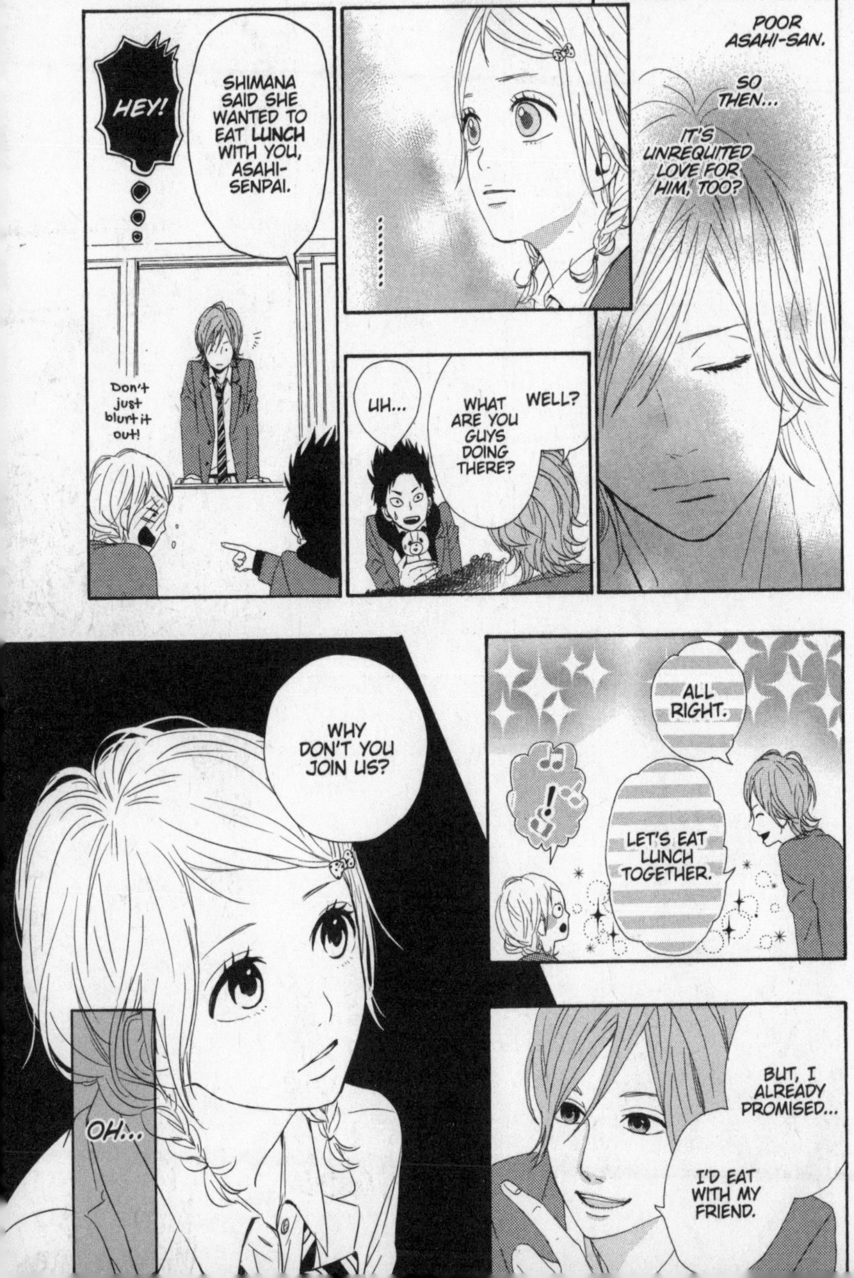
POOR ASAHI-SAN.
SO THEN...
IT'S UNREQUITED LOVE FOR HIM, TOO?
......
WELL?
WHAT ARE YOU GUYS DOING THERE?
UH...
SHIMANA SAID SHE WANTED TO EAT LUNCH WITH YOU, ASAHI-SENPAI.
HEY!
Don't just blurt it out!
ALL RIGHT.
LET'S EAT LUNCH TOGETHER.
!
BUT, I ALREADY PROMISED...
I'D EAT WITH MY FRIEND.
WHY DON'T YOU JOIN US?
OH...

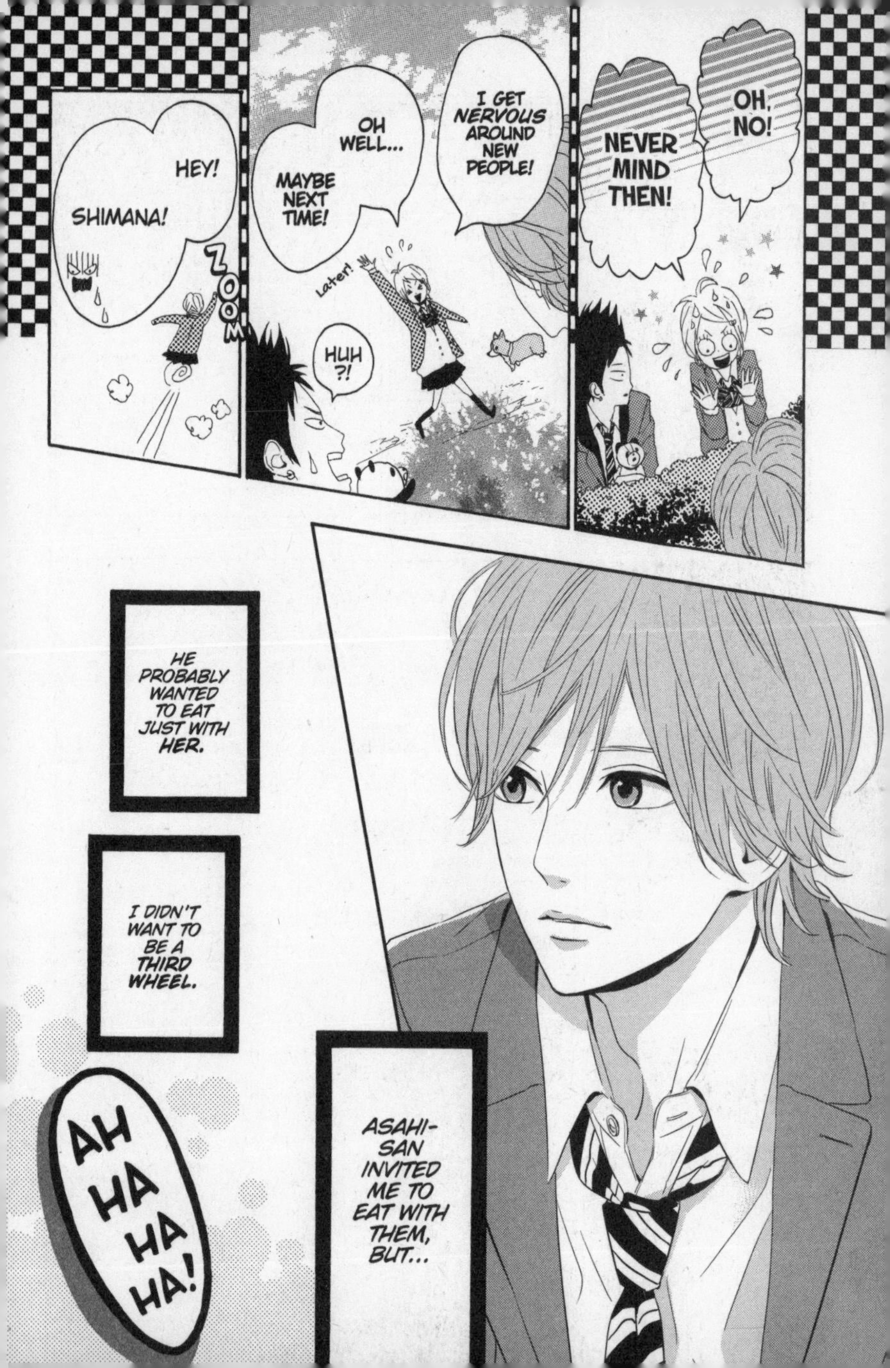
OH, NO!
NEVER MIND THEN!
I GET NERVOUS AROUND NEW PEOPLE!
OH WELL... MAYBE NEXT TIME!
Later!
HUH ?!
HEY! SHIMANA!
ZOOM
ASAHI-SAN INVITED ME TO EAT WITH THEM, BUT...
I DIDN'T WANT TO BE A THIRD WHEEL.
HE PROBABLY WANTED TO EAT JUST WITH HER.
AH HA HA HA!

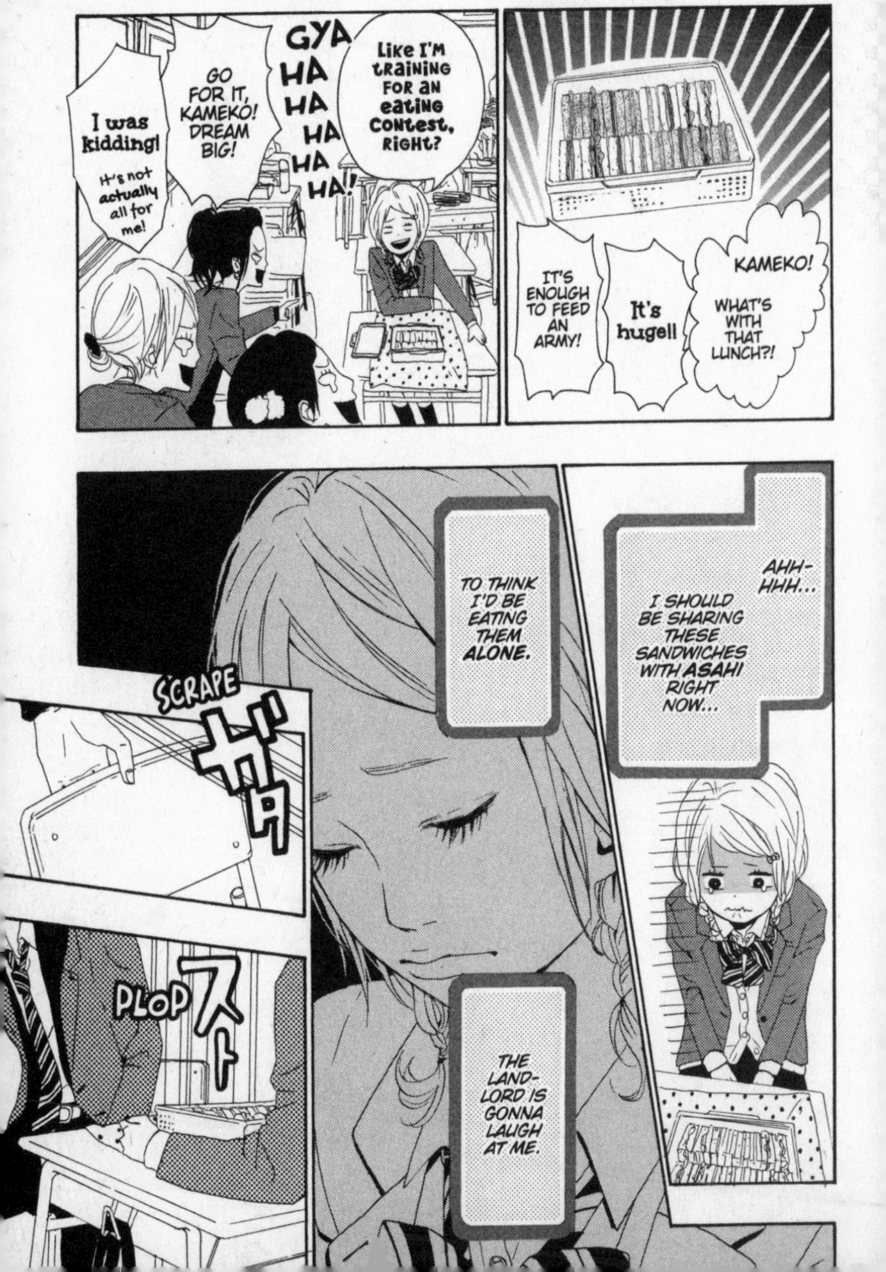
KAMEKO! WHAT'S WITH THAT LUNCH?!
It's huge!!
IT'S ENOUGH TO FEED AN ARMY!
Like I'M training for an eating Contest, Right?
GYA HA HA HA HA HA!
GO FOR IT, KAMEKO! DREAM BIG!
I was kidding!
It's not actually all for me!
AHH-HHH...
I SHOULD BE SHARING THESE SANDWICHES WITH ASAHI RIGHT NOW...
TO THINK I'D BE EATING THEM ALONE.
THE LAND-LORD IS GONNA LAUGH AT ME.
SCRAPE ガタ
PLOP スト

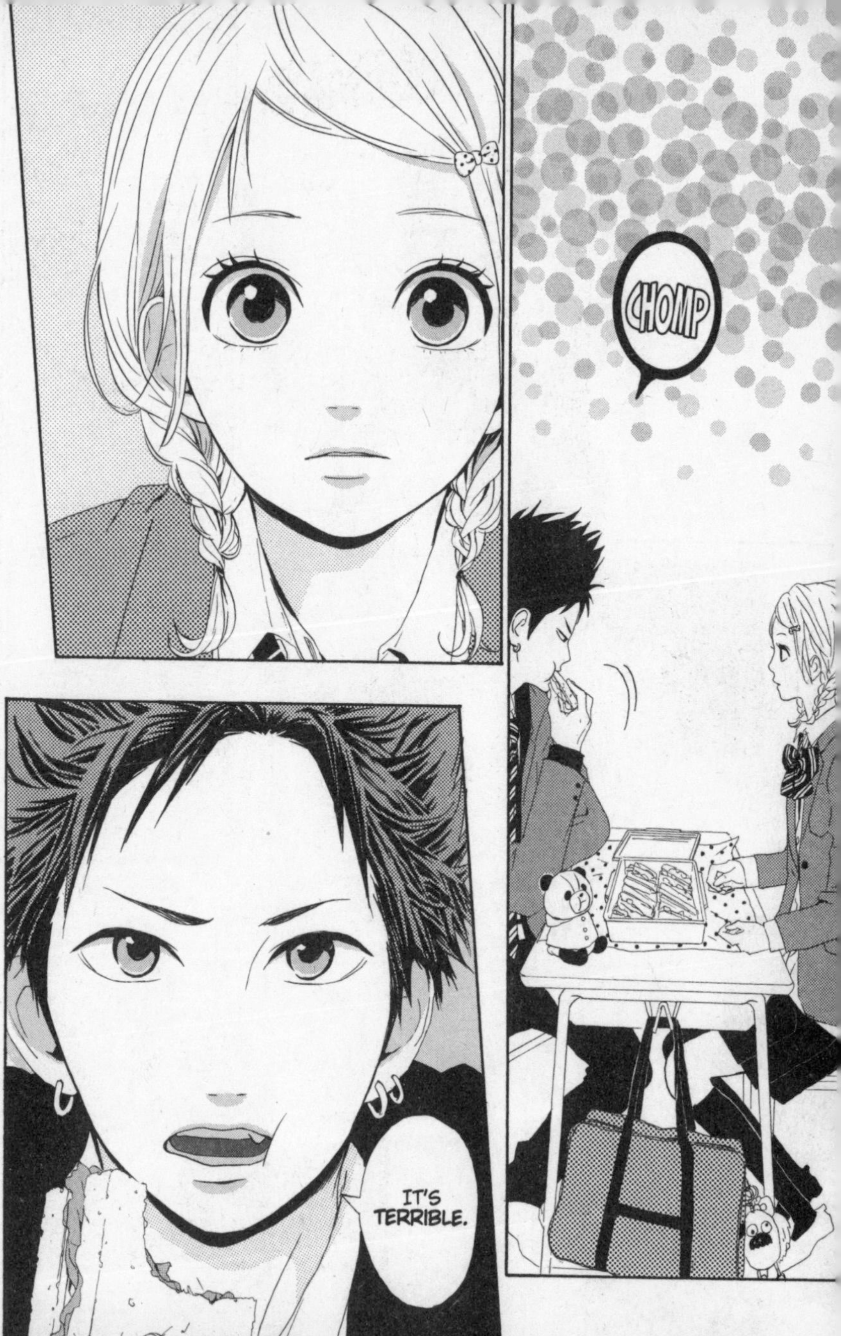
CHOMP
IT'S TERRIBLE.

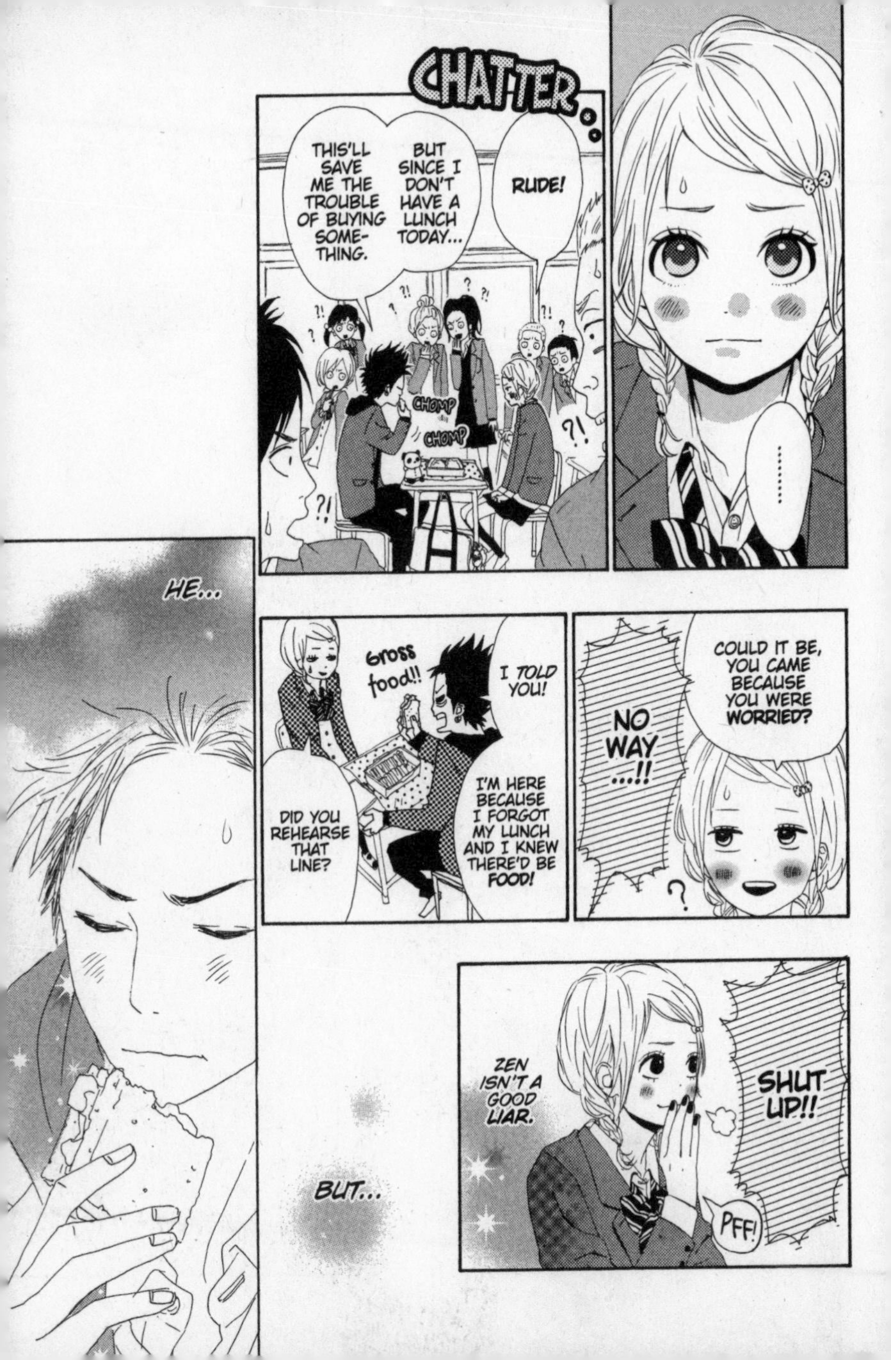
......
CHATTER...
RUDE!
BUT SINCE I DON'T HAVE A LUNCH TODAY...
THIS'LL SAVE ME THE TROUBLE OF BUYING SOME-THING.
?!
?
?!
?
?!
?!
?
CHOMP
CHOMP
?!
?!
COULD IT BE, YOU CAME BECAUSE YOU WERE WORRIED?
NO WAY ...!!
?
I TOLD YOU!
I'M HERE BECAUSE I FORGOT MY LUNCH AND I KNEW THERE'D BE FOOD!
Gross food!!
DID YOU REHEARSE THAT LINE?
SHUT UP!!
PFF!
ZEN ISN'T A GOOD LIAR.
HE...
BUT...

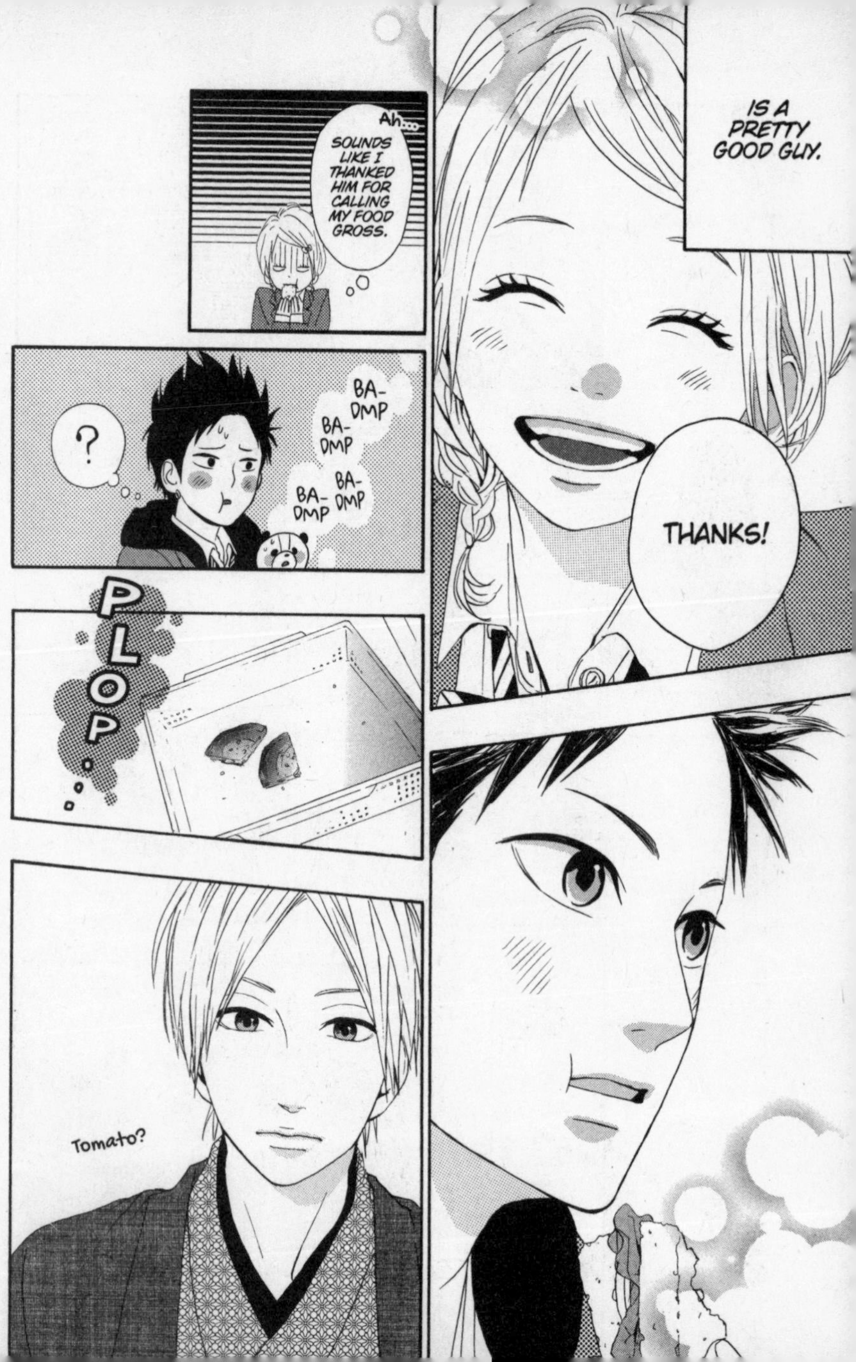
IS A PRETTY GOOD GUY.
THANKS!
Ah... SOUNDS LIKE I THANKED HIM FOR CALLING MY FOOD GROSS.
?
BA-DMP BA-DMP
BA-DMP BA-DMP
PLOP
Tomato?

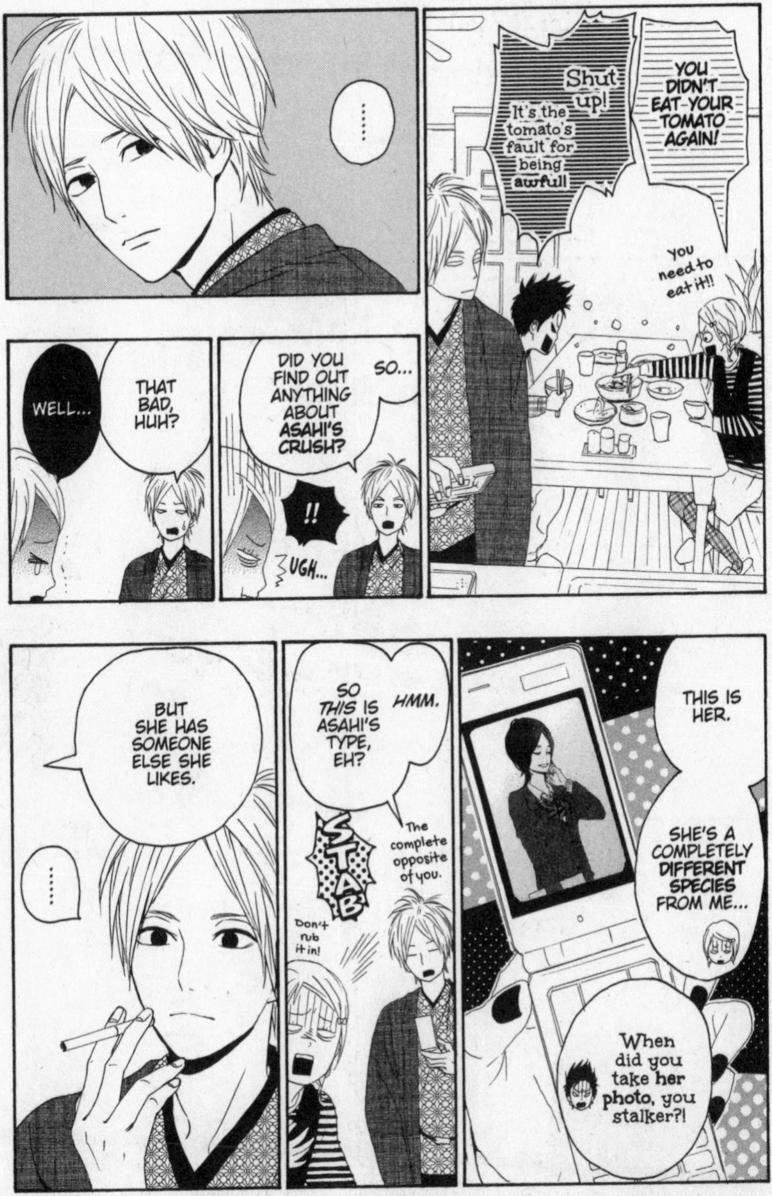
YOU DIDN'T EAT YOUR TOMATO AGAIN!
Shut up! It's the tomato's fault for being awful!
You need to eat it!!
......
SO...
DID YOU FIND OUT ANYTHING ABOUT ASAHI'S CRUSH?
!!
UGH...
THAT BAD, HUH?
WELL...
THIS IS HER.
SHE'S A COMPLETELY DIFFERENT SPECIES FROM ME...
When did you take her photo, you stalker?!
HMM.
SO *THIS* IS ASAHI'S TYPE, EH?
STAB
The complete opposite of you.
Don't rub it in!
BUT SHE HAS SOMEONE ELSE SHE LIKES.
......

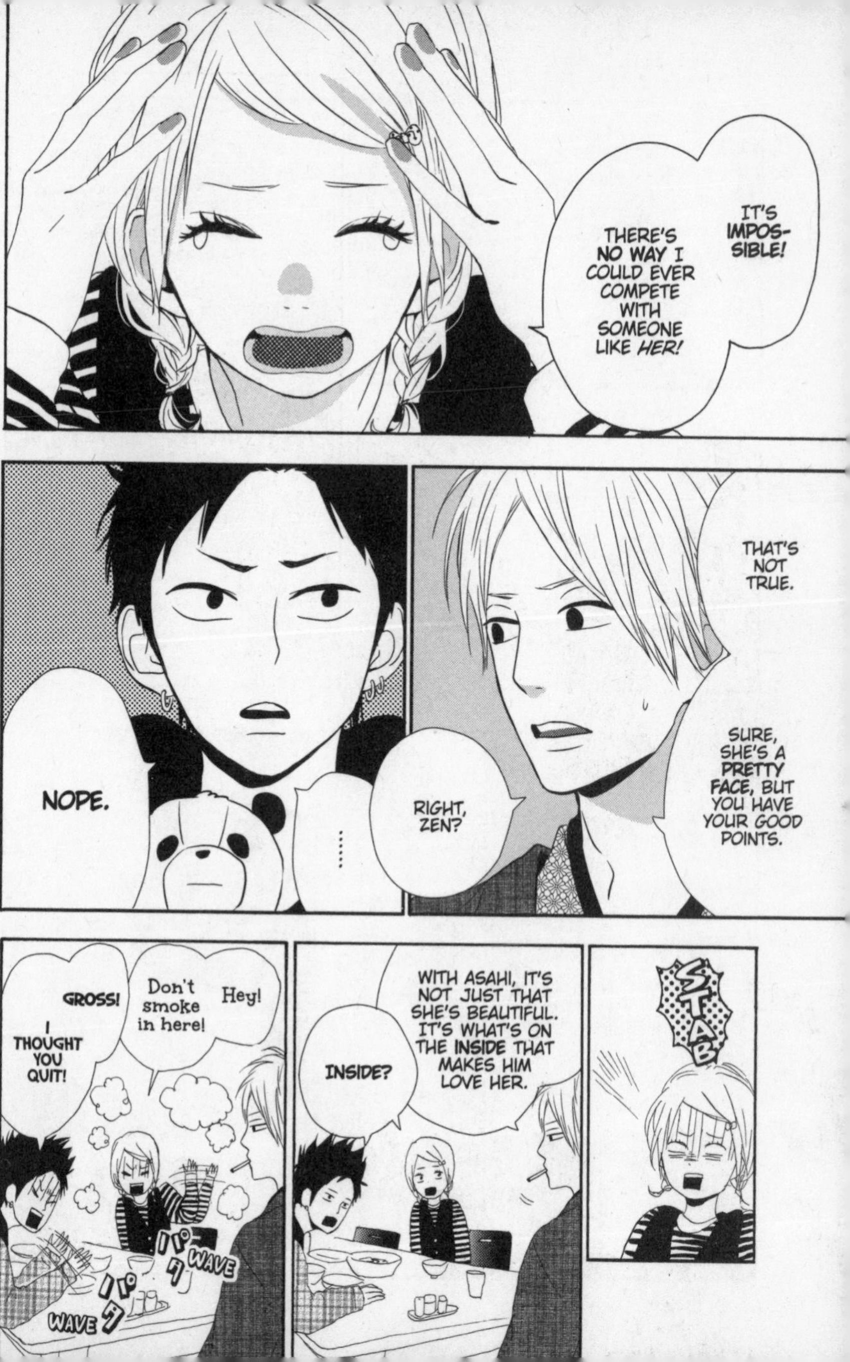
IT'S IMPOS-SIBLE!
THERE'S NO WAY I COULD EVER COMPETE WITH SOMEONE LIKE HER!
THAT'S NOT TRUE.
SURE, SHE'S A PRETTY FACE, BUT YOU HAVE YOUR GOOD POINTS.
RIGHT, ZEN?
......
NOPE.
STAB
WITH ASAHI, IT'S NOT JUST THAT SHE'S BEAUTIFUL. IT'S WHAT'S ON THE INSIDE THAT MAKES HIM LOVE HER.
INSIDE?
Hey!
Don't smoke in here!
GROSS!
I THOUGHT YOU QUIT!
WAVE
WAVE

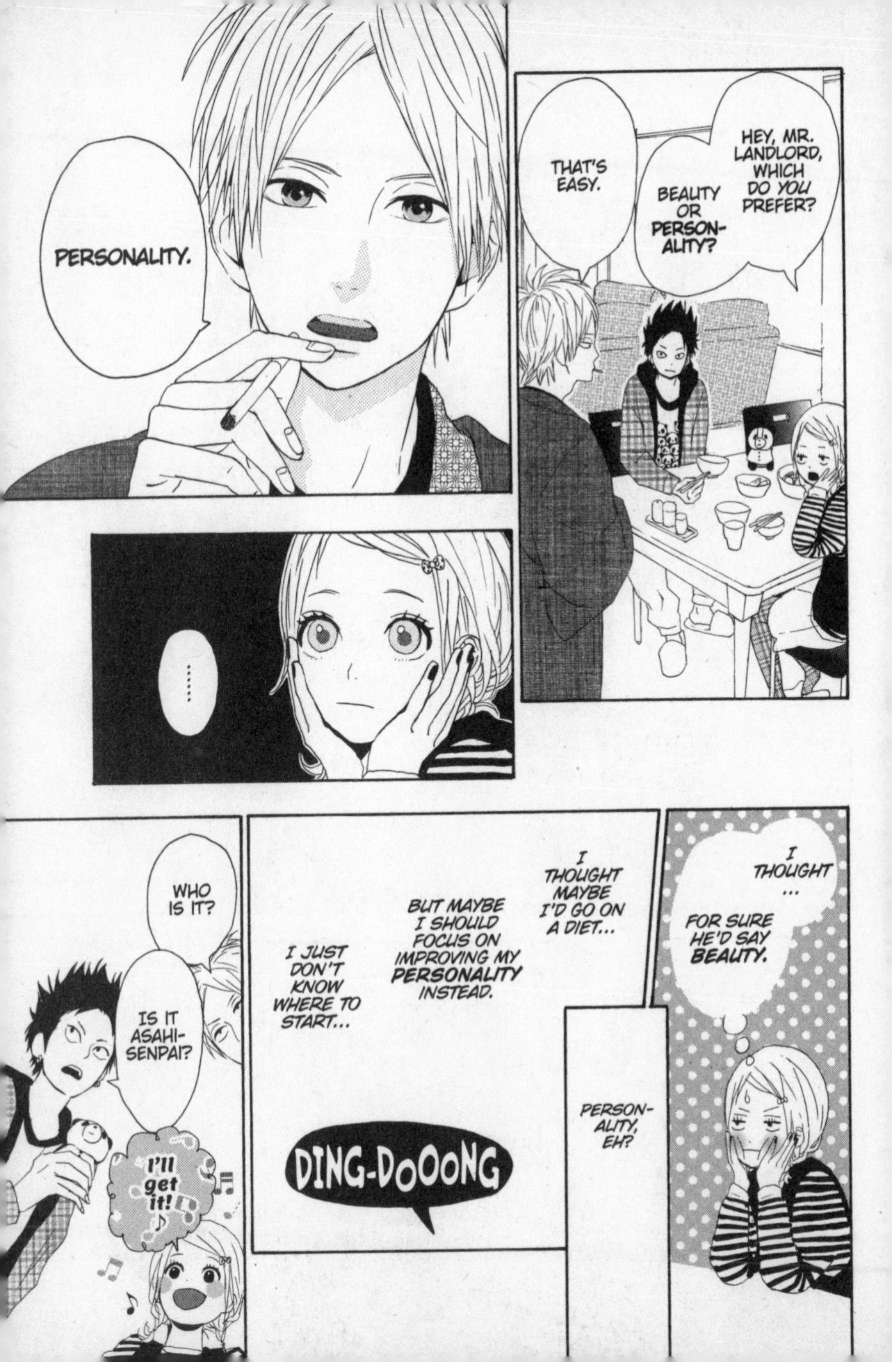
HEY, MR. LANDLORD, WHICH DO YOU PREFER?
BEAUTY OR PERSONALITY?
THAT'S EASY.
PERSONALITY.
......
I THOUGHT...
FOR SURE HE'D SAY BEAUTY.
PERSONALITY, EH?
I THOUGHT MAYBE I'D GO ON A DIET...
BUT MAYBE I SHOULD FOCUS ON IMPROVING MY PERSONALITY INSTEAD.
I JUST DON'T KNOW WHERE TO START...
DING-DOOONG
WHO IS IT?
IS IT ASAHI-SENPAI?
I'll get it!

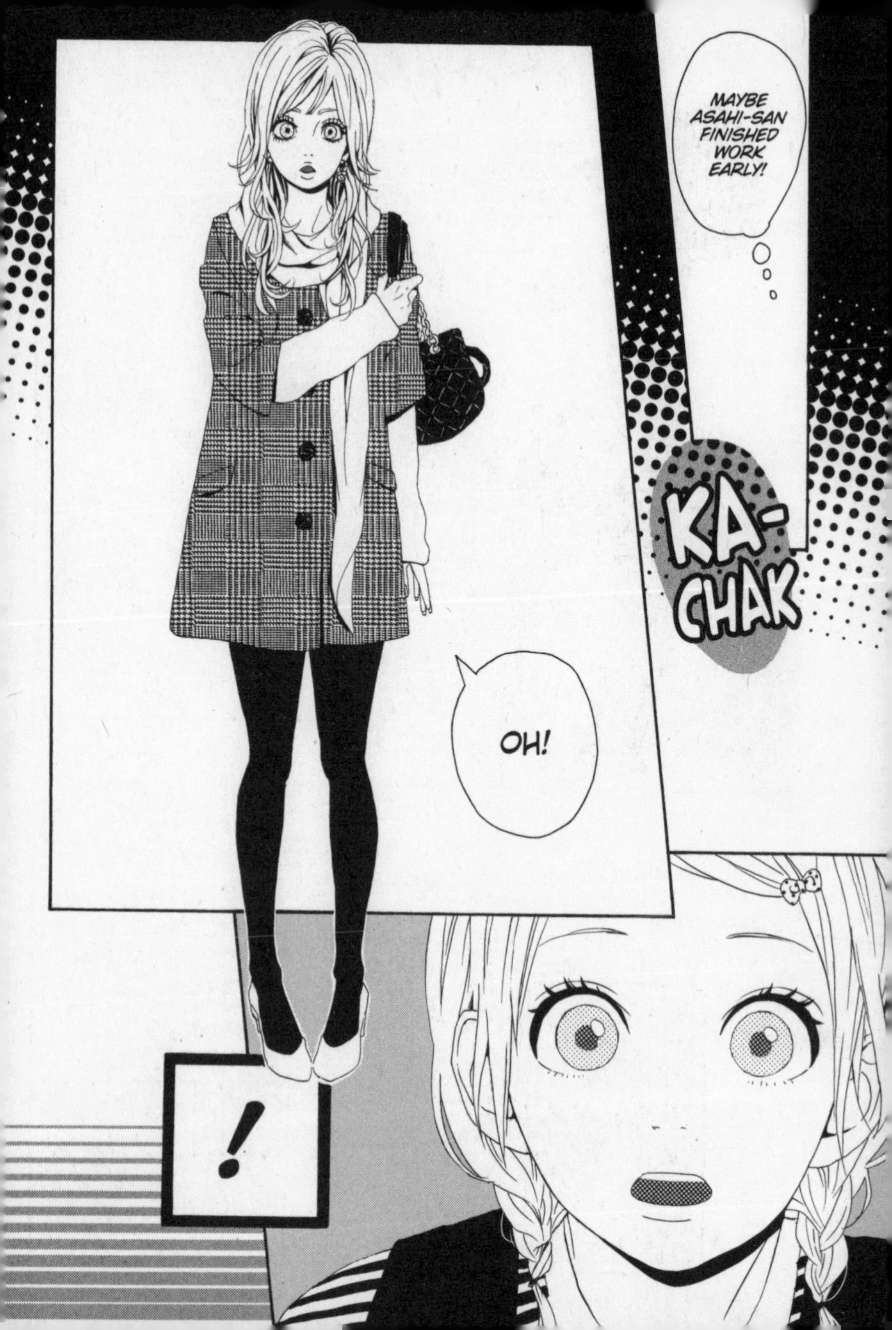
MAYBE ASAHI-SAN FINISHED WORK EARLY!
KA-CHAK
OH!
!

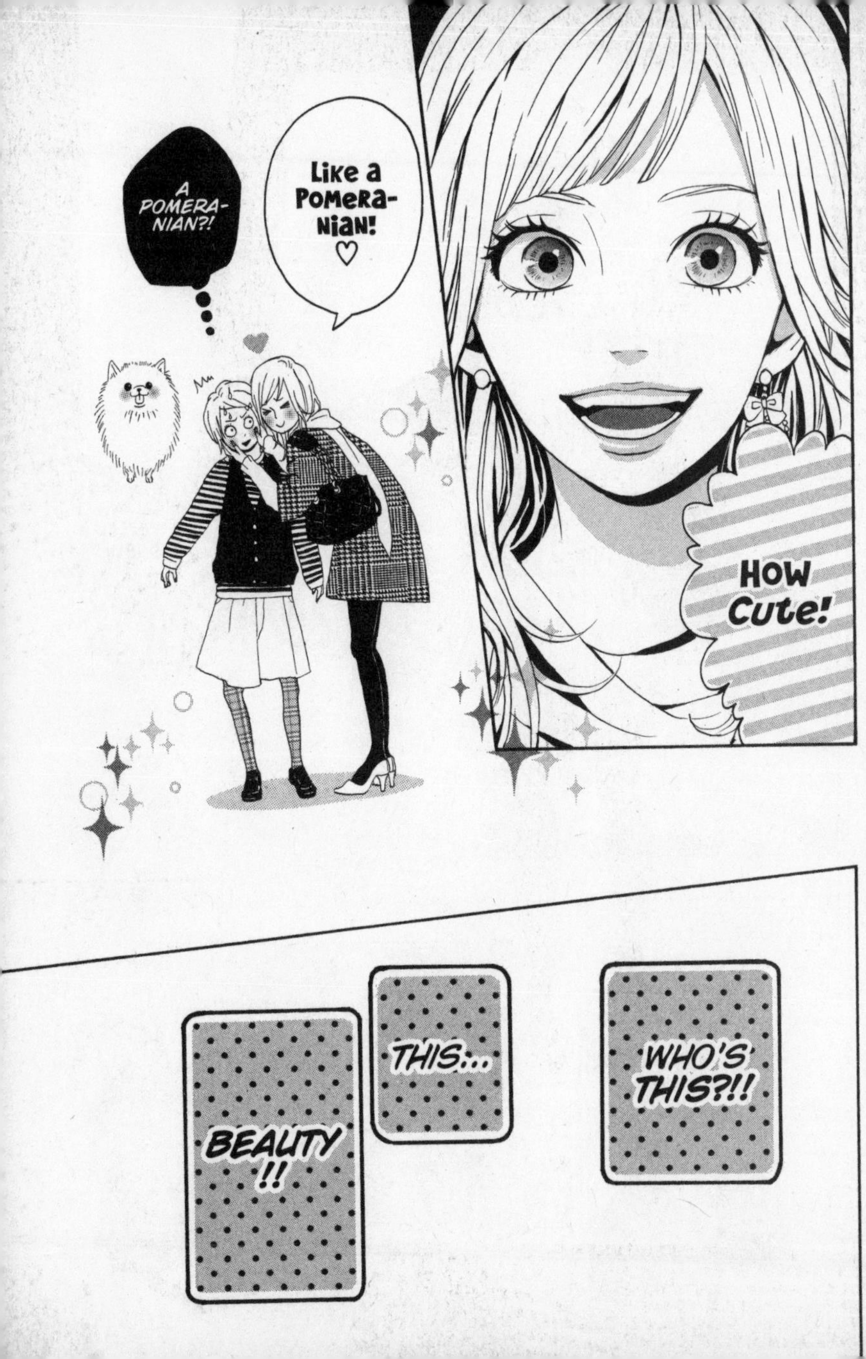
HOW Cute!
Like a POMERA-NIAN! ♡
A POMERA-NIAN?!
WHO'S THIS?!!
THIS...
BEAUTY !!

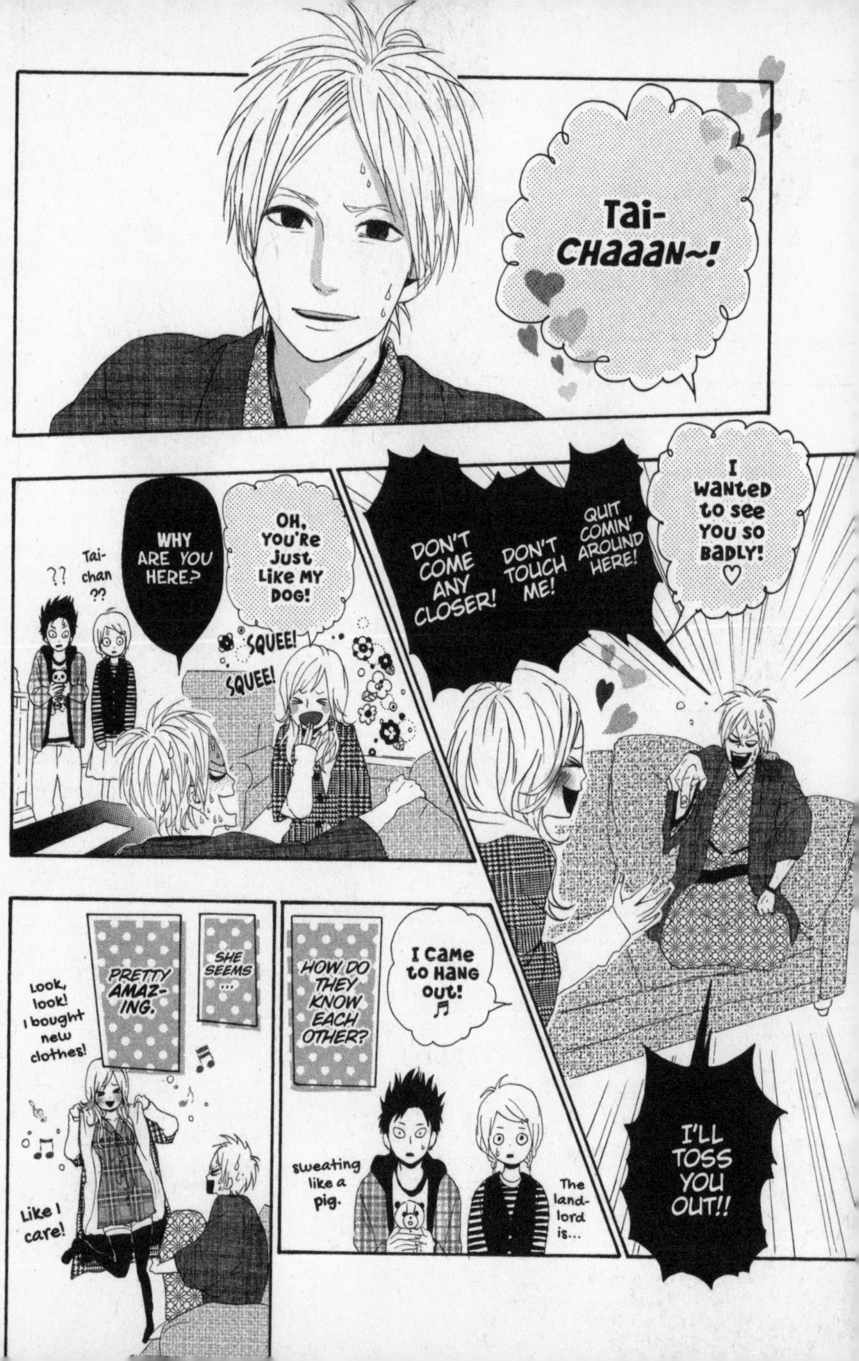
Tai-CHaaan~!
I wanted to see you so badly! ♡
QUIT COMIN' AROUND HERE!
DON'T TOUCH ME!
DON'T COME ANY CLOSER!
I'LL TOSS YOU OUT!!
OH, You're Just Like MY DOG!
SQUEE!
SQUEE!
WHY ARE YOU HERE?
Tai-chan ??
??
I Came to HANG out! ♬
HOW DO THEY KNOW EACH OTHER?
The land-lord is...
sweating like a pig.
SHE SEEMS ...
PRETTY AMAZ-ING.
Look, look! I bought new clothes!
Like I care!

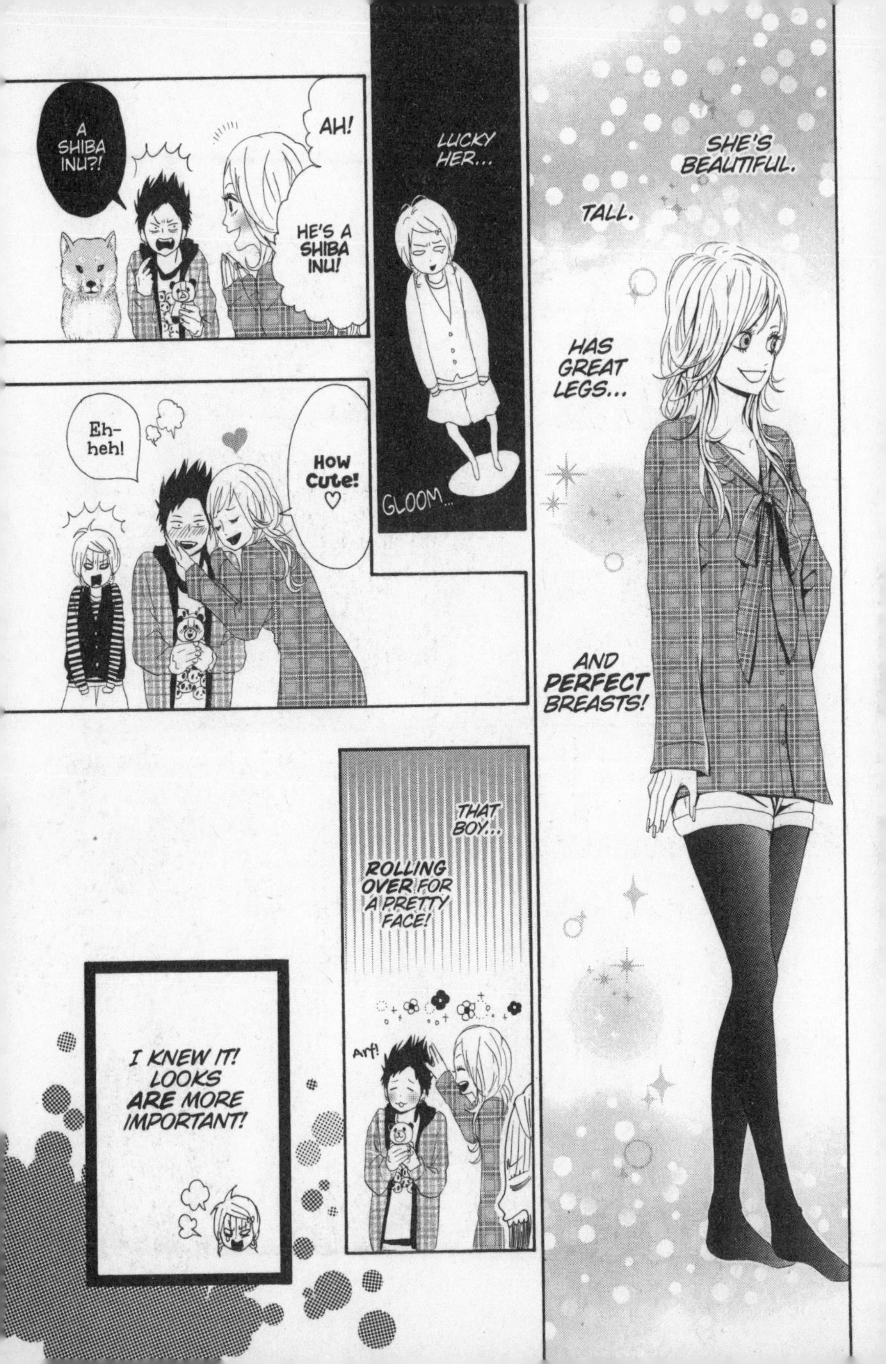
SHE'S BEAUTIFUL.
TALL.
HAS GREAT LEGS...
AND PERFECT BREASTS!
LUCKY HER...
GLOOM...
AH!
HE'S A SHIBA INU!
A SHIBA INU?!
HOW Cute! ♡
Eh-heh!
THAT BOY...
ROLLING OVER FOR A PRETTY FACE!
Arf!
I KNEW IT! LOOKS ARE MORE IMPORTANT!

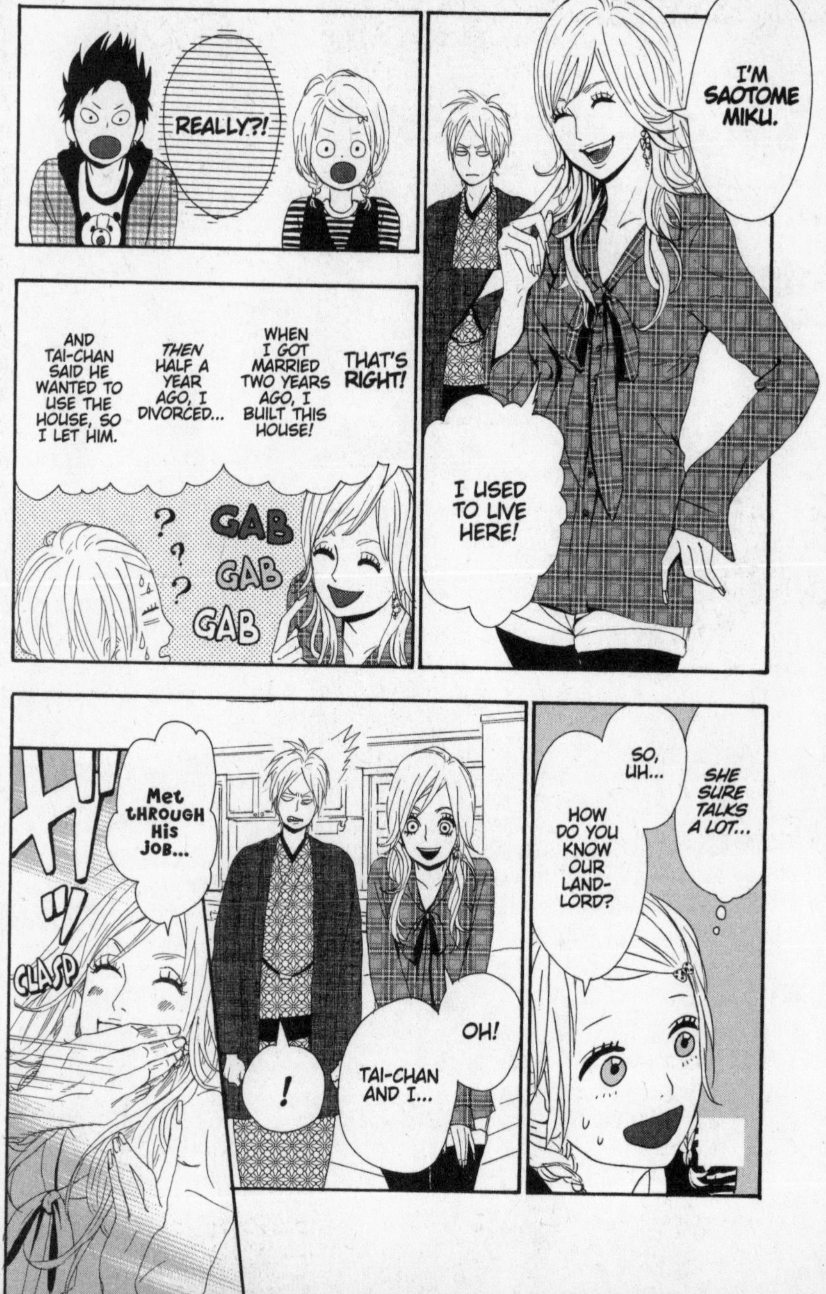
I'M SAOTOME MIKU.
I USED TO LIVE HERE!
REALLY?!
THAT'S RIGHT!
WHEN I GOT MARRIED TWO YEARS AGO, I BUILT THIS HOUSE!
THEN HALF A YEAR AGO, I DIVORCED...
AND TAI-CHAN SAID HE WANTED TO USE THE HOUSE, SO I LET HIM.
GAB
GAB
GAB
? ? ?
SHE SURE TALKS A LOT...
SO, UH...
HOW DO YOU KNOW OUR LANDLORD?
OH!
TAI-CHAN AND I...
!
Met THROUGH His JOB...
CLASP

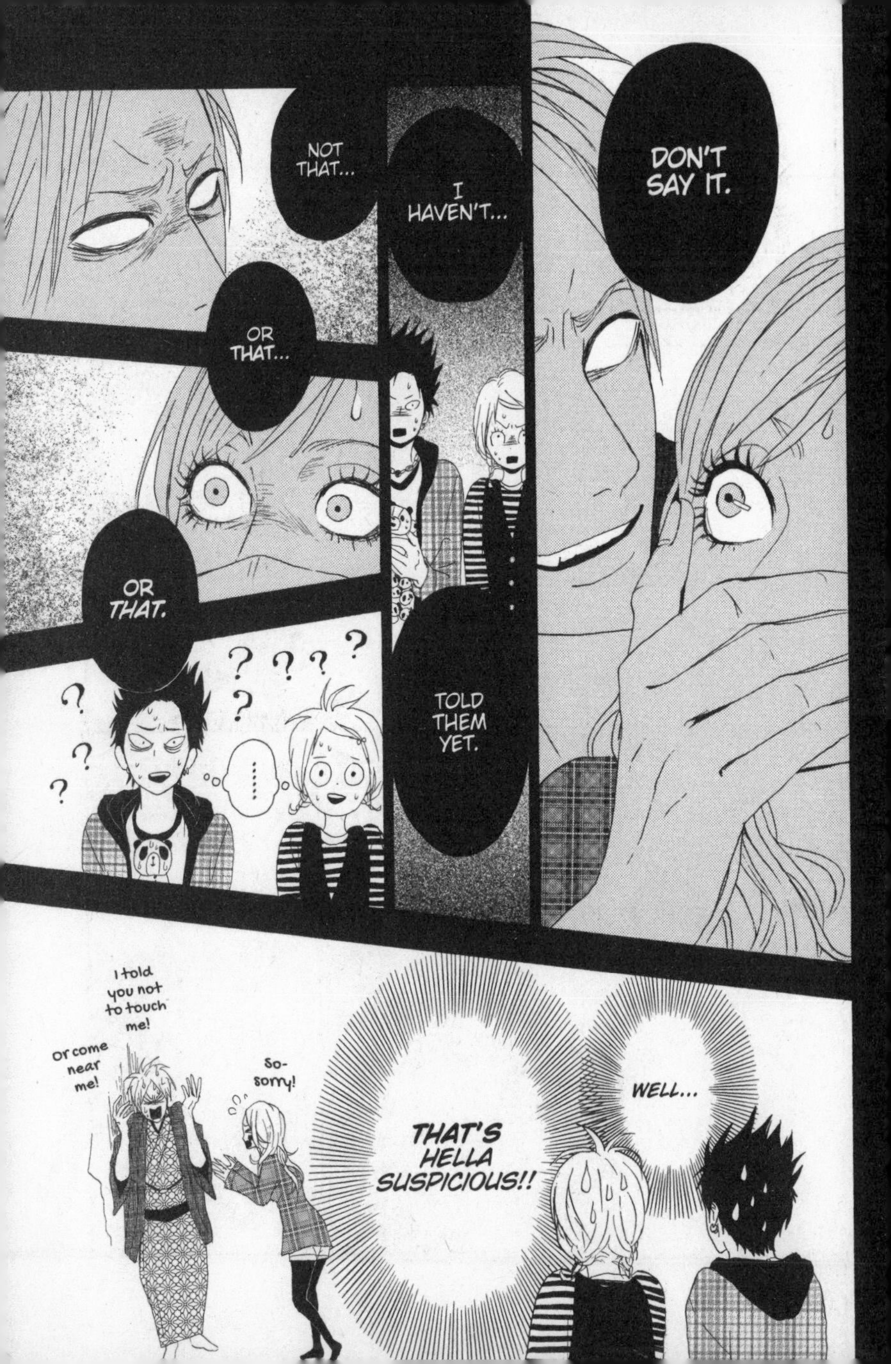
DON'T SAY IT.
I HAVEN'T...
TOLD THEM YET.
NOT THAT...
OR THAT...
OR *THAT*.
......
WELL...
THAT'S HELLA SUSPICIOUS!!
So-sorry!
I told you not to touch me!
Or come near me!

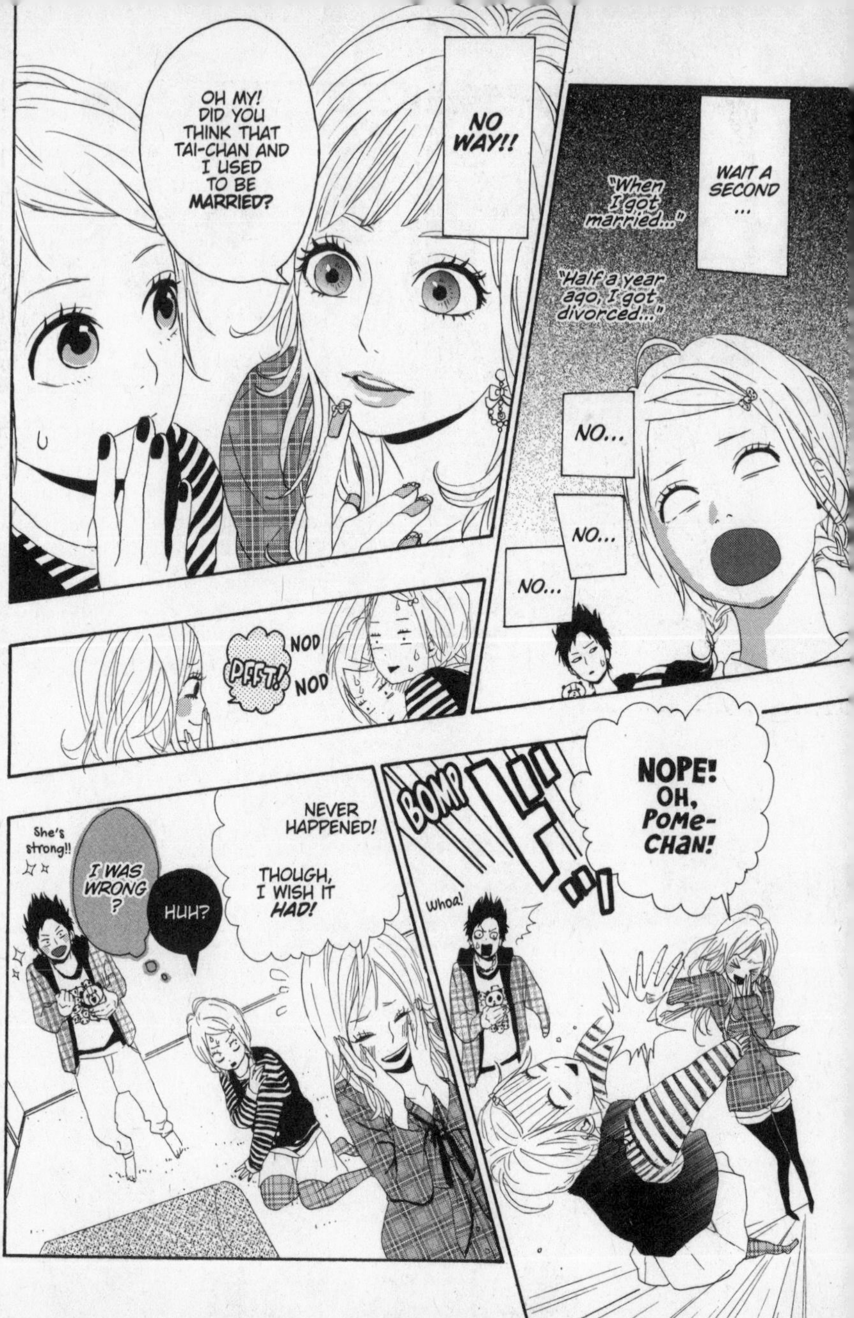
WAIT A SECOND ...
"When I got married..."
"Half a year ago, I got divorced..."
NO...
NO...
NO...
NO WAY!!
OH MY! DID YOU THINK THAT TAI-CHAN AND I USED TO BE MARRIED?
NOD
NOD
PFFT!
NOPE! OH, POME-CHAN!
BOMP
Whoa!
NEVER HAPPENED!
THOUGH, I WISH IT HAD!
HUH?
I WAS WRONG?
She's strong!!

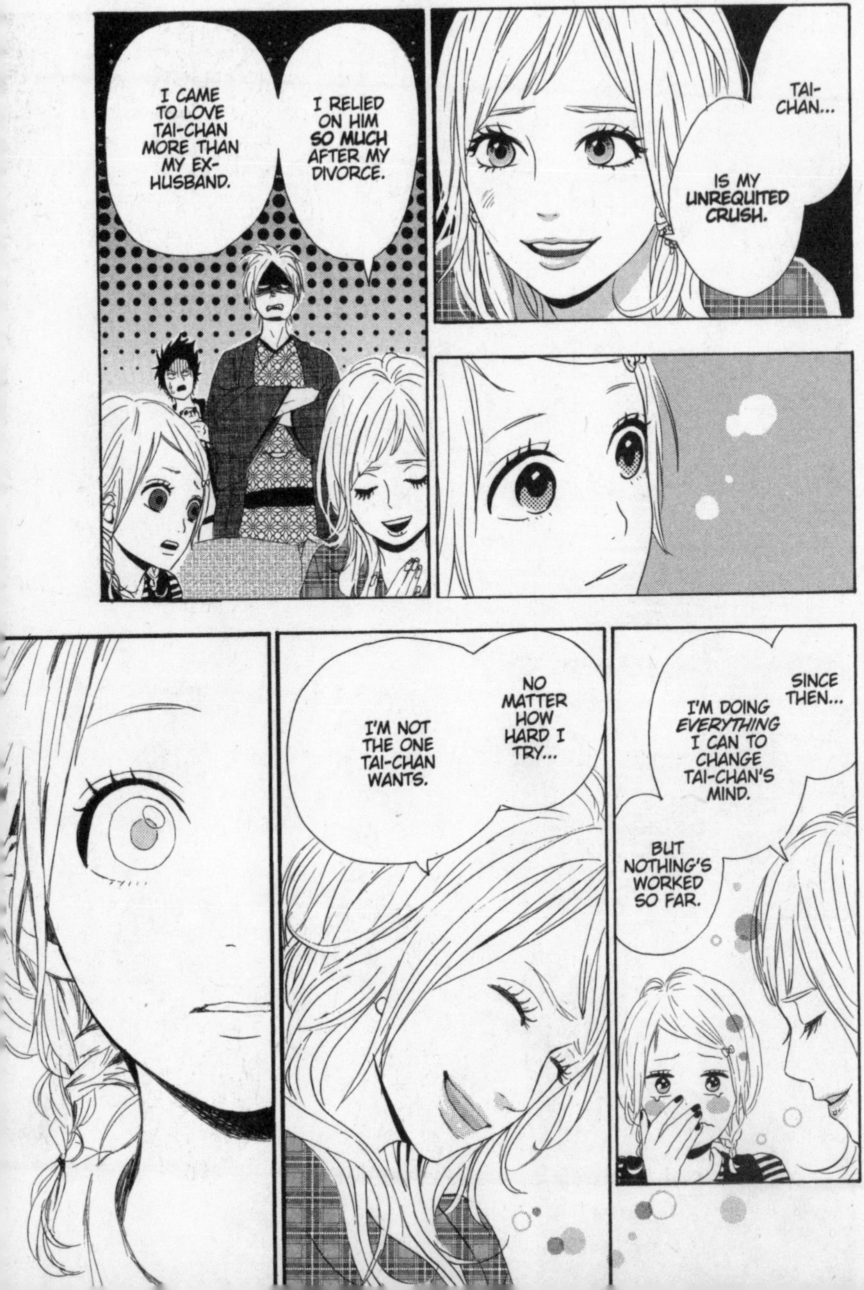
TAI-CHAN...
IS MY UNREQUITED CRUSH.
I RELIED ON HIM SO MUCH AFTER MY DIVORCE.
I CAME TO LOVE TAI-CHAN MORE THAN MY EX-HUSBAND.
SINCE THEN...
I'M DOING *EVERYTHING* I CAN TO CHANGE TAI-CHAN'S MIND.
BUT NOTHING'S WORKED SO FAR.
NO MATTER HOW HARD I TRY...
I'M NOT THE ONE TAI-CHAN WANTS.

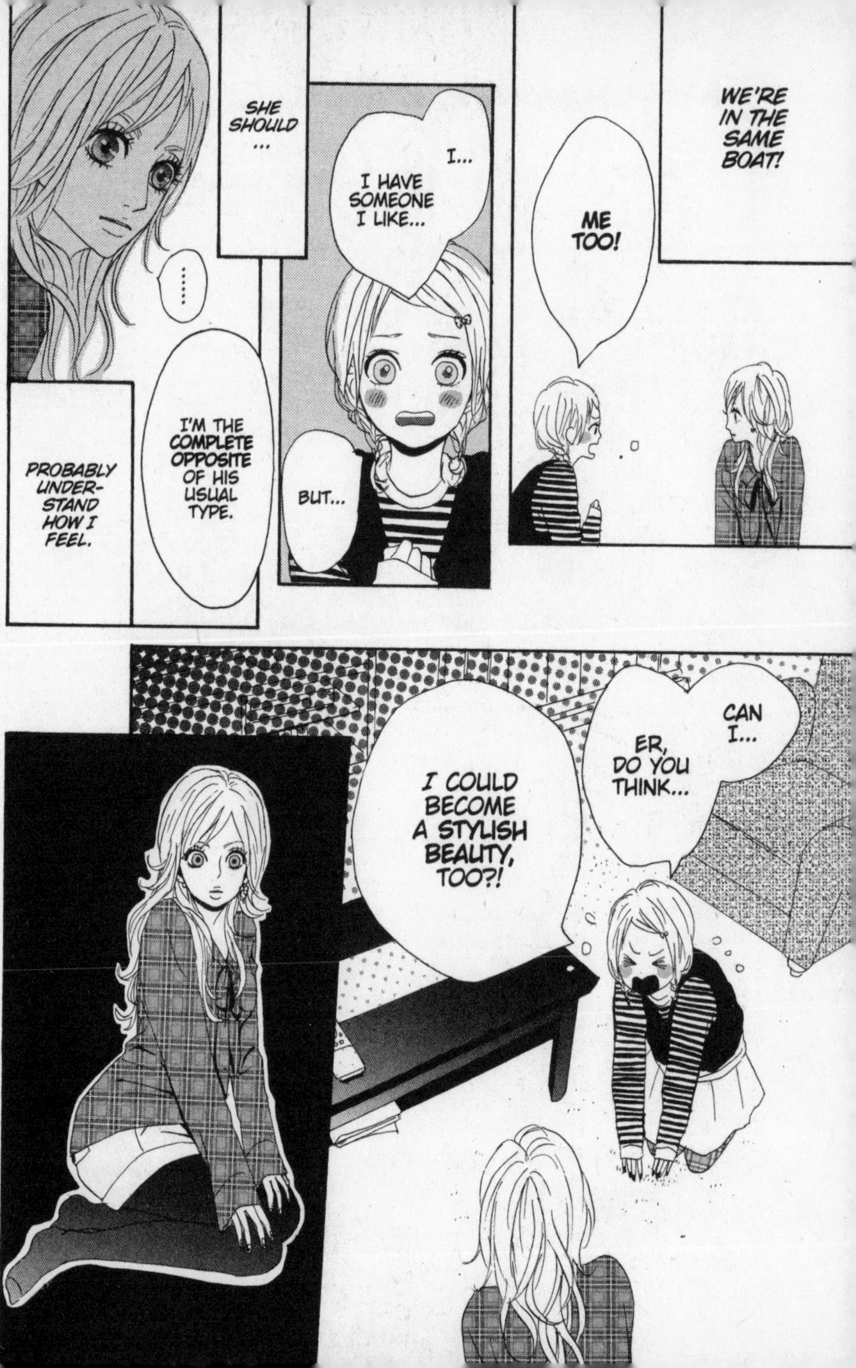
WE'RE IN THE SAME BOAT!
ME TOO!
I... I HAVE SOMEONE I LIKE...
BUT...
SHE SHOULD ...
......
I'M THE COMPLETE OPPOSITE OF HIS USUAL TYPE.
PROBABLY UNDER-STAND HOW I FEEL.
CAN I... ER, DO YOU THINK...
I COULD BECOME A STYLISH BEAUTY, TOO?!

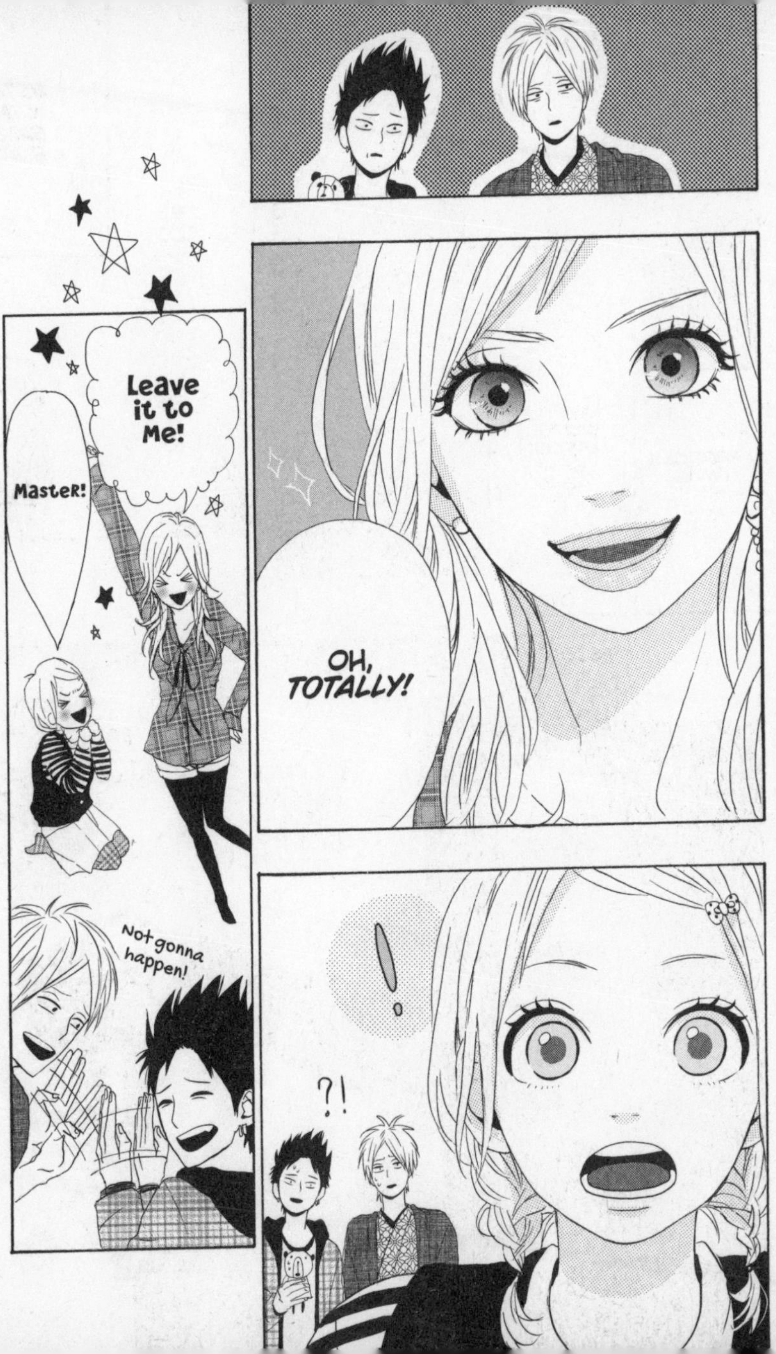
OH, TOTALLY!
?!
Leave it to Me!
MasteR!
Not gonna happen!

Meaningless Doodle

Bedtime!

Dreamin' Sun

4th DOOR

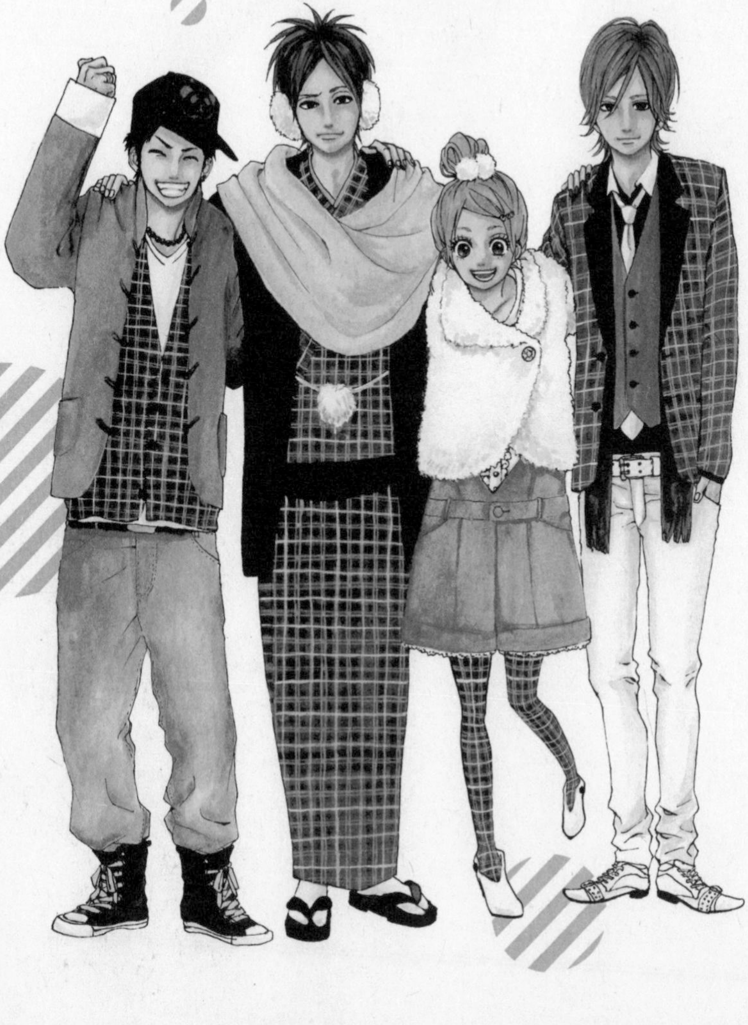

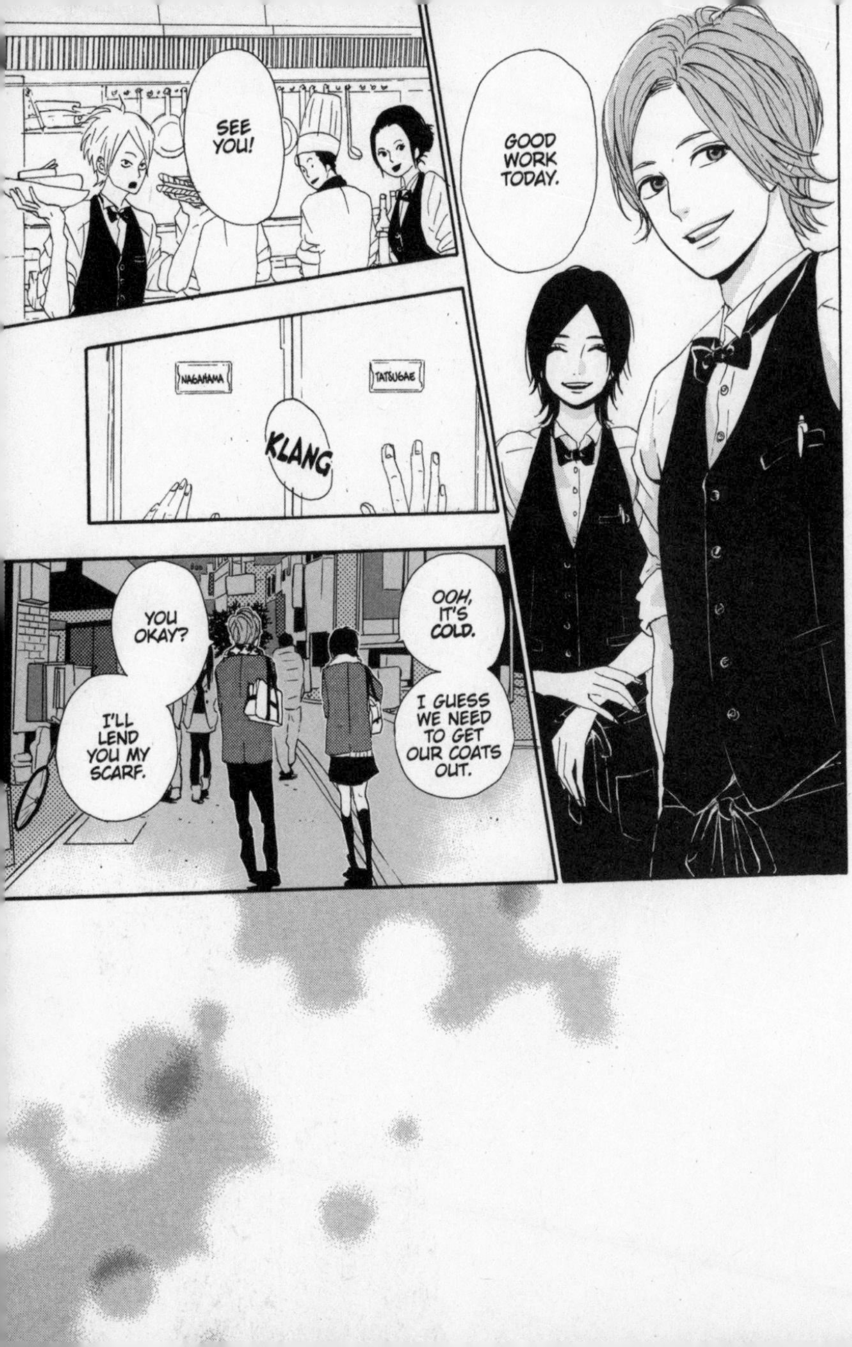
GOOD WORK TODAY.
SEE YOU!
NAGAHAMA
TATSUGAE
KLANG
OOH, IT'S COLD.
I GUESS WE NEED TO GET OUR COATS OUT.
YOU OKAY?
I'LL LEND YOU MY SCARF.

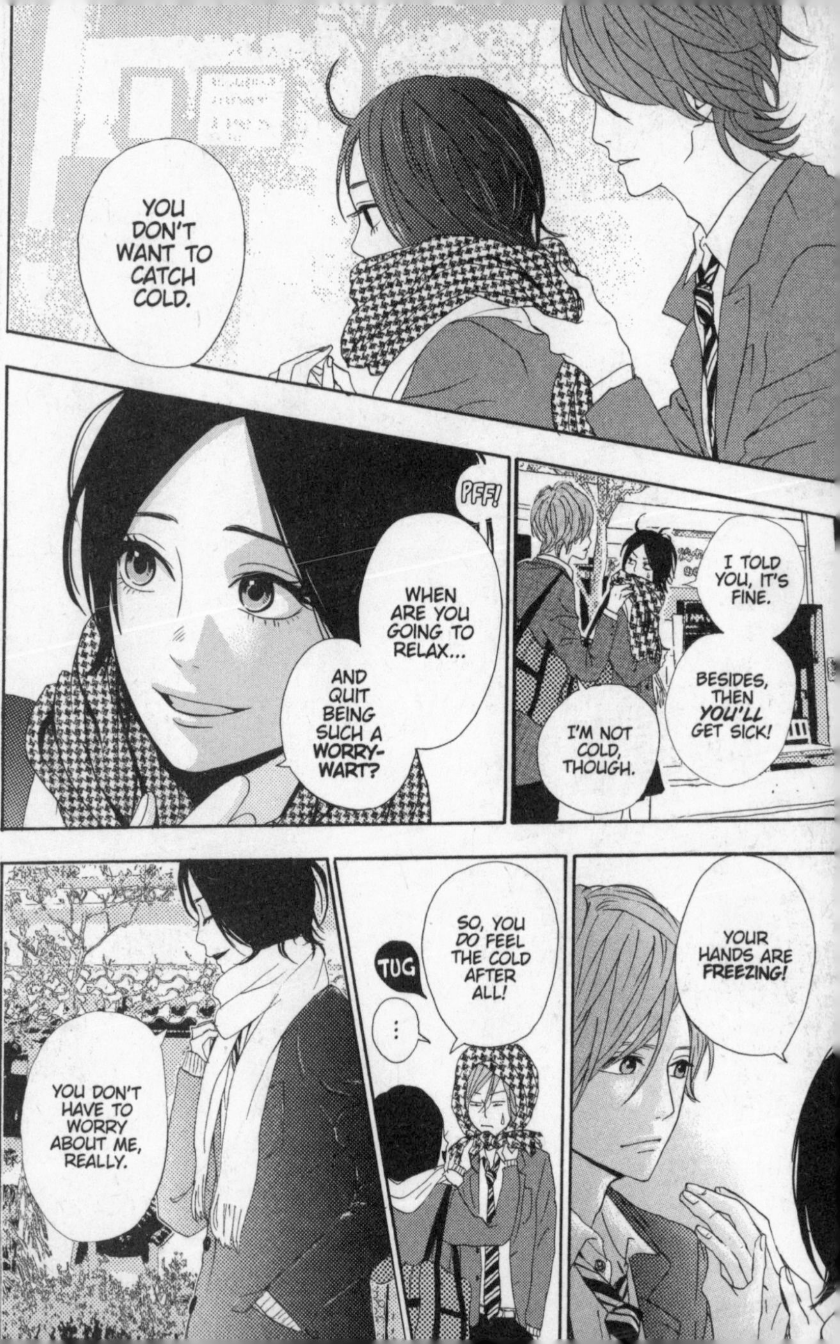
YOU DON'T WANT TO CATCH COLD.
I TOLD YOU, IT'S FINE.
BESIDES, THEN *YOU'LL* GET SICK!
I'M NOT COLD, THOUGH.
PFF!
WHEN ARE YOU GOING TO RELAX...
AND QUIT BEING SUCH A WORRY-WART?
YOUR HANDS ARE FREEZING!
SO, YOU *DO* FEEL THE COLD AFTER ALL!
TUG
...
YOU DON'T HAVE TO WORRY ABOUT ME, REALLY.

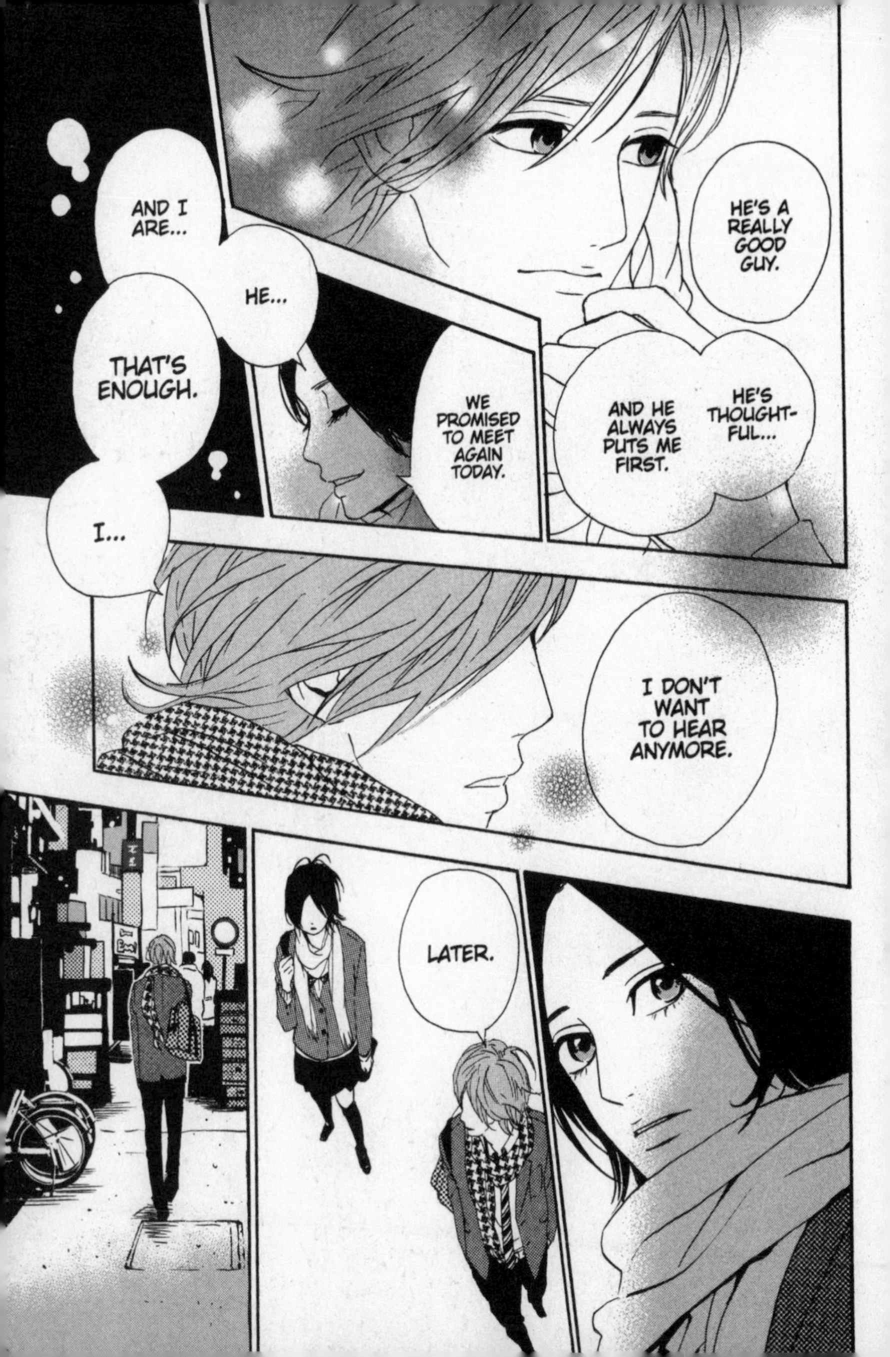
HE'S A REALLY GOOD GUY.
HE'S THOUGHTFUL...
AND HE ALWAYS PUTS ME FIRST.
WE PROMISED TO MEET AGAIN TODAY.
HE...
AND I ARE...
THAT'S ENOUGH.
I...
I DON'T WANT TO HEAR ANYMORE.
LATER.

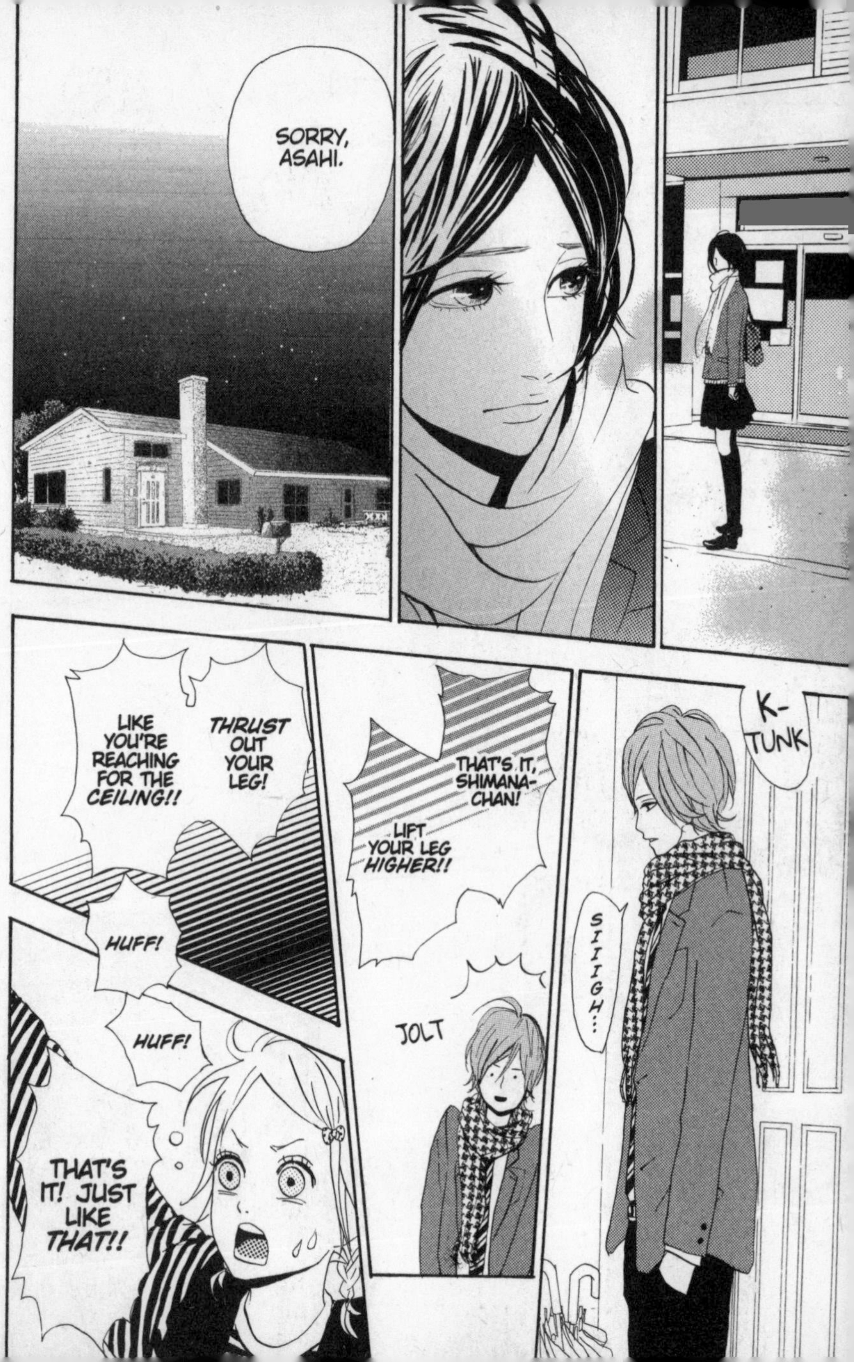
SORRY, ASAHI.
K-TUNK
SIIIGH...
THAT'S IT, SHIMANA-CHAN!
LIFT YOUR LEG HIGHER!!
JOLT
THRUST OUT YOUR LEG!
LIKE YOU'RE REACHING FOR THE CEILING!!
HUFF!
HUFF!
THAT'S IT! JUST LIKE THAT!!

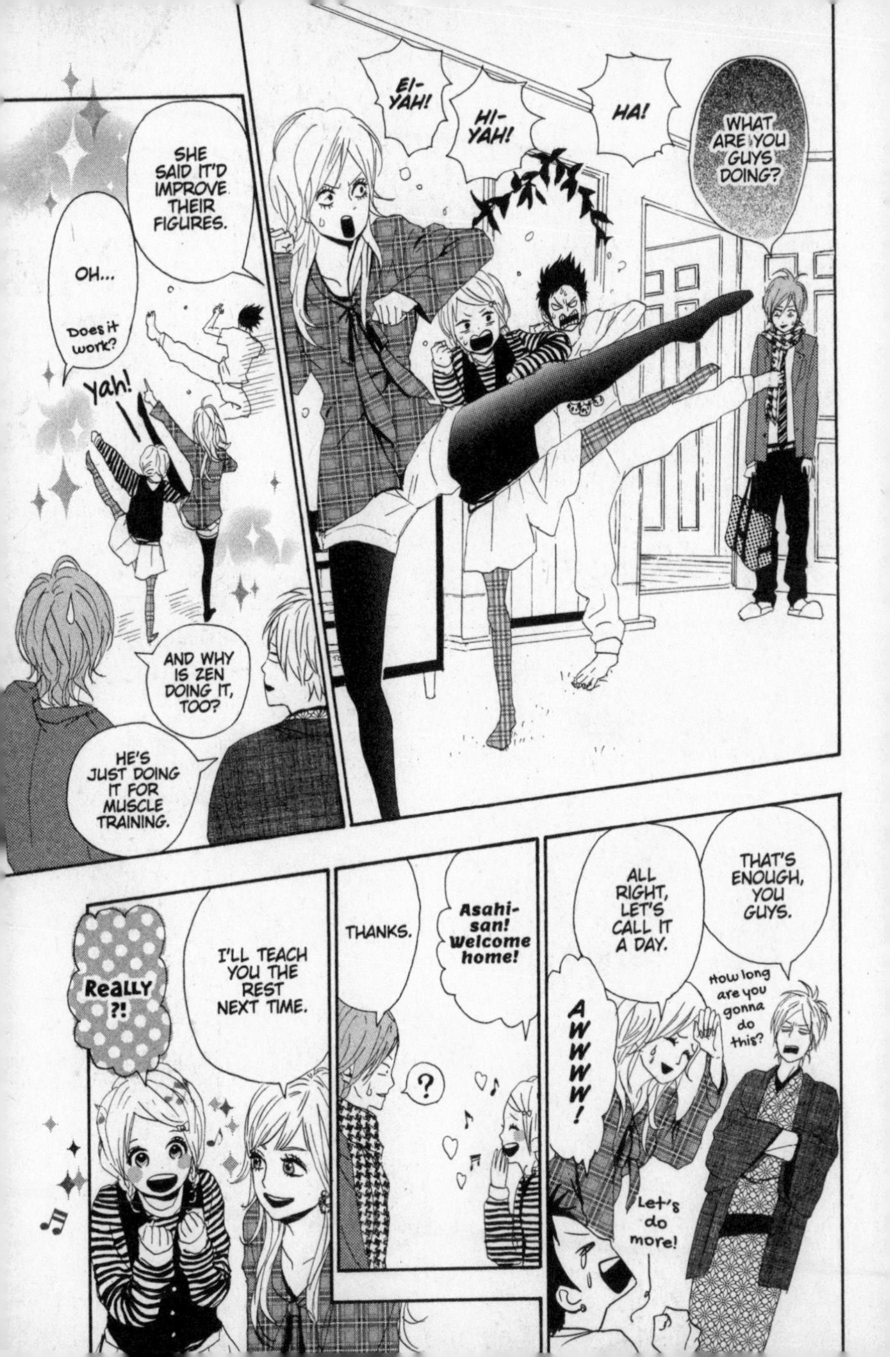

WHAT ARE YOU GUYS DOING?
HA!
HI-YAH!
EI-YAH!
SHE SAID IT'D IMPROVE THEIR FIGURES.
OH...
Does it work?
Yah!
AND WHY IS ZEN DOING IT, TOO?
HE'S JUST DOING IT FOR MUSCLE TRAINING.
THAT'S ENOUGH, YOU GUYS.
ALL RIGHT, LET'S CALL IT A DAY.
How long are you gonna do this?
AWWWW!
Let's do more!
Asahi-san! Welcome home!
THANKS.
?
I'LL TEACH YOU THE REST NEXT TIME.
Really?!

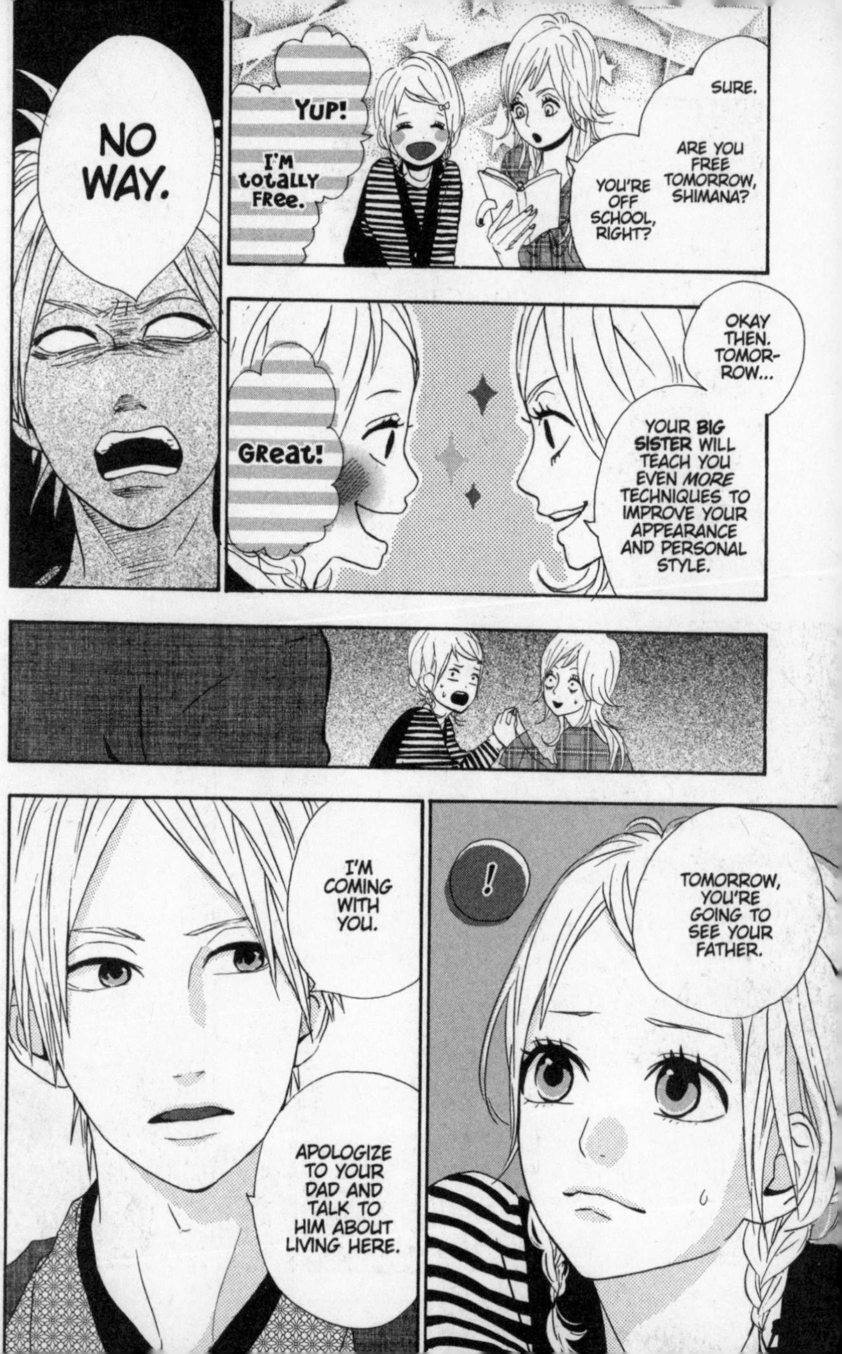
SURE.
ARE YOU FREE TOMORROW, SHIMANA?
YOU'RE OFF SCHOOL, RIGHT?
YUP!
I'M totally Free.
OKAY THEN. TOMOR-ROW...
YOUR BIG SISTER WILL TEACH YOU EVEN MORE TECHNIQUES TO IMPROVE YOUR APPEARANCE AND PERSONAL STYLE.
GReat!
NO WAY.
!
TOMORROW, YOU'RE GOING TO SEE YOUR FATHER.
I'M COMING WITH YOU.
APOLOGIZE TO YOUR DAD AND TALK TO HIM ABOUT LIVING HERE.

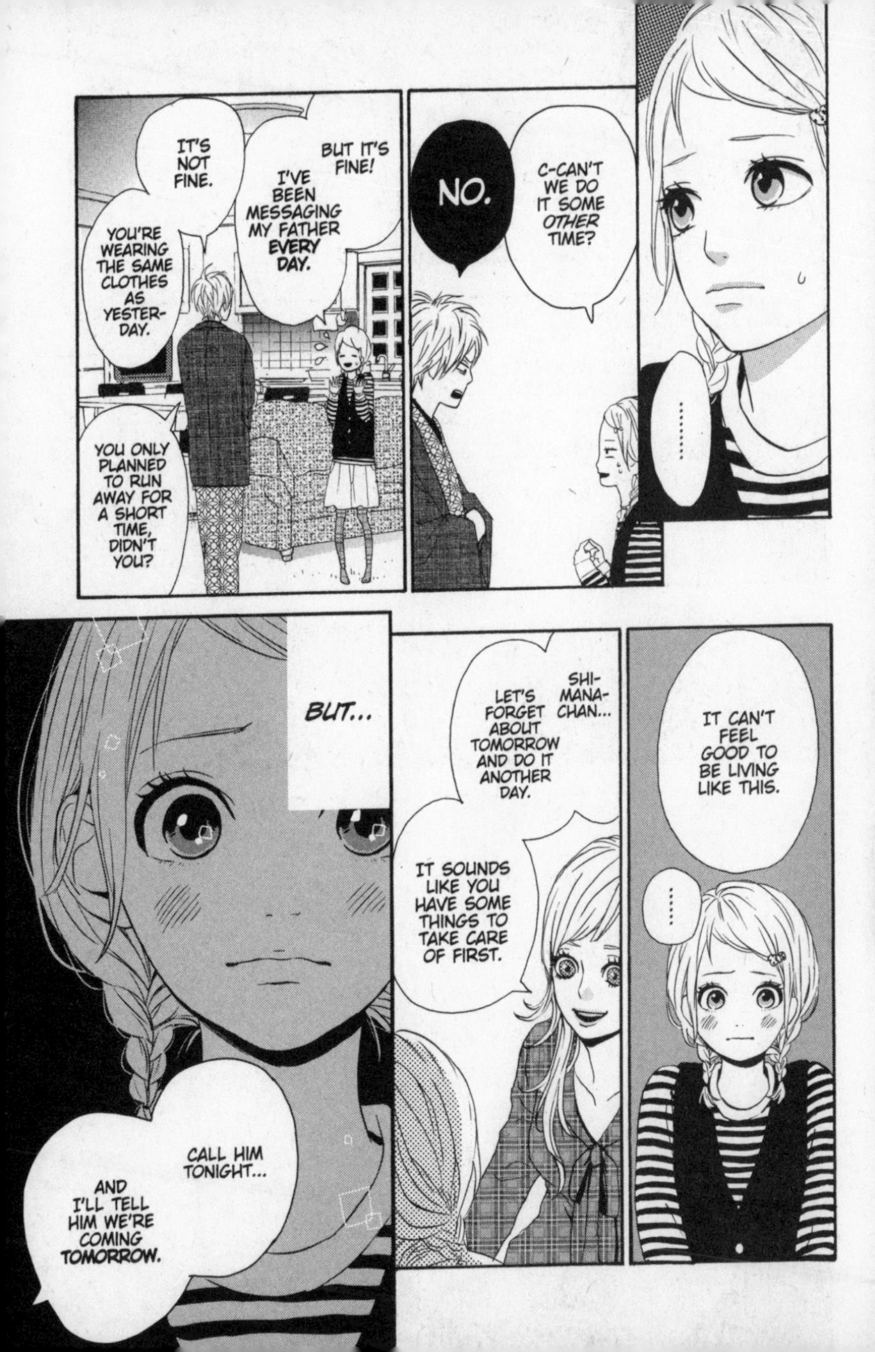
......
C-CAN'T WE DO IT SOME OTHER TIME?
NO.
BUT IT'S FINE!
I'VE BEEN MESSAGING MY FATHER EVERY DAY.
IT'S NOT FINE.
YOU'RE WEARING THE SAME CLOTHES AS YESTER-DAY.
YOU ONLY PLANNED TO RUN AWAY FOR A SHORT TIME, DIDN'T YOU?
IT CAN'T FEEL GOOD TO BE LIVING LIKE THIS.
......
SHI-MANA-CHAN...
LET'S FORGET ABOUT TOMORROW AND DO IT ANOTHER DAY.
IT SOUNDS LIKE YOU HAVE SOME THINGS TO TAKE CARE OF FIRST.
BUT...
CALL HIM TONIGHT...
AND I'LL TELL HIM WE'RE COMING TOMORROW.

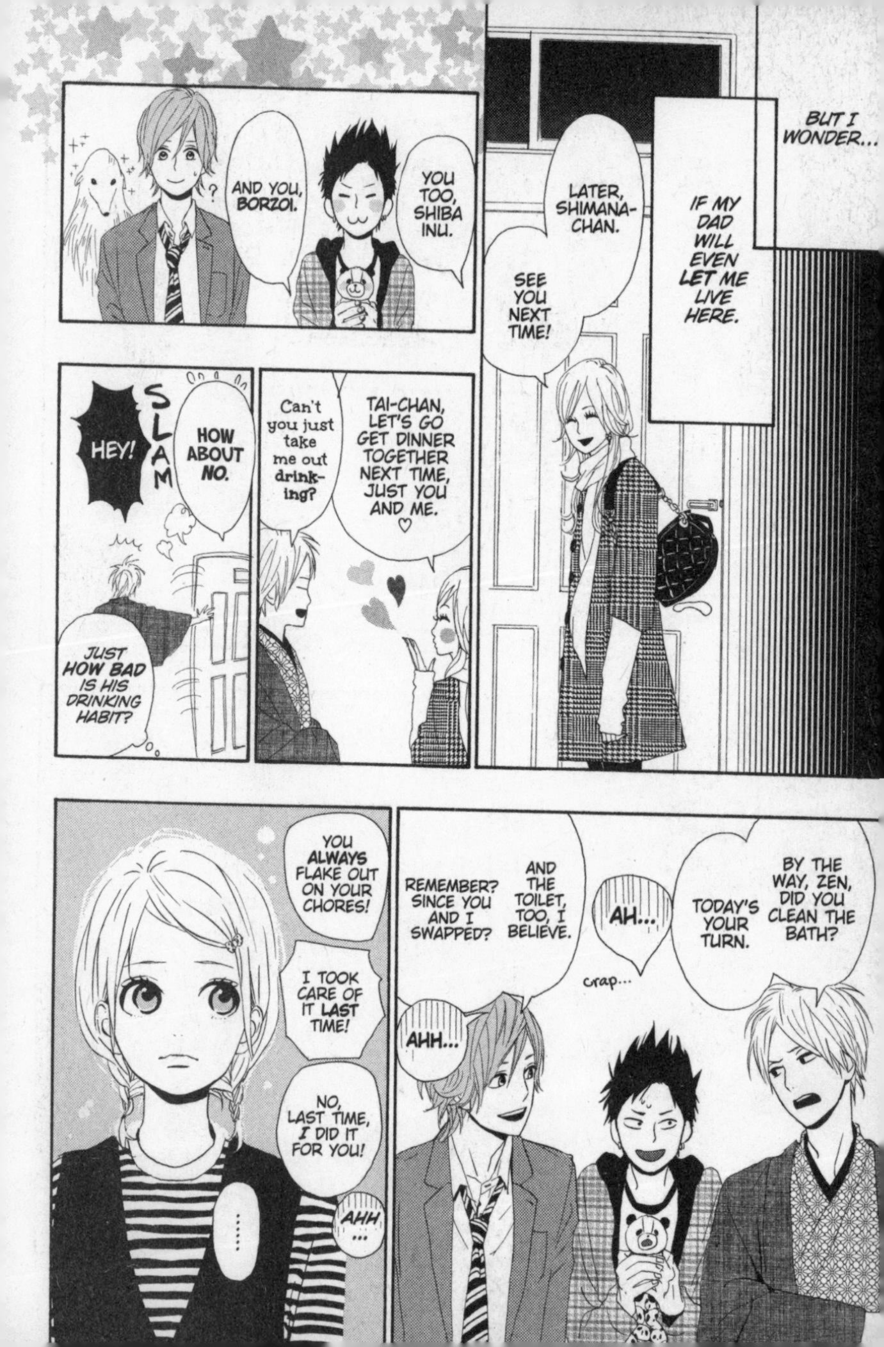
BUT I WONDER...
IF MY DAD WILL EVEN LET ME LIVE HERE.
LATER, SHIMANA-CHAN.
SEE YOU NEXT TIME!
YOU TOO, SHIBA INU.
AND YOU, BORZOI.
TAI-CHAN, LET'S GO GET DINNER TOGETHER NEXT TIME, JUST YOU AND ME. ♡
Can't you just take me out drinking?
HOW ABOUT NO.
SLAM
HEY!
JUST HOW BAD IS HIS DRINKING HABIT?
BY THE WAY, ZEN, DID YOU CLEAN THE BATH?
TODAY'S YOUR TURN.
AH...
AND THE TOILET, TOO, I BELIEVE.
REMEMBER? SINCE YOU AND I SWAPPED?
crap...
AHH...
YOU ALWAYS FLAKE OUT ON YOUR CHORES!
I TOOK CARE OF IT LAST TIME!
NO, LAST TIME, I DID IT FOR YOU!
AHH...
......

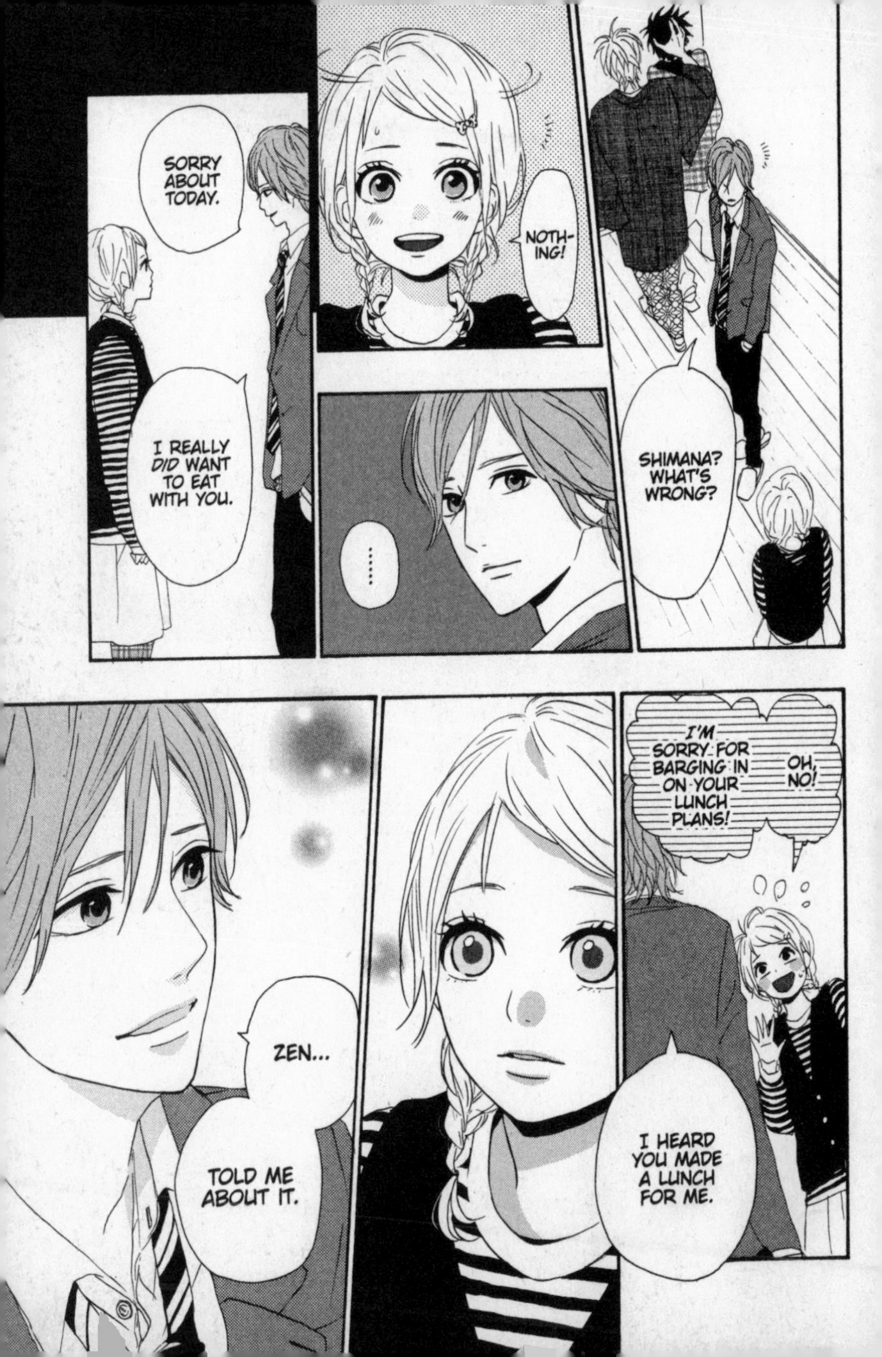
SHIMANA? WHAT'S WRONG?
NOTH-ING!
......
SORRY ABOUT TODAY.
I REALLY *DID* WANT TO EAT WITH YOU.
OH, NO!
I'M SORRY FOR BARGING IN ON YOUR LUNCH PLANS!
I HEARD YOU MADE A LUNCH FOR ME.
ZEN...
TOLD ME ABOUT IT.

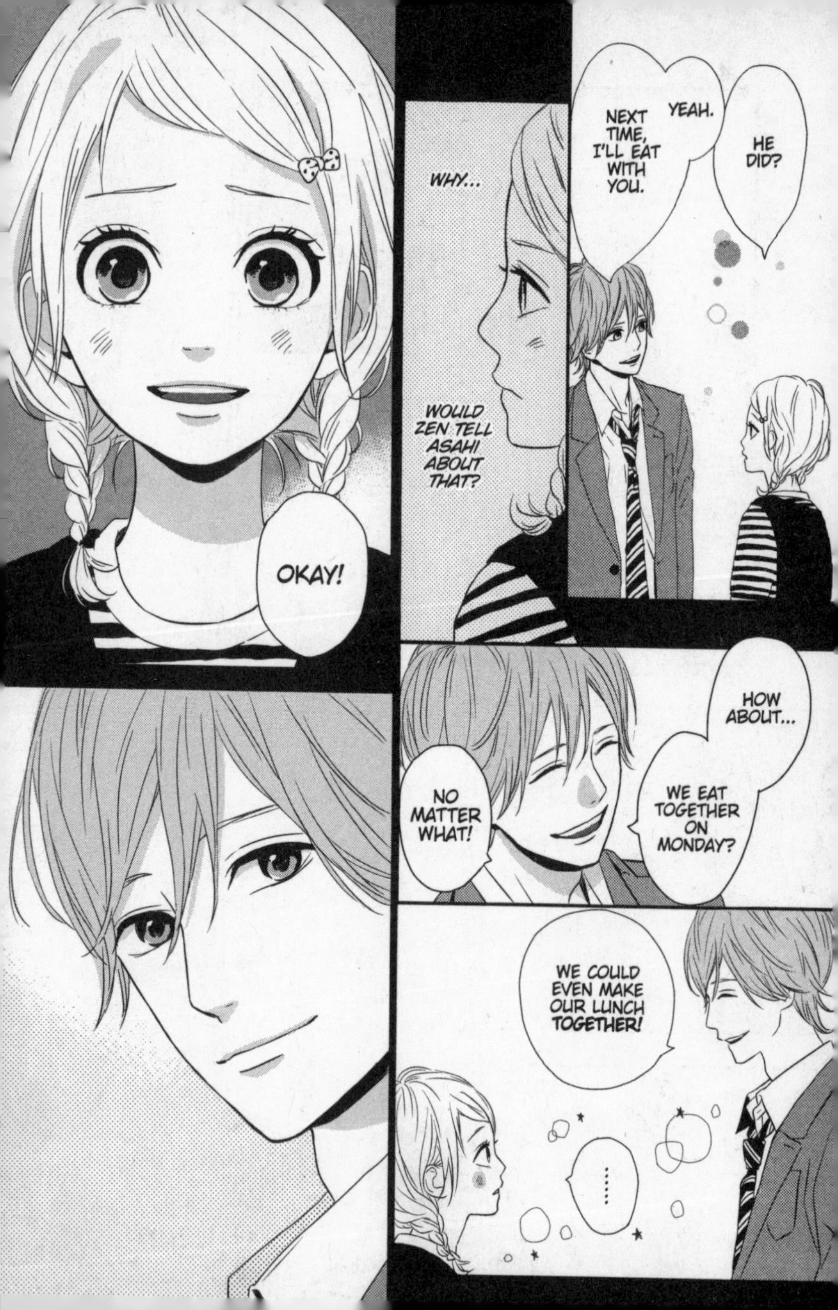
HE DID?
YEAH.
NEXT TIME, I'LL EAT WITH YOU.
WHY...
WOULD ZEN TELL ASAHI ABOUT THAT?
OKAY!
HOW ABOUT...
WE EAT TOGETHER ON MONDAY?
NO MATTER WHAT!
WE COULD EVEN MAKE OUR LUNCH TOGETHER!
......

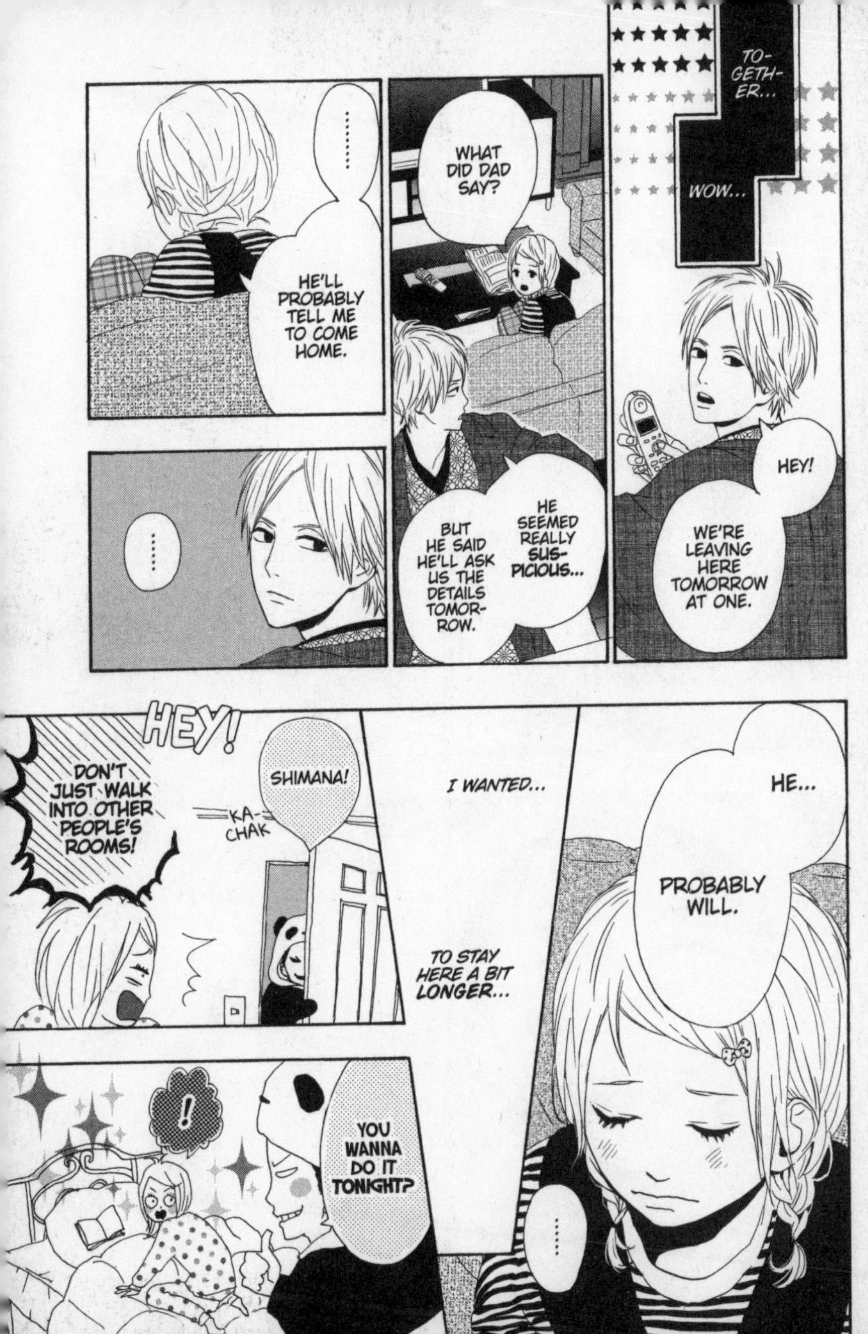

TO-GETH-ER...
WOW...
HEY!
WE'RE LEAVING HERE TOMORROW AT ONE.
WHAT DID DAD SAY?
HE SEEMED REALLY SUS-PICIOUS...
BUT HE SAID HE'LL ASK US THE DETAILS TOMOR-ROW.
......
HE'LL PROBABLY TELL ME TO COME HOME.
......
HE...
PROBABLY WILL.
......
I WANTED...
TO STAY HERE A BIT LONGER...
SHIMANA!
KA-CHAK
HEY!
DON'T JUST WALK INTO OTHER PEOPLE'S ROOMS!
YOU WANNA DO IT TONIGHT?
!

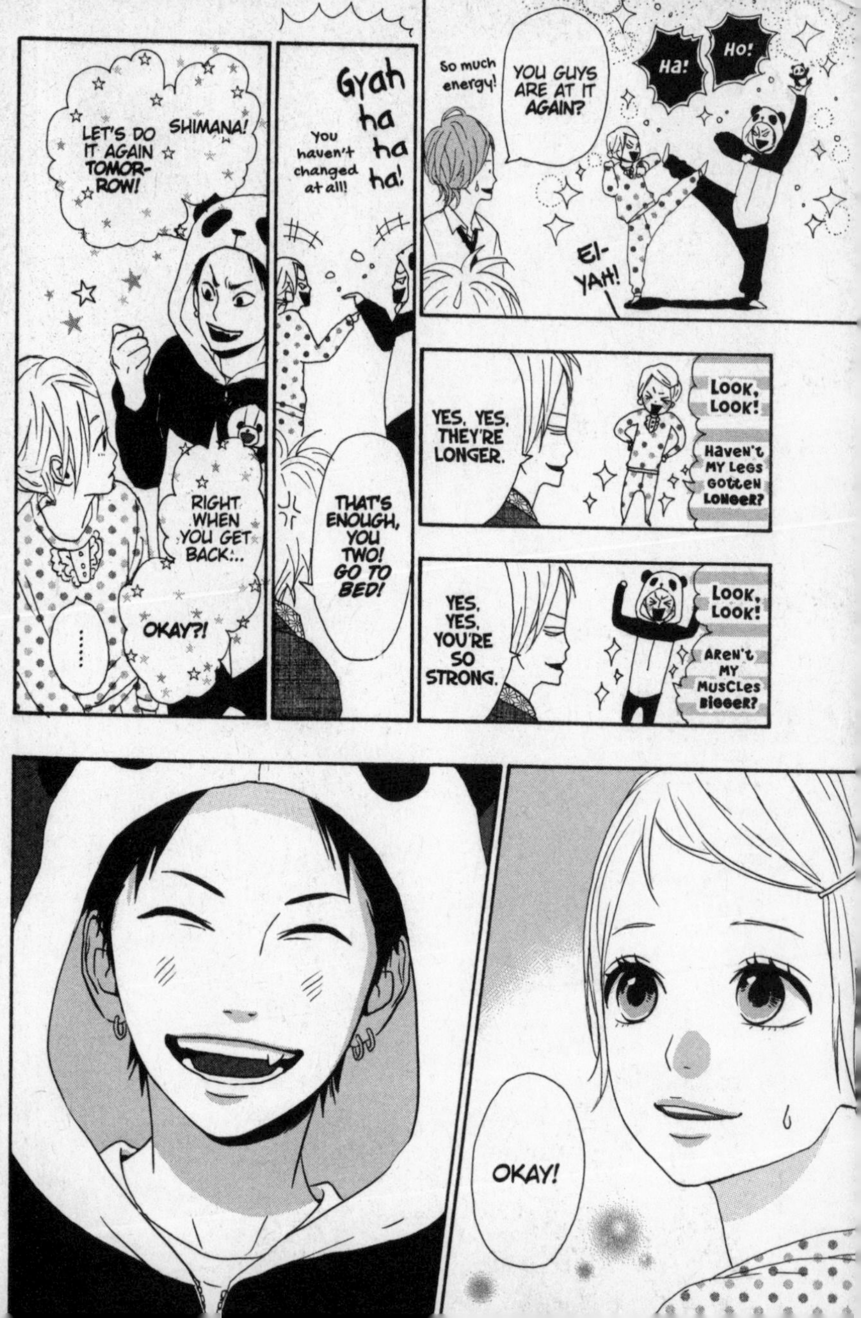

Ho!
Ha!
YOU GUYS ARE AT IT AGAIN?
So much energy!
EI-YAH!
LOOK, LOOK!
HAVEN'T MY LEGS GOTTEN LONGER?
YES, YES, THEY'RE LONGER.
LOOK, LOOK!
AREN'T MY MUSCLES BIGGER?
YES, YES, YOU'RE SO STRONG.
Gyah ha ha ha!
You haven't changed at all!
THAT'S ENOUGH, YOU TWO! GO TO BED!
SHIMANA!
LET'S DO IT AGAIN TOMORROW!
RIGHT WHEN YOU GET BACK...
OKAY?!
......
OKAY!

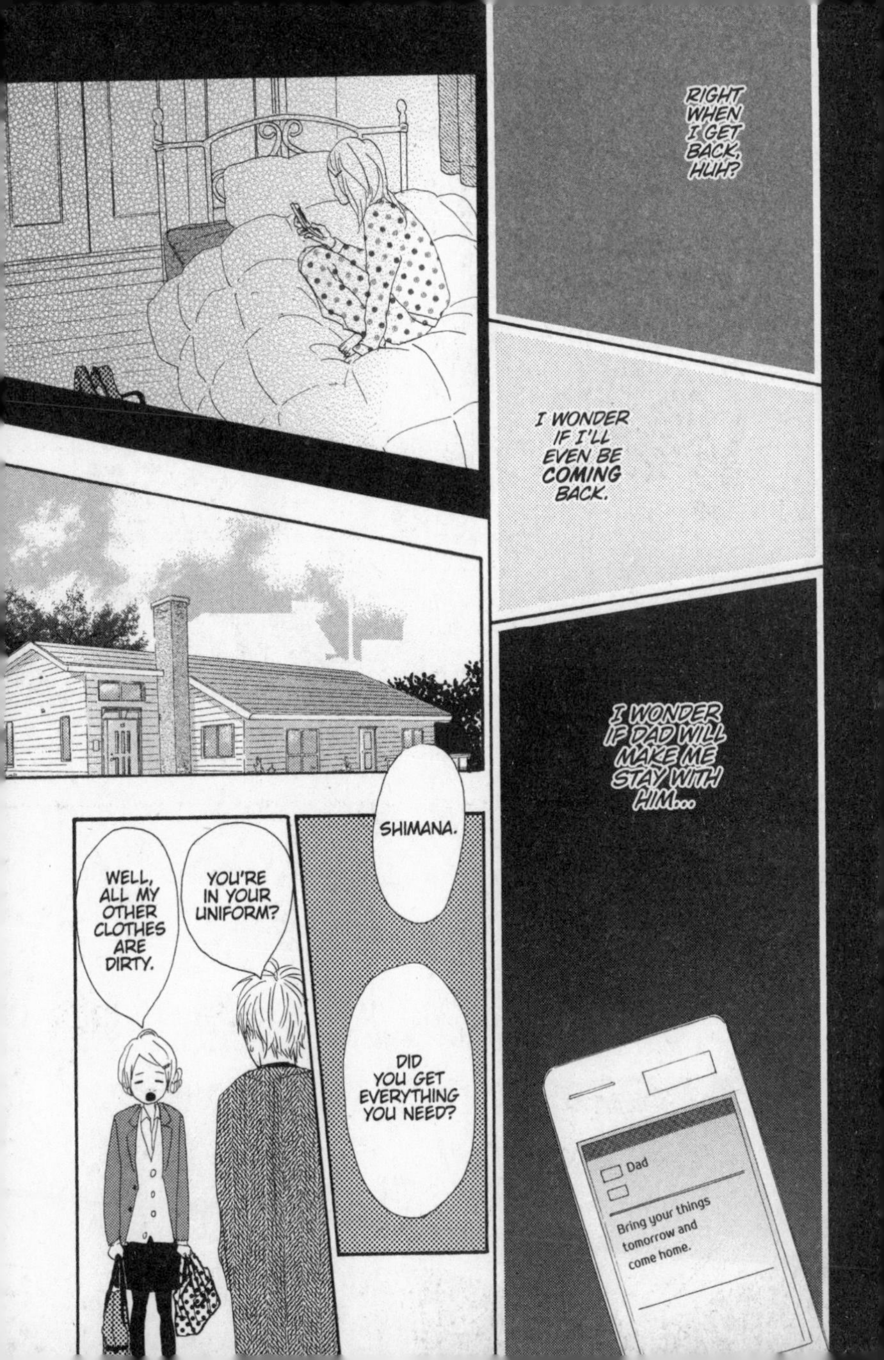
RIGHT WHEN I GET BACK, HUH?
I WONDER IF I'LL EVEN BE COMING BACK.
I WONDER IF DAD WILL MAKE ME STAY WITH HIM...
Dad
Bring your things tomorrow and come home.
SHIMANA.
DID YOU GET EVERYTHING YOU NEED?
YOU'RE IN YOUR UNIFORM?
WELL, ALL MY OTHER CLOTHES ARE DIRTY.

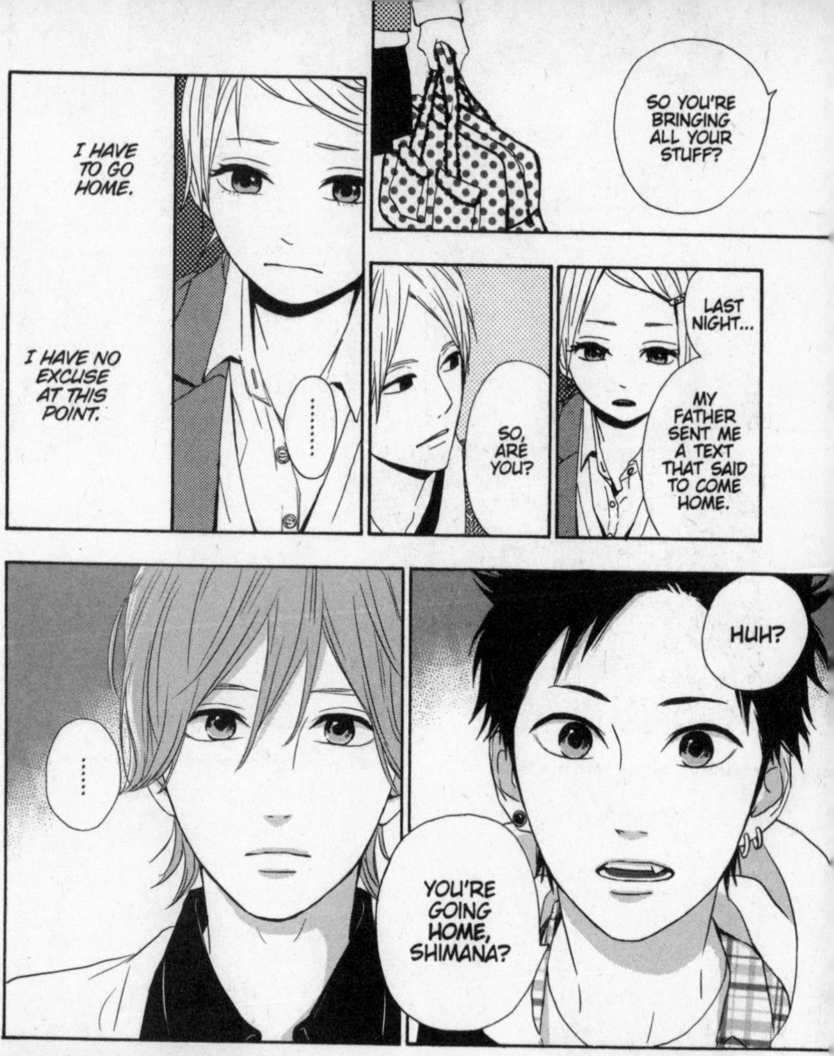
SO YOU'RE BRINGING ALL YOUR STUFF?
LAST NIGHT...
MY FATHER SENT ME A TEXT THAT SAID TO COME HOME.
SO, ARE YOU?
I HAVE TO GO HOME.
......
I HAVE NO EXCUSE AT THIS POINT.
HUH?
YOU'RE GOING HOME, SHIMANA?
......

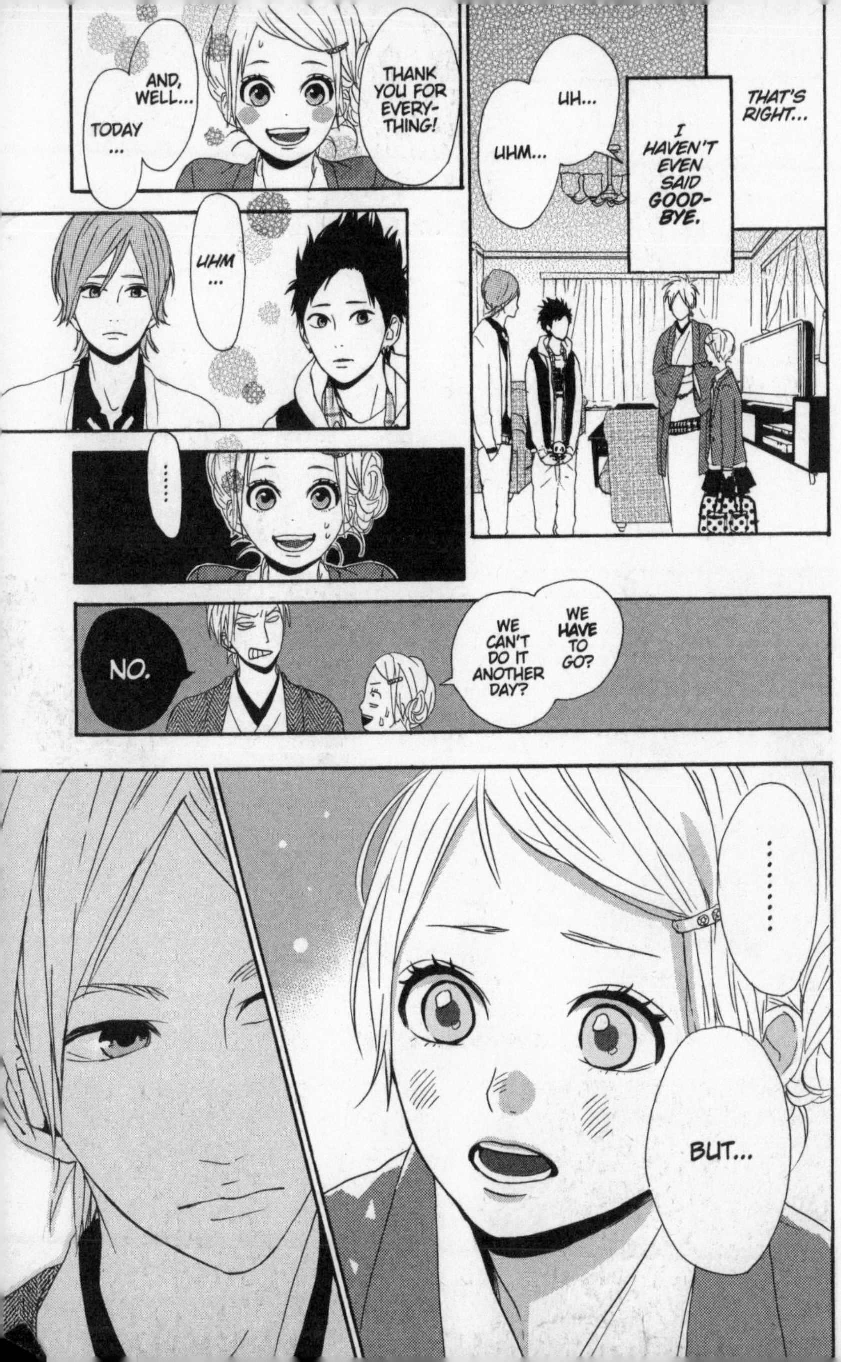
THAT'S RIGHT...
I HAVEN'T EVEN SAID GOOD-BYE.
UH...
UHM...
THANK YOU FOR EVERYTHING!
AND, WELL...
TODAY ...
UHM ...
......
WE HAVE TO GO?
WE CAN'T DO IT ANOTHER DAY?
NO.
......
BUT...

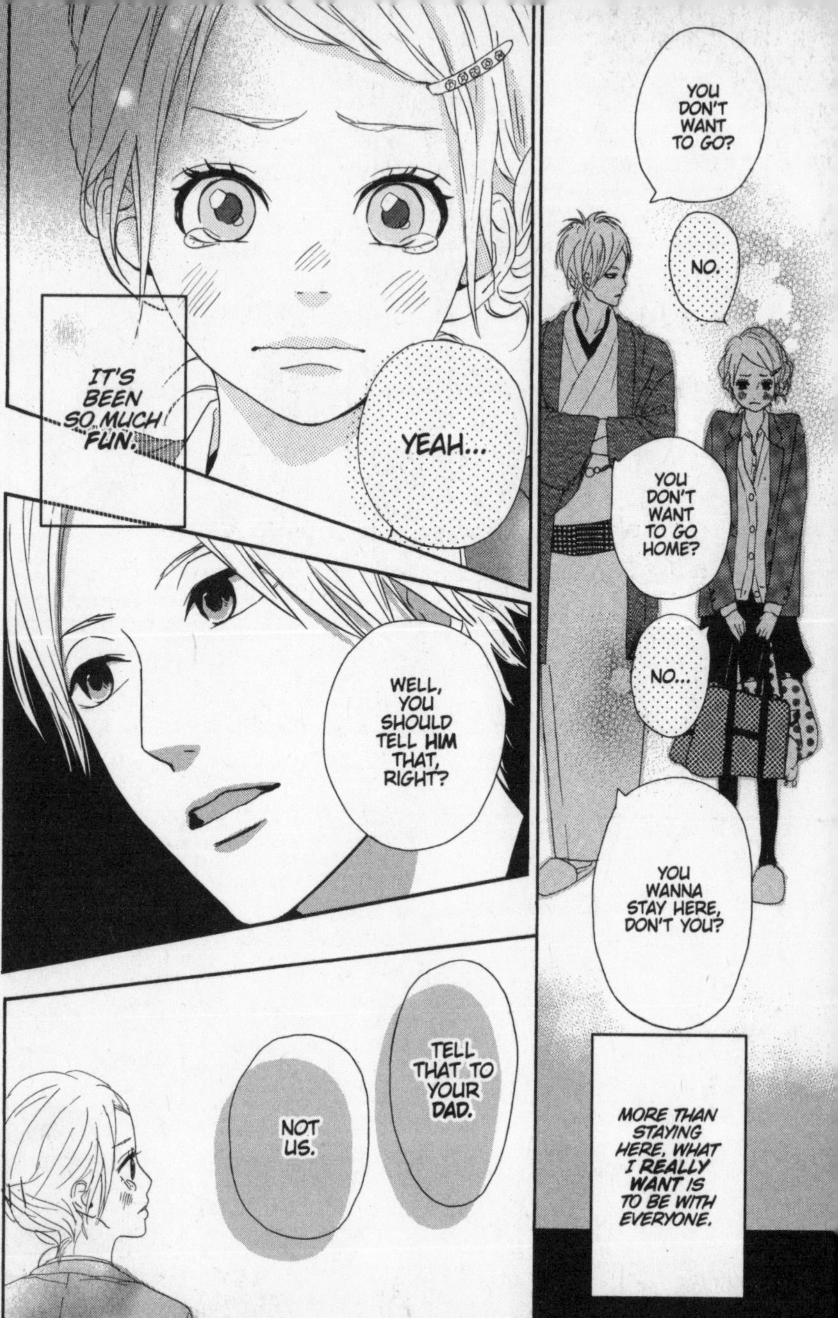
YOU DON'T WANT TO GO?
NO.
YOU DON'T WANT TO GO HOME?
NO...
YOU WANNA STAY HERE, DON'T YOU?
MORE THAN STAYING HERE, WHAT I REALLY WANT IS TO BE WITH EVERYONE.
YEAH...
IT'S BEEN SO MUCH FUN.
WELL, YOU SHOULD TELL HIM THAT, RIGHT?
TELL THAT TO YOUR DAD.
NOT US.

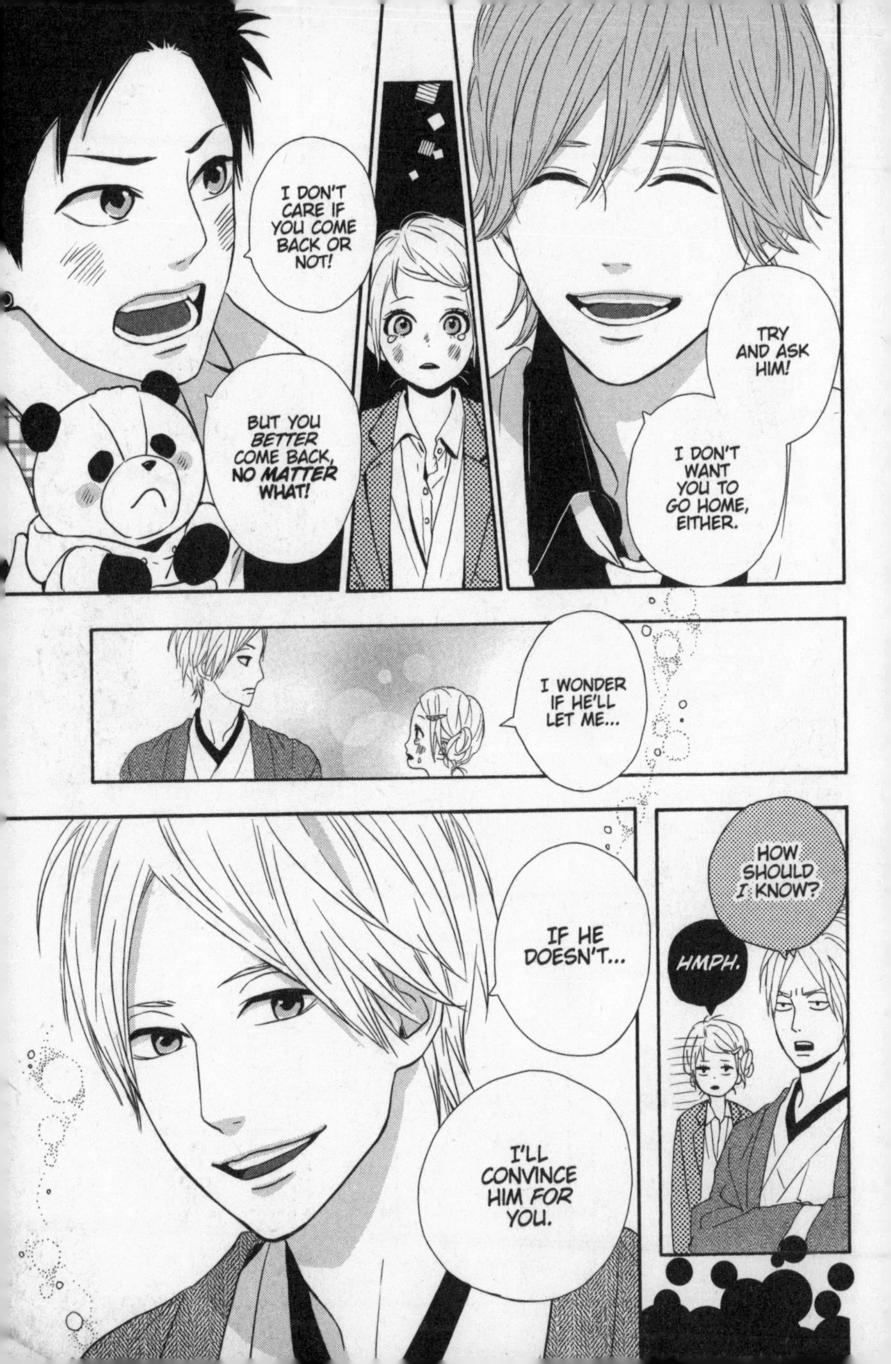
TRY AND ASK HIM!
I DON'T WANT YOU TO GO HOME, EITHER.
I DON'T CARE IF YOU COME BACK OR NOT!
BUT YOU *BETTER* COME BACK, NO *MATTER* WHAT!
I WONDER IF HE'LL LET ME...
HOW SHOULD *I* KNOW?
HMPH.
IF HE DOESN'T...
I'LL CONVINCE HIM *FOR* YOU.

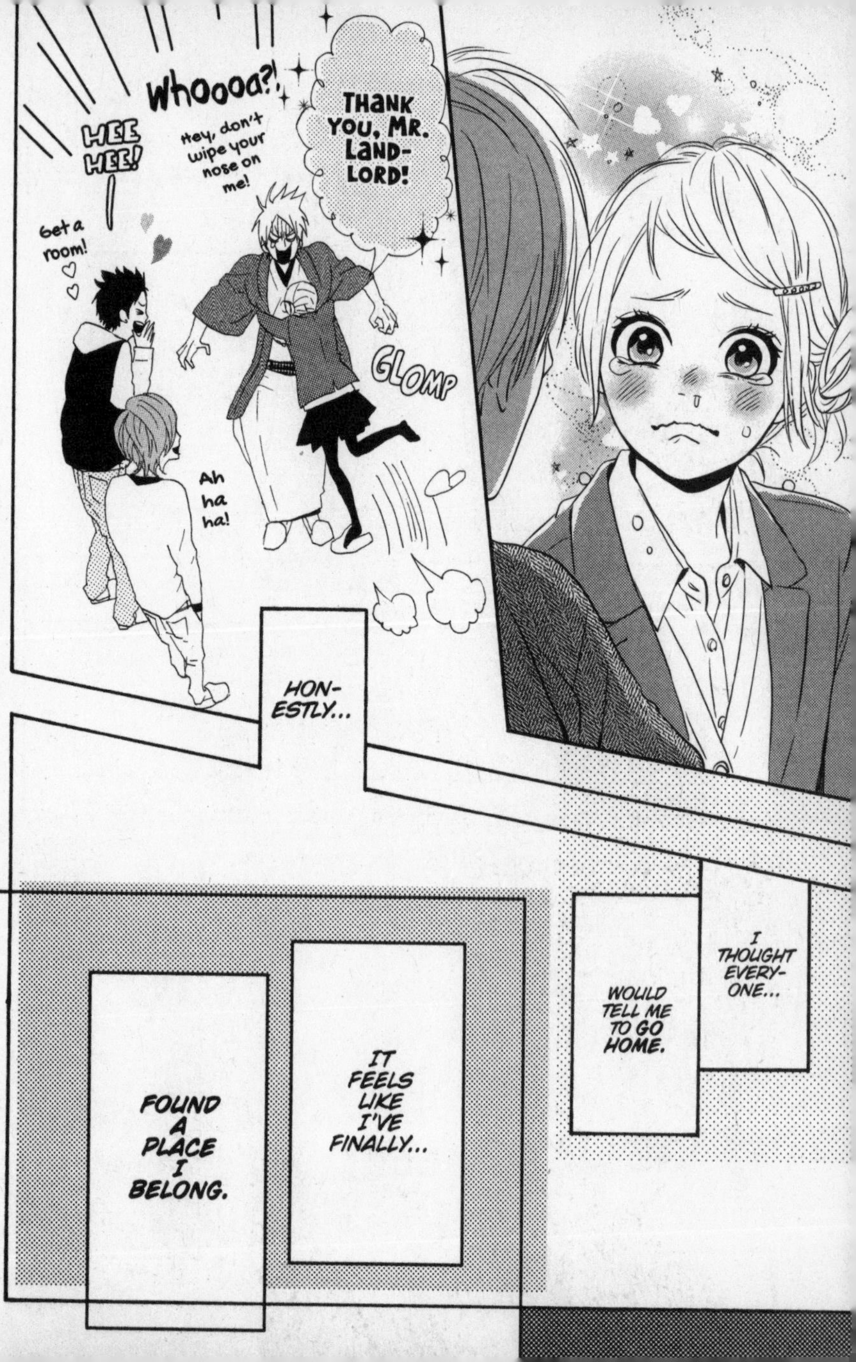
THANK YOU, MR. LAND-LORD!
Whoooa?!
Hey, don't wipe your nose on me!
HEE HEE!
GLOMP
Get a room!
Ah ha ha!
HON-ESTLY...
I THOUGHT EVERY-ONE...
WOULD TELL ME TO GO HOME.
IT FEELS LIKE I'VE FINALLY...
FOUND A PLACE I BELONG.

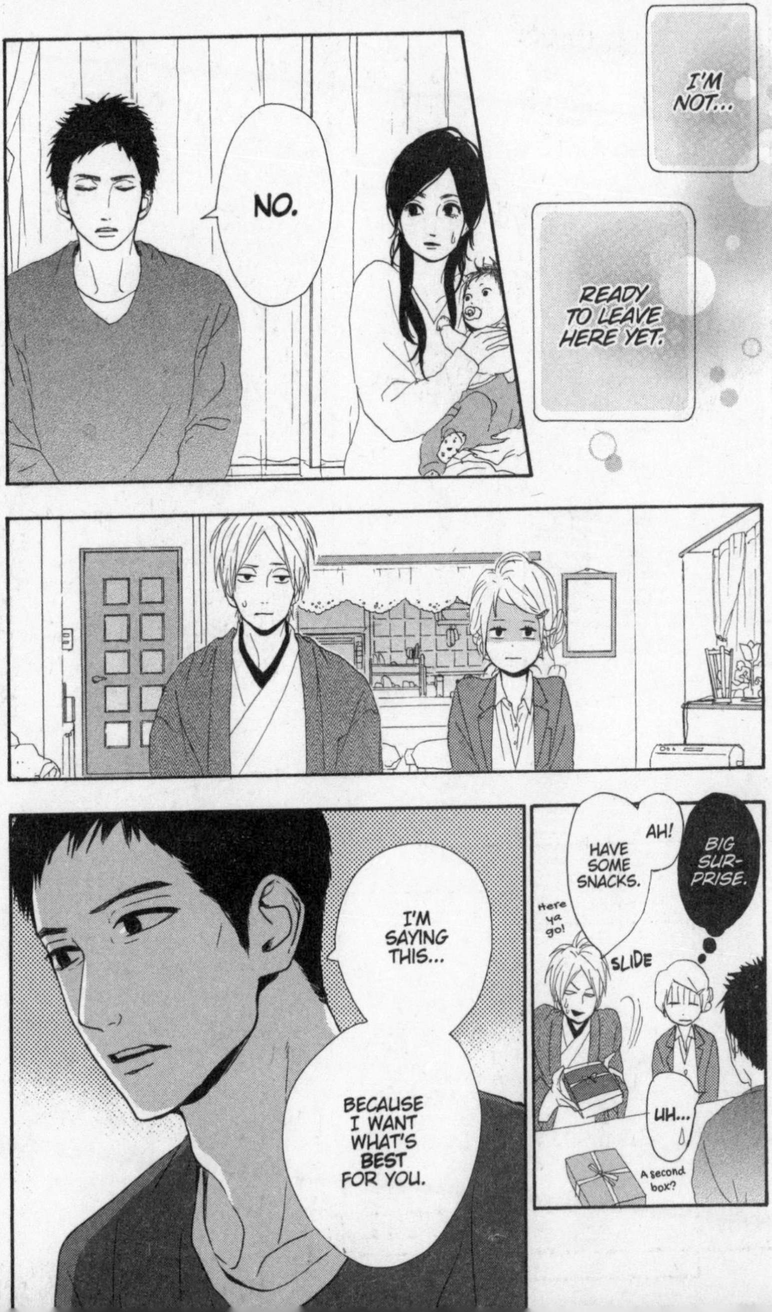
I'M NOT...
READY TO LEAVE HERE YET.
NO.
BIG SUR-PRISE.
AH!
HAVE SOME SNACKS.
Here ya go!
SLIDE
UH...
A second box?
I'M SAYING THIS...
BECAUSE I WANT WHAT'S BEST FOR YOU.

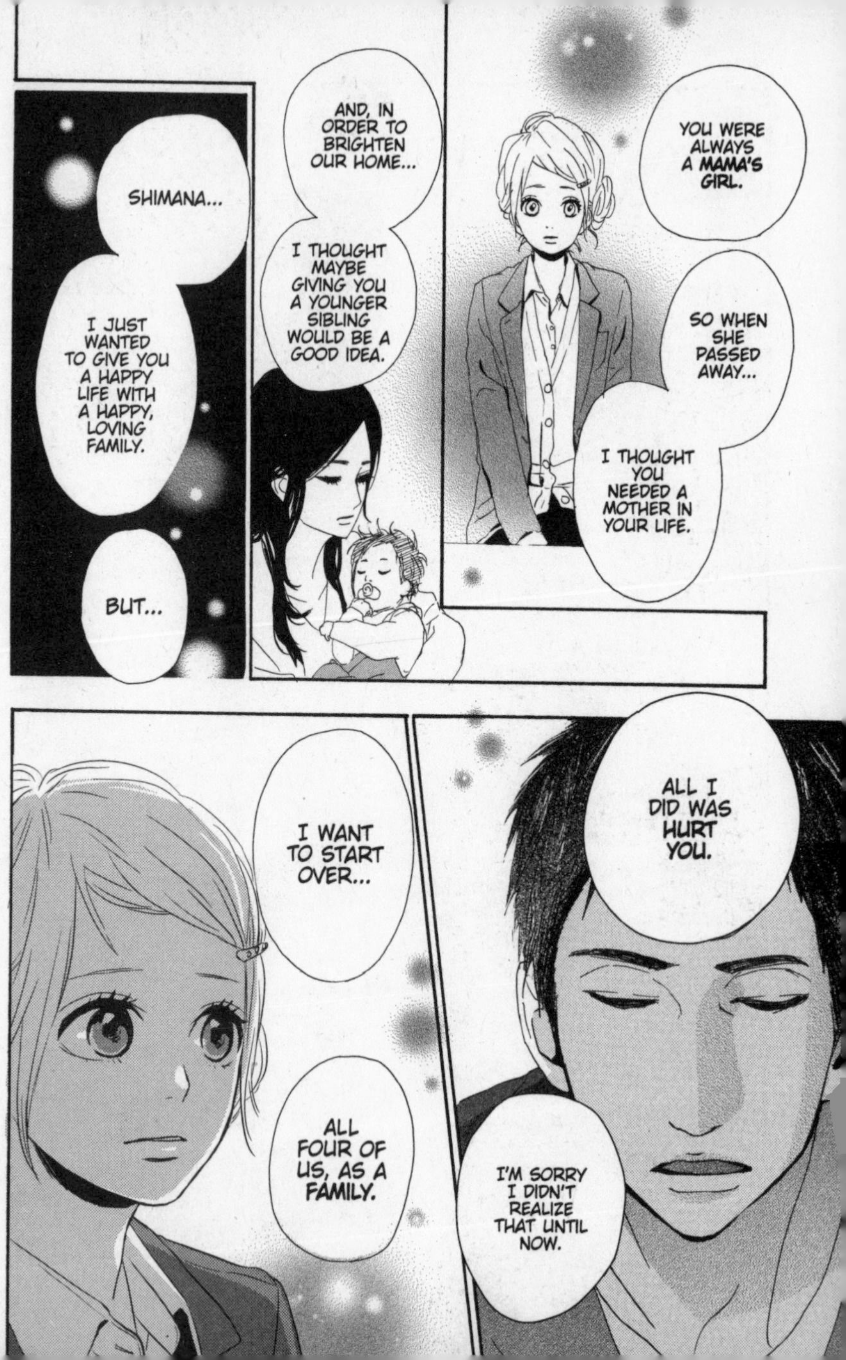
YOU WERE ALWAYS A MAMA'S GIRL.
SO WHEN SHE PASSED AWAY...
I THOUGHT YOU NEEDED A MOTHER IN YOUR LIFE.
AND, IN ORDER TO BRIGHTEN OUR HOME...
I THOUGHT MAYBE GIVING YOU A YOUNGER SIBLING WOULD BE A GOOD IDEA.
SHIMANA...
I JUST WANTED TO GIVE YOU A HAPPY LIFE WITH A HAPPY, LOVING FAMILY.
BUT...
ALL I DID WAS HURT YOU.
I'M SORRY I DIDN'T REALIZE THAT UNTIL NOW.
I WANT TO START OVER...
ALL FOUR OF US, AS A FAMILY.

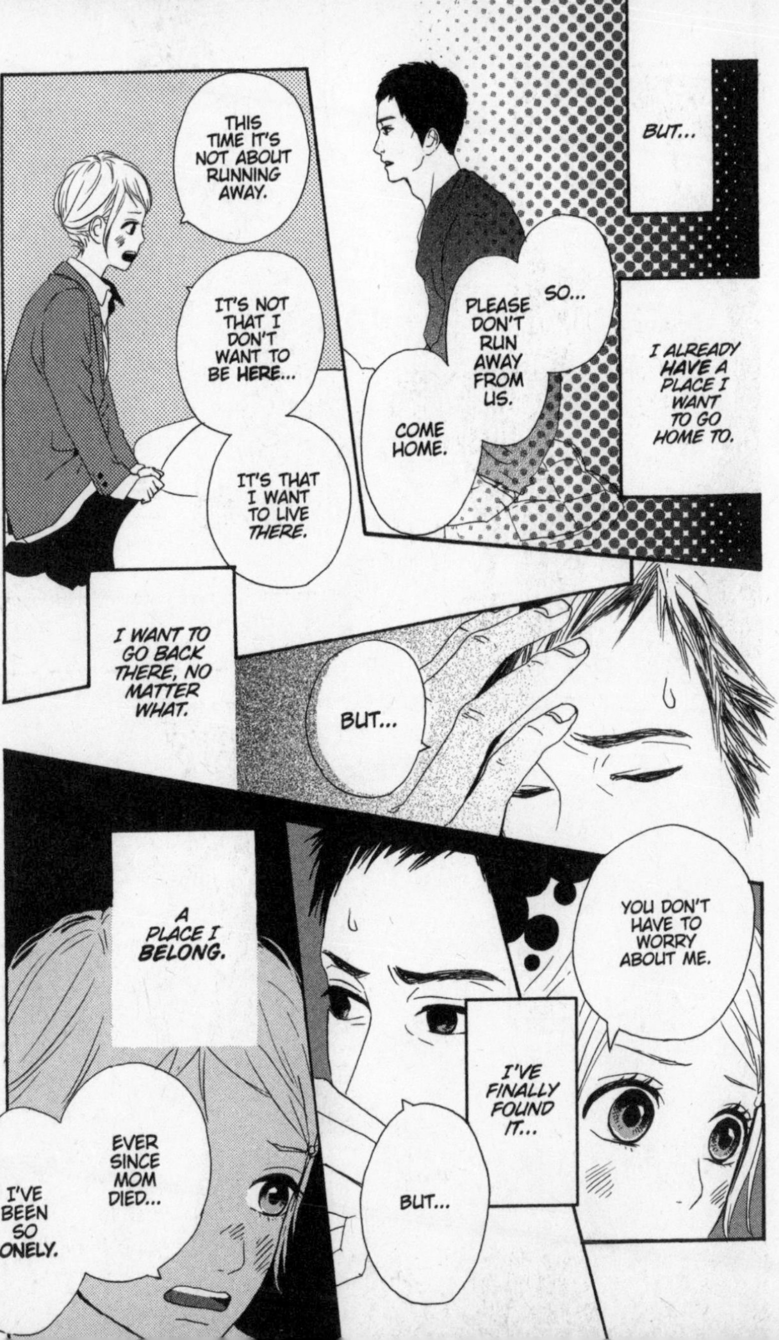
BUT...
I ALREADY HAVE A PLACE I WANT TO GO HOME TO.
SO...
PLEASE DON'T RUN AWAY FROM US.
COME HOME.
THIS TIME IT'S NOT ABOUT RUNNING AWAY.
IT'S NOT THAT I DON'T WANT TO BE HERE...
IT'S THAT I WANT TO LIVE THERE.
BUT...
I WANT TO GO BACK THERE, NO MATTER WHAT.
YOU DON'T HAVE TO WORRY ABOUT ME.
I'VE FINALLY FOUND IT...
A PLACE I BELONG.
BUT...
EVER SINCE MOM DIED...
I'VE BEEN SO LONELY.

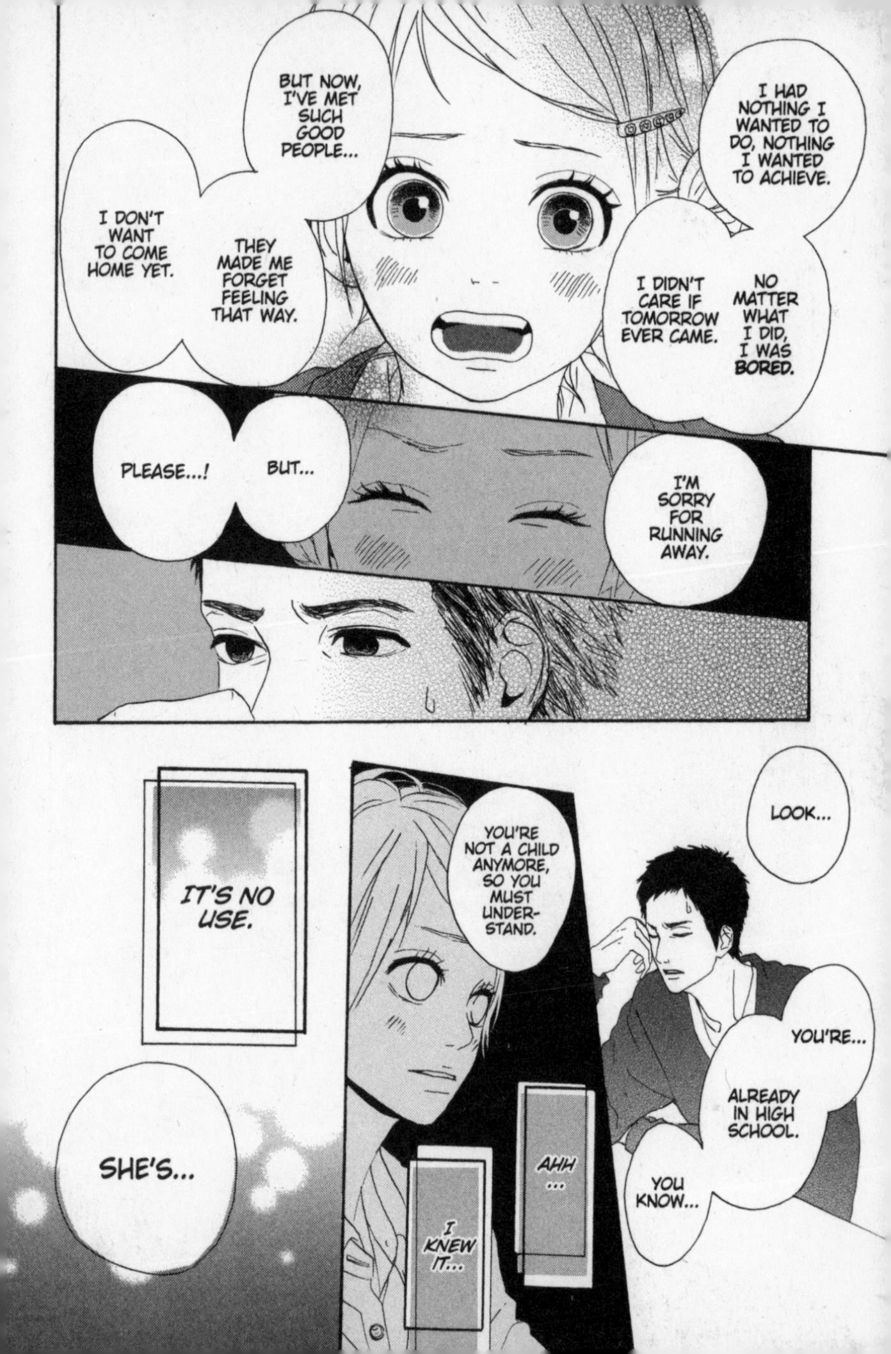
I HAD NOTHING I WANTED TO DO, NOTHING I WANTED TO ACHIEVE.
NO MATTER WHAT I DID, I WAS BORED.
I DIDN'T CARE IF TOMORROW EVER CAME.
BUT NOW, I'VE MET SUCH GOOD PEOPLE...
THEY MADE ME FORGET FEELING THAT WAY.
I DON'T WANT TO COME HOME YET.
I'M SORRY FOR RUNNING AWAY.
BUT...
PLEASE...!
LOOK...
YOU'RE...
ALREADY IN HIGH SCHOOL.
YOU KNOW...
YOU'RE NOT A CHILD ANYMORE, SO YOU MUST UNDERSTAND.
AHH ...
I KNEW IT...
IT'S NO USE.
SHE'S...

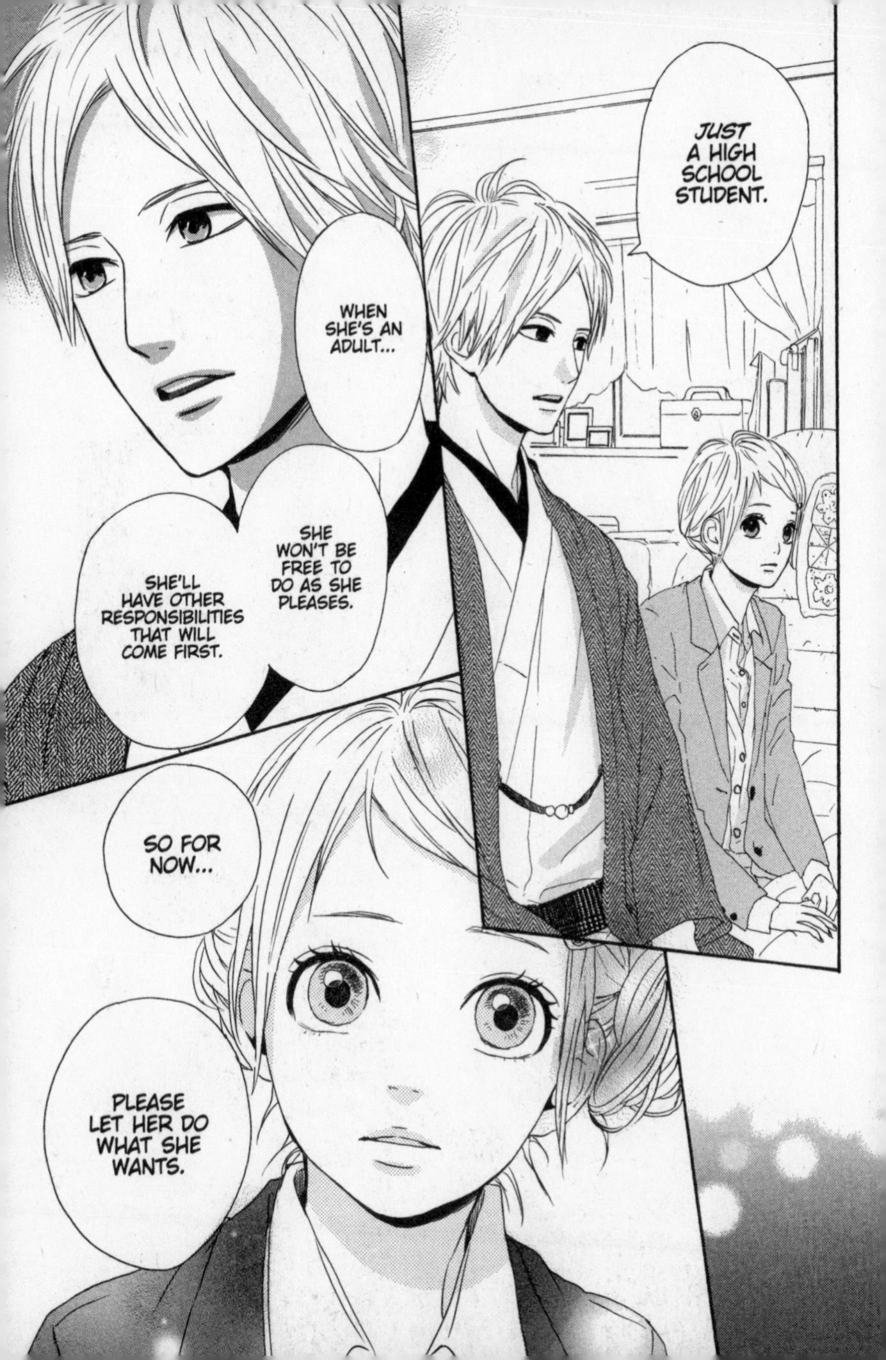
JUST A HIGH SCHOOL STUDENT.
WHEN SHE'S AN ADULT...
SHE WON'T BE FREE TO DO AS SHE PLEASES.
SHE'LL HAVE OTHER RESPONSIBILITIES THAT WILL COME FIRST.
SO FOR NOW...
PLEASE LET HER DO WHAT SHE WANTS.

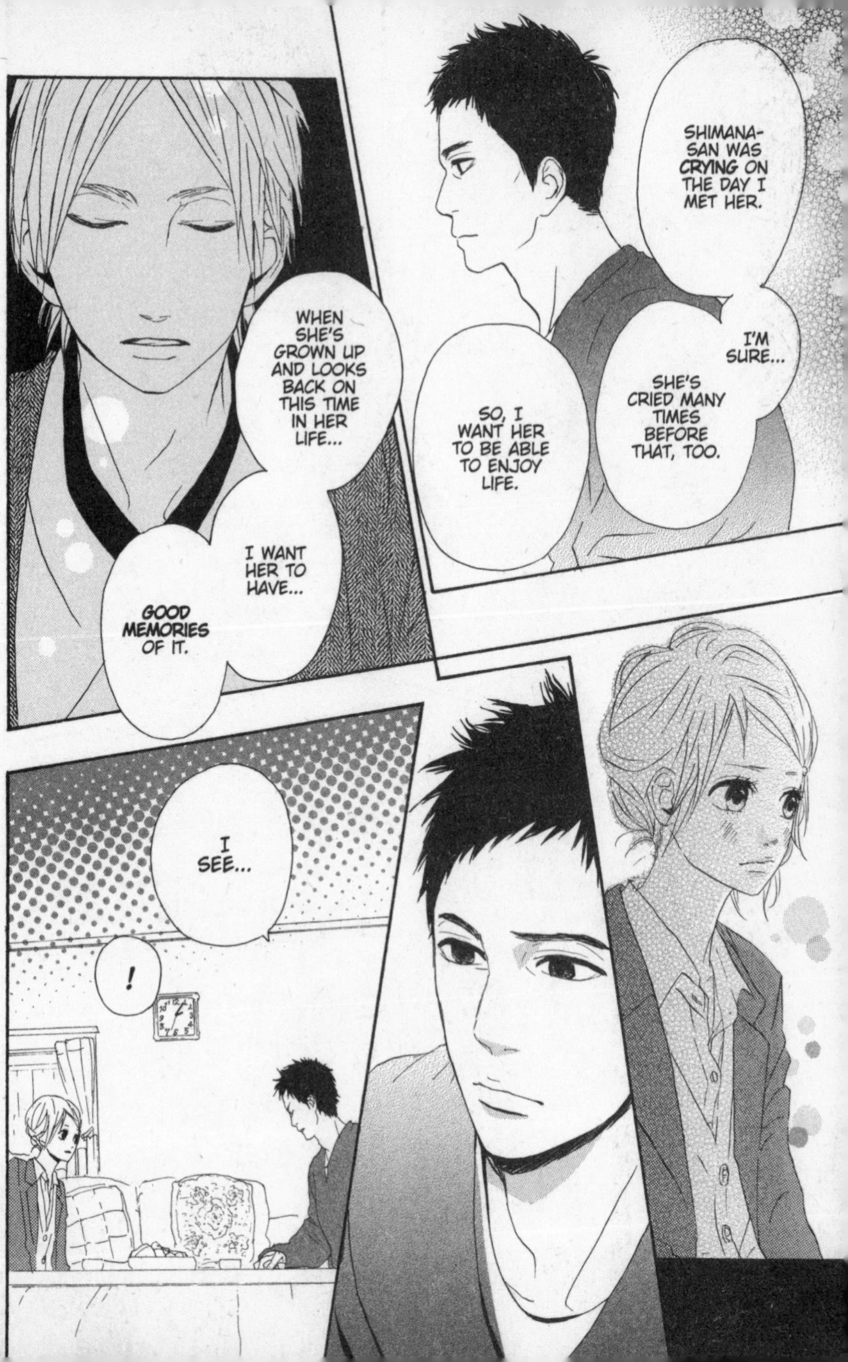
SHIMANA-SAN WAS CRYING ON THE DAY I MET HER.
I'M SURE...
SHE'S CRIED MANY TIMES BEFORE THAT, TOO.
SO, I WANT HER TO BE ABLE TO ENJOY LIFE.
WHEN SHE'S GROWN UP AND LOOKS BACK ON THIS TIME IN HER LIFE...
I WANT HER TO HAVE...
GOOD MEMORIES OF IT.
I SEE...
!

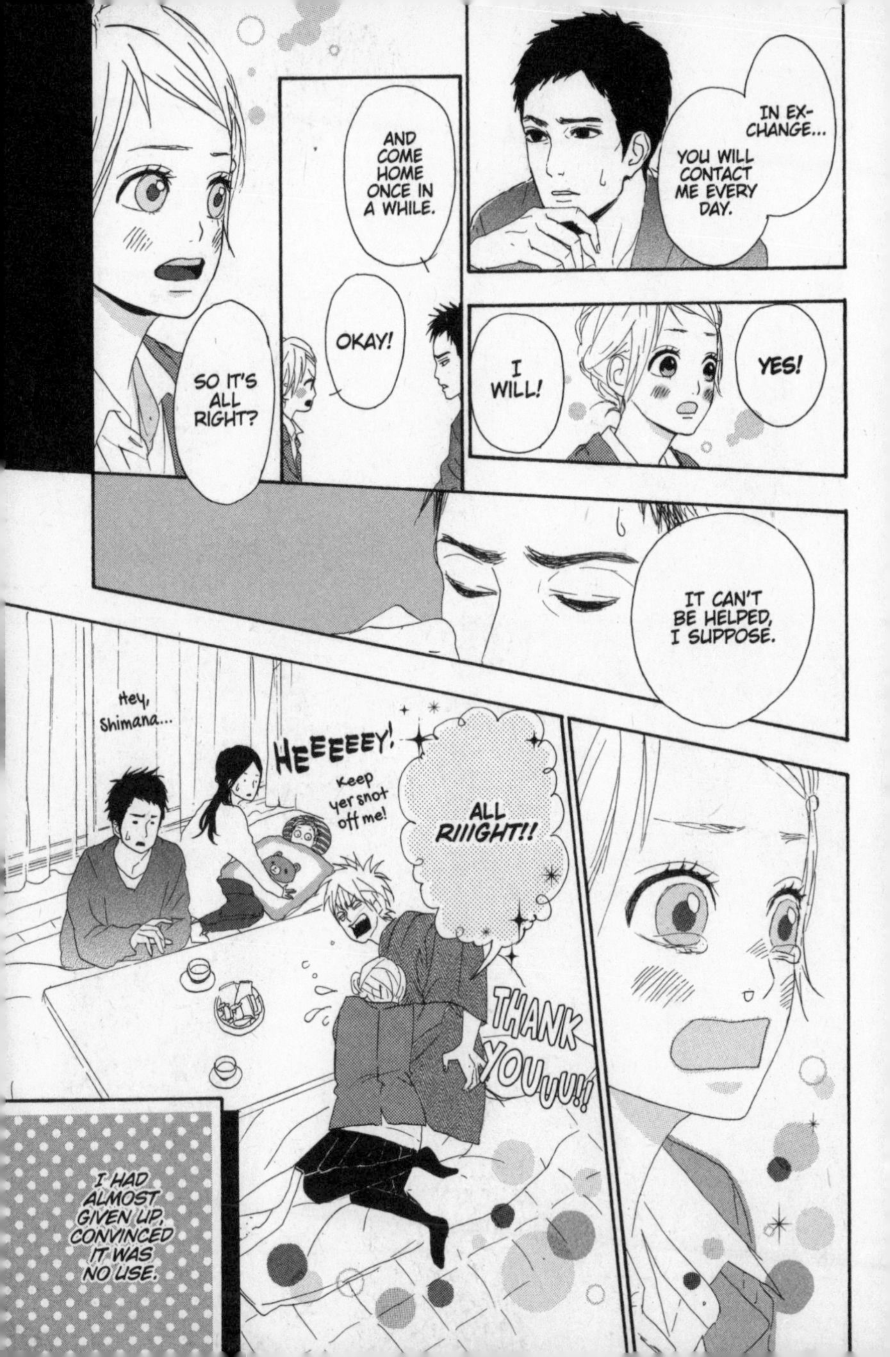

IN EX-CHANGE... YOU WILL CONTACT ME EVERY DAY.
YES!
I WILL!
AND COME HOME ONCE IN A WHILE.
OKAY!
SO IT'S ALL RIGHT?
IT CAN'T BE HELPED, I SUPPOSE.
THANK YOUUU!!
ALL RIIIGHT!!
HEEEEEY!
Keep yer snot off me!
Hey, Shimana...
I HAD ALMOST GIVEN UP, CONVINCED IT WAS NO USE.

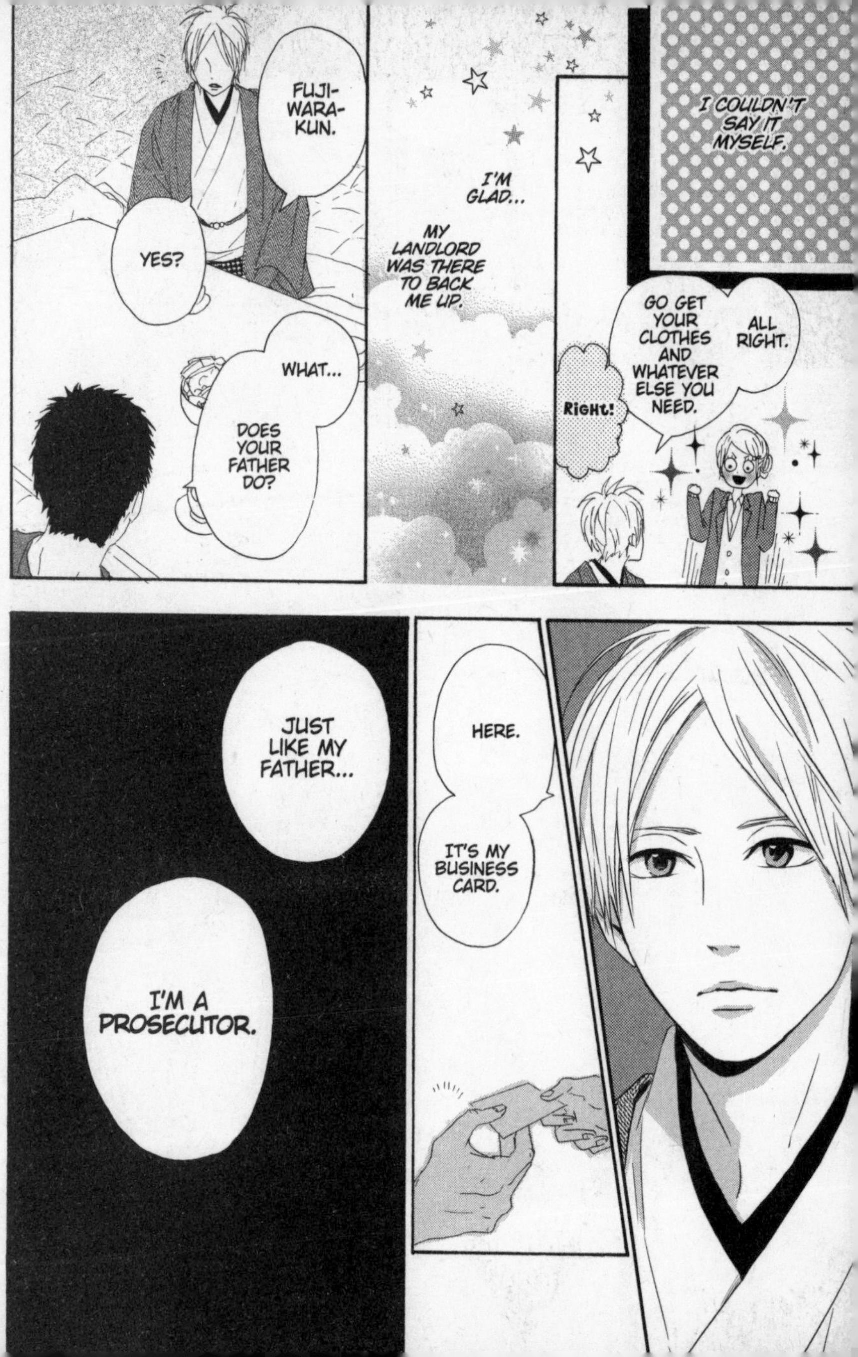
I COULDN'T SAY IT MYSELF.
ALL RIGHT.
GO GET YOUR CLOTHES AND WHATEVER ELSE YOU NEED.
Right!
I'M GLAD...
MY LANDLORD WAS THERE TO BACK ME UP.
FUJI-WARA-KUN.
YES?
WHAT...
DOES YOUR FATHER DO?
HERE.
IT'S MY BUSINESS CARD.
JUST LIKE MY FATHER...
I'M A PROSECUTOR.

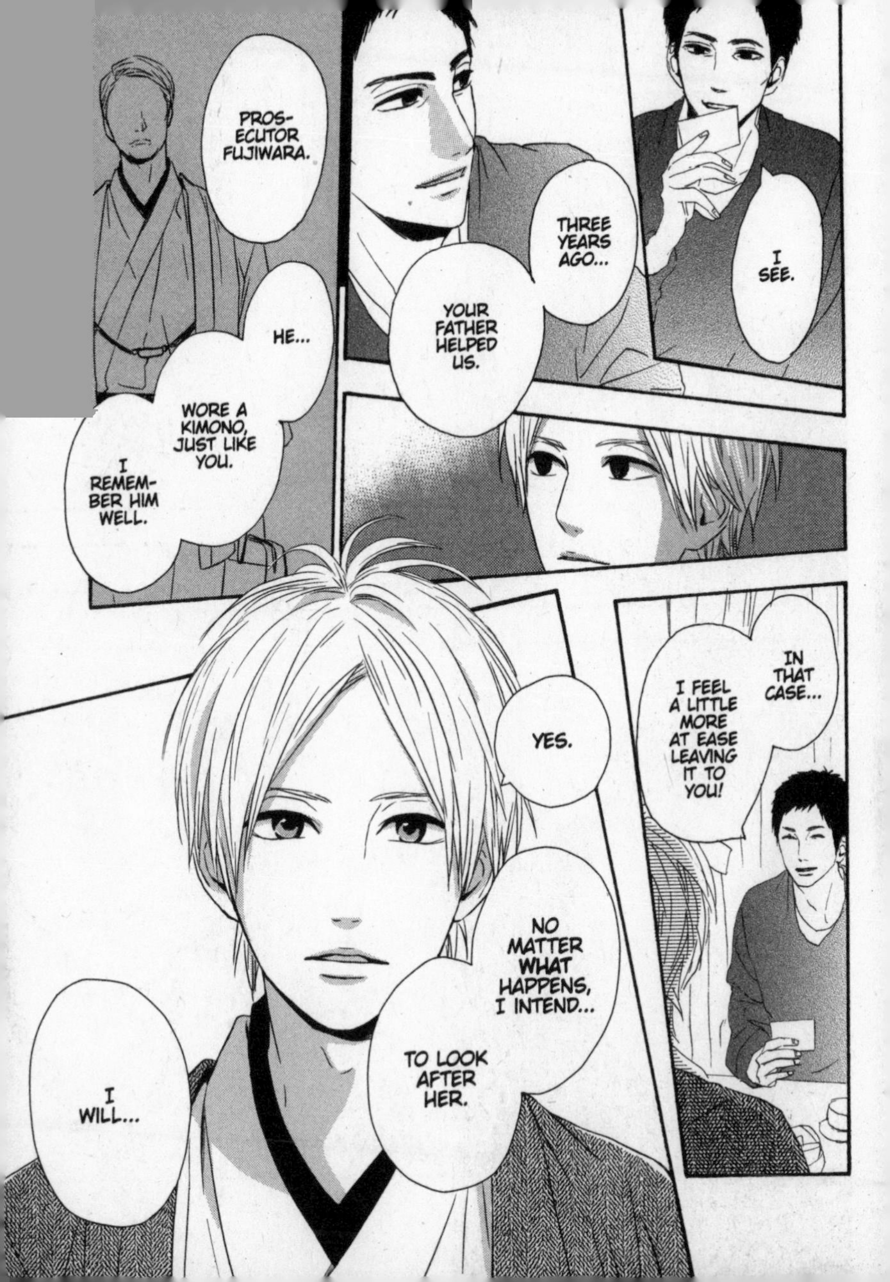
I SEE.
THREE YEARS AGO...
YOUR FATHER HELPED US.
PROSECUTOR FUJIWARA.
HE...
WORE A KIMONO, JUST LIKE YOU.
I REMEMBER HIM WELL.
IN THAT CASE...
I FEEL A LITTLE MORE AT EASE LEAVING IT TO YOU!
YES.
NO MATTER WHAT HAPPENS, I INTEND...
TO LOOK AFTER HER.
I WILL...

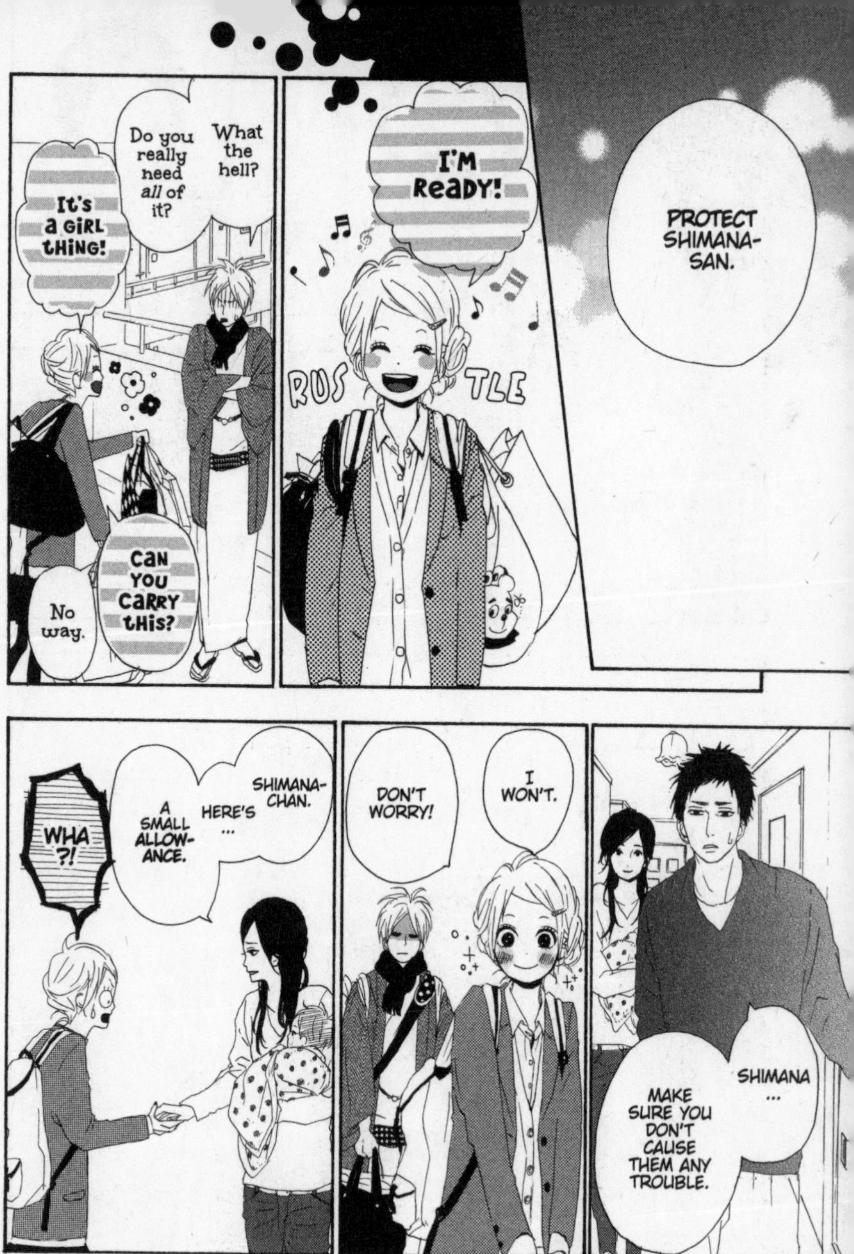
PROTECT SHIMANA-SAN.
I'M READY!
RUS TLE
What the hell?
Do you really need *all* of it?
It's a girl thing!
Can you carry this?
No way.
SHIMANA...
MAKE SURE YOU DON'T CAUSE THEM ANY TROUBLE.
I WON'T.
DON'T WORRY!
SHIMANA-CHAN.
HERE'S...
A SMALL ALLOWANCE.
WHA?!

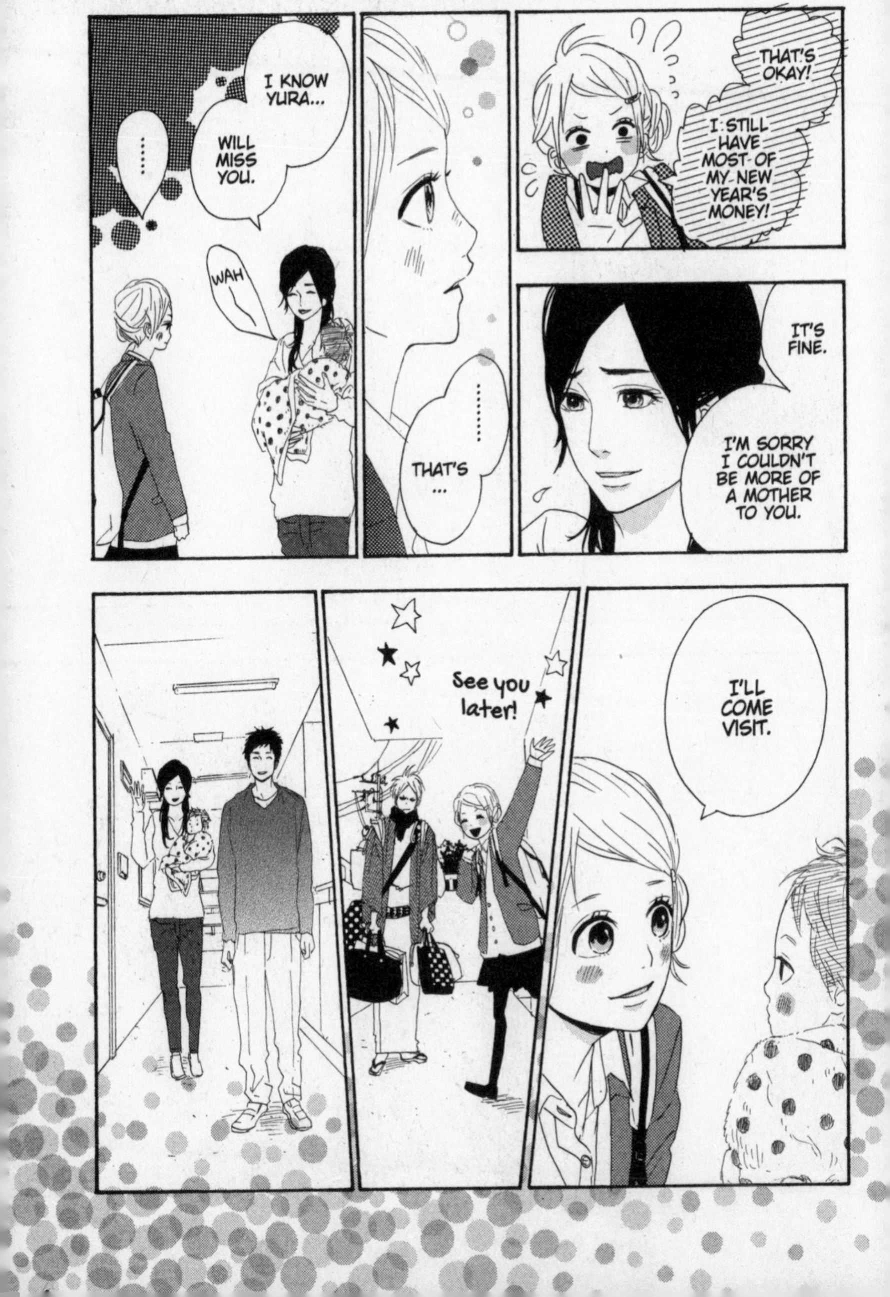
THAT'S OKAY!
I STILL HAVE MOST OF MY NEW YEAR'S MONEY!
IT'S FINE.
I'M SORRY I COULDN'T BE MORE OF A MOTHER TO YOU.
......
THAT'S ...
I KNOW YURA...
WILL MISS YOU.
......
WAH
I'LL COME VISIT.
See you later!

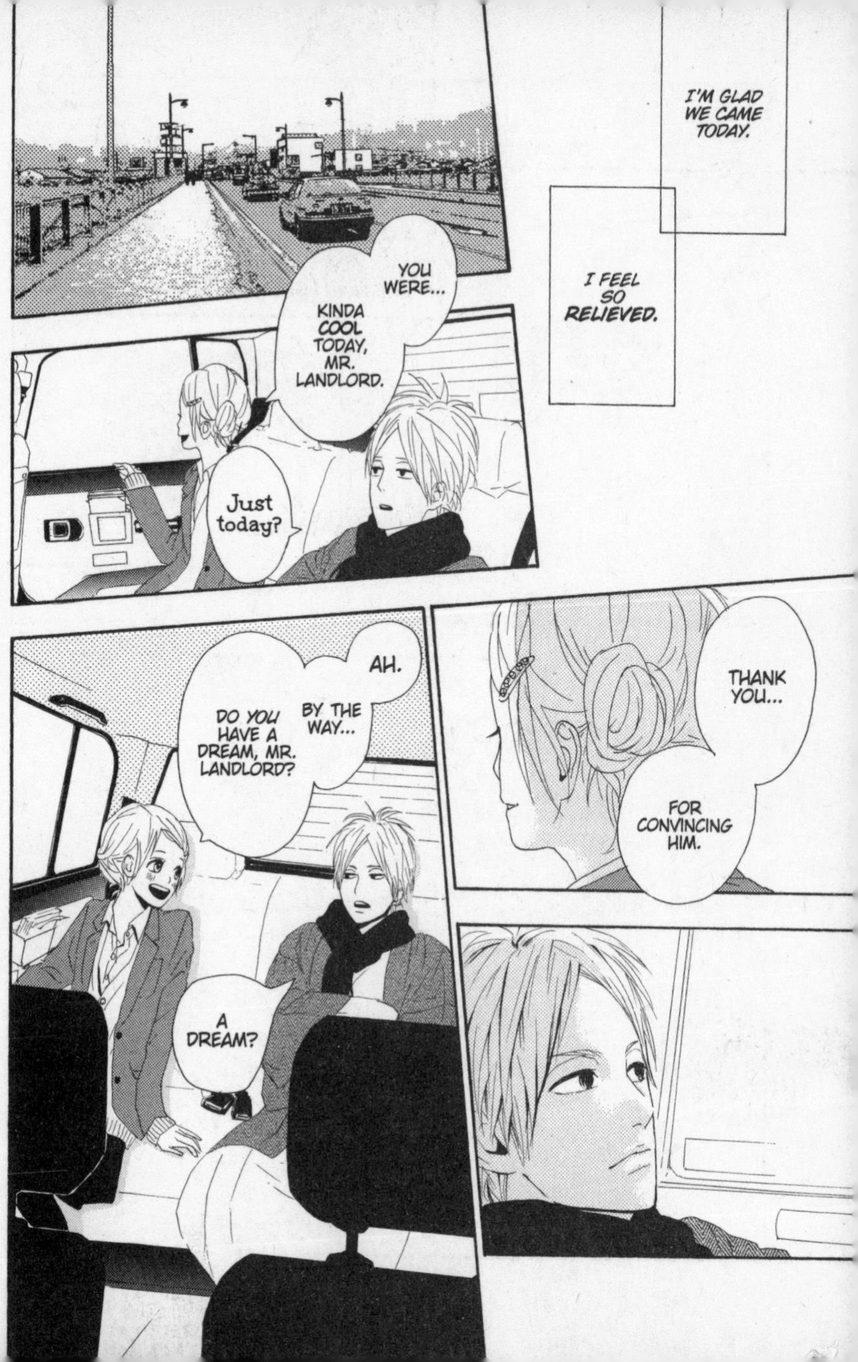
I'M GLAD WE CAME TODAY.
I FEEL SO RELIEVED.
YOU WERE...
KINDA COOL TODAY, MR. LANDLORD.
Just today?
THANK YOU...
FOR CONVINCING HIM.
AH.
BY THE WAY...
DO YOU HAVE A DREAM, MR. LANDLORD?
A DREAM?

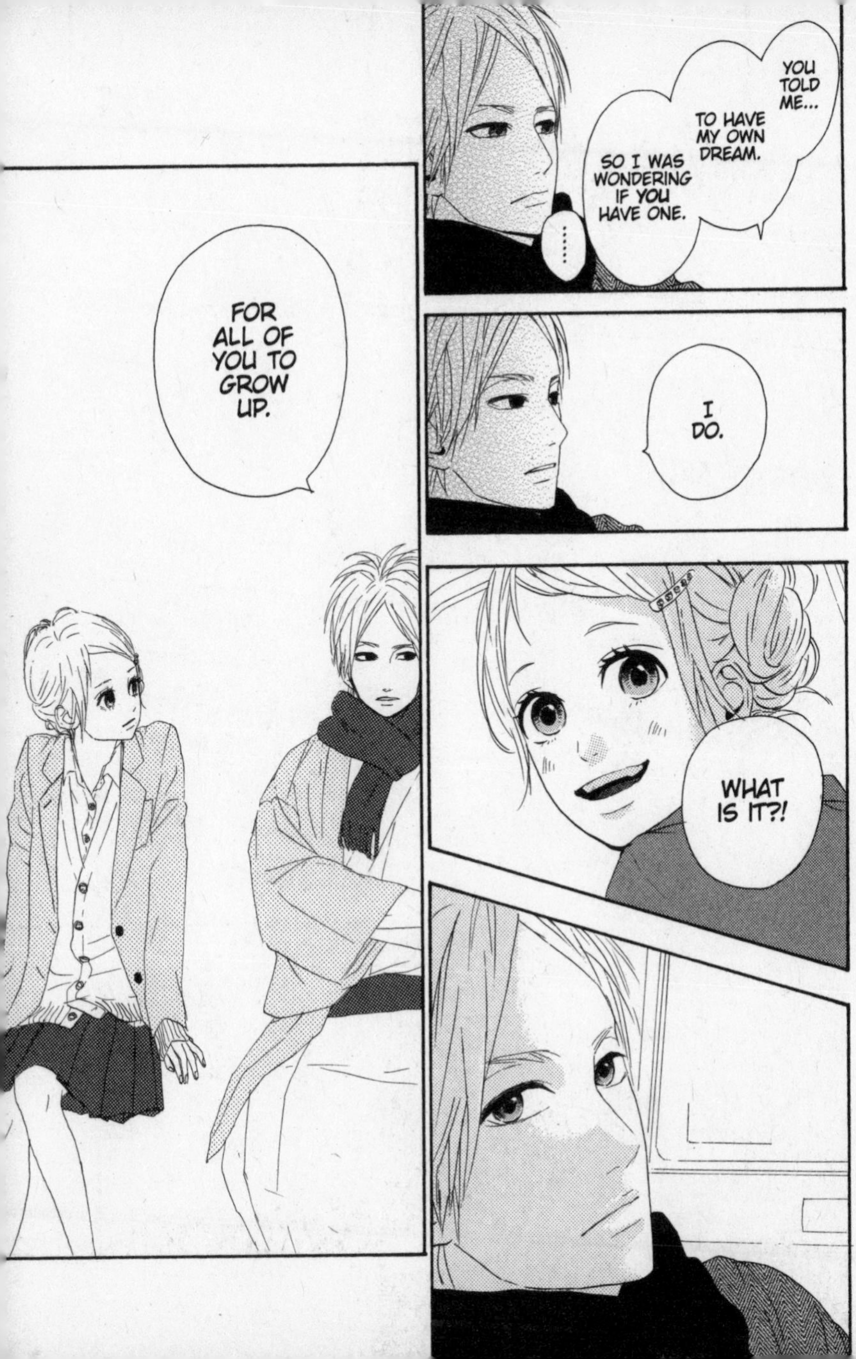
YOU TOLD ME...
TO HAVE MY OWN DREAM.
SO I WAS WONDERING IF YOU HAVE ONE.
......
I DO.
WHAT IS IT?!
FOR ALL OF YOU TO GROW UP.

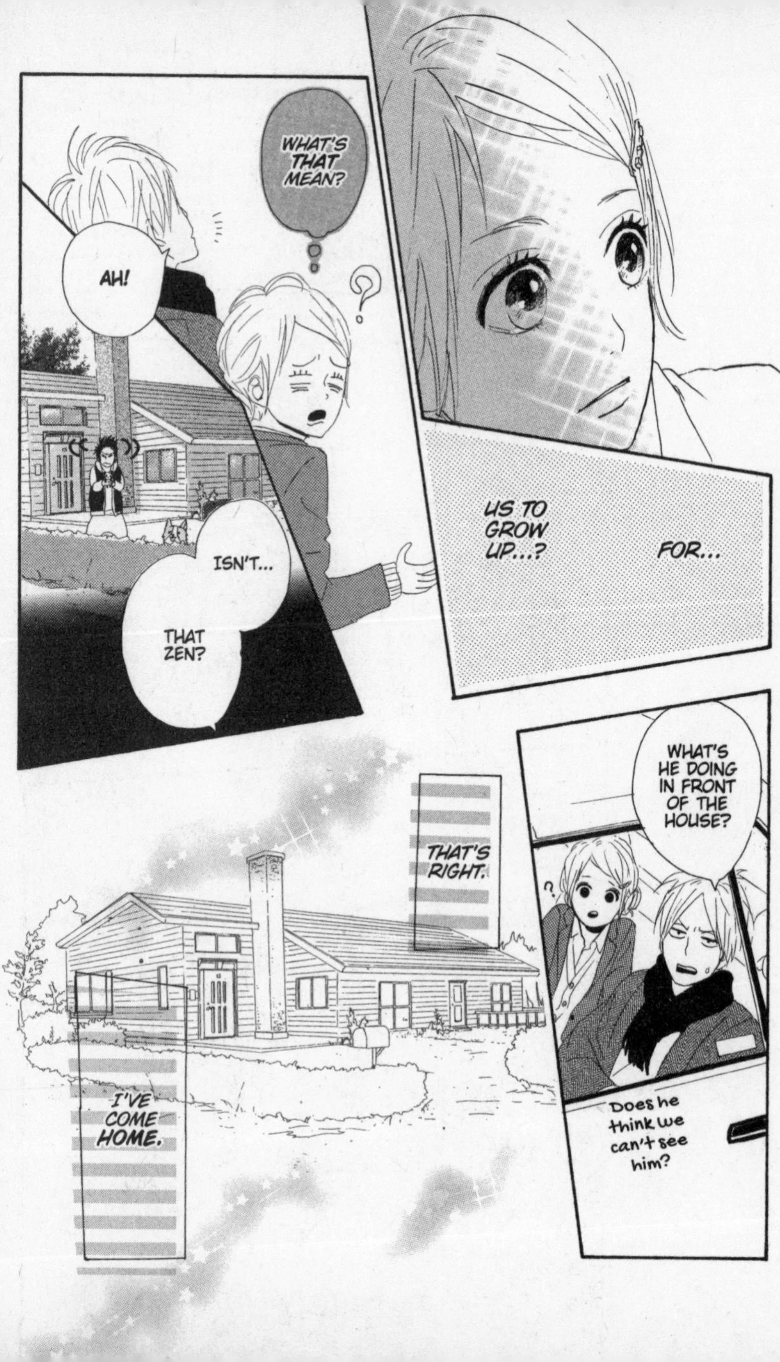
FOR...
US TO GROW UP...?
WHAT'S THAT MEAN?
AH!
ISN'T...
THAT ZEN?
WHAT'S HE DOING IN FRONT OF THE HOUSE?
Does he think we can't see him?
THAT'S RIGHT.
I'VE COME HOME.

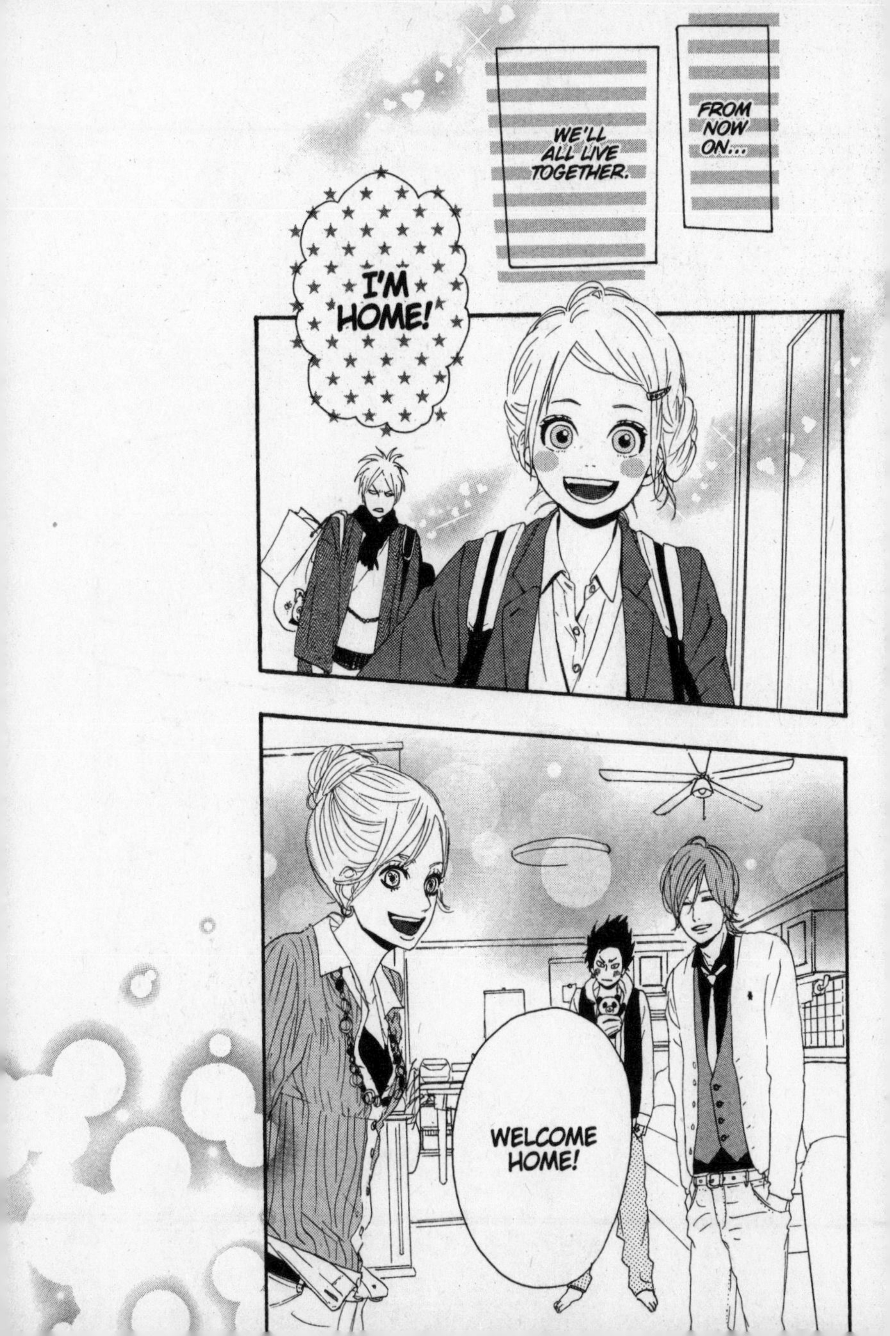
FROM NOW ON...
WE'LL ALL LIVE TOGETHER.
I'M HOME!
WELCOME HOME!

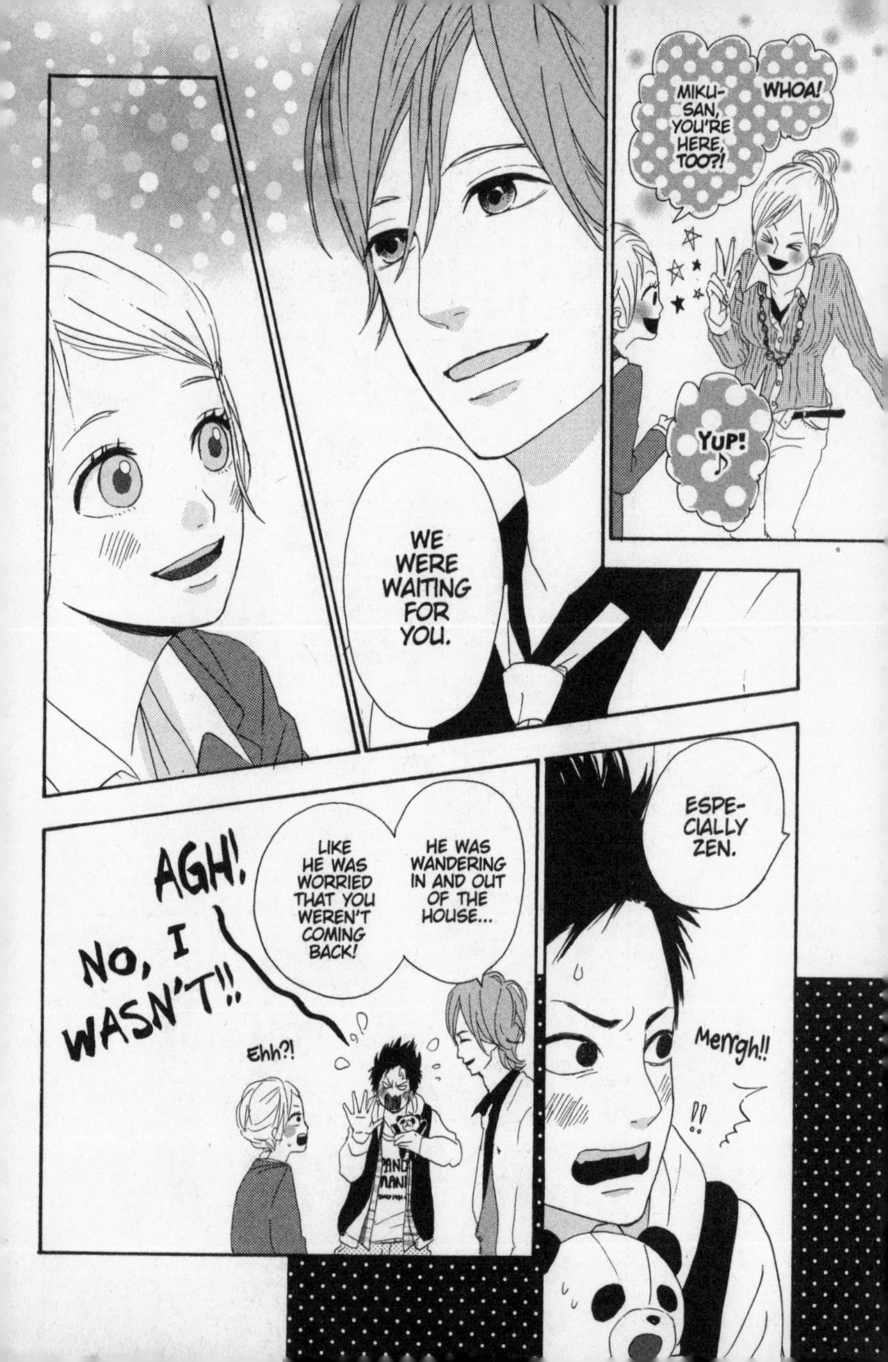
WHOA!
MIKU-SAN, YOU'RE HERE, TOO?!
YUP! ♪
WE WERE WAITING FOR YOU.
ESPE-CIALLY ZEN.
Merrgh!!
!!
HE WAS WANDERING IN AND OUT OF THE HOUSE...
LIKE HE WAS WORRIED THAT YOU WEREN'T COMING BACK!
AGH!
NO, I WASN'T!!
Ehh?!

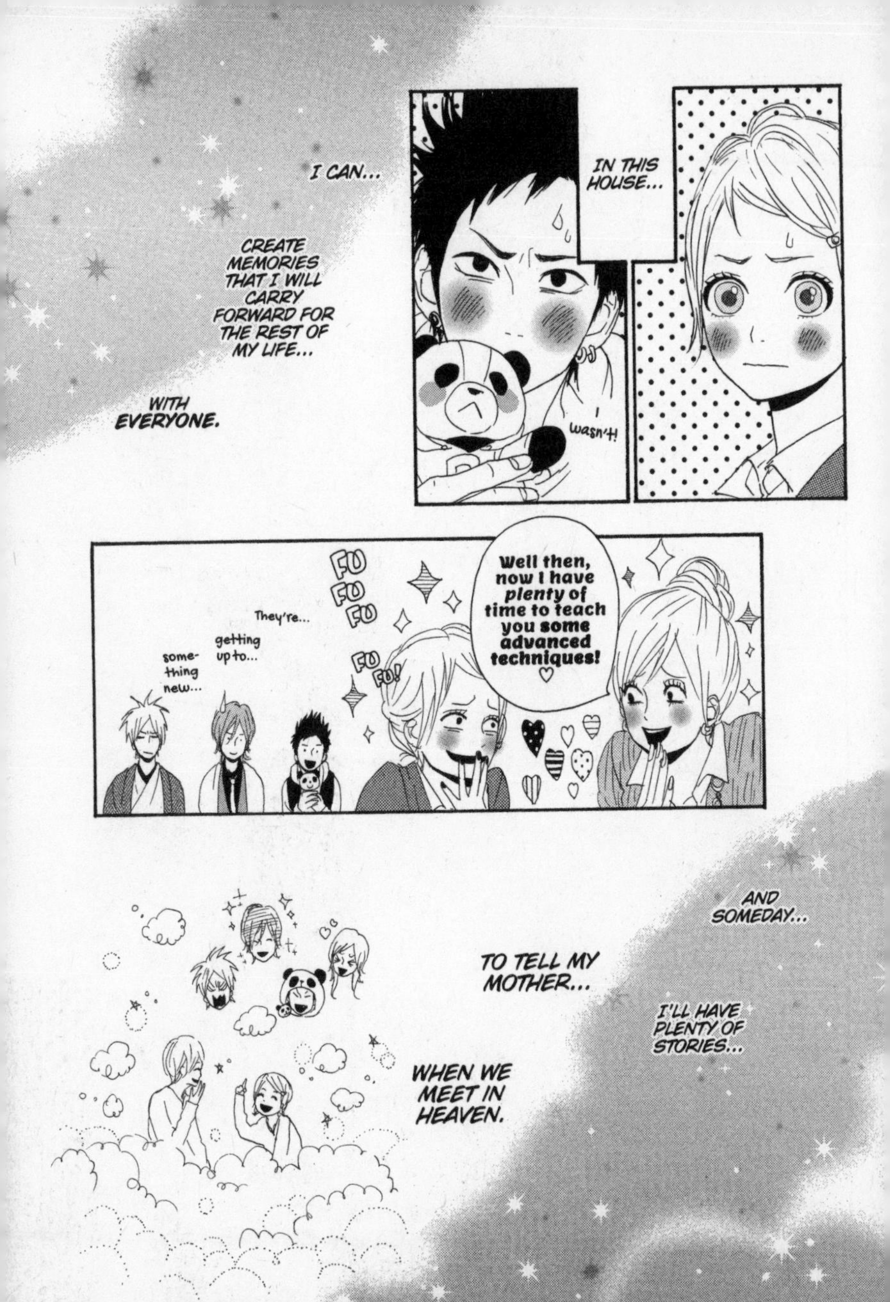
IN THIS HOUSE...
I wasn't!
I CAN...
CREATE MEMORIES THAT I WILL CARRY FORWARD FOR THE REST OF MY LIFE...
WITH EVERYONE.
Well then, now I have *plenty* of time to teach you some advanced techniques! ♡
FU FU FU
FU FU!
They're...
getting up to...
something new...
AND SOMEDAY...
I'LL HAVE PLENTY OF STORIES...
TO TELL MY MOTHER...
WHEN WE MEET IN HEAVEN.

‹‹to be continued››

Meaningless Doodle

La la la la la~!

La la la la~!

Phweet!

BONUS MANGA

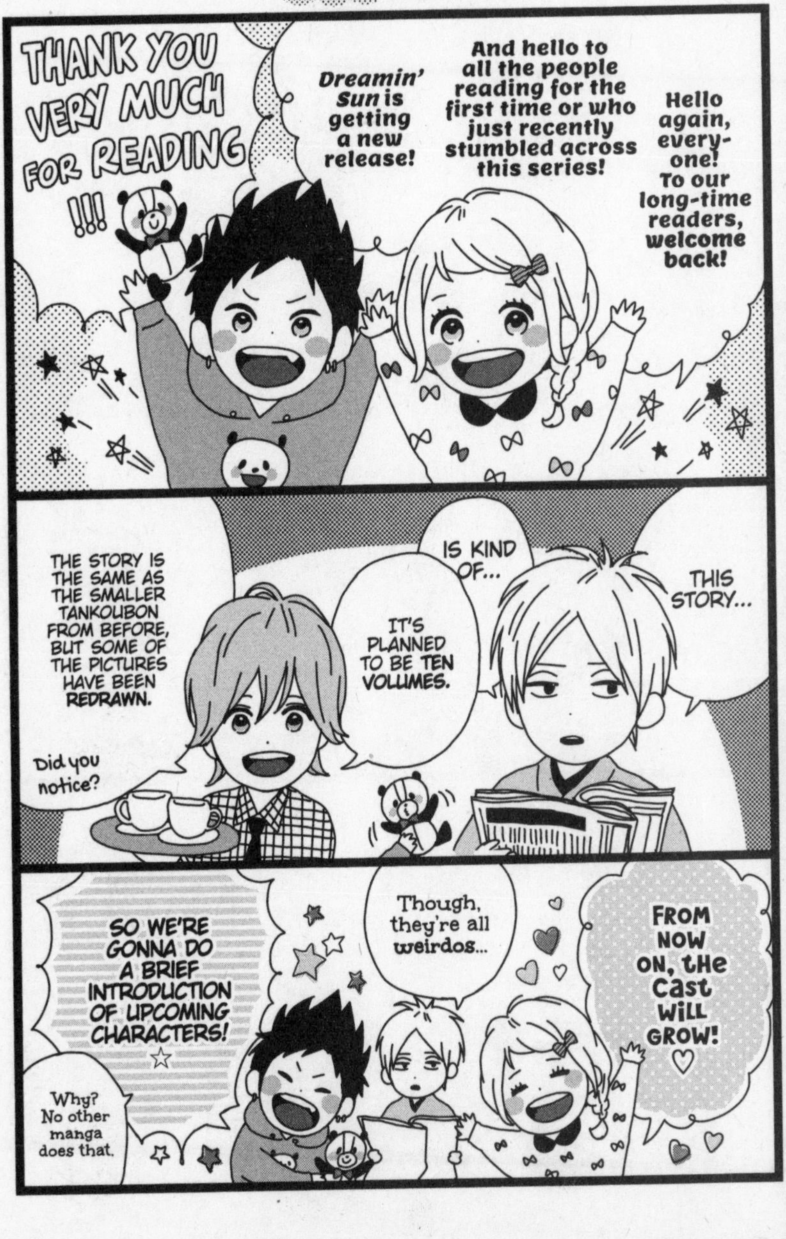
Hello again, everyone! To our long-time readers, welcome back!
And hello to all the people reading for the first time or who just recently stumbled across this series!
Dreamin' Sun is getting a new release!
THANK YOU VERY MUCH FOR READING !!!
THIS STORY...
IS KIND OF...
IT'S PLANNED TO BE TEN VOLUMES.
THE STORY IS THE SAME AS THE SMALLER TANKOUBON FROM BEFORE, BUT SOME OF THE PICTURES HAVE BEEN REDRAWN.
Did you notice?
FROM NOW ON, THE CAST WILL GROW! ♡
Though, they're all weirdos...
SO WE'RE GONNA DO A BRIEF INTRODUCTION OF UPCOMING CHARACTERS! ☆
Why? No other manga does that.

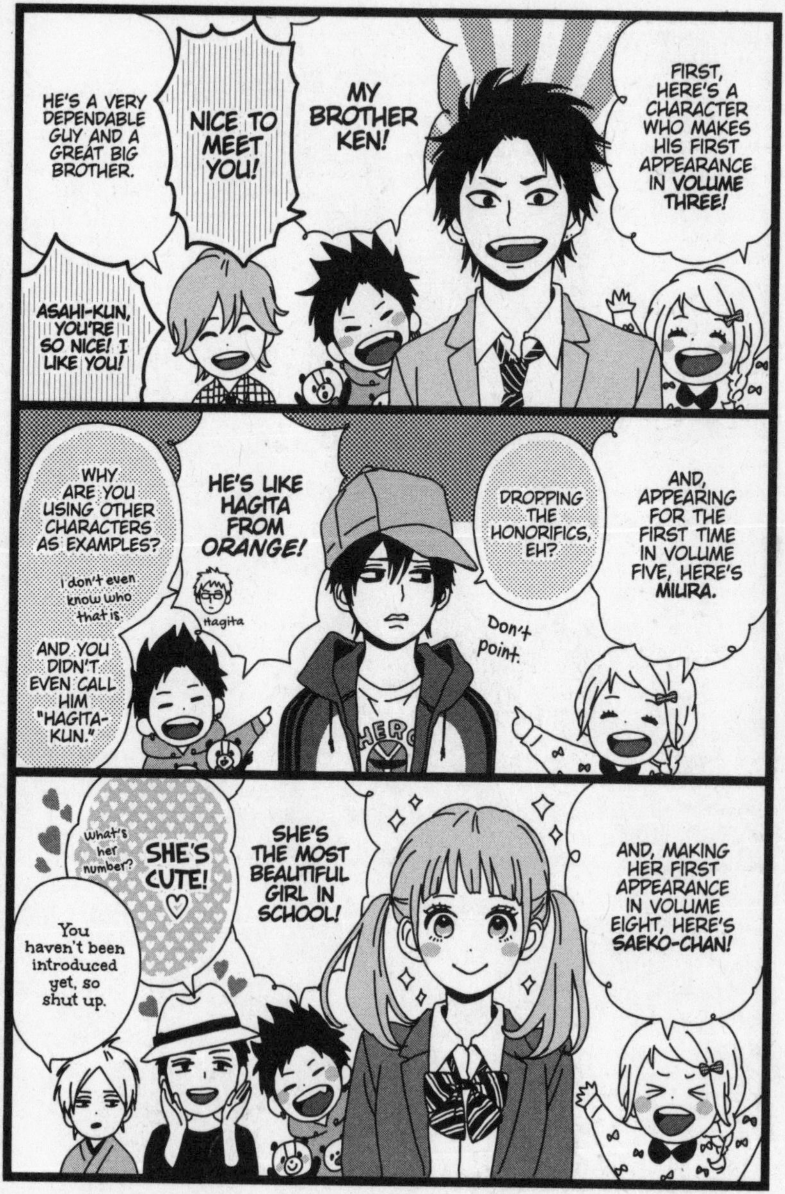
FIRST, HERE'S A CHARACTER WHO MAKES HIS FIRST APPEARANCE IN VOLUME THREE!
MY BROTHER KEN!
NICE TO MEET YOU!
HE'S A VERY DEPENDABLE GUY AND A GREAT BIG BROTHER.
ASAHI-KUN, YOU'RE SO NICE! I LIKE YOU!
AND, APPEARING FOR THE FIRST TIME IN VOLUME FIVE, HERE'S MIURA.
DROPPING THE HONORIFICS, EH?
Don't point.
HE'S LIKE HAGITA FROM ORANGE!
Hagita
WHY ARE YOU USING OTHER CHARACTERS AS EXAMPLES?
I don't even know who that is.
AND YOU DIDN'T EVEN CALL HIM "HAGITA-KUN."
AND, MAKING HER FIRST APPEARANCE IN VOLUME EIGHT, HERE'S SAEKO-CHAN!
SHE'S THE MOST BEAUTIFUL GIRL IN SCHOOL!
SHE'S CUTE!
What's her number?
You haven't been introduced yet, so shut up.

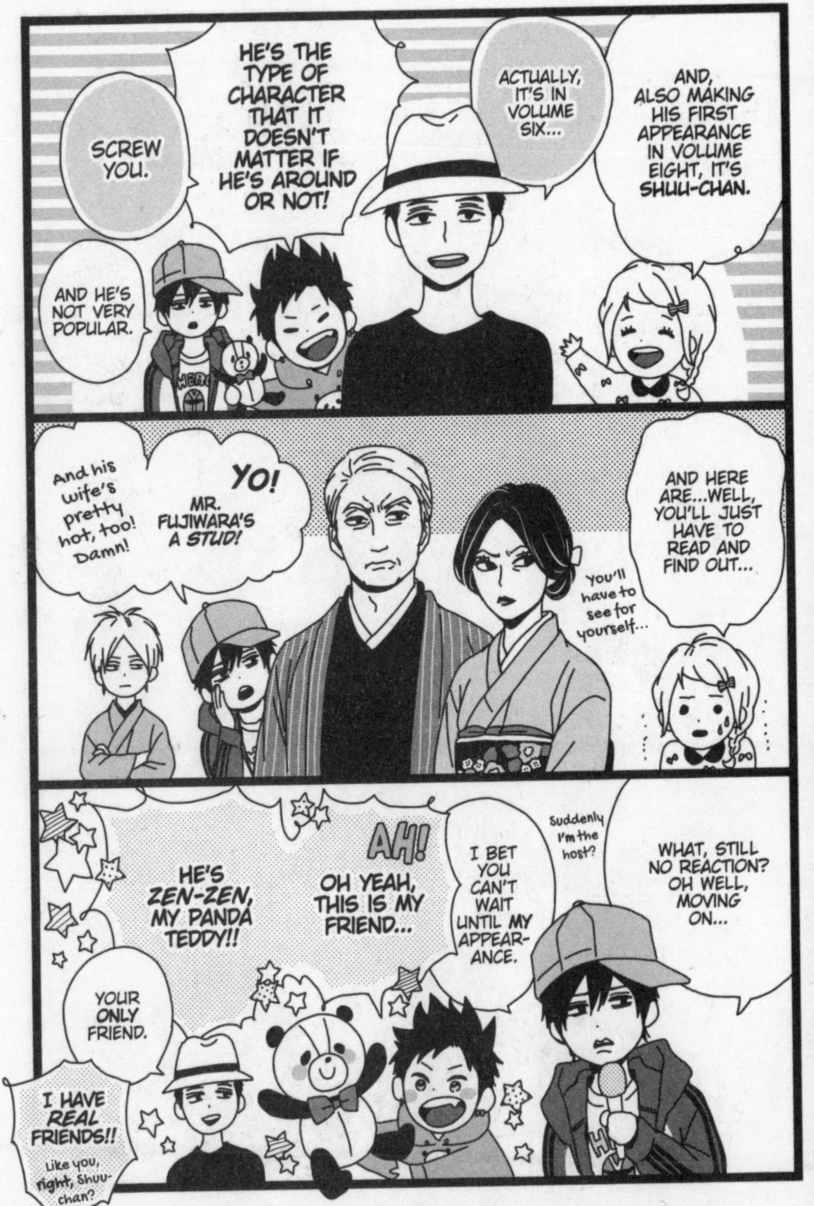
AND, ALSO MAKING HIS FIRST APPEARANCE IN VOLUME EIGHT, IT'S SHUU-CHAN.
ACTUALLY, IT'S IN VOLUME SIX...
HE'S THE TYPE OF CHARACTER THAT IT DOESN'T MATTER IF HE'S AROUND OR NOT!
SCREW YOU.
AND HE'S NOT VERY POPULAR.
AND HERE ARE...WELL, YOU'LL JUST HAVE TO READ AND FIND OUT...
You'll have to see for yourself...
YO!
MR. FUJIWARA'S A STUD!
And his wife's pretty hot, too! Damn!
WHAT, STILL NO REACTION? OH WELL, MOVING ON...
Suddenly I'm the host?
I BET YOU CAN'T WAIT UNTIL MY APPEARANCE.
AH!
OH YEAH, THIS IS MY FRIEND...
HE'S ZEN-ZEN, MY PANDA TEDDY!!
YOUR ONLY FRIEND.
I HAVE REAL FRIENDS!!
Like you, right, Shuu-chan?

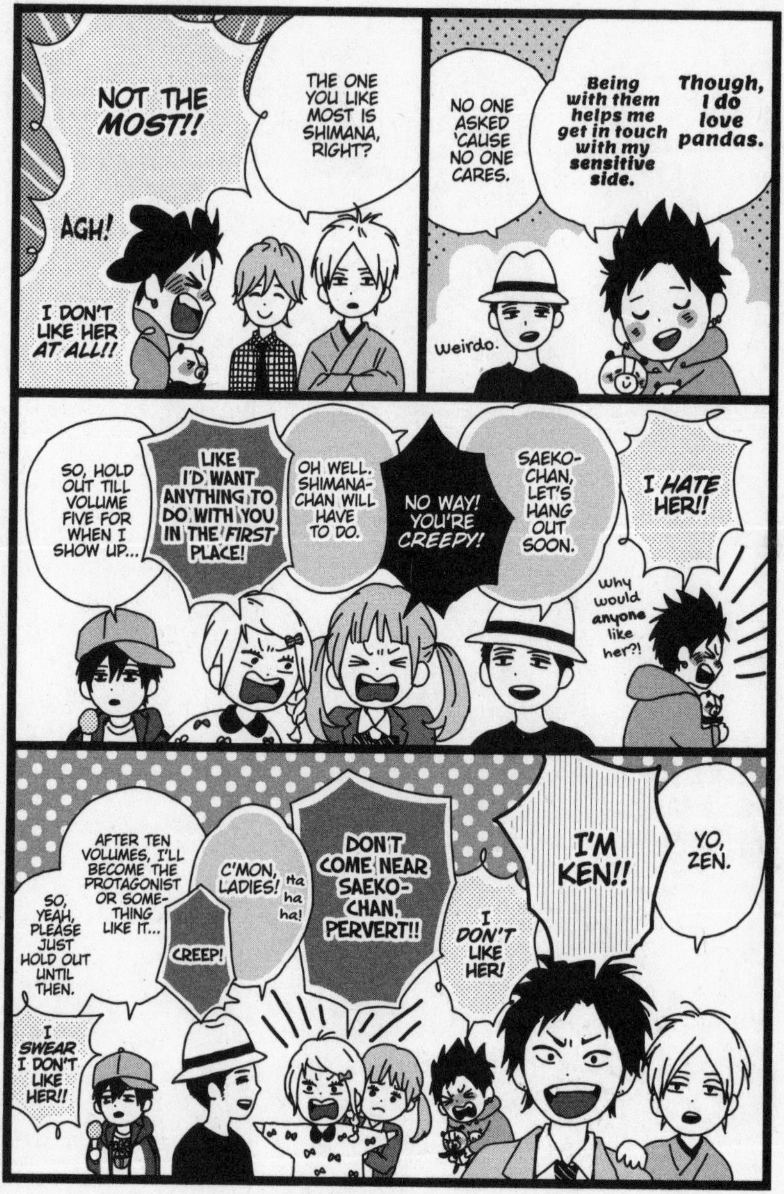
Though, I do love pandas.
Being with them helps me get in touch with my sensitive side.
NO ONE ASKED 'CAUSE NO ONE CARES.
Weirdo.
THE ONE YOU LIKE MOST IS SHIMANA, RIGHT?
NOT THE MOST!!
AGH!
I DON'T LIKE HER AT ALL!!
I HATE HER!!
Why would anyone like her?!
SAEKO-CHAN, LET'S HANG OUT SOON.
NO WAY! YOU'RE CREEPY!
OH WELL. SHIMANA-CHAN WILL HAVE TO DO.
LIKE I'D WANT ANYTHING TO DO WITH YOU IN THE FIRST PLACE!
SO, HOLD OUT TILL VOLUME FIVE FOR WHEN I SHOW UP...
YO, ZEN.
I'M KEN!!
I DON'T LIKE HER!
DON'T COME NEAR SAEKO-CHAN, PERVERT!!
Ha ha ha!
C'MON, LADIES!
CREEP!
AFTER TEN VOLUMES, I'LL BECOME THE PROTAGONIST OR SOMETHING LIKE IT...
SO, YEAH, PLEASE JUST HOLD OUT UNTIL THEN.
I SWEAR I DON'T LIKE HER!!

THE END

THE FIND POKO GAME

POKO
↓

Poko is hidden throughout the manga! Find him!

In this volume there are 7 Pokos!

hint: He's not in the house.

The New Release Version of the Hit Romantic Comedy!

With its redrawn artwork, it's even cuter than before!

"I want to...
have more confidence in myself."

Thanks to some wise words from her landlord, Shimana's father has accepted her new living situation. Unable to work up the courage to ask Asahi on a date, Shimana goes shopping with Miku and the others as part of her self-improvement plan. When she sends Asahi a picture to show him her new look, what will his response be...?!

Includes *Dreamin' Sun* chapters 5~9, plus a bonus manga!

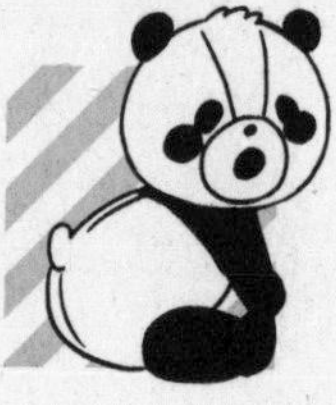

Ichigo Takano presents

Dreamin' Sun 2

Coming Soon!

Story & Art by *orange*'s Ichigo Takano!

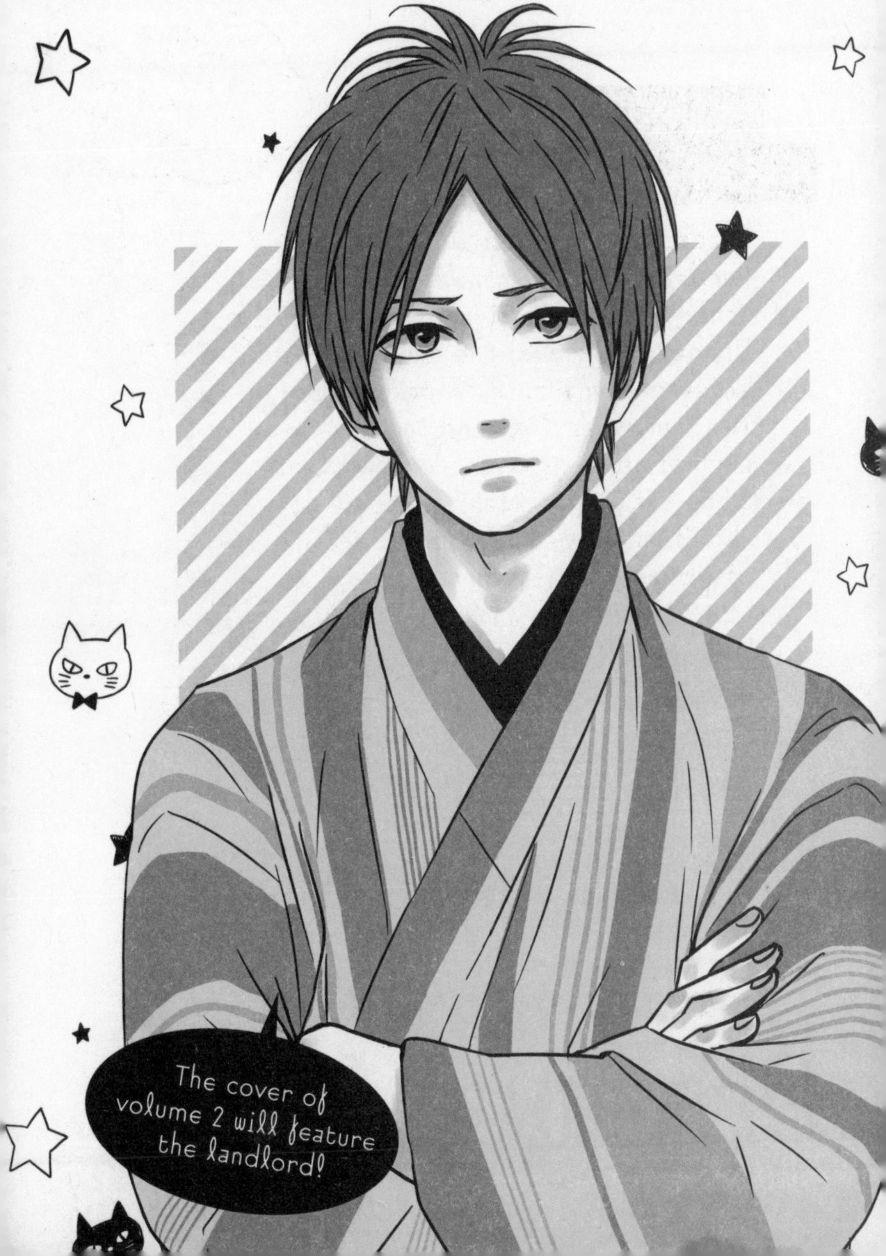
The cover of volume 2 will feature the landlord!

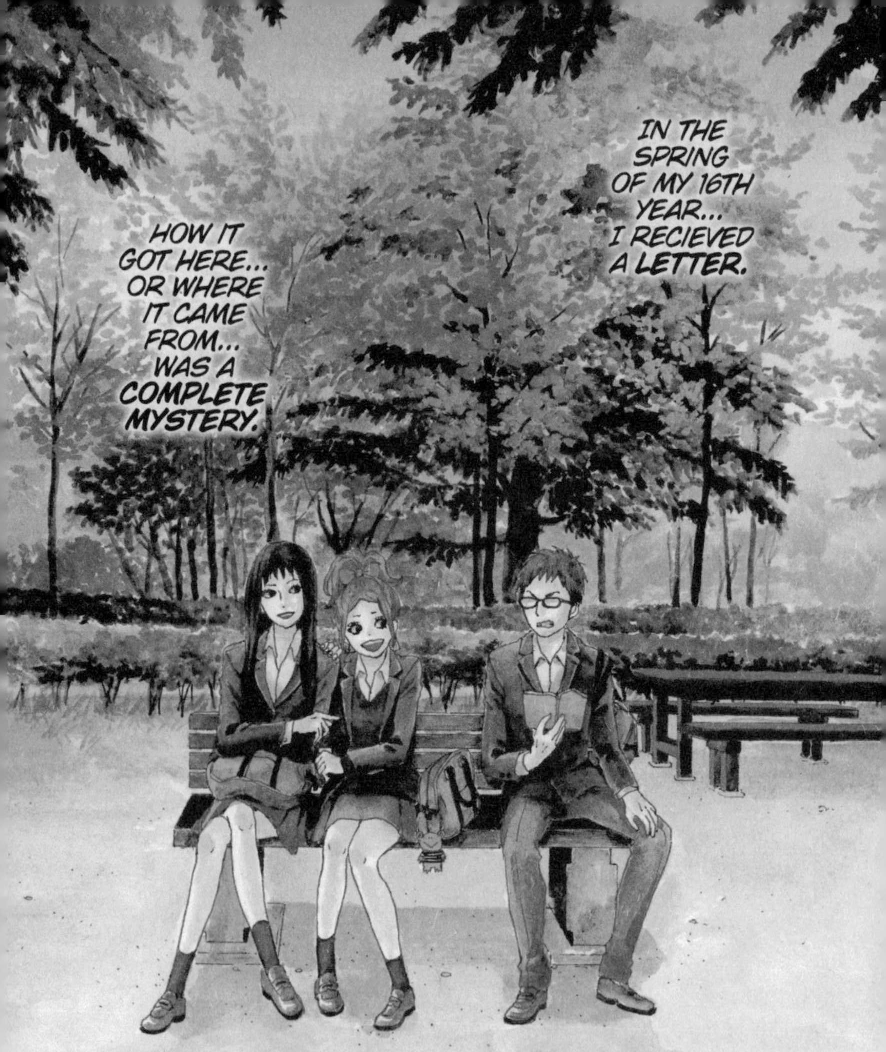
IN THE SPRING OF MY 16TH YEAR... I RECIEVED A LETTER.
HOW IT GOT HERE... OR WHERE IT CAME FROM... WAS A COMPLETE MYSTERY.

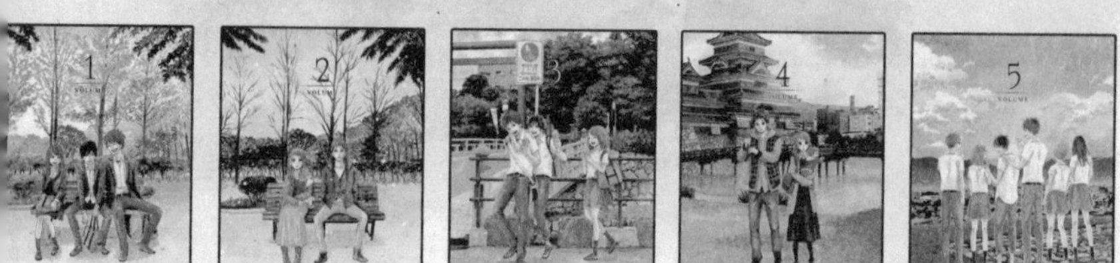
orange
ICHIGO TAKANO